ELUSIVE EQUALITY

ELUSIVE

DESEGREGATION AND RESEGREGATION
IN NORFOLK'S PUBLIC SCHOOLS

EQUALITY

JEFFREY L. LITTLEJOHN AND CHARLES H. FORD

UNIVERSITY OF VIRGINIA PRESS | CHARLOTTESVILLE AND LONDON

University of Virginia Press

© 2012 by the Rector and Visitors of the University of Virginia

All rights reserved

Printed in the United States of America on acid-free paper

First published 2012

9 8 7 6 5 4 3 2 1

Library of Congress Cataloging-in-Publication Data

Littlejohn, Jeffrey L., 1973–

 Elusive equality : desegregation and resegregation in Norfolk's
public schools / Jeffrey L. Littlejohn and Charles H. Ford.

  p.   cm.

Includes bibliographical references and index.

ISBN 978-0-8139-3288-0 (cloth : alk. paper)

ISBN 978-0-8139-3289-7 (e-book)

 1. School integration —Virginia — Norfolk — History.

2. Segregation in education —Virginia — Norfolk — History.

3. African Americans — Education —Virginia — Norfolk —
History. 4. Public schools —Virginia — Norfolk — History.

I. Ford, Charles Howard, 1964– II. Title.

LC214.23.N75L58 2012

379.2'6309755521 — dc23   2012001540

CONTENTS

ACKNOWLEDGMENTS

HISTORIANS HAVE FEW FRIENDS, but they do have many sources. This aphorism is doubly true in reference to this long-gestating project, which is bound to make Norfolk's civic oligarchy a little less comfortable. Our most significant ally in this business of muckraking has been Cassandra Newby-Alexander, professor of history at Norfolk State University, who has always been willing to speak truth to power. We benefited enormously from her encyclopedic knowledge of the port city and its secrets, both "open" and otherwise. Local archivists also aided and abetted our research. In particular, we depended on the assistance of Sonia Yaco at Old Dominion University and Tommy Bogger at Norfolk State University. Sonia's help in navigating her newly acquired Norfolk school board papers was especially timely, while Tommy combined his historical and archival experience to help us understand the complexity of the local African American leadership. In addition, we were lucky to have the help of a wonderful team of librarians at the Norfolk Public Library: Robert Hitchings, William Troy Valos, William Inge, and Peggy Haile McPhillips were indispensible. Robert's deep knowledge of genealogy solved many of our mysteries, while Troy and William found forgotten documents and photographs with aplomb. Peggy also led us to sources that we had earlier overlooked. We could not have been as thorough as we were without the invaluable guidance and insight of these friends.

Outside of Tidewater, John N. Jacob, head of the Lewis Powell, Jr., Archives at Washington and Lee University's School of Law in Lexington, Virginia, was most gracious in scouting and copying key documents from the Powell and Hoffman Papers housed there. Ted DeLaney, chair of the History Department at Washington and Lee, was the perfect Virginia gentleman in hosting the visits of Charles H. Ford to his lovely campus's archives. Ted also organized a most memorable and useful panel that included us at the annual meeting of the Southern Historical Association in Louisville, Kentucky, in November 2009. The comments provided there by eminent historians Patricia Sullivan and Raymond Arsenault were invaluable. In addition, the staff members of the Leyburn Library's Special Collections at Washington and Lee, the Library of Virginia in Richmond, and the Albert and Shirley Small Library at the University of Virginia in Charlottesville contributed to the success of this project.

We would like to thank the staff at the University of Virginia Press for their patience and guidance. In particular, Richard Holway, Ellen Satrom, Morgan Myers, and Raennah Mitchell helped tremendously. Copyeditor Robert Burchfield and map maker Chris Erichsen enhanced the project. And our colleagues Peter Wallenstein, James Hershman, Thomas Cox, Bernadette Pruitt, and Michael Martin helped at various stages of the book's production.

Furthermore, we would also like to thank the following underwriters of Jeffrey L. Littlejohn's frequent research trips to Hampton Roads and vicinity: Page R. Laws, dean of the Honors College at Norfolk State; the Colvin Gibson Funds of Norfolk State's Department of History; Norfolk State's Black History Month Committee; and his own Department of History at Sam Houston State University in Huntsville, Texas.

Several venues helped to enhance pieces of the work-in-progress. A special thanks goes out to the Virginia Foundation for the Humanities and the National Endowment for the Humanities, both of which supported Jeff's early research on this project. The Virginia Foundation gave additional support in 2009, when its radio program, *With Good Reason,* and program host Sarah McConnell allowed Charles to hone his knowledge of the role of white moderates during Massive Resistance. Cathy Lewis of WHRO in Norfolk also gave Jeff and this developing project ample publicity on both her daily noontime talk show and weekly evening public affairs program. Channel 48, the city of Norfolk's public access television station, ran several pieces that showcased research from the project, including the taping of a high-profile civic event commemorating the end of Massive Resistance that was put on by the Norfolk-Portsmouth Bar Association. Charles would especially like to thank local lawyer James R. Harvey III, of Vandeventer and Black, and the grandson-in-law of Judge Hoffman himself, for his key role in making that panel discussion a memorable success. And, last but certainly not least here, we would like to thank the stalwarts of the *New Journal and Guide,* publisher Brenda Andrews and reporter Leonard E. Colvin, for allowing us to comment on public education in Hampton Roads.

On a personal note, Jeff would like to thank his friends Vishal and Tera Shah and Alek and Katie Collins, who opened their homes to him on numerous occasions so he could complete the research for this book. He would also like to express his deepest thanks and love to his wife, Mary, and children, Greenley and Brant, who supported him throughout this long-running project. Similarly, Charles would like to thank his long-suffering partner Kevin A. Girard for putting up with his many hours at the office and library.

Finally, we would like to thank all of the living primary sources that made this project come alive: Geraldine Talley Hobby, Louis Cousins, LaVera Forbes, Patricia Turner, Andrew Heidelberg, Delores Johnson Brown, Johnnie Rouse, Olivia Driver Lindsay, Patricia Godbolt White, Len Holt, James Gay, John Osterhout, Ed Rodman, Lulu Thornton, James E. Spivey, Thomas G. Johnson Jr., Vincent Thomas, King Davis, Paul Riddick, W. Randy Wright, W. T. Mason Jr., and Ellis James. While some of our interviewees may not appreciate our most critical interpretations, we made all of our arguments to the best of our abilities. We hope that our analysis will be taken seriously, and not personally. If any errors of fact or interpretation remain in our narrative, then we apologize in advance for lingering infelicities of both content and style.

ELUSIVE EQUALITY

INTRODUCTION

HE MOST POPULAR vignettes in the history of Norfolk, Virginia, usually consist of the yellow fever disaster of 1855, Civil War and world war tributes, urban renewal, and, of course, the school closures crisis of 1958–59. These stories are the first to be related to newcomers and tourists, and, thankfully for the historian, all have been analyzed from a variety of perspectives by the area's primary local newspaper, the *Virginian-Pilot*. In this tradition, reporter Denise Watson Batts recently provided an in-depth look at the school closures timed to come out on the fiftieth anniversary of those fateful events. In five parts, we revisited once again the impact of *Brown v. Board of Education* (1954), the state's closure of six public schools in Norfolk to prevent desegregation, and the nearly 10,000 displaced students. Undermining that tradition, however, was Batts's especially adept narrative style that brought to life the experiences of the students and their families. She did not simply rehash the familiar sequence of high politics in Richmond and at city hall that had manufactured the crisis; instead, she focused on the children and families as they experienced the crisis. The responses to Batts's narrative, however, were mixed. Some online readers welcomed her fresh approach to an important epoch, but many more questioned the timing of the series during the historic candidacy of African American Barack Obama for the presidency of the United States. In this vein of commentary, Batts's coverage was part of the liberal media's politically motivated effort to galvanize black voters and disrupt hard-won racial harmony. The vehemence of the negative responses was unexpected by the reporter herself, who happens to be a longtime resident and native of the port city.[1]

Batts's series was embraced, however, by Norfolk's official establishment, which had set up a civic commission of notables to commemorate the event. The commission's ostensible charge was to present all aspects of the crisis, but its title — the End of Massive Resistance — consciously or unconsciously fed into the confines of the long-held view of the school closures as an unfortunate detour in the port city's inevitable progress toward prosperity, equity, and inclusion for everyone. This came out in the most minute of details. For example, the official Martin Luther King, Jr. Unity March and Program on January 19, 2009, took hundreds of folks, both white and black, past the official End of Massive Resistance sites: the *Virginian-Pilot* office of Pulitzer Prize–winning editor Lenoir Chambers, Judge Walter E. Hoffman's federal courthouse, the Martin Luther King Jr. Memorial, and the Bute Street Baptist Church. Special guests—city officials, the Norfolk 17, and members of the white "Lost Class of '59"—were given laminated parking passes, which featured a facsimile of the front page of the *Virginian-Pilot* of February 3, 1959. The headline read: "Schools Desegregated Peacefully: All Norfolk Classes Again Open; Negroes Pass Quiet Crowds." Above the facsimile was a February 1, 2008, quotation from Mayor Paul Fraim declaring that the separate and unequal Norfolk of fifty years earlier was "gone forever." The official story of the city moving forever upward had been captured here concisely in this souvenir for the VIPs.[2]

Beginning with the Unity March and Program, the consequent commemoration spawned a rich array of events, including a well-attended community forum with nationally known pundit Juan Williams as moderator, and chief justice of the Virginia Supreme Court Leroy Rountree Hassell Sr., William and Mary's Arthur B. Hanson Professor of Law Davison M. Douglas, and Charles H. Ford himself as the panelists. Good and important changes did come from these events; the cowardice, noted by Attorney General Eric Holder Jr., of Americans in reference to race seemingly started to dissipate, at least in the port city, according to the Norfolk Historical Society's Louis Guy, a member of the commission. Accordingly, the living members of the Norfolk 17, the first cohort of African American transfers to previously all-white schools, effusively thanked the commission and its collaborators; in turn, the commission, local universities, and others showered them with long-withheld attention and reverence. Members of the 17 and members of their longtime nemesis, the white "Lost Class of '59," began real friendships, with fifty-year-old ice finally starting to melt. Most unlikely was the scene of an elderly and repentant Judge Hal Bonney Jr., who was the most fire-breathing of local segregationists in the late 1950s, suddenly seeing the light on the road to Damascus, or, at least, to the black church of Patricia Turner, a leading member of the Norfolk 17, and seeking forgiveness there for the sins of his youth. Thus, the primary goal of the commission and of "the Virginia way" had been secured: increasing racial harmony at both the individual and collective levels. At its final meeting, members of the commission lavishly congratulated themselves and declared "mission accomplished." At that same meeting, Mayor Fraim, a white moderate from the wealthy west side, and the Reverend Joseph Green, the elderly African American cochair of the commission, cautioned that there was much work left to be done in improving racial relations, but they and the other commissioners never seriously addressed the difficult demographic, economic, or racial issues that continue to forestall true educational equality and integration. That would have been too uncomfortable for the commissioners and the historical figures seeking closure. Here the commemoration was in a long line of similar episodes from local history: twentieth-century Norfolk had always congratulated itself on achieving racial equipoise, while keeping elite whites firmly in control. That civic patting-itself-on-the-back happened after equalization efforts in the 1940s, after token desegregation in the 1960s, after apparent compliance with busing mandates in the 1970s, and after returning to neighborhood schools in 1986. In each case, as we shall see, true equity and integration were frustrated, even if (and in part because) interracial dialogues, forums, committees, and other such window dressing increased.[3]

While the commemoration sought closure, its most problematic and controversial by-product had to have been the Virginia Stage Company's *Line in the Sand,* an original play by northern transplant Chris Hanna loosely based upon the prelude and duration of the school closures crisis. This play dramatically improved in both its historical and dramatic quality from its initial drafts, but it remained anchored in traditional historiography and local myth on opening night in late February 2009. Despite featuring a stunning portrayal of African American activist Vivian Carter Mason, *Line in the Sand* stuck to the familiar parameters of the official school closures story. In this tale, local authorities, including Mayor W. Fred Duckworth, were forced to the brink of madness by evil external forces in the guise of the Byrd machine. Meanwhile, the city's white professionals — exemplified by the Norfolk Committee for Public Schools (NCPS), U.S. District Judge Walter E. Hoffman, and 100 businessmen who petitioned to reopen the schools — came to their senses and challenged the state's discriminatory school-closing policies. This heroic story of local progressivism came to its "logical" ending, the *Virginian-Pilot*'s venerable critic Mal Vincent noted, on February 2, 1959, the alleged day of the end of "Massive Resistance."

White redemption with its heavy dose of legal history weighed down the play's second part, in which an insipid and anticlimactic coda replaced one initial draft's having an African American man shoot the mayor (who was actually murdered for unknown reasons in 1972, a decade after he left office). Other versions had the same black man with the mask of a white woman's face shoot Duckworth, while the most problematic rendition had a member of the Norfolk 17 forgive the fallen mayor for his segregationist sins. Thankfully, public input and pressure from the commission excised those unfortunate detours of fantasy, but the improved result only underscored the historiographical and municipal need to go beyond reenacting the crisis onstage. Indeed, obsessing on this particular crisis and its characters without looking at what happened before and after distorted and trivialized the struggles for educational equity and inclusion that have been going on for at least a century. Most sinister, such a contained and safe commemoration absolved Norfolk's whites and blacks from taking any more efforts toward equity and inclusion in the future.[4]

On the other hand, local African Americans have constructed their own celebratory narrative that is almost as limiting as the official story. On Freedom Sunday, July 6, 2008, the First Baptist Church on Bute Street — the place of refuge for the seventeen African Americans locked out of white schools in 1958–59 — hosted a well-attended tribute to those pioneers whose sacrifices and achievements cannot be overstated. Meanwhile, Lisa Godley and Barbara Hamm Lee at WHRO-TV, the local public television station, coproduced a prosaic if passable documentary, *The Norfolk 17: Their Story,* which aired just in time for the actual anniversary. Members of the 17 themselves have also published accounts of their experiences, and their testimonies have finally begun to challenge the long-held view that Norfolk's desegregation proceeded smoothly after "the late unpleasantness" of the school closings. Simultaneously, the city council entertained ideas from architecture students at Hampton University for a proposed monument honoring the Norfolk 17 along the port city's new light-rail tracks downtown; the monument would be a permanent testimony to civic progress amid the hustle and bustle of modern public transportation. This attention is wonderful and long overdue, even if surviving members of the 1959 class of Booker T. Washington High School felt left out of the festivities for the Norfolk 17 and let commission member Marvin Lake know their feelings publicly. That alleged snub did create a tiny tempest in a teapot during the summer of 2009, but it underscored a much, much greater point: spotlighting and canonizing only the Norfolk 17 ignores all of the other African American students, parents, and leaders who had fought and who continue to fight for their civil rights and equal opportunities.[5] Also, this persistent pocket of the "accomplishment school" of black history obscures the fact that several of the 17 did not graduate from desegregated schools and that there were many other African Americans who had applied but who were turned down without explanation. Most African American students and parents did not apply for transfers, and African American opinion was sharply divided over goals and strategies over the long term. Looking at the Norfolk 17 in isolation obscures that multilayered complexity. Finally, this recognition of the 17 also leads directly to the celebration of federal district court judge Walter E. Hoffman, who ordered the desegregation of Norfolk's schools and thus the end of legalized Jim Crow. We do not deny the greatness of Hoffman as a jurist, but we do present a more nuanced and humanized portrait of him than the plaster-of-Paris pariah who braved social ostracism to uphold the rule of law. This spotlight only on the heroic Hoffman of 1958 and 1959 ignores his deep-seated opposition to real integration that came only with crosstown busing, a change that Hoffman and the rest of white officialdom in Norfolk loathed.[6]

Dispelling these persistent myths has been made difficult by those in power still comfortable with the way things were and are in the port city. For example, when we began this project, Jeffrey Littlejohn's repeated inquiries to the Norfolk school board to release its files on desegregation and busing yielded few documents. Most of the records were archived off-site, lost, or misplaced, he was told. Similarly, at the *Virginian-Pilot*, his inquiries into their photographs from desegregation and busing episodes were initially met with the same kind of nonchalant disregard. Of course, when official Norfolk and Virginia needed filler for their proclamations, articles, and websites regarding these events, they borrowed liberally from our early efforts: one proclamation about the Norfolk 17 issued by the General Assembly is a verbatim plagiarism of Littlejohn's online descriptions.[7] Nevertheless, when we enlisted the help of power brokers — both black and white — and as the municipal commemoration drew near, suddenly the records and photographs began to surface. The microfilmed official school board minutes up until 1968 finally made their way to the Norfolk Public Library, even if the official ones from 1969 to 1993 had been mysteriously thrown out without any repercussions. More galling than even that was the transfer of Norfolk's public school records to Old Dominion University's Special Collections. These were the same records that we at historically black Norfolk State University had been told did not exist. Thanks to the cooperation of Old Dominion's archivist Sonia Yaco, however, we were able to exploit this treasure trove, making our book the first large-scale study to use this invaluable archival resource. Combining the results of oral interviews, court transcripts, archival collections, and accounts from the three major newspapers in the area — the African American weekly, the *Journal and Guide*, as well as the *Pilot* and the surprisingly rich *Ledger-Dispatch* — we connect the school closures crisis with its broader historical and social context. Our approach makes this work the most comprehensive, multidimensional, and unsentimental analysis of the century-long struggle to gain educational equality in Norfolk.[8]

Tracing this struggle requires a chronological approach, which highlights the many social, legal, and political developments that took place in Norfolk over the last century. We begin in chapter 1 with a discussion of the city's segregated schools and early local efforts to equalize them. Building on previous work by Earl Lewis and other scholars, we provide an urban geography that connects the white and black communities of the 1930s with the more familiar "Massive Resistance" narrative of the 1950s.

Our second and third chapters expose the emptiness of Norfolk's vaunted self-image as a progressive port, showing the long and painful path from *Brown v. Board of Education* (1954) to the infamous school closures in September 1958. Focusing on the key roles played by the National Association for the Advancement of Colored People (NAACP), Mayor W. Fred Duckworth, and the local students and families who were involved, these chapters show how the segregationists in power overreacted and overplayed their hand. At the same time, these chapters suggest that, despite popular notions to the contrary, white moderates and segregationists shared the same goal: stopping any real integration.

In chapters 4–7, we examine the causes and consequences of the city's heated battle over crosstown busing. The tragic irony of this story is that without busing, Norfolk's schools never would have been truly integrated, and with busing, so many whites left the city that integration became virtually impossible. In fact, the most recent figures show that the district is more segregated today than at any time since 1970. It is thus vital that we study the confrontations and compromises of the past, so that we may make informed and egalitarian policy decisions in the future. Our epilogue juxtaposes the vaunted "urban advantage" of Norfolk's public schools in the "Age of Obama" with continuing gaps and disparities in reference to race and class. It offers neither a sugarcoated happy ending nor a vituperative indictment, but the balance only possible through a thorough, sober look at where we have been.[9]

CHAPTER ONE

DISCRIMINATION
AND NORFOLK UNDER THE OLD
   DOMINION, 1938–1954
DISSENT

I
T CERTAINLY WAS UNUSUAL. On June 25, 1939, at St. John's African
Methodist Episcopal (AME) Church in Norfolk, Virginia, over 1,200 African Americans signed a petition requesting that the city's school board
rehire chemistry teacher Aline Black, who had recently been dismissed
from her position at nearby Booker T. Washington High School. Just prior
to the St. John's meeting, "a large number of Negro children, led by a Negro
Boy Scout Drum and Bugle Corps, marched from the Dunbar School into
the church, carrying banners." Their procession route took them from the
western edges of the mainly black Huntersville neighborhood through "the
Harlem of the South," Norfolk's vibrant Church Street business district.
Their banners and placards skillfully alluded to current events — like the
rise of dictatorships in Europe — to stress the significance of the plight of
Black, who had lost her annual contract with the school board when she
challenged the district's policy of separate and unequal salary scales for
white and black faculty members. Accordingly, the march to St. John's, the
largest and oldest African American church in Norfolk, made for powerfully
and intentionally corrosive street theater as the children walked past with
their signs that stated, among other things: "'Dictators — Hitler, Mussolini,
Norfolk School Board,' . . . 'The Right of Petition Ought Not To Be Denied American Citizens,' 'Our School Board Has Vetoed the Bill of Rights,'
. . . 'The School Board's Method of Dealing With Colored Teachers is Un-
American.'"[1] Framing the school board's racism as foreign and totalitarian
made for good politics, while having over 100 children demonstrate was an
absolute stroke of genius on the part of the local organizers: insurance sales-
man David Longley, dentist Dr. Samuel F. Coppage, attorney P. B. Young
Jr., and railway mail clerk Jerry O. Gilliam.[2] Their casting of children in

the march either consciously or unconsciously mocked the prevailing white Virginian view of blacks as unwanted and perpetually immature wards who would never dare to criticize the white establishment that ran the state.

Whatever its dramatic intentions, this children's procession was quite a spectacle, as collective demonstrations of African Americans protesting injustices were only too rare in Jim Crow Virginia, which had long prided itself on ostensibly harmonious and, in the judicious phrasing of historian J. Douglas Smith, "managed racial relations." In return for fewer lynchings and hate crimes, Virginia's blacks were supposed to be grateful and to show their gratitude by not challenging the separate and unequal status quo.[3] That certainly extended to the sphere of public education, where teachers were paid differently because of race and, to a lesser degree, because of gender. This institutional inequality had long been resented, if accepted, by nearly all black teachers who were eager to eke out some kind of professional career within the confines of Jim Crow. That was the case in Norfolk until the NAACP encouraged the impeccably qualified Black, a twelve-year veteran of the school system and an Ivy League graduate, to petition, in October 1938, and, then, in March 1939, to file suit against the Norfolk School Board. Backed by her team of lawyers that featured Thurgood Marshall, Black's defiant courage weakened the precepts of local paternalism that had always denied African American agency. Although she lost her case on June 1, 1939, just bringing it publicly emboldened and inspired others, if only temporarily and dramatically at St. John's later in the month. On the other hand, the school board's subsequent mistreatment of Black lessened black deference to white leadership. The school board not only released her without legitimate cause two weeks before the actual court decision, but then it had the audacity to charge her $4.01 for the school day that she had spent in Judge Allan Reeves Hanckel's circuit court. This overreaction was obviously crass and displayed a seemingly un-Virginian kind of pettiness, which did worry the devotees of "managed racial relations" as much as it seemed to galvanize the crowd at St. John's.[4]

Historians have closely analyzed the immediate causes and consequences of the Aline Black lawsuit and its even more famous follow-up, *Alston v. School Board of the City of Norfolk* (1940), but they have never connected the themes, individuals, institutions, and strategies featured in these familiar landmark events with similar ones found in such dramas as the school closures crisis and the advent of busing that would happen later in the century.

On June 25, 1939, local residents held a demonstration at St. John's African Methodist Episcopal Church to protest the dismissal of teacher Aline Black. (Courtesy of the National Association for the Advancement of Colored People)

The best secondary accounts of NAACP activity and twentieth-century African American life in Norfolk are those set during the Depression and World War II, and they end just before the *Brown* decision. Then, African American agency and sources are strangely either omitted or pushed to the margins in Norfolk's transformation from prewar backwater to postwar "Sunrise City by the Sea." This has led to unfortunate errors and gaping holes in the current historiography. Most significantly, J. Douglas Smith contends that lessening black deference and its obverse, growing white Negrophobia, had eroded the "managed racial relations" of elite paternalism in the Old Dominion to the point that it was no longer relevant by the 1950s. While no one would dispute that "the Virginia way" and its particular expressions in Norfolk changed dramatically between 1909 and 2009, this and subsequent chapters show the continued uses, transpositions, and reconstitutions of Virginian paternalism in Norfolk, particularly in the key sphere of public education, well past its alleged death. For instance, a major component of maintaining white supremacy was the interracial or biracial committee of notables, a frequent white resort to calm black anger or resentment that, in turn, would be refitted or rejected by black leaders for their own purposes from the 1940s onward. Indeed, while the St. John's protest showed a rare degree of unity among local and national black leaders, division and diversity of opinions among local blacks about how best to achieve equal educational opportunities were the norms both before and well after that protest, providing periodic and, occasionally, key comfort to the defenders of the racial status quo. Furthermore, as Mark V. Tushnet has shown, a major component of preventing salary equalization from coming after the successful *Alston* case was the practice by school boards of what the NAACP's 1941 pamphlet, *Teachers' Salaries in Black and White,* called "intimidation, chicanery, and trickery of almost every form imaginable."[5] Finally, in providing a usable touchstone for much-needed analyses of later events, this chapter offers an urban geography of Norfolk under Jim Crow, building upon and tailoring the pioneering work of historian Earl Lewis and urban studies analyst Forrest White Jr. in order to comprehend the local desires for equalization and then for desegregation. This setting of the stage is necessary to understand the later periods of desegregation, integration, and resegregation that have been treated separately and unevenly, if at all, by scholars of Virginia history.

TO TRACE THESE continuities first requires a closer look at the St. John's rally and its immediate effects. While Norfolk's self-presentation as the "All-American City" was still a generation away, its leaders did worry about damage control in the wake of the board's decision to release Black. Both in its article on the mass protest and its editorial a day later, the *Virginian-Pilot* was clearly more concerned about what it deemed as the harmful effects of the *Black* case on the maintenance of a humanized and workable segregation than it was about achieving real salary equalization. For example, in its coverage of the event, it placed the reactions of two prominent local whites at the rally—the Reverend Gerald Evans Hopkins, of Le Kies Methodist Church, and W. D. Keene Jr., federal customs inspector and executive secretary of Norfolk's own Interracial Commission—before the coverage of the petition or the speech by Walter E. White, the executive secretary of the NAACP. The attenuated nature of the support that these two white leaders offered in defense of the rally was even more revealing than its textual placement, however. As a resident of the streetcar suburb of Colonial Place, Keene insisted that he was there as an individual and not as a representative of the commission, which was to meet on this issue later in the week.

The Reverend Hopkins was also a member of this body, but he apparently did not feel the need to make a disclaimer about representing it. Hopkins might have been more socially confident and aware than his cautious colleague; he lived in Ghent proper, one of the "best" addresses in the city, even if his church was across the Hague waterway in the working-class Atlantic City neighborhood. At any rate, Keene's reticence was not entirely necessary, since the commission would soon vote to support Black, and its chair, Juvenile and Domestic Relations Court Judge Herbert G. Cochran, would petition the school board to reinstate her.[6]

For his part, the Reverend Hopkins endorsed the particulars of the petition, but he also told the black audience members that they should work to understand and forgive the errant school board. Hopkins stated, "Remember there are at least two sides to each question. In their minds these members of the school board, some of whom I know personally and admire, think they are doing the right thing." In other words, according to Hopkins, the audience members and marchers at St. John's were to forgive the board members in the same unconditional way that Christ had forgiven the sins of the members of the crowd. To do otherwise would have upset the "managed racial relations" that the interracial commissions of the 1920s and 1930s were supposed to ensure. Hopkins admitted that his sympathy for the goals of the petitioners was not shared by a majority of the white residents of Norfolk, but he predicted that his position would become much more commonplace with an increase in both the practice of Christianity and the "general educational level of our white people."[7]

More reflective of mainstream white opinion on this matter was the editorial in the *Ledger-Dispatch,* the smaller, more conservative, and less fashionable white newspaper in the city. It vehemently denied that the school board "was venting something like spleen" and did not appreciate the board being portrayed as "a public enemy." Still, the editorial was "uncertain" about the decision to release Black, but it suggested that she ought to have expected that move, given her "contumacious attitude." A "contumacious attitude" was unacceptable for any employee, but it was certainly beyond the pale for a black woman in Norfolk who dared to challenge the system.[8]

Like Keene and Hopkins and unlike the *Ledger-Dispatch,* the famed editor of the *Virginian-Pilot,* Louis Jaffe, urged the board to reconsider its decision by "doing the right thing" and rehiring Black, if for the same concerns about racial harmony, not racial equality. Like Hopkins, Jaffe knew the board members personally, finding them to be "public-spirited individuals who are above the temptation of petty reprisal." He blamed the state government for pressuring the school board in Norfolk to act as its "catspaw" in "the pay-parity controversy." The board members were not to blame. Their unfortunate detour from reason, to Jaffe, nevertheless did "untold damage to the city's interracial relations." The decision to fire Aline Black had only stirred up trouble in the form of the "formidable" parley at St. John's, which, gratefully to the editor, only witnessed "a few sharp and resentful words" and largely was free of "provocative or abusive polemics."[9]

While firmly grounding their remarks in the tropes and images of American secular religion so beloved by Jaffe, the black speakers at St. John's were not content with waiting either for white people to get educated or for them to do the right thing. With a new world war between the democracies and dictatorships about to erupt in Europe, P. B. Young Sr., the longtime editor of the city's black weekly, the *Journal and Guide,* clearly defined the *Black* case as a fight between "Democracy" and "Autocracy." In this same martial vein, Walter White referred to a different Jesus than did the Reverend Hopkins, preferring those present to chase the moneychangers out of the temple instead of instinctively turning the other cheek. Thurgood Marshall similarly reminded everyone to fight as well as to pray, joking that that was what blacks did in "civilized countries" such as his neighboring Maryland where, according to him, all teachers had tenure after three years of service. He boasted of a "war-chest" to carry on the appeals process as well as to assist the now-unemployed Black. To Marshall and every other African American speaker, including the Reverend Walter L. Hamilton of Shiloh Baptist Church, the best way to get rid of the rascals on the school board was to vote for a new city council, which would then appoint new members to the board who were more accountable to the city's black citizens.[10]

This threat was much more credible by the late 1930s than at any other time since the Readjuster era of the early 1880s, as locally based white politicians such as Colgate W. Darden Jr. had to compete in contested federal elections for black votes. The federal courts had struck down Virginia's white primary in 1929, opening the way for the semblance of biracial New Deal coalitions even in the Old Dominion.[11] It is true that poll taxes and voter apathy had artificially depressed the numbers of eligible black voters in Norfolk, as a 1941 survey done by Luther Jackson, a professor of history at all-black Virginia State College in Petersburg, would conclude. Yet that same study and its ensuing campaign to get out the black vote would contribute to the long-term trend of more African American taxpayers and voters in the port city than ever before.[12] While electoral victories seemed within reach for black leaders in Norfolk once again, however, clear-cut mandates for dismantling Jim Crow remained elusive, and both the local and national NAACP deduced that the best venue to seek equality under the law in the short term remained the courts, even if Aline Black had lost in the first round. They firmly believed that they would eventually win, even if it took many years.[13]

This confidence and corresponding, if temporary, unity was certainly on display at the national NAACP's annual convention held in nearby Richmond a few days after the St. John's protest in Norfolk. Roughly 5,000 delegates as well as the mayor of Richmond, J. Fulmer Bright, and the governor of Virginia, James C. Price, gathered at an "immense" auditorium, while thousands more listened outside to the convention's celebrity speakers via a public address system. Mayor Bright even published a letter of welcome to the convention in the *Richmond Afro-American,* the capital's black weekly. The leading white celebrity at the show, however, was none other than First Lady Eleanor Roosevelt, who was invited to speak and present opera singer Marian Anderson with the NAACP's Spingarn Medal Award. This recognition was for Anderson's ultimate public relations victory during the previous spring over the Daughters of the American Revolution (DAR), which had refused to allow her to perform at their hall because she was black. Roosevelt had resigned from the DAR in protest over Anderson's mistreatment, and she had been instrumental in getting Anderson to sing at the Lincoln Memorial instead. While basking in that shared triumph, Roosevelt did go ever so carefully beyond just celebrating the resolution of the Anderson controversy. In remarks carried by both the Columbia Broadcasting and National Broadcasting companies' radio networks, the First Lady elliptically referred to the necessity of "educational reform" for the "preservation of democracy," a coded endorsement of the NAACP's equalization efforts.[14] In their speeches, Charles Houston, the NAACP's chief counsel, and Walter White were far less circumspect than Eleanor Roosevelt had been. While Houston unequivocally endorsed the Supreme Court's recent decision in *Gaines v. Missouri,* White, to "tumultuous applause," beseeched Governor Price to "do his utmost to render justice" in reference to the Aline Black case.[15]

It had taken the NAACP many months to achieve that moment of local consensus and national awareness evident at both St. John's and in Richmond, but that unity of purpose among local and national black leaders was fleeting and ultimately unsatisfying to both. While black teachers in Norfolk worked with the national NAACP to secure pay parity in local schools, the city's most prominent African American leader, P. B. Young Sr., worked out a conciliatory deal of his own with the white power structure.

A native of small town North Carolina, Young had been in Norfolk since the Jamestown Exposition of 1907. By the 1930s, he and his family lived on Chapel Street between two black neighborhoods: Uptown and Huntersville. The *Journal and Guide*'s offices were located just a short walking distance away at 721 E. Olney Road, a convenient location near the Church Street business district. Working close to home, Young was never really interested in making big profits. He was concerned with wielding power and shaping opinion, however. Over his thirty-year career as a newspaperman and banking executive, Young had become very influential in explaining the actions of whites to blacks and vice versa. He was more than a big fish in a small pond, however, having achieved a degree of statewide and national prominence as a trustee of the Jeanes Rural School Fund as well as one of the best black colleges in the nation, Howard University in Washington, D.C. Such power in a segregated setting did not come without its price in integrity and consistency. Young was no "Uncle Tom," but he could certainly and convincingly act in that role if he could win real, if piecemeal, concessions from whites. His definitive biographer, Henry Suggs, has aptly characterized Young as a "militant accommodationist," and, true to form, in the pay-parity cases, he at first played the militant, only later to switch to the accommodationist role when it looked like the best possible settlement was near.[16]

Indeed, Young as "militant" was just as believable to contemporaries as was his trimming of news articles to please skittish white patrons and advertisers. As the *Journal and Guide* grew in circulation from 20,000 subscribers in 1933 to over 65,000 in 1944, his paper unequivocally backed the teachers and gave detailed coverage and editorial support to their cause. The founder of Norfolk's local branch of the NAACP in 1917, Young did not always agree with either local or national activists, but he took the time to moderate a session on civil rights at the 1939 Richmond convention. A few days later, he sent off a spirited and thoughtful response to a condescendingly racist letter to the editor from a white lawyer, W. H. Venable, an exchange that appeared in the *Ledger-Dispatch* at the height of the Aline Black controversy. Here Young directly rebutted the most egregious pretensions and posturings of "the Virginia Way." He was very proud of that reply, which bestowed renewed credibility to him as a "race man"; he had the entire exchange reprinted in full in the *Journal and Guide* a few weeks later. Being seen as a "race man" was particularly important to a Virginia gentleman of mixed heritage who was so light in appearance. Accordingly, the *Journal and Guide* styled itself as "Tidewater Virginia's Largest Business Owned ENTIRELY and EXCLUSIVELY by Negroes." On the other hand, the seasoned and savvy editor was capable of overcoming his own considerable ego to work with local NAACP chair Jerry O. Gilliam, via his son, helping to put on the St. John's protest. He had clashed with sometime rival Gilliam over tactics and methods in the past, but, in confronting their common white enemies downtown, those differences were forgotten, at least for the time being.[17]

While the elder Young stayed in the spotlight, behind the scenes P. B. (Bernard) Young Jr. was more uniformly forceful than his father, even in the immediate months after the Hanckel decision in the *Black* case. The tone and content of Bernard Young's eloquent letters and telegrams — many of them marked personal and confidential — to the lawyer Thurgood Marshall and other NAACP officials show both the strength of his embrace of the teachers' cause throughout 1939 and, correspondingly, his suspicions about the collective resolve of black teachers in Norfolk to see justice done. For example, on October 13, 1939, Bernard Young wrote Marshall to urge him to "begin to use some pressure tactics" on the Norfolk Teachers Association (NTA), the local professional organization for faculty members at black public schools, in order to get the NTA to join a second pay-parity lawsuit. This was not the way that it was supposed to be. Ever since the NAACP had begun its drive for teacher pay equity in Virginia in Buckingham County in 1931, the organization had thought that it had the best chance for a breakthrough in Norfolk, largely because of its local branches' strong and growing connections among the city's teachers. Black teachers and leaders in Norfolk had even lobbied for equal pay on their own just before the onset of the Great Depression, and the ensuing pay cuts of 1932 had rubbed salt into these festering wounds of racial insult. Yet that earlier perception of local black teachers as "race men and women" was not completely panning out in 1938 and 1939 due to pressures, both real and internalized. Many black teachers understandably did not want to be dismissed for their support of this litigation; getting paid between two-thirds and three-quarters of what their white counterparts were receiving during the Depression was better than being unemployed. Many of them probably realized that they did not have the credentials of Aline Black, and thus if dismissed, they would not enjoy a particularly soft landing. While the NAACP paid for a year of Black's graduate study at the City University of New York after she lost, that golden parachute would not be there for every rank-and-file teacher whose contract could be withdrawn.[18]

Given that probability, some African American teachers from the outset denied that the "contumacious" chemistry teacher represented their position; they allegedly stated that they were satisfied with their salaries. Even before the Hanckel decision, Norfolk lawyer and NAACP worker T. Ione Diggs had told the *Richmond Afro-American* that she knew of several teachers who had gone to the school board to distance themselves from the NAACP's lawsuit.[19] These same teachers may have been the source of the rumors in April 1939 about Aline Black getting an unconfirmed job offer from President Gandy of Virginia State College in return for dropping her legal action. Gandy quickly denied it, and the damaging rumor about Black being an opportunist went away just as quickly.[20] Regardless of the teachers' stance toward the litigation, however, the pending case did bring unwanted and harassing scrutiny to local black schools. As J. Robert Smith, the editor of the *Afro-American,* candidly put it, "white supervisors are now busy finding more dirt in the nooks and corners of classrooms than they have found before since the existence of schools in old Norfolk." The black teachers of Norfolk knew that their jobs were on the line.[21]

In view of these high stakes, some of these teachers were leery of the competence and commitment of the NAACP's local counsel, W. L. Davis, for the proposed second round. He had been pushed upon them, and intimidated teachers ironically pushed back. Davis quickly withdrew after being insulted by the unexpected questioning of his professional ability, but his critics did not care. They did not want to lose again, especially if this second lawsuit in Norfolk was going to proceed with or without their support. Accordingly, the NTA held closed-door meetings to vent these feelings and frustrations. This secrecy concerned Bernard Young in part because these meetings were closed to members of the black press such as himself. He and his father could no longer monitor the teachers' support of the necessary litigation, support that was key to any chance of victory. Young insisted that he and his family newspaper — unlike the rival and more outspoken *Afro-American,* which had its own loyal Tidewater audience — would never air the intramural wranglings of black teachers. They understood that the appearance, if not the reality, of black unity was needed to confront white oppression, but those teachers apparently did not trust even the relatively cautious *Journal and Guide.*[22]

Bernard Young had heard some pretty disturbing news through the grapevine. Forced to rely upon secondhand information, he had learned "from reliable sources, that at a recent meeting four women principals of the old school not only voted against the association's joining in the fight officially, but took the floor in an attempt to swing a majority with them." He was relieved to find out that this defeatist faction had been ultimately beaten, but Young was fully aware that the key to any victory, however small, was an emboldened and unified NTA. As he candidly wrote Marshall, "until the teachers are of one mind in this matter, whichever side we take, we are apt to be like Presbyterians — damned if we do and damned if we don't."[23]

Most worrisome to Young was his perception that the prospective new plaintiff, Melvin O. Alston, was not cooperating fully in the NAACP-led effort. A business education teacher at Booker T. Washington High School for five years in 1939, Alston had been a stalwart officer of the local NAACP branch — he was its vice president in 1939. Like many of his colleagues, however, Alston apparently disliked attorney Davis and favored closed-door sessions of the NTA to maintain local control. The previous fall, Alston had offered himself as the sacrificial lamb in another pay-parity case, but he understandably wanted some monetary cushion if he was actually fired because he had assumed this high-profile role. A graduate of Virginia State College and the Teachers College of Columbia University in New York City, he was a trailblazer, but he was not naive. One factor that may have emboldened him to stick his neck out in the fall of 1938 was the expected release of at least part of his father's estate to him, a prospective inheritance that would allow him some degree of financial independence in the face of possible dismissal. But that prospect still remained up in the air through the next year, and he needed a more reliable source of alternative money if he was to go forward. He liked living on O'Keefe Street in the heart of middle-class Huntersville; therefore, he still wanted some written assurance from Thurgood Marshall that he would get the amount of his annual salary from the NAACP "in the event I lose my job." At first, it did not matter because the national NAACP went ahead and picked Black over him largely because of happenstance. She apparently met and impressed Marshall when he was in town in October 1938 looking for a plaintiff. At the same time, Alston had apparently telephoned Marshall to file his own petition, but the lawyer had not been at home. Whatever the case, Marshall's initial selection of Black did not make Alston jealous or unhappy; he cheered her cause from the sidelines.[24]

When the first round of Black's lawsuit began in late May 1939, Marshall really did not expect to win. He believed that the elderly Judge Hanckel would find against Black, and he simply wanted to create a usable record for an appeal. Marshall's strategy seemed to be working when the school board admitted that it had discriminated against African American teachers. But the school board's attorneys insisted that such discrimination was legal, and Judge Hanckel upheld their demurrer. This ruling was expected in part not only because Judge Hanckel was of the generation that had built Jim Crow in Norfolk but also because, before he arrived in the city during the 1890s, he had been shaped by a long lineage of South Carolina planters.

Despite Marshall's plan to appeal the Hanckel decision, he soon elected to drop the case since Black no longer worked for the district and could not effectively challenge its pay practices. In light of this disturbing legal situation, Marshall decided to file a second, fresh pay-parity suit, and he immediately sought out Alston, who, in turn, insisted that, if he was to be the new plaintiff, then his cooperation was "contingent upon a written promise to me signed by the proper person, to the effect that I shall be compensated to the extent of one thousand dollars ($1,000) immediately upon temporary or permanent loss of [my] present teaching position." One month later, Alston suddenly got cold feet and backed out, stating that his refusal was "definite and final." In late August, Marshall then arranged to meet Alston after Labor Day when school was in session. The NTA consequently met to endorse the new suit at a meeting at Dunbar School, and Alston emerged as the new plaintiff. Bernard Young had nothing about which to worry: Alston would weather the storms of his eventually successful suit and would go on to become the first teacher in the Norfolk system, white or black, to get his doctorate in education in 1944.[25]

After finalizing the Alston choice, Marshall and his team — which, by this time, featured Dean William H. Hastie of Howard University Law School and Oliver W. Hill of the Virginia State Conference of NAACP branches—prepared to argue their new case before U.S. District Judge Luther Bynum Way, whom President Herbert Hoover had appointed in 1931. Way was best known for his hard line against "white slavery," but he ended up being almost as blind to the legacies of African American slavery in Norfolk as Judge Hanckel had been. In February 1940, Way ruled against Alston, citing the teacher's signing of a discriminatory contract as proof that he had consented to the unequal pay scale that was based upon race. In other words, Alston had waived his constitutional rights by taking his job. Judge Way also denied the class-action nature of the lawsuit, discerning the case as a simple suit between Alston and his employer. Nonetheless, Way, unlike Hanckel, did see the unequal pay scale as problematic, and he went on to criticize the school board's revenge against Aline Black. This time, Marshall and his team saw an opening in Way's comments and immediately filed an appeal to the Fourth Circuit Court of Appeals.[26]

On first glance, this venue seemed to be as inhospitable to the NAACP and its plaintiff as the courtrooms of Hanckel and Way had been. On this appellate bench sat the recently confirmed Armistead Dobie, the son of Norfolk's former school superintendent Richard Dobie—the very official who had maintained and solidified the unequal pay scale in question during his tenure as superintendent from 1896 to 1922. A former Confederate private, the elder Dobie's life and work gave little hope to the plaintiff and his attorneys about how his son would rule. Even more potentially hostile than Armistead Dobie was his most famous colleague, John J. Parker, whose elevation to the U.S. Supreme Court in 1930 had been successfully blocked by the civil rights organization because of his alleged racist rhetoric during a political campaign. Probably embarrassed by his youthful utterances, Parker was wedded to "the Virginia way" of courtly civility, however, and his gracious treatment of the NAACP lawyers during the case was part of that manner. Accordingly, he had ruled against Richmond's residential segregation law years earlier because it was too explicitly oppressive.[27]

While reflecting the conventional prejudices of the day, nevertheless, all three appellate judges on the Fourth Circuit—including Hoover appointee Morris A. Soper—firmly believed in actualizing the "separate but equal" doctrine that was established by the U.S. Supreme Court in *Plessy v. Ferguson* (1896). In June 1940, they found that Norfolk had not done its part to keep the segregated system running appropriately. The city paid black high school teachers an average of $699 per year, while comparably trained white teachers earned $970. This gross discrepancy challenged the strictures established in the *Plessy* ruling, and thus the judges of the Fourth Circuit issued a unanimous ruling for Alston and the NAACP. Noting that Norfolk's obvious and admitted discrimination violated both the due process and equal protection clauses of the Fourteenth Amendment, the judges found that Alston had not "waived" his constitutional rights when he signed his contract. In fact, he had not yet signed his upcoming contract, and he was not asking for back wages stemming from previous discriminatory contracts. He was only asking that his and other future annual contracts be equalized. Following the Fourth Circuit Court's approval of Alston's position, the U.S. Supreme Court passed on the case in October 1940. This set the stage for protracted and dramatic negotiations between the major players in this story — the school board, the municipal government, the teachers, the Youngs, the local NAACP, and Marshall and his team of attorneys.[28]

The NAACP's victory inside the courtrooms turned out to be unsatisfying outside, as Norfolk's racial managers compromised with the Youngs and the teachers. Key here were C. Alfred Anderson, Norfolk's main legal counsel, and Charles B. Borland, former police chief and current city manager. They offered the NTA a verbal pledge to boost the salaries of black teachers gradually, but the NAACP insisted that the pledge be immediate and in writing. The gradual scheme put forth by Anderson and Borland was a deal shaped by P. B. Young Sr. behind the backs of the NAACP lawyers; Marshall was livid when he found out about this seemingly secret dimension. Marshall thought that he had worked too hard only to be undermined by the leading intermediary of "the Virginia way" in Norfolk. On the other hand, Young did not want the prospect of real concessions from white officialdom to be wasted on some quixotic pursuit of ideological purity. He knew that most of the promises of "managed racial relations" in the Old Dominion were empty, but he also believed that the court-ordered basis of the city's desire to settle guaranteed actual progress. He hoped not only to raise the teachers' salaries but also to get the city to throw in a badly needed elementary school for blacks as part of any final resolution. Marshall vehemently disagreed with Young's self-invited intervention, and the young attorney immediately went to confront the old newspaperman. As Henry Suggs has relayed, what followed was a rather heated and embittered exchange between the two former allies, with choice words being expressed on both sides. At the consequent mass meetings of teachers, their arguments and accusations became public, magnifying the differences between blacks, while ironically making the white compromisers look good. At these gatherings, the teachers at first went with Young's position, only to accept a written plan crafted by the NAACP (yet almost identical to the city's earlier verbal pledge) in February 1941.[29]

Good things did come out of the final decree. Teacher salaries became more equal during World War II. Both plaintiffs — Aline Black and Melvin Alston — retained their professional credentials and returned to the classroom. In fact, when the dust had finally settled, Black was rehired at Booker T. Washington High School for the 1941–42 school year, after completing some graduate study in New York City. She would teach there until her retirement in 1969, thirty years after her legal showdown. Meanwhile, Alston received his doctorate and left Norfolk voluntarily, serving as a professor at historically black Florida A&M College by the 1950s. Both Black and Alston would be honored by the local NAACP in 1959 for their contributions to the struggle for equalization, but their individual accomplishments did not fully compensate for the sense of collective loss.[30] Despite the hopes of the Youngs, the elementary school in Uptown or Huntersville failed to materialize, even if the city did build two black elementary schools with federal funds in 1942 — one in the new Liberty Park housing project in eastern Brambleton and the other being the Tucker School across the Elizabeth River in Campostella.[31] Thanks to the Youngs, the local NAACP was temporarily eclipsed. And, most important to every African American in Norfolk, including the Youngs, black schools in Norfolk remained separate and very unequal. With this unsettling realization came a lingering feeling that local African American leaders, including many teachers, had sold out the broader cause of racial equality to feather their own personal nests. Such a quick compromise after a legal victory would not be repeated.[32]

THE SENSE OF BETRAYAL within African American communities in Norfolk was amplified by the "savage inequalities" in the "conscripted city" that went well beyond the question of teachers' salaries. These broad ranges of inequalities stemmed from the deep and reinforced legacy of slavery and subsequent racial discrimination. Nevertheless, to understand the particulars of this legacy in Norfolk requires a look at the city's urban geography during the first half of the twentieth century, a geography that was changing as the city grew both in population and land area. The best place to begin this survey is at the workplace of Aline Black and Melvin Alston — Booker T. Washington High School — in 1939. It is hard to imagine today that this cramped factory-like fortress was ever considered one of the largest and best-equipped black schools in the South, but it is important to note that, just a generation earlier, Norfolk did not even offer a public high school for blacks. While it is true that Norfolk Mission College under the auspices of the Presbyterian Church offered a private secondary school for blacks in the port city from 1887 to 1916 and that St. Joseph's would offer a Catholic alternative from 1915 onward, a public high school for blacks only came to Norfolk with the annexation of Huntersville in 1911. Here the port city acquired the Barboursville School, which was founded in 1906 and would be renamed the J. T. West High School the year after annexation. Its energetic principal, David Gilbert Jacox, had urged the renaming to honor John Thomas West, the white former superintendent from Norfolk County who had insisted on adequate, if not equal, school facilities and faculties for blacks. While showing more than the expected amount of deference to whites, Jacox was a great teacher, and he hired a dedicated and relatively well-credentialed staff.[33]

Finding adequate facilities, not faculties, therefore, would be a recurrent problem in the evolution of secondary education for Norfolk's blacks. The physical plant of West High School proved to be woefully problematic, even though the school had received accreditation in 1914 and had graduated its first class that same year. West High School was far too small for the city's growing student population, and even the school board noticed. At first, the board thought that an annex should be added to the existing school, but, even after the annex opened in early 1916, it still was not sufficient. Plus, the condition of the sidewalks and streets leading to the building was notoriously terrible, even by the relatively less exacting standards of those times. An opportunity, then, suddenly presented itself. When Norfolk Mission College closed later that same year due to financial reasons, its building was sold to the city, which promptly shifted high school instruction for blacks from West High School to the former Mission College site. The highest grades of the Lott Carey and S. C. Armstrong schools for blacks (the seventh and eighth grades) were also moved there. West High School remained open as a neighborhood mainstay for the lower grades long after its shelf life had expired: it would not have indoor bathrooms until the mid-1930s, and parents and children would still be complaining about its dreadful sidewalks and grounds well into the late 1950s.[34]

While West High School kept its name if not its dignity, the new consolidated secondary institution was christened Booker T. Washington High School in honor of the famed black leader who had visited Norfolk just before his death in 1915. Washington had a loyal and active following among Norfolk's African Americans, a following that included P. B. Young Sr., of course. So, the renaming was welcomed by blacks, for it honored one of their own, and the relocation was just as popular among local African Americans for it kept the mission of the Mission College going even after the failure of the former school. The reconditioned site soon proved to be too "old and inadequate" for either parents or administrators, however. For his part, the chair of the school board thought that its setup for liberal arts instruction did not match its new namesake's alleged preference for vocational and industrial training for blacks, a preference eagerly embraced by Virginia's managers of white supremacy. Accordingly, with their vision of constructing a practical investment that maintained the racial status quo for another generation, the city and school board spent $486,000 to build, in 1923, what they boasted was "the largest school building in the city" and "the finest and largest school for colored children" anywhere. This new Booker T. Washington High School would get a Grade A accreditation from the Southern Association of Colleges and Schools (SACS) in 1932, even if the accreditation only meant that it was one of the best schools in an unequal system.[35]

This boosterism about the new building was not restricted to whites; its biggest champion initially was African American educator Winston Douglas, who would serve as the principal of Booker T. Washington High School from 1927 into the 1960s. Douglas is probably best known for his key role in getting Richmond-based Virginia Union University to open up a junior, satellite branch in Norfolk in 1935, an offshoot that eventually became the Norfolk Division of Virginia State College in 1944. Yet, in his day, he was best known as a no-nonsense administrator, and he really liked where he worked. For example, in December 1930, in the *Journal and Guide,* he gushed: "Its sixty-five class rooms and shops, spacious halls, and splendid auditorium present an impressive picture to the visitor. Especially striking are the shops, with their modern electrical machinery and the home economics rooms with their immaculate up-to-date furnishing, where large numbers of students are enthusiastically at work in the practical art courses." In that same valentine, however, Douglas damned other less attractive aspects of his school with fainter praise. Most revealing was his characterization of the office-size school library as merely "very creditable." Even through his veil of appreciation, Douglas admitted that its holdings were primarily acquired via private fund-raisers arranged by the school librarian and were only supplemented by state and local moneys. He did not mention that Booker T. did not have a full-time librarian; it would take four more years for Vivian Tucker to be selected for that position. He was quick to mention, however, the $600 that the school board had spent on acquiring books for his library over the previous three years. After praising his white bosses in the deferential way conventional to the time — "our officials are to be commended for a spirit of fairness and a sincere interest"— he opined that "while the schools are not all that we might wish, they are functioning admirably so far as resources will permit." He further predicted that "some very necessary improvements" would only come about if "the citizens of Norfolk, white and colored alike, are willing to make the sacrifice necessary."[36]

A few of those "very necessary improvements" did come, but Douglas's blitheness about the conditions at Norfolk's black schools would be dampened by an ever-expanding student enrollment and rising expectations about what even black schools should offer. As early as 1936, he himself was complaining about overcrowding; in 1945 and 1949 he led a chorus of complaining petitioners to the school board, foreshadowing the student-led protests of a generation later. While not all of its students had a seat, the facilities at Booker T. were gradually expanded, even if they failed to keep up with both demand and expectations. The biggest news for the black high school in 1939, therefore, was not the fallout from the *Black* and *Alston* cases, but it was rather the expansion of its library and the building of its cafeteria, both of which were formally dedicated in November 1940.[37] Douglas viewed these improvements as "much needed," and he noted that they "had been actively sought by colored citizens over a period of fifteen years." Yet those citizens had to be disappointed with the meager improvements they received. A photograph of the inside of the cafeteria, taken not long before it opened, revealed a dank, dungeonlike hole featuring a poor use of space with folding chairs and spartan tables crammed together in an uncomfortable mess. It was not well designed, but at least it was better than nothing.[38]

Overcrowding at Booker T. Washington stemmed from the fact that Norfolk directed all black students in the city to one high school; as the city expanded, the overcrowding obviously grew worse. The largest acquisition of black residents and neighborhoods came in 1911 in a new wave of annexations: that of Lamberts Point to the north and west of downtown and, most important, that of Barboursville, Huntersville, Cottage Heights, Lindenwood, Douglas Park, Washington Heights, and the Church Street business district on the city's eastern flank. From colonial times, black people and neighborhoods were scattered throughout the port city, but their greatest concentrations within the 1845 borders of the central core were in Uptown, or the old Fourth Ward, which was just to the east and north of the commercial district downtown. A century later, these areas, the oldest predominantly black ones in Norfolk, had turned into the nation's worst slums with back alleys, rickety frame row houses, and windowless tenements. Yet even they were not completely segregated, having both poor black and white residents until their clearance under postwar urban renewal. Indeed, there were not exclusively African American ghettoes in Norfolk in the northern metropolitan sense until after the city had embarked on its zeal for public housing projects during and after World War II. As middle-class and working-class blacks left the older, more crowded Uptown area after 1900, they settled in Lindenwood, Cottage Heights, and Huntersville, all of which featured lovely single-family bungalows with well-kept yards and gardens, despite the fact that the city government in the early 1920s had decided to place an unsightly garbage dump in their midst.[39]

Unlike the annexation efforts of 1911, most of the municipal annexations between 1887 and 1959 actually reduced the percentage of African American residents in Norfolk. The port did attract black migrants from rural Virginia and North Carolina, but many merely used it as a way station on their way north. On the other hand, most of the annexed areas had overwhelming white majorities that stayed in place. In 1930, the population was 65.9 percent white and 33.9 percent black, with 0.2 percent being in the "other races" category. By 1940, the white majority had grown to 68.1 percent, and the Tanner's Creek annexations of the 1950s, even with the black neighborhoods of Oakwood and Rosemont, brought with them many more whites than blacks. This increasing white majority, even as the number of blacks in the city correspondingly increased, ensured a paradoxical blend of African American agency and deference. As Jane Reif of the Virginia Council on Human Relations noted in 1960, the racial ratios in Norfolk allowed blacks

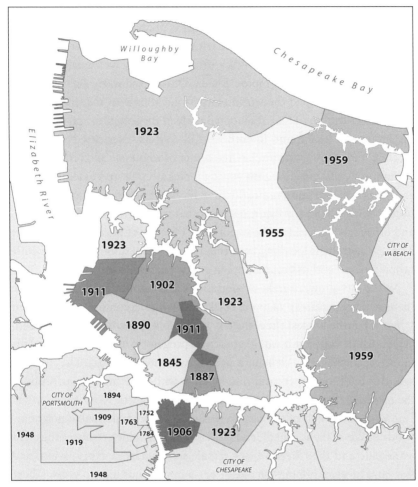

The annexations of adjacent territories by Norfolk occurred in several stages between 1887 and 1959, as this map illustrates. (Courtesy of the City of Norfolk)

to test the boundaries of Jim Crow, while those same ratios benefited the white managers of "the Virginia way."[40]

While annexations whitened the city's population, the overall demographic growth of the port city was almost geometric. In 1900, Norfolk had 46,624 residents.[41] By 1930, thanks to both migrations and annexations, the seaport's population had tripled to 129,710 people. And the growth continued. A decade later, the city had an official count of 144,332 that only swelled with Norfolk becoming the "conscripted city" of World War II. In 1950, Norfolk had 213,513 residents, almost five times as many as people as in 1900.[42]

This ever-expanding nexus of "Maritime Dixie" featured various industries, naturally related to Norfolk's direct proximity to the strategic and lucrative waterways of Hampton Roads. During the world wars, the U.S. government developed the world's largest naval base in the northwestern quadrant of the city. This presence would feed the shipping and shipbuilding industries, long found in both Norfolk and its sister city, Portsmouth. Norfolk, though, was the undisputed center of wholesale and retail trade in Hampton Roads, providing the setting for local, state, and federal agencies as well as regional communication and banking networks. Railroads connected Norfolk with the Piedmont and other interior regions, carrying coal and other raw materials to be exported. This type of nexus thus made the port city a strategic location, both economically and militarily, even before urban renewal and its accompanying public relations offensives.[43]

As the city grew, rounds of migrations and annexations brought with them a dizzying array of both black and white communities and their schools. For the longest time, the city of Norfolk was confined to a boundary drawn in 1845, but it would absorb its progeny — mainly, the neighboring streetcar suburbs — at a quick pace between 1887 and 1923. The streetcar suburbs, built for upper- and middle-class white commuters, surrounded the city in an arc going from one side of the Elizabeth River to the other. Due west and north of the city were the especially fashionable neighborhoods of West Ghent, Ghent, and North Ghent, in which many of the city's white elite and their live-in black female servants lived. Norfolk annexed this land in 1890, hoping for these bedroom communities to grow. Ghent proper, south of Olney Road with its stately Mowbray Arch, would be developed first, sprouting the largest concentration of single-family, late-Victorian mansions in the city. North Ghent would be developed largely between 1899 and 1920, with West Ghent following largely in the 1920s. Two more downscale neighborhoods also came into their own about the turn of the century within the original annexation zone of 1890. Directly across Mowbray Arch and alongside the Elizabeth River was working-class Atlantic City, a relatively gritty mix of industrial, commercial, and residential areas that were mostly white with a minority of black residents and workers. Then, there was East Ghent, which stretched from the other side of Colonial Avenue on the west side to the mainly black neighborhoods of the Fourth

Ward, or Uptown and Huntersville, farther east. It developed to accommodate a mixture of apartments and modest homes and a sprinkling of black residents. Farther north of the Ghents, across the train tracks and facing the Lafayette River, were the solidly middle-class and nearly all-white suburbs of Park Place, Colonial Place, Old Dominion Place, Virginia Place, Villa Heights, and Riverview, the lands for which had been annexed by Norfolk in 1902. On the other hand, due south of downtown and across the Elizabeth was Berkley, a suburb connected by ferry and annexed in 1906 from Norfolk County. It had the most black people of any of the "white" suburbs, including hardscrabble Atlantic City.[44]

Directly east of the 1845 borders of Norfolk laid Brambleton, the port's first suburb that predated both the Civil War and streetcars. It had middle- and working-class housing and was annexed in 1887, three years before Ghent. Unlike Ghent proper, it bordered mainly black neighborhoods such as Huntersville. A growing black middle class eventually sought homes in adjacent Brambleton, and, in turn, its white population would fight a losing battle from the 1920s to the 1940s to keep the neighborhood segregated at the Corprew Avenue line. By the mid-1950s, Brambleton would feature two leading black churches in the struggle for educational equality — Grace Episcopal and Shiloh Baptist, whose buildings had hosted formerly white congregations — and the campus of the Norfolk Division of all-black Virginia State College, which had formerly been a segregated nine-hole golf course for whites only.[45]

The biggest wave of annexations occurred in 1923, when an even larger arc of surrounding land, this time mostly from Princess Anne County, was added to the city. This new chunk stretched from Norfolk Highlands and Campostella across the Elizabeth River to the south all the way around the city's borders to the tony and restricted suburbs of Larchmont and Edgewater to the west. In between lay the mainly white and middle-class Chesterfield Heights (just east of Brambleton) through the leafy Lafayette Residence Park (across the Lafayette River from Park Place) and then through the mostly black Titustown section of Sewells Point. The mostly white resort areas of Ocean View and Willoughby Spit were added to the far north, as was the land that would eventually become the naval base and its surroundings. The outer borders of Norfolk would now go from Chesapeake Bay on the north to and beyond the Elizabeth River to the south.[46]

As in the case of Huntersville, along with these new lands for the city came new public schools, both white and black. The only school built for blacks originally in Norfolk was the Cumberland Street School, or S. C. Armstrong School, which began in 1886. As noted earlier, the all-black Barboursville School, or West High School, became Norfolk's with the acquisition of Huntersville in 1911, as did the "B" Avenue School, or soon-to-be-renamed Joseph C. Price School, on Church Street. The Douglas Park School, named for abolitionist Frederick Douglass yet usually spelled with only one *s*, emerged in annexed northern Brambleton as black families moved in from the Fourth Ward. Its neoclassical facade could not hide its unfortunate location in the very midst of heavy industrial sites. Around the same time, the equally modest Abraham Lincoln School sprang up in working-class Berkley. Slightly to the east, the Campostella School also catered to blacks across the Elizabeth River; in 1933 it would be renamed after the first principal of the Armstrong School: Richard Allen Tucker. About a decade before the renaming of the Campostella School, J. J. Smallwood Elementary, a black school in western Norfolk, which got its name from a noted African American temperance activist, came with the Lamberts Point annexation. Arguably the worst one of the bunch, however, was the Oakwood Elementary School, which came with the Tanner's Creek annexations a generation later. Even though its latest incarnation opened in 1952 under the auspices of Norfolk County, the Oakwood School had split shifts exclusively from day one.[47]

Other black schools were hand-me-downs from whites, who had either rejected their lack of modern facilities or who had abandoned their adjoining neighborhoods. The Queen Street School, later renamed the J. H. Smythe School, was the first of these; it was a four-room, two-story Italianate cottage built in 1856 as one of the first four public schools in the city. It had very little space and potbellied stoves for heating well into the twentieth century. Accordingly, due to its structural deficiencies, it was designated a black school in 1900 and would continue as such until 1954. Nearby, the slightly larger Princess Anne Avenue School, later renamed the Lott Carey School, was built in Uptown itself in 1895 to serve the small number of whites living in the mainly black neighborhood. Because it was in a largely African American neighborhood, it was reassigned to black students in 1909. This process of conversion of obsolete or underused facilities from white to black use continued all the way to the end of legalized segregation. In 1935, thirty-two-year-old Henry Clay Elementary School for whites became the Laura E.

Titus Elementary School for blacks. The name "Henry Clay" was then eventually assigned to an even older downtown white school, which was converted due to dwindling enrollment to African American use in 1954 and would be torn down only in 1964.[48] Two elderly white schools named for Confederates — Stonewall Jackson and John Goode — were assigned to black pupils in 1949. Underutilized Ruffner Junior High on the edges of Brambleton was converted in 1952, followed by the equally aged Gatewood Elementary in Berkley in 1958 and the nearly half-century-old James Madison Elementary near Lambert's Point in 1960.[49]

This official preference for putting African American students into obviously old white schools was not just applied to outdated buildings that had once been for whites; in one notorious case, it was done with a building that had been thought too inadequate for "normal" blacks. Here the rejected Norfolk Mission College site at the corner of Princess Anne and Chicazola Streets, which had been thought too small for Booker T. Washington students, was turned into the Paul Laurence Dunbar School primarily for African American youth who were over-age or had mental disabilities. Because of the districtwide lack of facilities for black students, however, Dunbar also took in the overflow of "normal" black students from other schools on part-time shifts. According to the 1928 superintendent's report, more than 450 pupils were enrolled at this "Special School," which was deemed to have "made a contribution to the system in relieving the normal classes . . . of markedly over-age pupils and the attending problems of these who are 'misfits.'" The district had not done, of course, any alumni survey of Dunbar's graduates, but "personal reports of these former pupils indicate that the school is functioning to a degree in fitting these pupils for some position in life." Yet the failure and dropout rates there were much higher than at any other school, either black or white. Predictably, Dunbar did not have a white equivalent, but its multiple uses, including being the only "Open-Air" place for tubercular black children, was very much typical for African American educational facilities in Norfolk. Dunbar's role as the staging ground for the protest procession to St. John's in 1939 becomes then much more poignant in this context; its students and teachers acutely knew the confining limits of Jim Crow. The Dunbar School was finally closed in 1955 because its walls were literally falling down. The Dunbar example also helps to underscore the fact that, in contrast to the retrofitting of old white schools for black children, no black schools were ever converted to white use.[50]

In this dual system of separate and unequal, the white flagship school had to be Matthew Fontaine Maury High School, which had lunch facilities, indoor bathrooms, a beautiful library, a theater-style auditorium, and marble floors and columns from its opening in 1911. The original white public high school for Norfolk had been placed in Brambleton in 1894, but a devastating fire at that building in 1908 forced the school to be located temporarily at the Omohundro School, or John Marshall School, in East Ghent until it moved into the new Maury building in the same neighborhood three years later. The new Maury High School was impressive. In the official 1919 survey of Virginia's public schools, Maury's facilities were rated at a nearly perfect 962 out of 1,000 points, while Booker T. Washington High School, then still trapped in the old Mission College site, lagged behind at 577.[51] Junior high schools for whites, such as Ruffner and Blair, relieved any incipient overcrowding pressures at Maury in 1923; Booker T. Washington would have to wait another generation to have Jacox Junior High in the early 1950s to take away its intermediate grades. Other facilities helped Maury to remain top-notch. Granby High School, which opened in 1939, took the white high school students from the northern parts of the city; Norview High School, built by Norfolk County in 1954 and acquired by the city in 1955, did the same for white students from the Tanner's Creek annexation areas. Norview prided itself on being one of the most spacious school buildings in the Old Dominion. Neighborhood high schools thus had become gradually available for whites under Jim Crow, but the same was not true for many black students. In contrast to its pampered sister, Maury, Booker T. Washington served black secondary students from all over the city well into the 1960s.[52]

The school building booms of the 1910s and 1920s, therefore, helped to relieve the overcrowding at white schools much more so than at their black counterparts. Even the superintendent's report for 1924–28 admitted this trend; it noted that "the decrease in the number of part-time pupils in the white schools has been more than counterbalanced by the increase of part-time pupils in the colored schools." In 1928, 31 percent of the black students in elementary schools were on part-time session because of the lack of adequate classroom space.[53] The building of Liberty Park School in the 1940s, followed by Lindenwood, Diggs Park, Bowling Park, and Young Park in the next decade, was just not enough to meet the rising demand. Four of the above — Liberty Park, Diggs Park, Bowling Park, and Young Park — were designed specifically for their adjoining new housing projects for poor and

The opening of Jacox Junior High School in 1949 helped to relieve some of the crowding at Booker T. Washington High School, but cramped conditions remained the norm in the band room and other locations, as this 1954 photograph clearly demonstrates. (Courtesy of the *New Journal and Guide*)

working-class blacks within the city limits. African American families outside these new ghettoes had to find the most convenient local school outside their own neighborhood. In contrast, even whites in the relatively less favored northern part of the city had their own intermediate school by 1955: Northside Junior High. In general, therefore, more and varied facilities actually strengthened the local application of separate and unequal.[54]

PRESIDING OVER the dual system throughout these times of expansion were three administrators who had come to Norfolk from other parts of the South: Superintendents Crowdley Mason from Georgia, Edward S. Brinkley from Maryland's Eastern Shore, and John J. Brewbaker from Appalachia. While each administrator was a transplanted outsider, each believed in and exhibited the paternalism of "the Virginia way": extending small concessions to black teachers, parents, and students whom they hoped would appreciate their stage-managed benevolence. Mason graced the dais at the dedication of Booker T. Washington's overdue library and cafeteria; Brinkley ensured the already-won implementation of pay parity; Brewbaker would generate a host of biracial committees and events. Each also knew when to draw the limits of that benevolence. Mason fired Aline Black; Brinkley rebuffed Winston Douglas's initial complaints; Brewbaker stalled the implementation of the *Brown* decision.[55]

J. J. Brewbaker, however, was the best racial manager of the three, which may come as a surprise given his humble origins. He came from the Shenandoah Valley of rural western Virginia, having been born near Buchanan in Botetourt County on June 6, 1895. He went to public schools there and graduated from Buchanan High School in 1915. He then matriculated at nearby Roanoke College in Salem, Virginia, and graduated in 1918. After graduation, Brewbaker briefly served with the U.S. Army in France, returning home to become the assistant cashier in the Bank of Buchanan. He left banking for good in 1922 to become the principal of Buchanan High School, the place from which he had graduated just seven years earlier. There was no black equivalent of Buchanan High in Botetourt County in those days, and, through the next decade, this persisted even though the student population there was at least 13 percent black during the 1936–37 school year. In contrast, Botetourt had three other accredited high schools for whites. At any rate, Brewbaker would run Buchanan High until 1926, when he began a short stint as principal of St. Paul High School in Wise County, Virginia, before moving to Norfolk in September 1927.[56]

For the next thirty-three years, Brewbaker would serve in a variety of administrative positions in Norfolk's schools. From 1927 to 1939, he was principal of the Robert E. Lee Elementary School in East Ghent, and later, from 1939 to 1942, he served in the same role at James Madison Elementary School and the Maury Night School. His administrative positions allowed him to live at the relatively respectable address of 422 Westover in East Ghent through the Depression and beyond. He also fit graduate work into his busy schedule, receiving a master's degree in education from the University of Virginia in 1939 and taking graduate-level courses at the Teachers College of Columbia University in New York City. Upon the accession of Superintendent Brinkley in 1943, Brewbaker became assistant superintendent, serving as such until Brinkley's death in 1949. When he succeeded Brinkley later that year, Brewbaker was fifty-four years old and had been in the school system for over twenty years.[57]

Mason, Brinkley, and Brewbaker loved to showcase their successes, but their own reports accepted the only too obvious inequities that they themselves saw as natural and customary. Most revealing of these racial disparities were their official publications for the district. At least four times during the Jim Crow era — in 1925, 1928, 1937, and 1951 — the Norfolk superintendents went to the trouble of showcasing their schools in print. The results gave the illusion of inclusion, while textually and pictorially placing blacks in their "proper" place. For example, the 1925 effort featured photographic glimpses within white schools and one of its black counterparts: the newly built Booker T. Washington High School. At no time in this particular survey were the schools explicitly identified as white or black: it was assumed that readers would know that Booker T. Washington was exclusively for black students and that the rest were for whites. The many photographs in this overview captured some of the elegant murals and sculptures that adorned the hallways of a number of white schools. They were designed to evoke historical and literary tropes that were part and parcel of largely academic curricula. In contrast, the single featured classroom of Booker T. Washington was a workshop designed to inculcate artisanal trades thought fit for blacks. Another picture showed the black high school's oddly shaped auditorium, which even then would have had a hard time of seating all of its students.[58] These obvious inequities were also evident in the 1924–28 report, which was driven by statistics more than pictures. Most revealingly, the report showed that music instruction was new for black children in Norfolk that school year. It assumed that the reader knew that such instruction had been available to white children in the port city for at least a generation earlier. It was only natural. Yet here, even among the equalizing "accomplishments," the district admitted achievement, attendance, access, and equity gaps between whites and blacks in clinical tables and graphs. It probably admitted too much for the racial managers of "the Virginia way."[59]

Deliberately returning to the more accessible format of pictorial content, the 1937 report devoted exactly two pictures and three pages to a separate and brief "chapter" on black schools and students. Here the children singularly appear in vocational roles appropriate to their gender: girls engaged in dressmaking, and boys learning carpentry and bricklaying. Academics were seemingly for whites only. Earlier, in the discussion of white schools, this survey declared that a library was "a necessity for every modern school," belying the fact that Booker T. Washington's "real" library would not be ready for another three years.[60]

Most indicative of illusionary inclusion, however, was Brewbaker's 1951 report, a triumph of style over substance compared to the naively honest publications of the Mason era. With midcentury modern graphics, it had no special section on blacks, and it did seemingly integrate twenty-five pictures of African American students, teachers, and parents among the 121 photographs used overall. A few of its pictures actually featured blacks in academic roles and classes, but the majority of them still had black students in customary vocational settings. The report was bold enough to have three pictures that featured both whites and blacks together, but even these pictures reflected the conventional racial order. In one, a white nurse helps a black child, and, in another, a tall white woman literally talks down to happy black mothers. The final "integrated" picture has Brewbaker sharing the stage with a smiling black man before the Bi-Racial Council as it gave its seemingly integrated stamp of approval to the district's determination to maintain Jim Crow.[61]

In reaction to the continuing racial disparities within the district and the corresponding indifference and/or legerdemain shown by white officials, black deference in Norfolk was definitely on the wane. Given this backdrop, the *Black* and *Alston* cases become more much understandable and were part of a continuum of African American resistance to the managers of white supremacy, who, in Norfolk, merely stepped up their game in response. Resolving the thorny issue of pay parity only let the managers off the hook, at least temporarily, for the long-term structural issues of overcrowding and broader educational equality. The final settlement of the *Black* and *Alston* cases — and then the domestic ramifications of World War II — had crosscutting effects on this waning of discrimination by consent. The war, in particular, was both a curse and a blessing to those wanting better schools and living conditions for Norfolk's blacks.

On the positive side for those seeking educational equality, World War II not only created the city's new progressive self-image, but it also shaped the cohort of homegrown black attorneys — particularly Victor Ashe, J. Hugo Madison, and Joseph A. Jordan Jr. — who would challenge that civic self-satisfaction in the decades to come. The most audacious of this dynamic trio in the beginning was Victor Ashe, who came out of Atlantic City, St. Joseph's

Catholic, Villanova, and then the war to run for city council in 1946 to force Norfolk's courthouse crowd to envision a day of black representation in municipal government. J. Hugo Madison, the vice president of Booker T. Washington's class of 1939, left the Norfolk Division of Virginia Union for military duty only to team up with Ashe and the local NAACP to challenge the legality of day-to-day discrimination after the war. One of their first targets was the total ban on blacks in Seashore State Park in northern Princess Anne County; their courtroom experiences in those cases would serve them well in the long struggle for educational equity to come. Their efforts would be aided by the fortitude and judgment of fellow lawyer and NAACP stalwart Joseph A. Jordan Jr., who was the most scarred by the war, having been severely injured in France and relegated to using a wheelchair. Overcoming this painful disability, however, gave Jordan ample energy and edge to become the most militant of the trio, while preparing him to become Norfolk's first African American city councilman in the twentieth century.[62]

While forging the black leadership of the future, the war and its aftermath made Norfolk the national showcase for urban renewal. That was an unlikely twist for the port city. During the Depression, Norfolk had some of the densest and worst slums in the United States, and its schools ranked in the bottom percentiles of nearly every important category. Deemed the "wickedest city" in the United States in the 1890s, Norfolk remained, during the first half of the twentieth century, truly a dumpy, shady place, a fourth-rate Sodom by the sea with its very own notorious red-light districts along East Main Street and Granby Street. Numbers rackets and cheap bars cluttered its downtown neighborhoods. It was no wonder, then, that Norfolk had the highest incidence of venereal diseases in the country.[63] Professor Ernest W. Gray of the all-white Norfolk Division of William and Mary in 1939 found his city's "main sin," however, to be "apathy"; he found little civic engagement for "peace, racial relations, parks and playgrounds, slum clearance, municipal reform, and removal of poll taxes."[64] Prewar Norfolk was indeed "the Big Easy" of the East, without the charm of New Orleans.

Urban renewal begun during and after the war dramatically changed that corrupt and lazy image, at least in the minds of the city fathers. Charles B. Borland's Crime Conference of 1937 began to convince municipal officials to get rid of the slums that they thought had produced the crime wave. A year later, business leaders pooled resources via a renewed Community Fund to combat the most obvious social ills. Yet only the war and the consequent influx of workers, both military and civilian, galvanized Norfolk's white bourgeoisie to act. Working together, they established the Norfolk Housing and Redevelopment Agency (NHRA), a model of good-government paternalism in line with "the Virginia way." To accommodate the conscripted and their families, this agency created low-cost, if racially segregated, housing projects for both blacks and whites that were far better constructed than the haphazard tenements of old. These seemingly successful ventures would be the preface to Redevelopment Project #1, the very first initiative to be funded under the federal housing act of 1949.[65] Flush with confidence over these successes, Norfolk's white bourgeoisie enabled the election of their own to municipal government, casting the elections of lawyer Richard D. Cooke, car dealer Pretlow Darden, and sand-and gravel magnate John Twohy II to municipal office in 1946 in the guise of "the People's Ticket." Opponents more aptly characterized Cooke-Darden-Twohy as "the Silkstocking Ticket," but they could not stop this speeding train of notables and experts. As the *Pilot* reported much later, there was "a distinct minimum of status quo stubbornness," as "the People's Ticket" accomplished many of their goals in their four years in office.[66] Even the persistent holdovers of the old regime such as Corporation Court Clerk William L. Prieur Jr. — the local chieftain from Senator Harry Byrd's political machine — did not stand in the way of progress. Indeed, both "the People's Ticket" and its handful of critics were tied to Harry Byrd by patronage and thus reflected his conventional and reflexive attachment to Jim Crow. After all, the changes pushed by the NHRA only reinforced and strengthened overt racial segregation in housing. For their part, black leaders were grateful for the inclusive tone of the good-government renaissance, which had led to the hiring of the city's first black police officers in 1945. The Youngs, among others, were invited to be on advisory committees to oversee, among other things, the markedly better, if segregated, housing.[67]

Indeed, abetting these changes in style and, to a lesser extent, substance in reference to racial matters were the increasingly common biracial committees or councils that were to advise white officials on matters that affected poor whites and blacks. Most helped to implement and not to influence already determined policy. Yet one extraordinary African American woman tried to turn this tool of oppression on its head and milked it for all that it was worth: Vivian Carter Mason. Central to the multidecade struggle for educational equality in Norfolk, she would draw upon her experiences outside the city to outmaneuver the co-opting tactics of its racial managers. Born in 1900 in Wilkes-Barre, Pennsylvania, Vivian Carter was the daughter of a Methodist minister and music teacher. She learned early on from her parents that a good education was necessary to have the confidence to challenge white supremacy. After her family had moved to a predominantly white neighborhood in Auburn, New York, she successfully challenged one of her white teachers who had inculcated his class with the then-orthodox idea that slavery was not so bad. Young Vivian shamed her teacher into reading Booker T. Washington's autobiography, *Up From Slavery,* and he apparently recanted. In 1925, Carter graduated from the prestigious University of Chicago with a degree in social work. She was ready to do battle with both the systemic racism and sexism of her day, and her marriage that same year to a fellow classmate and businessman, William T. Mason Sr., brought her to his hometown: Norfolk, Virginia. While having and raising their only child — William T. Mason Jr. — in Norfolk, the new Mrs. Mason worked at the local black branch of the Young Women's Christian Association (YWCA) as its program director in the late 1920s. She was very leery of raising her son, however, within the pernicious context of separate and unequal. Accordingly, in 1931 she whisked her child away to a private school in New York City and stayed with him there. Her husband, a West Indian immigrant and real estate/insurance executive, was secure and wealthy enough to agree with her. Once in New York City, Vivian Carter Mason would be no stay-at-home mother. She would go on to become the first black director within New York City's Department of Welfare, to earn two master's degrees, to serve on the boards of the National Association of Colored Women (NACW) — which, in 1935, became the National Council of Negro Women — and the national YWCA, and to found the Committee of 100 Women, a biracial organization that shepherded the participation of disadvantaged children of whatever background at summer camp.[68]

Mason returned to Norfolk from New York City in the mid-1940s, after her son's graduation from high school and a back injury she suffered in a terrible train wreck. She was not about to let that injury slow her down though. Instead, she used her array of Gotham experiences to reform "the little Manhattan by the Bay." Conditions for poor blacks in Norfolk had worsened since the 1920s, in her mind, and the best way to address this problem was to energize the wives and mothers of Norfolk's resurgent bourgeoisie, both white and black. Care of and advocacy on behalf of the poor and defense-less had long been seen as a feminine sphere of action, and Mason wanted to make sure that poor blacks were not left out of the city's planned renaissance. By involving civic matrons, access to influential husbands, brothers, and sons would be assured, and beneficial policies would be enacted.[69]

At least, that was Mason's hope when, on April 17, 1945, she invited eighteen women — seven black and eleven white — to form the Women's Council for Interracial Cooperation (WCIC). Mason was elected the council's first chair, and her activism and northern exposure influenced its stated goals, which went beyond the usual "Virginia way."[70] Yet even this forward-thinking council could not change the renaissance's preference for legal segregation in Norfolk. It is true that the WCIC helped to push the NHRA to create better housing and opportunities for poor blacks, but the women were most effective in pushing for little bits of equalization, not whole-scale integration. In December 1947 and through the spring of 1948, for example, the WCIC successfully lobbied for doors on the stalls of the girls' toilets at Booker T. Washington High School as well as for separate bathrooms for teachers there.[71] Small victories were real victories, nonetheless. Mason was emboldened to run with the chauvinistic P. B. Young Sr. as "black Silkstocking" alternatives for city council in 1952, but she would leave Norfolk once again in 1953 to become the president of the National Council of Negro Women, headquartered in Washington, D.C., only to return four years later — just in time to play a critical role in ending the city's Massive Resistance to school desegregation in 1959.[72]

Vivian Carter Mason had tried to recast the old idea of the biracial committee and make it work for progress rather than simple racial management by whites. The Silkstockings, though, merely regrouped at the prospect of real equality. They sanctioned the ceding of outdated white facilities or outnumbered white outposts to blacks in return for increasing residential segregation. In 1946, the same year of "the People's Ticket" and Ashe's candidacy for city council, municipal leaders gave the green light to middle-class blacks to complete their migration into Brambleton, the city's first streetcar suburb. Grace Episcopal and Shiloh Baptist moved into formerly white buildings. White residents fled; Ruffner, on the edges of Brambleton, was assigned to blacks in 1952. The Norfolk Division of all-black Virginia State College moved from one white hand-me-down (Vincent de Paul's hospital in Uptown) to another — the all-white nine-hole golf course and country club in Brambleton. These calculated retreats were even evident in the most violent racial incidents in Norfolk of the 1950s — those having to do with working- and middle-class blacks moving into adjacent white neighborhoods in the Tanner's Creek annexation areas. In 1954, black families who had been displaced by urban renewal and failed to find available housing in Oakwood, Rosemont, and Chesapeake Manor Gardens crossed the traditional racial barrier of Widgeon Road to seek housing in Coronado, a small, white, mainly military enclave adjacent to Norview High School. Harassment of black buyers descended into random acts of violence, which the outgoing Norfolk County police did little to stop. When the new mayor, W. Fred Duckworth, refused to help, P. B. Young Sr. turned to the Silkstockings for assistance. Order was restored, whites fled Coronado, and it became a black neighborhood by 1960. But residential segregation in other parts of the city increased, so abandoning Coronado was a small price to pay for the city's elite.[73]

Urban renewal was then deliberately used to forestall integration. Federal funds were used to demolish relatively integrated frontiers such as Broad Creek Village and Atlantic City, while the same funds "protected" Ghent proper and western Norfolk from black migrations. To the Silkstockings and their friends, integration was regressive, and segregation was progressive. Armed with the sophisticated analysis from an expert from Princeton University (Charles K. Agle), they treated those directly affected by renewal and removal with a veneer of respect, holding meetings and taking tours. "Bulldozer" Duckworth, the mayoral successor to the Silkstockings in 1950, was more brutally honest than his upscale predecessors; the end results of both administrations was the same: the removal and containment of black people. Mayor Duckworth is sometimes portrayed incorrectly as an atavistic legacy from racially divisive times, but he merely executed the ambitious plans of the progressive "People's Ticket" with aplomb. And Duckworth was not that different from the business leaders whom he replaced. Like Pretlow Darden, he was a car dealer, too. Indeed, the most prominent of the Silkstockings — the Darden brothers — were just a generation removed from being Carolina peasants, but successful businesses and Colgate's marriage to a DuPont helped them to assume the mantle of being local aristocrats, even if their stockings were of recent vintage. Whether the Silkstocking or Duckworth administration, however, the city fathers knew that they knew best; black insurgents Ashe, Mason, and Young need not have applied for city council. Given this Hobson's choice of paternalistic pity or overt contempt, black leaders chose the least hostile coterie of racial managers in order to contain the damage done by the city's renaissance.[74]

FIRMLY WEDDED TO "the Virginia way," Norfolk officialdom believed that the pretense of separate and equal preserved what they perceived as the progress of the previous generation. This ran true for both the Silkstocking and Duckworth administrations. Accordingly, any compliance with the Supreme Court's decision in *Brown v. Board of Education* (1954) would ruin those carefully crafted improvements. The most complete version of this line of argument is to be found in Superintendent Brewbaker's February 1957 affidavit defending the school board against African American students wanting to transfer to all-white schools. Here he highlighted with detailed statistics his district's attempts to equalize facilities, salaries, faculty workloads, and curricula over the preceding two decades. He first made sure to address the main reason for the *Black* and *Alston* cases, noting that teacher pay parity had been reached in Norfolk without resorting to integration.[75] Next, he pointed out that statistics on per-pupil expenditures clearly demonstrated that Norfolk had overcome the discriminatory practices of the previous generation. In fact, by 1955–56 the district spent $8.25 more for each black child than it did for each white child. This increase in expenditures for black children resulted in large part from the reduction of student-teacher ratios at black schools. For instance, in 1955–56 black secondary schools had smaller classes than their white counterparts, with teacher loads at black schools averaging 18.6 pupils, while their white counterparts averaged 20.5.[76] Of course, this use of statistics was misleading. It did not account for the fact that, by the 1950s, many black teachers with impeccable and, at times, overqualified credentials had been employed in their teaching positions for many more years than more transient whites just being hired into the system. Nor did Superintendent Brewbaker take the time to explain that the district's decision to pay black veteran teachers on par with their white counterparts had dramatically altered per-pupil expenditures at black schools, given the fact that personnel made up the largest expense within the district.[77]

Despite these technicalities, Brewbaker insisted that the quality of the curricula in black schools was just as varied and effective as the curricula in their white counterparts. There were really no differences, he said; both white and black schools offered a wide array of academic and vocational tracks by the 1950s. This rich uniformity was due to white action and black consent; as Brewbaker noted, "through workshops, in-service programs, and system-wide committees, curriculum production has moved on a common front which negates any consideration of differentiation in curriculum offerings between the two races." Since the course offerings were equal if separate, library services, audiovisual aids, and textbooks were distributed equally without regard to race, according to the superintendent. Brewbaker's own exhibits attached to his affidavit, however, inadvertently revealed inequities in course offerings, particularly in upper-level electives. For example, white high schools routinely offered both "English Literature and Its World Relations" and "Advanced Grammar and Composition," but no black school scheduled these courses for 1955–56. If there was "sufficient request and need," then the black schools had the qualified teachers who could teach these classes, of course. The obvious implication was that, to the white-dominated school system, there were not enough black high school students prepared to go beyond the basics of comprehension and writing. Similarly, white high schools offered "Advanced Algebra," "Business Law," "Psychology," and advanced foreign language instruction in Latin, Spanish, and French; no black school did. The inability to find faculty members to teach distributive education at the black schools in 1955–56 took that option off the table for their students. In contrast, that same year black schools offered less-academic courses in plumbing, bricklaying, and keyboard harmony that no white schools did. While the core basics were the same, the devil of curricular inequality was in the details.[78]

While glossing over those details, Brewbaker blamed any racial divide on standardized tests on "the degree of cultural and home environmental development" that he found to be lower in black communities. On those tests for 1955–56, for example, black sixth graders on average were achieving at the same level as white fourth or fifth graders. Black eighth graders on average were achieving at the same level as "typical" white sixth graders in the system. Accordingly, Brewbaker noted, the bottom one-fourth of white students in the sixth and eighth grades were performing at the same level of the bottom three-quarters of black students in the same grades. The top one-fourth of black students, in turn, performed as well as three-quarters of the whites in the sixth and eighth grades. To the superintendent, Norfolk had done all that it could do to equalize educational opportunity within its dual system, and it was up to black children and parents to take advantage of

their "equal facilities, services, and excellently trained teachers." By stress-
ing the racial gaps in learning outcomes rather than in inputs, he skillfully
shifted the blame for the effects of racial oppression to its intended victims,
who, in his opinion, were not doing the best with what they had.[79]

While touting his district's equalization record for the federal court,
Brewbaker had fully anticipated local litigation by listing his own furtive
moves toward desegregation, steps that amounted to no more than procedural window dressing. In a revealing internal memorandum, a virtual note
to himself, from April 1956 (nearly a year before his affidavit), he described
his district's own calculated and modulated use of the interracial or biracial
committee concept, straight from the shopworn playbook of "managed racial relations." For instance, the superintendent noted his first accomplishment in "racial integration" dating from August 1949 as the holding of one
big annual meeting of all principals, supervisors, and other administrative
personnel instead the scheduling of two separate ones — one for whites and
one for blacks — as had been the case during the Mason and Brinkley years.
During this Administrators' Conference, Brewbaker maintained that "each
discussion panel, committee, and study group is well integrated in regard
to race."[80]

Accordingly, the success of the Administrators' Conference from August
1949 onward led to the establishment of other committees, working groups,
workshops, councils, and meetings "on the bi-racial plan." In particular,
standing citywide committees of faculty members and principals who wrote
curriculum guides or who addressed professional issues were carefully balanced between white and black members. Since 1952, there had been "joint
relationships in meetings of all of the heads of departments in the secondary
schools." There were "joint" meetings held every month for the guidance
counselors of the junior and senior high schools to get together and to share
notes. Social studies teachers had even held their very own "joint" meetings "on several occasions." Indeed, this enthusiasm for "joint" meetings
among teachers was quickly formalized. The Teachers' Advisory Council,
"a bi-racial board of fifteen members which makes recommendations to the
Superintendent and School Board on matters pertaining to teacher welfare,"
featured an African American chairman, six black teachers and principals,
and nine white teachers and principals by 1956.[81]

Students and other stakeholders were also swept up in the fetish for biracial gatherings of limited duration and power, at least according to the su-

perintendent. The City-wide Student Council Association was "biracial"; all student councils in the district from both white and black high schools had two representatives to the association, whose meetings were "joint." This arrangement had been ongoing since 1952, and students themselves had suggested it. Similarly, the Citizens Committee for Traffic Safety featured at least three representatives — "one boy, one girl, and a teacher" — from the physical education departments of both white and black high schools. This committee, which met monthly in the city council chamber and which had up to 150 members, also included representatives from major civic leagues and clubs, ostensibly without regard to race. Brewbaker pointed out that via this committee, both white and black schools "put on a Safety Program each month in competition for the temporary possession of a silver cup." He went on to note, "The Negro schools win the cup just as often as the white. The Negroes are highly respected by the entire group of 150 for their competence and know-how."[82]

The most prominent, at least on paper, of these biracial committees, however, was the Norfolk Citizens Advisory Council, which had been established in 1951. It reported to and advised the superintendent and the school board on strategic planning for the district. Reflecting roughly the racial makeup of the overall student population at the time, the council had fifteen white and eleven black members, leaders who, in their various communities, brought with them a variety of "professional, business, and cultural" perspectives to the table. In his memo, Brewbaker touted the fact that an African American had served as the council's chairman for at least the first two years of its existence. Less promising was his following notation of the council's unanimous vote to disband voluntarily on August 19, 1955. While dissolving itself, the council "recommended that the School Board appoint a special committee or advisory group to study and make recommendations to the School Board in the matter of integration," an implicit admission of its irrelevance.[83]

The council's recommendation shows that the "biracial" groups sponsored by the school district were not designed to usher in the desegregation and/or equalization of schools; rather, they were designed to humanize segregation by allowing "joint" meetings on highly ceremonial and limited occasions. Moreover, they were designed with the clear purpose of delaying any real desegregation or equalization by giving the appearance of consensual participation. Blacks did participate in these machinations, knowing the committees' real agenda yet hoping to use these forums for their own purposes. Yet for those whites in Norfolk concerned about the complete maintenance of Jim Crow at all costs, these biracial committees of the school system were incorrectly seen as the tip of the iceberg of widespread race-mixing. Given the emergence of Massive Resistance by 1956, even the council's delaying tactic of yet another advisory committee was not followed through on, as the next chapter will show. The masks required by "the Virginia way" had begun both to slip and to change.

There were only two steps toward "racial integration" that Brewbaker had listed that did not revolve around forming another biracial committee. These measures were less consequential and more revealing than those establishing the committees. For example, he recorded that "the Cerebral Palsy Clinic at the J. E. B. Stuart School is not segregated as far as the clinical and therapeutic services are concerned." By 1956, white and black students as patients used the same waiting and examination areas at the Colonial Place school. But even there for the relatively deracinated people with disabilities, the teaching of academic subjects was strictly just for the white students. This clinical experience was the only sustained incidence of face-to-face desegregation in Norfolk's schools beyond the highly self-conscious biracial committees.[84] Brewbaker also went as far to note that his school district's publications, such as its newsletters and directories, did not have separate and unequal sections for blacks and whites. In the 1955–56 edition of the schools directory, he boasted, the schools appeared in alphabetical order without regard to race. The fact that he felt compelled to mention that unremarkable ordering as progress underscores the hollowness of the school district's reputation for being especially liberal or moderate in racial matters.[85]

Yet Brewbaker was certain that pushing too hard on desegregation would threaten draconian cuts in state aid, given that the General Assembly and governor had issued dire warnings threatening to punish school boards that complied with the *Brown* decision. He outlined the possible cuts to come: an across-the-board reduction of the teaching staff by 25 percent (without regard to race), an even more sweeping reduction for the budget line for instructional supplies by 50 percent, closing the system's health services, foregoing all new equipment purchases, and abandoning the Cerebral Palsy Center at the J. E. B. Stuart School and all education for homebound children, among other measures. If those cuts were to take effect because of

Massive Resistance, Brewbaker reasoned, then desegregation should be sacrificed to preserve the trends toward equalization within the dual system.[86]

Nevertheless, calling the bluffs of both Brewbaker and the state was worth it to the local African American students, parents, and attorneys who went to court to secure the students' constitutional rights. Black leaders and community members understandably remained skeptical of a system that had remained unequal despite equalization. Black parents wanted their children to attend the school closest to their home, and students were tired of crowded and antiquated facilities. They would not be impressed or bought off with crumbs. On the other hand, "equalization" had given Jim Crow a second wind in Norfolk, and the city's racial managers were not about to give up without a fight of their own.

CHAPTER TWO

COURAGE
AND MODERATION'S FAILURE
IN NORFOLK, 1954–1958
CONVICTION

I T SEEMED SO REASONABLE, and thus so Virginian, a response at the
time. In May 1954, following the U.S. Supreme Court's decision in *Brown
v. Board of Education,* Professor Herbert A. Marshall encouraged his all-
black class at the Norfolk Division of Virginia State College to consider
the possible impact of the recent ruling outlawing segregated public schools.
As the class progressed, a student noticed that a visiting white journalist,
James E. Mays from the *Norfolk Virginian-Pilot,* had entered the room.
"What do you think will be the outcome of the court's decision?" the student asked Mays. The reporter seemed to be taken aback. Mays "replied
weakly," stating, "The only thing that I can say is that the whole question
will just call for a lot of good, solid, common, everyday horse sense when
the inevitable problems come up. If both sides will use restraint, I believe
that things may work out." Pragmatism and moderation were also reflected
in the classroom give-and-take, as the white observer recorded it. Marshall,
who had been employed at the all-black junior college since 1939 and was
the head of the social sciences department there, welcomed *Brown* as "a
step forward for democracy," but he cautioned his students about "over-
eagerness" in racial integration. Although the professor did not see *Brown*
as magically dispelling "the race problems" inherent in either customary or
codified white privilege, neither he nor his class viewed integration as particularly difficult or distant. For example, an "ex-GI" in the class talked of
his pleasant integrated experiences in the army; a navy wife pointed to her
attendance at mixed-race parties where "whites and Negroes alike had been
equally nice to her." After the class debated the tactical question of whether
blacks or whites should initiate integration, one student "sitting near [Mays]"
optimistically predicted, "Those things will work themselves out when the

time comes." In fact, Mays agreed with these lighthearted assessments, joking that, by merely being in the room, he had integrated that day's class.
Ominously, though, as Mays thanked the class, he "walked out into the
rain," foreshadowing the gathering storm that would soon engulf the city,
pushing the defenders of Jim Crow past the "measured reasonableness"
of "the Virginia Way" on to the impulsive and aggressive school-closing
tactics of the Massive Resisters.[1]

Norfolk seemed to be an unlikely place for Massive Resistance to take
its most dramatic stand. By the mid-1950s, it was a bustling port with the
world's largest naval base, which brought people from all over the country
to Tidewater because of the imperatives of the Cold War. Its school board,
in particular, was in the midst of a building boom to fit this increased demand from both whites and blacks. Like Atlanta, Norfolk seemed too busy
to hate. The city's white citizens — especially those in the middle and upper
classes — still saw themselves as above the unsavory vulgarity of the Deep
and Delta South in part because they thought that their version of paternalistic segregation had made Jim Crow kinder and gentler.[2] That heady
self-image combining a progressive future with an idealized past and present was to be severely tested as the city became the centerpiece in the state's
controversial stand against school desegregation.

At first, Norfolk's white elite did their best to ignore Governor Thomas
Stanley and his posturing against the *Brown* decision, which was seen as a
simple tactic to please whites in the Black Belt counties just south of the capital. Then, as the beginnings of actual if begrudging desegregation took hold
in nearby cities such as Louisville and Baltimore, many people came to the
conclusion that Norfolk would eventually follow suit. Just one year after the
Brown decision, school superintendent J. J. Brewbaker exchanged ideas with
the school superintendent of Baltimore about future desegregation strategies.[3] He even allowed the establishment of integrated summer workshops
for teachers at Lakewood School, a minor concession that was applauded by
the local chapter of the National Association for the Advancement of Colored People (NAACP).[4] For these small steps, he was praised nationally.[5] In
that same self-conscious vein of moderation, Lenoir Chambers, the editor
of the *Virginian-Pilot,* consistently urged Brewbaker to follow a measured
approach to *Brown,* recommending the use of "all deliberate speed" to make
the process as painless as possible.[6]

Yet despite all of the initial talk in Norfolk about going along with the

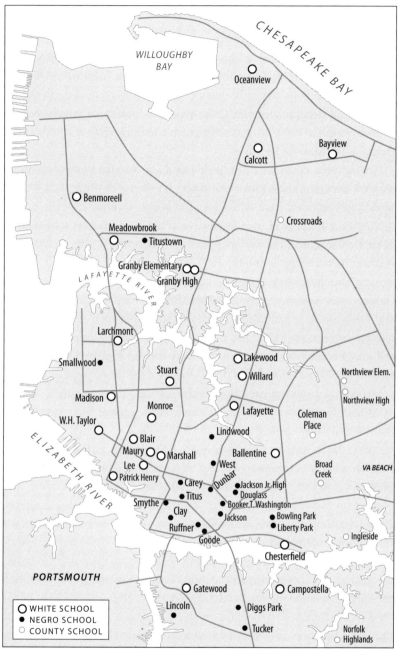

This map appeared in the *Norfolk Ledger-Dispatch* on May 18, 1954, immediately after the Supreme Court's decision in *Brown v. Board of Education*. The map shows the racial segregation in Norfolk's public schools that had developed over the previous five decades. (Courtesy of the *Virginian-Pilot*)

Supreme Court's decision, the backdrop of gubernatorial defiance and legislative delay finally blossomed with the overt intervention of Virginia's U.S.
senator Harry F. Byrd. His call for "Massive Resistance" against the *Brown*
decision in 1956 scared Brewbaker and bolstered those local officials such as
W. Fred Duckworth, the mayor of Norfolk, who wanted to continue separate
and unequal schools even if it meant closing them. While the Right Wing
rallied in both the city and the state, the middle caved in. The reasoned pleas
of Lenoir Chambers were not enough to calm the polarized atmosphere.
Indeed, most white moderates in Norfolk kept quiet until the actual closing
of the schools, and, even then, the proschools pressure group attracted a
relatively small number of foot soldiers. The so-called shouting mobs who
opposed the *Brown* decision did not really have to shout to keep blacks out;
rather, a silent majority of Byrd sympathizers simply affirmed the school
closings in a November 1958 referendum by a margin of three to two. Facing
the failure of white moderates to stem the tide of Massive Resistance prior
to the school closures crisis, African American students, their parents, and
their lawyers persistently nudged the district court in Norfolk to go beyond
furtive posturing and to proceed to actual compliance with the *Brown* decision. This chapter traces the strange and winding road to the school closures
crisis, an event made possible by African American activism as much as by
official brinkmanship.

WHILE MOST OF Norfolk's citizens did nothing to prevent the school closures crisis until it was too late, the sense of inevitable change toward some
kind of school integration, however token, was kept alive by two sources that
were not completely unrelated: Judge Walter E. Hoffman and the clergy of
the city, both white and black. Indeed, even before the precipitous appointment of Hoffman to the federal bench by President Dwight Eisenhower in
late June 1954, many leading clergymen in Norfolk had publicly embraced the
Brown decision. Some of the reasoning of prominent white clergy was surprisingly showcased in an article of May 24 in the *Norfolk Ledger-Dispatch*,
whose editorial board remained steadfastly opposed to desegregation in the
city. The ministers quoted in this piece saw no discrepancy between the
Court's ruling and Christian precepts; they went further to imply that resistance to *Brown* was un-Christian and thus uncivilized. For instance, the
Reverend Floyd Leggett, pastor of the First Christian Church, Disciples, told
his relatively well-to-do congregation in Ghent to avoid savage and volatile

Walter E. Hoffman was sworn in as a federal judge on September 4, 1954. (Courtesy of the *Virginian-Pilot*)

reactions to the decision that could only injure the children and other innocent people involved. Leggett was especially well positioned to influence key players in this unfolding drama, since he served as pastor to school superintendent Brewbaker as well as the chair of Norfolk's school board, businessman Paul T. Schweitzer. Similarly, the new Reverend Peyton Randolph Williams urged his flock at Christ and St. Luke's Episcopal Church, a pillar of the city's westside establishment, to use the judicial rebuke of accepted segregation as a time for needed self-reflection and communal improvement. To Williams, everyone had sinned, and thus everyone had to compromise. He therefore based his implicit support of some kind of compliance with *Brown* upon this conventional mainline Protestant idea: "Without some recognition of our own sinfulness, the democratic process is unworkable. We see that exemplified in the McCarthy hearings, where there is a persistent unwillingness to face one's own shortcomings while at the same time condemning others. We see it, too, in the boiling up of the controversy over segregation." Here, Williams criticized the guttural, tribal instincts that cropped up in the negative responses to *Brown* without ever coming out directly and supporting desegregation.[7]

African American ministers were understandably more direct than Williams was in their approval of *Brown* as an overdue application of Christianity. In the *Journal and Guide*, the reactions of local black ministers to *Brown* were prominently placed. That in itself was not unusual, but the unanimity and force of the printed opinions were especially pointed. The black-owned weekly — and its readership — had long moved past accommodating to Jim Crow, noting almost offhand that "the court's action was apparently no surprise to the majority of the clergymen." In fact, Norfolk's black ministers linked the *Brown* decision with the fundamental precepts of Christianity, Americanism, and anti-Communism, inverting the typical conservative trinity of the day for their side. In particular, the Reverend Richard B. Martin, the rector of Grace Episcopal Church, a congregation that featured many of the city's wealthiest blacks, exclaimed that the school desegregation cases had created a critical moral juncture for Americans. "Democracy has been asked to articulate its creed and to declare its position before the court of Christian conscience. The decision is life and death. The judgment hall is global." Martin discerned, "In the decision of the Supreme Court, our democracy chooses life, and the invulnerability of truth and righteousness has proved once again that truth presents a case from which there can be no ultimate appeal."[8]

In the immediate afterglow of the *Brown* decision, there was little concern of an imminent backlash in Norfolk. Superintendent Brewbaker himself was "not surprised at the decision." Indeed, just a few weeks earlier he had listened to Director Lyman B. Brooks of the Norfolk Division of Virginia State College talk about the future necessity of integration as a prerequisite for academic success before an all-black graduating class at Booker T. Washington Night School. Brewbaker liked the court's provision for gradual implementation, predicting, "It would not be too difficult to work out." In fact, he and J. Farley Powers, the chairman of the Norfolk School Board, believed that the residential patterns in Norfolk corresponded so well with existing school assignments that most schools would "go on as they have been." Only the high schools could be considered for racial mixing in the future, but the white high schools would retain overwhelming white majorities even with integration. Agreeing with editorials in both the *Virginian-Pilot* and the *Norfolk Ledger-Dispatch*, Brewbaker thought that violence and other draconian responses might happen elsewhere, but they would erupt only in places where whites were in the minority. That obviously did not include Norfolk because, to him, the city would have a white majority for the foreseeable future.[9]

Brewbaker's upbeat, if circumspect, assessment of the *Brown* decision was in part based on the successful implementation of token integration in the local Catholic schools. Even before the Diocese of Richmond, which included Norfolk and its environs, decided to desegregate all of its schools with their 21,000 students, Francis Joseph Blakely, the priest at Blessed Sacrament Catholic Church near the naval base, had encouraged an African American student to attend the new yet still lily-white Blessed Sacrament Elementary School in November 1953. This action would only come to light in July 1954, when the forces of Massive Resistance had begun to mobilize with gubernatorial approval.[10] In April 1955, the Norfolk Catholic High School Board announced that incoming freshmen coming from all-black St. Joseph's would be allowed to enroll at Norfolk Catholic in the fall; twelve transfers followed through on the offer. A year later, the official line in the local media and in the ecclesiastical hierarchy had pegged this gradual desegregation as a success; the athletic boys had fit in particularly well. Yet the students themselves, both black and white, admitted that the social interactions between whites and blacks were quite limited at Norfolk Catholic, with students of both races puzzled by a reporter who asked them if they had visited the home of someone of the opposite race. It had never occurred to some of them that such a visit could take place.[11]

Given the cultural limitations at the local Catholic schools, there were going to be problems with public school integration even in "liberal" Norfolk. In April 1954, President Eisenhower, via Rear Admiral T. B. Brittain of the U.S. Navy, had ordered the integration of the five-room elementary school at Benmoreell on the naval base as part of a wider executive order ending segregation on military posts. Benmoreell was a housing project built by the navy for the families of the enlisted men. Designed to be temporary during World War II, the project dipped into nearby all-black Titustown, and thus its elementary school was on the racial frontier seemingly bound for desegregation anyway. After the war, however, because Norfolk supplied both the teachers and other resources at the Benmoreell school, a federally owned facility, Brewbaker insisted that he must abide by state segregation law pending the Supreme Court's decision in *Brown*. This meant that the first and second graders of black sailors had to attend the closest black school, Titustown Elementary. This minor standoff did not last long, however; in 1956 the district conveniently closed Benmoreell Elementary because it was a tiny firetrap fit for no one.[12]

Now that the *Brown* decision was here, however, almost everyone, including Virginia's governor, Thomas Stanley, and Attorney General J. Lindsay Almond Jr., wanted a commission to ponder the situation and recommend what to do next. In April, the *Virginian-Pilot* had endorsed the call for such a body headed by former governor Colgate W. Darden Jr. At the same time, the *Journal and Guide* noted that the establishment of such a commission was in the Republican Party's state platform in the last gubernatorial election and had even been considered in the last session of the General Assembly. This, then, was certainly nothing new, but to have someone such as Darden, who was now the president of the University of Virginia and whose family was part of Norfolk's power elite, to advocate it meant that it would actually happen. After the *Brown* decision, the courthouse crowd and even the *Ledger-Dispatch* came around to this pragmatic and prudent step, but those truly committed to segregation did so for obstructionist reasons. Dropping the mask of moderation after failing to get black leaders to accommodate to legal segregation in late May, Governor Stanley emerged as one of those diehards. When he named a thirty-two-member committee to consider school desegregation on August 30, 1954, it was packed with white legislators from the Black Belt, the most vehement supporters of Jim Crow. Thus, the so-called Gray Commission, named after its chairman, Garland Gray, was designed to be an obstacle to integration, rather than a tool to implement the Supreme Court's order in the recent *Brown* decision.[13]

ALTHOUGH IT WAS by no means clear at the time, as the Gray Commission got under way, President Eisenhower changed the dynamics of the desegregation debate when he appointed Walter E. Hoffman to be a federal district judge for eastern Virginia on June 29, 1954. This was a new position created by Congress, and Hoffman fit the bill. As a prominent "gentleman jock" attorney from Norfolk, he was nicknamed "Beef" and had worked as a law partner with Edward ("Eddie") L. Breeden Jr., a prominent Democratic state senator. Despite his affiliation with the Republican Party, Hoffman had the support of leading figures in the state's political and legal circles, including Mayor Duckworth; W. R. C. Cocke, the president of the Norfolk and

Portsmouth Bar Association; and Richmond's Lewis Powell Jr., his former classmate at Washington and Lee Law School.

Hoffman would need all the support he could get. A few months after his appointment, a second *Brown* decision (commonly known as *Brown II*) brought the practical logistics of school desegregation to his courtroom. It would instantly make him the lightning rod for those who thought that even the obstructionist Gray Commission was too moderate, especially those in the newly established Defenders of State Sovereignty and Individual Liberties. This citizens' council gave a tincture of official Virginia respectability to the segregationist cause. Although not a formal member, Harry Byrd, of course, supported the essential elements of the Defenders' agenda, which was to stop school desegregation before it began. Hoffman had enough social and political gravitas not to be swayed by the Defenders and their nasty phone calls. In July 1955, he issued an order to desegregate Seashore State Park in Princess Anne County in what is now the city of Virginia Beach, weathering the bitter and personal threats coming from the citizens' council and associated others. The Seashore State Park decision was a bad omen for the Defenders, but they thought that they could outfox the judge by getting the governor to close that park down immediately. Stanley eagerly complied, and Seashore, only forty-five minutes from downtown Norfolk, remained closed until 1963. Despite Hoffman's steadfastness, the Seashore State Park case showed just how far the old order would go to preserve Jim Crow. If the governor could so cavalierly shut down a popular tourist destination to prevent integration, then he could be capable of shutting down public schools, the very incubators of the American way, to do the same.[14]

Supporters of *Brown* in Norfolk did not despair in the face of the new intransigence, even if self-described moderates had failed to temper the official reaction of the Massive Resisters. The Virginia Human Relations Council was formed in February 1955 as an integrated vehicle to aid in the smooth and gradual desegregation of the Commonwealth's schools. It was composed largely of professors, teachers, social workers, and, of course, the clergy.[15] The newsletter of the state conference of the NAACP, the *Candle,* referred in passing to a Norfolk–Newport News chapter of the council in March 1958. Nevertheless, an actual and active local branch in Norfolk was never really formed until well after the white schools had closed and reopened.[16] In that vacuum on the local left came women's groups — particularly the Women's Council for Interracial Cooperation (WCIC), the local chapter of the American Association of University Women (AAUW), and the Young Women's Christian Association (YWCA) — who became the leaders among elite whites and blacks with a handful of male allies, almost all of whom were clergy. For example, the WCIC sponsored a luncheon at the municipal airport in which Myrtle Crawford, professor of education at the Norfolk Division of Virginia State College and recent transplant from Louisville, spoke on the logistics of desegregation in her former city. Crawford and her husband, Floyd, would become stalwart members of Covenant Presbyterian, a middle-class African American congregation just across the street from the campus.[17] The president of the WCIC, Edith White, was married to Forrest White, the civic-minded doctor who would go on to play a major role in the reopening of the schools; in a March 1958 letter, she estimated the membership of that council in Norfolk as 360.[18] Much more circumspect and silent, however, was the more mainstream local chapter of the League of Women Voters, which was implored by its state leaders in 1957 to steer clear of desegregation and to concentrate on race-neutral education issues instead.[19]

While the WCIC took the lead in organizing elite whites and blacks, galvanizing rank-and-file African Americans frequently took place at church gatherings. For instance, a fund-raiser for buildings at St. Paul's Christian Methodist Episcopal (CME) Church was held at nearby Christ CME Church on Sunday afternoon, June 19, 1955. The first and main event to raise donations was a panel discussion on the ways that churches could facilitate integration, especially in the public schools in the wake of the Supreme Court's decision. The panel starred a diverse array of prominent African Americans in Tidewater: G. W. C. Brown, the supervisor of the Evening College at the Norfolk Division of Virginia State College; Leola Clark, president of the Crest Social Club; Willie Mae Watson, principal of Diggs Park School; and the Reverend E. C. Walton, pastor of First Baptist Church, located in the small town of South Hill in Mecklenberg County, Virginia.[20] Indeed, preparing oneself mentally and spiritually for integration was a common lecture topic for black ministers in the area.[21]

Local black business and fraternal leaders also actively urged compliance with *Brown*. In particular, the Norfolk-Portsmouth chapter of Frontiers appealed to human reason and business sense as well as Christian spirit in its calls for gradual and steady implementation. The Frontiers' membership included prominent academics such as President Brooks and G. W. C. Brown, as well as the treasurer of the state conference of the NAACP, Norfolk dentist Samuel F. Coppage. Dr. G. Hamilton Francis, a physician, chaired the Public Affairs Committee, which also featured real estate agent A. Sampson McFadden. Retired civil servant David I. Muckle of Portsmouth served as the chapter's president.[22] The Norfolk-Portsmouth Frontiers' newly elected treasurer in late 1957 also served as treasurer of the local Norfolk chapter of the NAACP; this busy individual happened to be Frank W. Merritt of North Carolina Mutual, the oldest and largest African American–owned insurance company.[23] Finally, local postman Joseph Simmons, the president of the Virginia State Elks, the second largest fraternal order among blacks in the Old Dominion, served as the first full-time NAACP Political Action Committee worker in early 1956.[24]

Interlinked with mostly black clergy, teachers, professionals, and businesspeople in Norfolk, the local, state, and national NAACP posed the greatest and most persistent threat to de jure segregation. The Virginia state conference, the nation's fourth largest,[25] had a goal of having 27,025 members in the Old Dominion in 1957,[26] and its leadership in Norfolk was especially effective. Robert D. Robertson spearheaded the city's chapter, which had 2,735 members as of September 15, 1958.[27] Herbert Marshall, the same college faculty member who had guided the classroom discussion right after *Brown,* headed the active youth and college division until 1958, when Robertson's wife, Roberta, became the enthusiastic mentor of local youth members.[28] Young people in the NAACP, however, were not just innocent pawns but rather served as foot soldiers in their own quest for full citizenship. Andrew Heidelberg, one of the seventeen African Americans eventually selected to desegregate the Norfolk schools, recalls that women from the local NAACP were trying to recruit him and his parents in the Chesapeake manor section of the city in the mid-1950s. He said that he was interested mainly to please his parents and the other adults, but other area youth were much more into activism to please themselves.[29] The Virginia Youth Conference was especially lively, with 114 dues-paying youth members in Norfolk in 1956.[30] Before he turned over the reins to Roberta Robertson in the spring of 1958, Herbert Marshall met with Herbert Wright, the youth secretary, to plan an ambitious series of programming and workshops statewide.[31] For both the junior and senior members of the local and state NAACP, John B. Henderson of Bank Street Baptist Church was their pundit and inspiration in the *Journal and Guide,* at times going beyond the restrained language of his boss, P. B. Young Sr., the paper's longtime owner. With black political power crippled by poll taxes and other gambits, Norfolk's NAACP, with the direct encouragement of the state conference and the national headquarters, would use the class action lawsuit as a most potent catalyst to prompt the conscientious Judge Hoffman into doing the heavy lifting of compliance if the legislature and school board would not.

Behind the scenes, however, local black opinion makers were not always on board with the contentious lawsuit strategy. For instance, in the optimistic days before the declaration of Massive Resistance, G. W. C. Brown himself, an officer of the state NAACP, clearly preferred the old biracial committee route of the 1940s over the prospect of a drawn-out battle in the courts. In a letter to Mayor Duckworth, he wrote, "All of these tensions of racial strife and conflict, threatened lawsuits and the like are unnecessary and costly. Our citizens—black and white alike—must learn to put the City of Norfolk ahead of race." He suggested the establishment of a Mayor's Committee on Human Relations to be the midwife during the birth of desegregation.[32] Duckworth ignored Brown's suggestion, however, and the educator was forced to approach Superintendent Brewbaker with the same suggestion a few months later. Brewbaker, unlike Duckworth, acknowledged receipt of Brown's letters and expressed his gratitude "to have something done in a sane, logical manner."[33] The declaration of Massive Resistance then intervened, poisoning any more backstage, local attempts to head off litigation. It was not until the eve of the school closures crisis in June 1958 that the biracial committee concept was briefly floated again, only to be rejected, this time by local black leaders in the face of the intransigence of local white officialdom.[34]

The most significant supporter of biracial tolerance, if not equality, was the *Virginian-Pilot*'s editor, Lenoir Chambers. "Isolated from the black community" without any real personal friendships with black leaders, Chambers consciously distanced himself and his paper from the NAACP as well as from the more white-centered Council on Human Relations.[35] Ironically, the most balanced and detailed coverage of the schools closures crisis was provided by the rival *Ledger-Dispatch,* whose segregationist editor, Frank Leslie, allowed his frontline reporters—one of whom was Unitarian Tony Stein—to tell their stories as they saw them without editorial interference.[36] The *Ledger-Dispatch*'s coverage was nominated for a journalism award, but it was Chambers of the *Pilot* who won the Pulitzer Prize for his editorials in 1960. Chambers's reasoned calls for the rule of law in racial matters stemmed from his long, low-profile service on behalf of civic racial harmony. He had been a member of Norfolk's Interracial Commission during the Aline Black and Melvin Alston cases, but he did not take a leading, public stand at that time. Twenty years later, he preferred token integration in line with *Brown* to calm racial tensions and to maintain the racial status quo over the risky and inflammatory gamble of defiance at all costs. In fact, Chambers's editorials proved to have a powerful influence on Judge Hoffman throughout the course of the school closures crisis.[37]

Pushed from all sides, Norfolk's school board hedged its bets, although its members clearly felt more pressure from the Defenders than from the NAACP or any potential federal force. In 1956, the board passed the school desegregation issue on to the state legislature, an action that board members understood as a stalling tactic. Later that year, however, the Gray Commission forced the hand of Brewbaker and Norfolk's school board chairman, Paul T. Schweitzer, with its local option scheme, kicking the decision on desegregation back to the local level. Angering the Defenders and Harry Byrd, the commission issued its final report in November 1955, calling on local school boards to design assignment plans for all pupils within their districts and suggesting that parents be allotted state vouchers to send their children to private, secular schools rather than integrated, public ones. Local control and parental choice, however truistic on first glance, were not sufficiently predictable to maintain a universal retention of the old order in Virginia.[38]

Disappointed especially by the deference to pragmatic local authorities who in "liberal" Norfolk could very well do the unthinkable, the extremists then took more drastic action, leaving no room for compromise. Senator Harry Byrd, via his machine and the Defender auxiliary, made it very clear: you were with them or you were against them. This simplistic and bombastic stance at first appealed to voters statewide. On January 9, 1956, in a statewide referendum, Virginia voters approved the most obstructionist of the Gray Commission's recommendations: the use of public moneys for private nonsectarian schools. Equally appealing at first to the old order was a young pundit's dusting off an antebellum argument for interposition, enlisting it in the rhetoric of defiance. A friend of Byrd eager to make a name for himself, James J. Kilpatrick of the *Richmond News Leader* launched an editorial campaign to redeploy the old constitutional doctrine of "interposition" in the Defenders' struggle. Purely secular and abstract, this old idea held that a state could protect its people from the federal government if the U.S.

government attempted to violate the people's fundamental rights. Only the *Ledger-Dispatch* embraced it in Norfolk, with most others either dismissing it or keeping silent given its powerful advocates. The *Virginian-Pilot*'s Lenoir Chambers was not afraid to speak up, however; he called interposition what it was: "an exercise in fantasy."[39] He was almost alone among white opinion shapers in Norfolk, however. Maverick Democrat Robert Whitehead, like Chambers, saw through the theatrics of Massive Resistance, but he represented Nelson County, not Norfolk, in the assembly, and his letter to Attorney General Almond did little more than vent his own steam.[40] The Norfolk Ministers' Association cautiously named a committee to study a possible response to the January 9 referendum, but that group only monitored the situation. The atmosphere was just too risky to do anything more.[41]

Even city councilmen in Norfolk who had earlier considered complying with *Brown* now lined up solidly with the majority for the referendum. For instance, during the summer of 1955, Councilman Ezra T. Summers had shared his own "voluntary choice method" of desegregation with his colleagues, who were both surprised and pleased by his suggestion to allow children the choice to enroll in either all-white, all-black, or integrated schools. Future mayor and councilman Roy B. Martin Jr. especially liked the ring of free choice, as he would a decade later. The council then forwarded the "Summers Plan" to the city manager, Sherwood Reader, and to the city attorney's office for their feedback.[42] Despite this initial burst of enthusiasm, this idea was forgotten due to the rightward shift in the political winds. By May 1956, Councilman Summers was telling the Cosmopolitan Club that he was for segregation period.[43] There would be no freedom of choice in Norfolk, at least for the time being. Accordingly, with Kilpatrick's and Byrd's assent, the Virginia General Assembly in February 1956 resolved to resist by all means necessary the federal government's usurpation of Virginia's sovereign powers, heavily drawing from the revived doctrine of interposition.[44]

On February 24, 1956, Byrd officially kicked off his crusade of Massive Resistance against the *Brown* decisions. That, of course, entailed building a coalition of the willing. Accordingly, on March 12, 1956, Byrd engineered the creation of the "Southern Manifesto," a polemic signed by both of Virginia's senators, all ten of the state's federal representatives, and eighty-nine other southern congressmen. The manifesto argued that both *Brown* decisions violated the U.S. Constitution and threatened the states and the people with the arbitrary use of national power. Its signers vowed to follow all possible legal avenues to bring back what the people — clearly understood as the white majority — wanted by turning the clock back to the *Plessy* era.

Following the official advent of Massive Resistance, the more moderate local option scheme was repudiated in part because it risked the prospect of integration in areas outside the Black Belt such as Norfolk. On August 27, 1956, with Byrd's full blessing, Governor Stanley issued the "Stanley Plan," which established a three-member, governor-appointed Pupil Placement Board. This impressive-sounding stalling tactic was meant to stop any and all attempts at integration by creating an "objective" body tasked to maintain "efficient" facilities. In Orwellian doublespeak, "objective" meant administration-approved, and "efficient" was a code word from the 1902 Virginia Constitution. Most heartening to the Defenders, the Stanley Plan also gave the governor direct authority to close any integrated public school in the state, going over the head of the seemingly spineless school boards, especially the moderate one in Norfolk. In contrast, Lenoir Chambers gasped at the real possibility that the Stanley Plan could close the schools and lose a whole generation, black and white, to ignorance and poverty.[45]

DISMAYED, IF NOT SURPRISED, by this flurry of official extremism, African Americans in urban Tidewater drew upon everlasting Scripture to be sure of victory over temporary political posturing. An editorial cartoon in the August 5, 1956, edition of the *Journal and Guide* by Jack Mimms graphically showed this point. In it, a smug white segregationist has closed his eyes to the truth. He is talking down to a black man with the hubristic comment, "Sure, you're a full-fledged American citizen, but I decide what you can or cannot do." The smiling faces of Adolf Hitler, Benito Mussolini, and Joseph Stalin, the disembodied heads of totalitarian atheism, flank the segregationist's side, underscoring what Mimms saw as the un-Christian and un-American aspects of that position. The African American man has his eyes opened to the unchanging truths of faith, even if he temporarily holds his hat in his hand, knowing that this oppression too shall soon pass. After all, a passage from Leviticus — "Ye Shall Not Oppress One Another"— is on his side.[46]

Lenoir Chambers was more secular in his pronouncements that counseled following the law. Without referring to Leviticus or other books of the Bible, he urged adoption of the Gray Commission's proposal over the Stanley Plan because it offered localities a choice on desegregation. Free choice, not state fiat, was all-American, and it had one big advantage to Chambers. Like most whites in Norfolk of that time, the *Pilot* editor did not know or want to know many black people: local option would prevent massive integration by providing an inoculation of desegregation in the urban areas where it was most feasible.[47]

Judge Hoffman probably preferred the local option idea for the same reasons as Chambers, but he had a job to do in carrying out the federal court decisions. *Brown II* had delegated the specific pace and logistics of desegregation to local district court judges, and black parents and children represented by the local, state, and national branches of the NAACP were willing to sue recalcitrant school boards and superintendents to get them moving. On May 10, 1956, ninety-six African American adults and schoolchildren — sixty-five students and thirty-one parents or guardians — formally requested that the federal district court issue an injunction ending racial discrimination in Norfolk's public schools. NAACP attorney Victor J. Ashe filed the suit in Judge Hoffman's jurisdiction on behalf of the plaintiffs and all other blacks in Norfolk in similar situations. The suit was nearly identical to one filed on April 26 asking for the desegregation of Newport News schools, and so Judge Hoffman eventually combined them, while keeping separate names for the cases.[48] The Norfolk suit was named *Leola Beckett v. The School Board of the City of Norfolk* because Beckett was the first child listed in alphabetical order of the sixty-five underage plaintiffs involved in the suit. Most interesting is that her name was not among the African American students seeking transfers in the summer of 1958 or later, yet her name would cling to the case until its final denouement in 1975.[49]

There was no indication that it would take that long to desegregate local schools. In fact, on January 11, 1957, in both the Newport News and Norfolk cases, the African American plaintiffs won their suits against the cities' school boards, which had followed the state's Pupil Placement Act in determining student assignments. Indeed, Judge Hoffman went further, declaring the Pupil Placement Act unconstitutional, since placement board members were instructed to consider the race of students in determining which school a particular child would attend. He ordered that the Norfolk School Board abolish its practice of assigning students to schools based upon race by the following academic year, beginning on August 15, 1957. In Hoffman's ruling, the first, seventh, and tenth grades would be the first to see at least a few blacks attending predominantly white schools.

Norfolk's superintendent appealed the decision, but not before he admitted to reporters that integration might be easily, if slowly, accomplished with the help of parent-teacher associations (PTAs) and other community organizations. Mrs. Stuart Grizzard, the president of the Norfolk City PTA, promptly gave him her support. Even so, however, the "moderate" Brewbaker was very willing to introduce new twists of segregation in his district, as when his assistant superintendent for curriculum and instruction, Herman Williams, announced that no black teachers would teach classes over the television, thereby preventing black teachers from instructing white students even if the teachers were not physically present.[50]

Judge Hoffman, for his part, also minimized the practical effects of *Beckett* in Norfolk. He bought Brewbaker's argument that the city had "substantially complied with the 'separate but equal' doctrine" and said that the city was "to be commended for its rapid strides in bringing about an equalization in physical equipment, curriculum, teacher load, and teachers' salaries." In fact, Hoffman declared, "If the 'separate but equal' doctrine were now in existence, there would be no grounds for any relief to be afforded" the African American plaintiffs. In other words, *Beckett* would mean no new court-mandated expenditures to enhance African American schools within the district. White taxpayers would not be unduly burdened by paying for bettering facilities or ending the dozens of part-time classes that African American children attended.[51]

While touting the board's willingness to equalize schools within the limits of Jim Crow, Judge Hoffman envisioned that new "redevelopment and housing plan[s]" might "substantially reduce the number of colored children who would ordinarily be assigned to [white public schools]." Such new residential developments would prevent the "threatening" four-to-one ratio of whites to blacks at elementary schools if *Brown* were implemented; even for Judge Hoffman, that a formerly all-white school could suddenly become one-quarter African American was too high a percentage.[52] Everything had to be as token and minimal as possible. Predictably, Chambers embraced Hoffman's vision, with its limited objectives. This meant that the plaintiffs' most powerful white allies were almost as tinged with racial isolation and superiority as their avowed enemies. For the parents and guardians who sued, therefore, their victory in this early battle was far from winning the much longer legal war.

Yet Hoffman was not entirely pleased with Brewbaker and his board; what especially angered the judge was the complete deference of the superintendent to the Byrd machine. Hoffman pointed out in open court that he would have entertained any plan with even the smallest of steps toward compliance, yet the board offered up only total "defiance of the Supreme Court."[53] He seemed to take that defiance personally, issuing "a grim warning" after just "going through the motions" of a court proceeding. When Brewbaker asked yet again "for more time" to ready parents and teachers for desegregation "before attempting to mix the children," Hoffman "snapped" back. He said this case was not about adults, but that it was squarely about children going to school. Defense attorneys for the board still tried to get Hoffman to delay. They just needed a few more weeks, months, or years to think things through. Fed up with the board's wasting of his time, Hoffman responded by setting a deadline for them of August 15, 1957. The courtroom theatrics between Hoffman and the defense attorneys were mainly procedural, intellectual, or legal exercises that did not delve into the everyday inequities in people's lives. If the board had just come up with the most skeletal and rudimentary plan, then Hoffman would have obliged them. He was obviously not in favor of complete integration, but he did have a job to do.[54]

The distance between their ostensible allies, Hoffman and Chambers, on the one hand, and the experiences of black people under legal segregation, on the other, was the least of the African American parents' problems in Norfolk. Indeed, even though the plaintiffs had won in court, in August 1957 the General Assembly tried to intimidate them by dragging a handful of the parents and their lawyers in front of Delegate James M. Thomson's ad hoc Committee on Law Reforms and Racial Activities, which was investigating NAACP practices within Virginia. At first, both local NAACP counselors, Victor Ashe and J. Hugo Madison, the main targets of the probe, refused to appear before the Thomson Committee. Accordingly, cited for contempt for failing to answer, Ashe and Madison were compelled to come before Judge Clyde H. Jacobs in Norfolk's circuit court, who told them that they had to respond to the committee's questions or be found guilty of contempt. In the meantime, one plaintiff out of the fourteen had already testified. All were advised to have counsel present before they endured the committee's needling; the *Journal and Guide* noted, right before this stunt, "Persons representing themselves to be investigators for the Thomson Committee, called on plaintiffs in the local school board action asking them questions about how and when they became plaintiffs in this action." Having been locked out from the closed-door executive session, the *Journal and Guide* guessed that this "gestapo-like" grilling would revolve around similar queries more designed to cow than to enlighten. The committee's official report snidely put down the motives of the plaintiffs, noting the wealth and position of some while underscoring the alleged stupidity of others. According to that official document, they were either too rich to need the free services of NAACP lawyers, or they were too dumb to know what the lawyers were really up to. Nevertheless, twelve plaintiffs proudly posed outside the session for a photo published in the African American weekly: Delphia Young, Louvenia Robinson, Mrs. James M. Turner, Robenia Deans, Sadie Barnes, Forest Gaines, Olea Beckett Hall, Delores Garrison, Sarah Cherry, Allee Christman, Doris Talley, and Mr. Talley.[55] The committee had obviously failed in its bid to scare them, and it would eventually sputter out that fall when it tried to go beyond its mandate to monitor all textbooks for any hint of racial egalitarianism that threatened white supremacy.[56]

While brushing off any legislative harassment, some African American parents in Norfolk refused to sign the pupil placement forms that went along with the Stanley Plan. Parents had to sign a yellow sheet issued by the placement board that officially assigned their children to a school, effectively giving their assent to segregated schools. In Richmond, a pilot program for the completion of these forms was tested in the spring, causing parents to try to get around signing "the blanks" and to still keep their children in school. The form was designed to go statewide in the fall.[57] In late May, the *Journal and Guide* had advised its readership to sign the forms because their children's education came first and because the placement board scheme would be eventually dissolved by the Supreme Court.[58] Most agreed, but that advice was too accommodationist for some. Two Booker T. Washington High School students, Samuel C. Merritt III, son of Mr. and Mrs. Samuel C. Merritt Jr., and Lewis Billups, grandson of Sally Taylor, were expelled after either their parents or guardians refused to sign the placement form. A third student, Sylvia Childs, was allowed to stay in school only after her uncle, the Reverend E. C. Walton, finally decided to sign the form "under protest."[59]

The parents who refused to sign eventually won an injunction from Judge Hoffman for their children to return to school, not just in Norfolk but also in similar cases in Suffolk and Nansemond County. In his order, Judge Hoffman wrote that the state had gone overboard in holding children accountable for the actions of their parents to prove a point that had already been ruled unconstitutional. Expulsion was not in the children's or the state's interests, to the judge, because it would lead to idleness and delinquency. The children should and would be in school except for the local authorities' enforcement of state pupil placement laws, which he had struck down earlier in the year. Obviously pleased with Judge Hoffman's decision, the *Journal and Guide* published a large photograph of the victorious black parents and their children who had refused to sign the state's placement forms.[60]

Compared to the well-publicized violence of Little Rock, Arkansas, however, Norfolk did seem to be on a more attainable, if halting, path toward some type of desegregation as late as 1957. While the port city waited a year because of federal appeals — the Fourth Circuit upheld Hoffman in August 1957 and the Supreme Court denied certiorari in October 1957 — Governor Orval Faubus of Arkansas challenged a federal court order to admit nine African American students to the all-white Central High School in Little Rock. Ultimately, President Dwight Eisenhower had to send federal troops to the Arkansas capital to make certain that the African American students could go to Central High. In stark contrast to the irrational drama in Little Rock, the black vote in Norfolk had helped to defeat a rabidly segregationist slate for the General Assembly.[61] Then, in November, the young African American attorney Edward Dawley Jr. ran as an independent candidate and received a surprisingly large amount of votes in a quixotic bid for the General Assembly. Along with his friend and fellow attorney, the equally brash Leonard Holt Jr., Dawley would go on to challenge the system in creative ways, which even the local chapter of the NAACP did not approve. For instance, in 1957, Dawley and Holt filed suit to desegregate the public toilets in the downtown courthouse building, even though their local African American lawyers' association (for which Dawley was president and Holt was secretary) refused to endorse their move.[62] Although Dawley and Holt ultimately lost their toilets case, many local figures welcomed their actions as a harbinger of better opportunities ahead. Surely, J. B. Henderson opined, the powers-that-be, worried about competing with the Russians after the surprise of Sputnik, could not be so dumb as to close the public schools, the incubators of future rocket scientists, to prevent desegregation.[63]

THE GENERAL ASSEMBLY session of January and February 1958 quickly proved that Virginia's political elite, led by its newly elected governor, J. Lindsay Almond Jr., would risk its economic and social well-being to maintain segregated public schools. On January 11, 1958, after winning a gubernatorial campaign in which he vowed that he would lose his right arm before seeing a single black child enrolled in Virginia's white public schools, Almond stressed the primacy of state over federal action in dealing with the issues facing public schools.[64] A cascade of laws strengthening Massive Resistance followed, highlighting the power and purpose behind the new Almond administration and its allies.[65]

Although cowed into inaction by Richmond and its local agents, J. J. Brewbaker was more immediately concerned about the pesky impatience of the African American plaintiffs and their attorneys. They just would not go away. One big reason for that peskiness was a belief by at least some of the would-be transfers that there would be no trouble in the transition. Here, reporter Jim Elliott of the *Ledger-Dispatch* cataloged the optimism of at least three black students hoping to go to Norview High School in the fall. The Welch sisters — Juanita, fifteen, and Evelyn, seventeen — and James L. Scott Jr., fifteen, all forecast a smooth transition. Evelyn noted that her older brother John had played basketball with boys from Norview without incident, and there seemed to be little concern about race. Evelyn, who was a self-described "average student," did worry a little about competing academically with white children for the first time, but she knew that she could compete through hard work and study. James and Juanita were also hopeful about the prospects of participating in extracurricular activities at Norview. James was a trombone player and hoped to audition for the school's band, while Juanita wanted to continue her student government and newspaper work there. She, however, did not see much racial mixing to be done at school dances or parties. Her oldest sister, Mary, a twenty-two-year-old high school graduate, interrupted at this point, suggesting that because whites and blacks largely mingled with their own people "even up North," there would be little social interaction with whites at Norview. Mary based this realism on living in Brooklyn, New York, for a while. The other adult quoted in the article — James L. Scott Sr., the father of James Jr. and a postal clerk — was also a little more hesitant on the transfer issue. But James Jr. had decided for himself, and that was enough for his parents.[66]

Although youthful optimism and parental courage pushed the system along, legal appeals had delayed the desegregation of schools in Norfolk by at least a year. As August 1957 came and went, Superintendent Brewbaker and the board hoped for yet another year of delay. Even so, on June

10, 1958, the superintendent did begrudgingly begin accepting applications for black students to transfer to white schools. He did not have to wait long for applicants, as their submitted requests "poured" in. By the afternoon of June 12, thirty-five African American transfers had turned in their completed paperwork, indicating their intention to go to "Norview Senior, Junior, and Elementary Schools, Granby High, Northside, Meadowbrook, Suburban Park, and other elementary schools." A reporter for the *Ledger-Dispatch*, Charlton Harrell, counted ten applications coming in that morning alone, with sixteen coming in the day before and nine on the very first day. He noted that many of these pupils lived closer to the all-white schools than the all-black ones. He also meticulously listed the names, ages, addresses, and occupations of each of the latest applicants. Publishing this type of detail in the local paper may have been done to intimidate or to discourage black parents and their children from submitting applications, but it does offer a glimpse of the would-be transfers and their families. For example, readers learned that the twenty-fourth and twenty-fifth applicants late on the afternoon of June 11 were the Bryant brothers of Oakwood: Walter Lewis, fifteen, and Daniel, six. Walter was hoping to go from all-black Jacox Junior High to Norview High; his little brother wanted to go to Norview Elementary. Students turning in applications the next morning were the Tatem siblings, Lawrence Pryor, Crystal Griffin, Calvin Winston, Daphne Perminter, Valerie Edmunds, and the Robinson children.[67] A day earlier, Harrell had provided a similar list accompanied by a stunning, front-page photograph of the Welch sisters — Juanita and Evelyn — in front of Norview High itself. That list featured Samuel C. Merritt III (the same Booker T. Washington student whose parents had refused to fill out the placement forms a year earlier), Melvin G. Green Jr., Cloyde and Thomas Reese, James L. Scott Jr., Claudia and Carol Wellington, Barbara Bond, Carole L. Branch, Margo D. Jordan (the young sister of her lawyer, Joseph A. Jordan Jr.), Patricia Godbolt, Juanita and Evelyn Welch, and Dorothy E. and Jeraldine V. Talley.[68] More than 100 similar requests over the next month were presented. By mid-July, 151 African American students had petitioned the Norfolk School Board seeking transfers into several of the all-white public schools in the city. In the midst of this rush of applications, on June 27, 1958, Judge Hoffman again reminded the superintendent and his board that Norfolk must act upon the transfer requests with speed and without regard to race.

On July 17, 1958, the very deadline for it to receive transfer applications,

Norfolk's school board issued a resolution listing the ten criteria that the board would use to determine a student's suitability for transfer.[69] These guidelines mentioned nothing explicitly about race; that would be "uncavalier" and unseemly and would obviously draw the ire of Judge Hoffman. Yet they were all about race, once placed into context. The first three assumed that there could be a Little Rock in Norfolk, and required that transferring students pose no threat to the safety or security of the children. Thus, for their own protection and instruction, the transfers were discouraged. Indeed, by August Norfolk's police chief told his commanding officers to reschedule previously scheduled vacations for any time other than August 20 through mid-September in anticipation of any "trouble" at the schools that fall.[70]

The last seven obstacles assumed that the academic, emotional, moral, physical, mental, and spiritual progress of white students, as well as of their surrounding communities, was far superior to that of their black counterparts. Implicit in the seemingly neutral wording was the fear that desegregating the schools would hold back the whites without helping the African American transfers, who were assumed to be too far behind to be helped anyway.

While publicly sticking to the ten-point list for denying African American transfers, the board then began to administer an intensive battery of interviews and tests designed to weed out any who remained. At the informal school board meeting held on July 17, 1958, Brewbaker passed out drafts of the forms and procedures to be followed. The draft memo to parents and guardians, dated July 21, 1958, stated, "Tests are to be administered to children who have applied or for whom applications have been made for admittance to schools previously attended by the opposite race." The memo tersely directed parents and guardians to take their applicants to the Office of Psychological Services at the John Marshall School at Fifteenth Street and Omohundro in East Ghent. While the parents and guardians waited in the school's auditorium, staff psychologists Robert J. Beard and Evelyn M. Dadmun proctored the exams and eventually gave the interviews. No slight was too petty for the board: all applicants scheduled to take their tests on July 29 (high schoolers) and 30 (middle schoolers) had to bring their own lunches. It was just another show of disrespect. Elementary school students were also to take the tests on July 31 and August 1 without being provided a lunch. Eleven beginning first graders were given the choice of being tested individually during the week of August 4. There were no makeups for the impromptu testing; any child who was not there to take the exam exactly as scheduled would not be able to take it at all.[71] Those rules also applied for the accompanying interviews, which were not particularly convenient. The interviews took place a little later in August on yet another day to be determined only by the board, causing more lost work time for parents. This may have been behind the failure of Samuel C. Merritt III to show up for his scheduled scrutiny on August 4—an absence that signaled the apparent death knell for his bid.[72]

Several African American parents with children applying for transfers balked at these unnecessary and insulting screenings, telling the *Journal and Guide* that they were "just going to ignore them" in the same manner as some students in the same situation in Charlottesville were doing.[73] Other parents wanted to know in advance what topics or kinds of questions would be on the test so they could prepare their children; Brewbaker brusquely rebuffed their attorney, Joseph Jordan Jr., when he asked the superintendent for a preview.[74] On July 28, accordingly, at least twenty-one of the would-be transfers asked the district court to throw out Norfolk's test-based filtering. Brewbaker countered this parental rebellion by saying that this kind of testing was routine for any students—white or black—wanting transfers that were unusual. He again refused to give out any information about the format or content of the tests to the plaintiffs' attorneys, Victor Ashe, J. Hugo Madison, and Joseph A. Jordan Jr.[75] The students could take the tests without a study guide or be automatically disqualified. Hoffman ultimately sided with the board here.

Most parents decided to let their children be tested, consequently, with the apparent blessing and tacit support of Robert D. Robertson, president of the local NAACP. However reluctant or ambivalent, these parental choices to comply with the board's process seemed to be a coordinated effort, as on Sunday afternoon, July 27, Robertson attended a meeting of "parents, friends of parents, and NAACP members" at Mt. Gilead Baptist Church in Oakwood to discuss going along with the procedures. On his end, Brewbaker decided to have thirty juniors and seniors report for testing and interviewing on Tuesday, July 29. Only sixteen of those thirty students actually showed up, with four of the fourteen absentees that day being litigants against the unnecessary testing in Norfolk's pupil assignment plan. One girl became ill about two-thirds of the way through the exam and had to leave.[76] The next day, just thirty-nine of the scheduled fifty-eight took the test; reporter Tony Stein of the *Ledger-Dispatch* noted that the participation rate was far different from Charlottesville, though, where a parental boycott led to no students taking the test.[77] On July 31, sixteen elementary school students out of twenty-nine scheduled took the test.[78] Three of the elementary school absentees were the children of Major Bennie Armstrong, director of administration at the Hampton Roads Army Terminal, who was suddenly reassigned to Fort Eustis on the Peninsula. The commanding officer of the terminal insisted that the reassignment had nothing to do with the desegregation issue, but, as a result, the applications for the Armstrong children to go to Meadowbrook Elementary were withdrawn.[79] Overall, by August 4, only 84 out of the 151 would-be transfers had taken the test as scheduled.[80] Two days later, the total reached 89, but, meanwhile, two students apparently dropped out or were disqualified for an unknown reason.[81] By August 15, when twenty-one people ranging from parents to school administrators and psychologists were subpoenaed to appear in court three days later, eighty-seven applicants had gone through both the testing and interviews.[82]

As matters moved slowly forward, resisters in Norfolk and Richmond tried to stop the desegregation process. In the first days of August, before any African American children had been assigned to white schools, a white couple in Norfolk — Mr. and Mrs. Coleman H. Coley — filed suit to block any such move. The Coleys were upset at the very real prospect that their child at Norview Junior High might be attending school with at least one black classmate. Circuit Court Judge Clyde Jacobs quickly threw out their request for an injunction, however, noting that the local school board had not yet formally violated the state's Pupil Placement Act. Despite Jacobs's ruling, the Virginia State Supreme Court of Appeals proved more willing to act. In fact, on August 18 the state's high court issued an injunction restraining the Norfolk School Board from "performing any act of enrollment" that was under the purview of the state's Pupil Placement Board.[83]

The moderate pose taken by the Norfolk School Board angered those on the left, too. For instance, in reference to the board's and the Commonwealth's latest ploys to frustrate even the most gradual implementation of the *Brown* decisions, the Reverend Henderson in the *Journal and Guide* blasted these delays in no uncertain terms. To Henderson, the board had picked the wrong side in the clear choice "between the Devil of rank Vir-

In July 1958, two young women traveled with their mother to John Marshall Elementary School in East Ghent, where the girls submitted to testing and interviews as part of the screening process required for all black students seeking admission to white public schools. (Courtesy of the *Virginian-Pilot*)

ginia racism and the deep Blue Sea of justice and equality as interpreted by the Supreme Court of this land of ours." To this NAACP leader and local pundit, there was no daylight between the positions of the board and the governor in that both were "diabolically shameful" and showed "an indecent and un-Christian lack of ethics." To Henderson and most black clergy, demonizing their opponents was directed at energizing their base and in encouraging more applications for transfers.[84]

While heating up the rhetoric and posturing on all sides, this polarization doomed any last-minute resort to the shopworn biracial committee approach to paper over the rough edges of racial division. In early June 1958, Lyman Beecher Brooks, P. B. Young Sr., and at least fourteen other promi- nent African American men — the Norfolk 16 — requested that the city council consider setting up a biracial group that would ease the racial ten- sions stirred by the court battles over desegregation. These were no "Uncle Toms" trying to enable white defiance: their number included Rev. Richard B. Martin, the pundit in the *Journal and Guide,* and J. Hugo Madison, one of the plaintiffs' attorneys. As noted earlier, even Brooks and Young had ties to the local chapter of the NAACP. Rather than forestall change, therefore, they hoped that a biracial committee would "calm the waters of disturbed opinion" in the inevitable transition to desegregated public schools.[85] This old chestnut of an idea, put forth this time by the black establishment, died in part because of Defender pressure on the council to appear unyielding to black leaders.[86] For his part, Brooks actually addressed the council on June 3 in reference to this proposed committee. In his remarks, he unfavorably compared "liberal" Norfolk to "conservative" Richmond, which allowed blacks to sit on important municipal boards and commissions.[87] Brooks would go on to repeat these sentiments in the *Virginian-Pilot* almost two weeks later.[88] At first, the council politely received his idea, but it was quickly forgotten.[89] Outside council chambers, the efforts of the Norfolk 16 were in- terpreted by both segregationists and integrationists as surrendering to the status quo. In response to a segregationist letter to the editor that appeared in the *Virginian-Pilot,* P. B. Young Sr. angrily dismissed the idea that the Norfolk 16 could tell the NAACP with its 3,500 local members to stop their legal action. Young noted that local blacks were as diverse in their opinions as any other Americans were: "They are not robots, subject to the will or order of just one, or of 16 of their number."[90]

Local integrationists ironically shared the segregationist view of this bi- racial committee, which they saw as a white flag. Indeed, Young's point about differences of opinion within African American circles was illustrated by the black Baptist ministers' unequivocal denunciation of the biracial committee concept, which they viewed as merely an attempt to exchange a little city patronage for the rights of black students and parents.[91] Attorney Ed Dawley, on the radical fringe, was even more troubled by the efforts of the Norfolk 16, condemning the internalized racism and big egos of these "leaders" via street theater.[92] In fact, it was clear that the most steadfast advocates of integration in Norfolk were not about to let their imagined caricature of P. B. Young Sr.

and company dilute the passion and determination of parents, students, and their pastors with the promise of a few high-profile appointments.

The persistence of local African American parents and students emboldened some key white ministers in Norfolk, who made it known that they would not be accessories for the Byrd machine. In particular, in the summer of 1958 "the Norfolk Presbytery, by almost unanimous vote, . . . voted to support the Supreme Court's schools desegregation decree and . . . warned churches in the Presbytery against allowing use of church facilities for 'private' school classes." What was so gratifying to the *Journal and Guide* was that "the voting on the resolution drawn by 85 ministers and elders was almost unanimous. There are 20 churches in Norfolk which are in the Presbytery, which has a membership of 57 churches overall."[93] This reflected an even greater support for public school desegregation among the southern and white Presbyterians here locally than in the southern white Presbyterian denominational assembly as a whole.

One Presbyterian pastor in Norfolk, however, actually went beyond lip service to bridge the racial religious divide: the Reverend William B. Abbot of Oakdale Presbyterian. Unlike the Reverend James C. Brewer, the well-known Unitarian leader of the Norfolk Committee for Public Schools (NCPS),[94] Abbot has been forgotten by historians. This is a mistake in part because it limits the parameters of white advocacy of real reform in Norfolk to simply keeping the schools open. In fact, Abbot pushed for far more robust social and political changes in the Old Dominion. In 1957, for instance, he not only attended but also addressed the state conference of the NAACP on "The Church Meets the Challenge of Compromise." The very act of speaking before the state NAACP was obviously rare for any white minister in Virginia, but Abbot took it a step further, calling for complete integration "without insincerity or evasion."[95] Later in 1958 he would go on to play a leading role in shaping the tone of the pastoral condemnation of the schools closure. A characteristically brash note to Senator Edward Breeden hinted at "cosmic support" for the schools reopening on a desegregated basis.[96]

While Abbot clearly and singularly pushed the envelope, his example helped bring less outspoken and more timid ministerial counterparts on board to oppose Massive Resistance. That collective influence of the opinions of local clergy had the effect of frustrating the segregationist Tidewater Educational Foundation, Inc. (TEF), which had expected to create all-white private academies on church properties to supplant the soon-to-be desegregated public schools. While it is true that, once the schools had closed, tutoring groups segregated by race met in all-white churches (and one all-black church for the Norfolk 17), these groups consciously distanced themselves from any relationship with outspoken segregationists and disbanded once the public schools opened again in February 1959. Consequently, when the TEF incorporated on June 27, 1958, it took considerable time to find an appropriate venue for its planned alternative instruction. Ultimately, the organization had to settle with Bayview Baptist Church, a working-class enclave on the very outskirts of town.[97] Bayview's pastor, the Reverend James F. Burks, was one of only two ministers in Norfolk—the other being Reverend R. Allen Brown of East Ocean View Presbyterian—to actively aid and abet Massive Resistance.[98]

Nevertheless, key lay support among the area's white Protestants sustained the TEF from its brief stay at Bayview Baptist to its eventual purchase of the Bruce Mansion along fashionable Mowbray Arch in Ghent for the all-white Tidewater Academy. Very significant in the making of the private Tidewater Academy was ironically a young public school teacher—twenty-five-year-old Hal Bonney, who taught history at Norview High School, a soon-to-be focal point in the schools closures crisis. Bonney was an outspoken segregationist and appeared on Edward R. Murrow's famed Columbia Broadcasting System (CBS) documentary *The Lost Class of '59* before becoming superintendent of Tidewater Academy.[99] Along with William H. McKendree, the local printer who was one of five directors of the TEF, and William Story, the extremist superintendent of adjacent South Norfolk County Schools, Bonney would soon rush to enroll white students displaced by the schools closure in Norfolk.

Indeed, McKendree was a leading member of the Defenders of State Sovereignty and Individual Liberties, which continued to organize in Norfolk. Dick Mansfield, a stringer with the *Virginian-Pilot* drafted a long intelligence telegram for the famed African American editor Earl Brown of *Life* magazine. Brown then forwarded this valuable information to Robert Carter, the NAACP's general counsel. In his report, Mansfield estimated that the Defenders' number in Norfolk at 4,400 and discerned, "This group has remained quietly active in parent-teacher assoc. activities and has gradually penetrated various social groups, its work carried on subtely [sic]." The telegram noted that the possible election of McKendree, "a member of the Defenders and a vocal foe of desegregation," as Norfolk's PTA president could happen, but it also noted that the city's "silent 'moderates'" reacted and rapidly came up with a then stealthy and publicly unnamed candidate of their own who might defuse any public controversy. The telegram predicted, however, that the very election of the moderate palatable to the PTA majority would produce "a nasty, in-fighting situation."[100]

JUDGE HOFFMAN for his part had had enough of local debates and delay. On August 19, 1958 — the day after the state appeals court had ordered a stop to the transfers — Hoffman issued his own mandate to the Norfolk School Board. He told the board to reconsider its August 18 rejection of all 151 African American transfer students. Hoffman further demanded that a new transfer report on the 151 applications be filed with him by August 29. He said he would not tolerate any more "pussy-footing around." The judge then declared that the school board needed "to act with dispatch" in the manner in which he had previously requested and, more specifically, to give the transfer requests a quick and serious review.[101]

On August 29, the members of the Norfolk School Board reported to Judge Hoffman that they would reluctantly and, against their better judgment, admit seventeen of the African American students to six of the city's all-white schools, which had a combined enrollment of over 10,000 students. Andrew Heidelberg, one of the chosen seventeen, later speculated that the acceptances were probably arbitrary and were not based on the "objective" scores of any test or interview. To Heidelberg, the board had selected those students who were either light-skinned (thirteen of the seventeen in his opinion) or who had names that were not very African American in nature such as his own and that of Alveraze Frederick Gonsouland.[102] One glance at a photograph of sixteen out of the seventeen in an event's program from early December 1958, however, shows that the board did not pick the transfers because many were light-skinned.[103] Most of the seventeen were like him: moderately brown to dark-skinned. The seventeen did have either very Anglo-Saxon or foreign-sounding names, but so did the less-celebrated would-be transfers listed in the newspaper and in the court transcripts who did not make the cut. Much more credible is Heidelberg's insight that social class had something to do with the final placement of the admittees; working-class Norview High School and Junior High School were designated for most of the black students, whereas Granby High School, in a "better" neighborhood, was slated to take only one transfer.[104] At any rate, the board had finally caved in on Hoffman's requirement for a plan, any plan; Richmond and its local tentacles were not pleased.

The counterrevolution then swung into motion, much more quickly than

The members of the Norfolk 17 posed for this photo in front of First Baptist Church (Bute Street) in 1958. The Norfolk 17 included (l–r): Andrew Heidelberg, Louis Cousins, Betty Jean Reed (front), Patricia Godbolt (back), Johnnie Rouse (front), Carol Wellington (back), Reginald Young (far back), Delores Johnson, Alvarez Frederick Gonsouland, LaVera Forbes (front), Edward Jordan (behind Forbes), James Turner Jr., Olivia Driver (back), Lolita Portis, Patricia Turner, Claudia Wellington, and Geraldine Talley. (Courtesy of Time-Life Pictures)

Brewbaker had processed the applications. Less than one month later, on September 27, 1958, Governor Lindsay Almond ordered that the six Norfolk schools slated for desegregation be closed immediately to avoid integration. On September 29, 1958, those six secondary schools were promptly shuttered, displacing 9,930 white students and seventeen black students. Meanwhile, Norfolk's two black junior highs, its only black high school, one of its white junior highs, and all of its segregated elementary schools remained open.[105] Eddie Breeden typed a revealing letter to Mayor Duckworth on that fateful September 29, hoping against hope that the governor would not act and that the schools would remain open. He never mailed it, however, and other moderate voices in power also shied away from direct confrontation. It was not elite Norfolk's shining hour.[106]

Indeed, the unthinkable had happened in Norfolk: the largest school closing of its kind would drag on for months, threatening to tarnish the city's relatively cosmopolitan reputation. Norfolk, of course, was not the only district in the Old Dominion to have its schools closed that fall. Warren County, Charlottesville, and Prince Edward County also actualized Massive Resistance via their schools, and the diversity of these locales — with their widely different racial and socioeconomic compositions — indicates the breadth and depth of popular and elite attachment to codified Jim Crow in Virginia. But even though Prince Edward County's closures would linger all the way into 1964, Norfolk's closures affected many more students than any of the other places, and, because of that, it became the new ground zero of the struggle for desegregated schools in 1958, supplanting Little Rock, Arkansas, from the previous academic year in public discourse and imagination over the issue.

How and why the schools closed abruptly in September 1958 and then reopened on February 2, 1959, is one of the subjects of chapter 3, but the underlying causes for this stunning overreaction were set into motion in the four years after *Brown*. The city's power elite and Judge Hoffman had tried to stem the tide of Massive Resistance even before it got going. Their minimal attempts at compliance with *Brown,* however, encouraged the NAACP and its clerical and white allies to push harder for integration, while simultaneously hardening the defenders of Jim Crow to even more radical acts of desperation. Moderation in this scenario led only to polarization; Norfolk, with its silent moderate majority, was the ideal testing ground in the cold, if not civil, war between those who wanted social justice and those who preferred the social injustice of custom and tradition.

CHAPTER THREE

CONFLICT
AND
DESEGREGATION'S DIFFICULT
BIRTH IN NORFOLK, 1958–1959
CONTINUITY

I T WAS NOT SUPPOSED to happen that way. The fix was already in when Norfolk's city council agreed to hear from those who opposed the closing of six all-white schools due to court-ordered desegregation. Just the night before in a closed dress rehearsal, the councilmen, along with school board members, legislators, and the Byrd machine's main lieutenant in Tidewater, Corporation Court Clerk William L. Prieur, had decided to pass the buck to Virginia's governor Lindsay Almond, whom they hoped or half-expected would reopen the schools on a segregated basis. This session on Tuesday, September 30, 1958, was merely supposed to be window dressing, a necessary formality, to allow those opposed to the school closures to vent — and vent they did. The passion and number of the petitioners demanding the reopening of the schools along with the prescribed admittance of seventeen carefully screened African American students was surprising to both the white and black journalists covering the council session. With about 150 people packing the council's chambers, the crowd posed a serious test for Norfolk's elected establishment. The impertinence of this unusually large gathering caused Mayor W. F. Duckworth to lash out at least two times. Once, as a youthful white attorney, Herbert L. Kramer, insisted that the city had no choice but to reopen the schools in compliance with Judge Hoffman's rulings, the mayor bristled, "It is silly for you to stand there and talk the way you are talking. It is an insult to my intelligence." His second reported flash of temper came when "the predominantly Negro side of the chamber" burst out into laughter. This public display of disaffection came after John Hall, only one of two Massive Resistance supporters to speak, wondered aloud if the Constitution had a Fourteenth Amendment. Hall was not really joking, even if his line of argument seemed absurd to the majority of those present. The mayor was not laughing, however. As the *Virginian-Pilot* observed, this spontaneous response from the audience forced Duckworth to bang his gavel repeatedly to regain order and then to threaten those whom he rightly suspected would laugh at similar comments in the future with ejection from the council's chambers.[1]

What really got the mayor going, however, was what he considered to be the self-serving, self-righteousness of all of the local preachers present. Early in the session, Edgar Potts, of Epworth United Methodist Church, presented a plea on behalf of seventy-six members of the all-white, all-Protestant Norfolk Ministers' Association, of which he was president. Potts requested that the city government move swiftly to reopen the schools in compliance with *Brown*, since the education of so many children was at stake. Avoiding the question of whether integration was desirable (at least in the official minutes), Potts underscored the bromide that American democracy depended upon public schools, which prepared "an informed electorate." American democracy, to Potts, was also based on Christianity, and thus the ministers "could only offer a Christian solution to the school integration crisis," which meant keeping the schools open, however integrated. The Reverend James Brewer, the Unitarian head of the Norfolk Committee for Public Schools (NCPS), pushed the other neutral-sounding pabulum of local rather than state control of the public schools, which Duckworth dismissed as unworkable without a big tax increase.[2]

The points raised by the ministers seemed to bait the council into blaming this whole mess squarely on the seventeen African American applicants, their parents, and their communities. George R. Abbott, the vice mayor, asked why seventeen African Americans should hold up the education of roughly 10,000 white children, who, to him, were far more valuable than catering to that troublesome handful of blacks. Whites were not applying to black schools to shut them down, so why should these seventeen African Americans cause this suffering to whites? Indeed, the council's answer came from Mayor Duckworth, who repeatedly insisted that the most painless way to resolve this standoff was to persuade the seventeen applicants to go back to their own segregated schools.[3] In an exchange not covered by the newspapers or the official minutes, the Reverend Moultrie Guerry of Old St. Paul's, one of the most venerable and respectable white churches in Norfolk, allegedly reiterated Potts's position, at which the mayor, who was well known for using racial epithets in public, blurted, "The best thing you preachers can do is to tell those 17 niggers to go back where they belong and we'll open the schools tomorrow." That particular volcanic flare set Guerry aback, but not before he came back by noting, "You can't halt progress. Even if those seventeen withdrew, there would be seventeen others to take their place."[4] The mayor probably knew that more applicants would be coming, and that is precisely why he could not stomach the lack of gratitude and deference that Norfolk's African Americans had for the racial status quo. In his response to the ministers, Duckworth argued that the National Association for the Advancement of Colored People (NAACP) — to him, "strictly a northern organization giving us a lot of trouble" — was behind this constant push for desegregation. Duckworth hated the organization and suggested that it did not reflect the silent majority of the city's African Americans, who were the direct beneficiaries of $50 million worth of governmental largesse spent on slum clearance and segregated schools. He stressed, "The City of Norfolk has done more for its Negroes . . . than any city in the South — barring none." And he had expected that area whites would have gotten better behaved and more obedient "citizens" as a result. Despite all of that patronage spent on Norfolk's African Americans, the mayor in exasperation pointedly noted, "They pay only 5 percent of the taxes and occupy 75 percent of the jail space."[5]

This slur on an entire community did not go unchallenged. Attorney Samuel Goldblatt, while agreeing with Duckworth that "the Colored people furnish a large contribution to the jail population," believed that racial disparities were not immutable and could be changed by giving integration a chance.[6] Yet the slur was best answered by the Reverend Richard B. Martin, the rector of Grace Episcopal Church, a congregation that featured stalwarts of the African American upper and middle classes, and a regular columnist with the *Norfolk Journal and Guide*. After expressing his due respect to the mayor and the councilmen present with a theatrical irony probably lost on those officials, Martin said, "I am very disturbed by your statements." He resented that Duckworth's distorted if pungent quoting of statistics made it seem as though African Americans were inherently criminal, having "no reason to . . . try to have character or to keep out of jail." To Martin, this phase in the struggle for legal equality was inevitable and "was not the result of the NAACP." He believed that "it would have come about with another organization as well . . . this is progress. This is the knock on the door of time. This is the twentieth century."[7]

However deluded Mayor Duckworth may have been about local African Americans, the city's chief executive was right in one sense. It was the Norfolk 17, their parents and guardians, their attorneys, and their NAACP supporters who were in the vanguard, pushing for compliance with *Brown v. Board of Education.* Indeed, the Norfolk 17 could have been the Norfolk 151 or more if the school board's legal and bureaucratic foot dragging had not severely restricted the ability of African American applicants seeking admission to white schools. Unfortunately, their story has been eclipsed in part by that of the white editor Lenoir Chambers of the *Virginian-Pilot,* who won a Pulitzer Prize in 1960 for his reasoned editorials both before and during the school closures crisis. By placing Chambers and other influential white moderates such as newspaper magnate Frank Batten at center stage, the usual narratives about desegregation in Norfolk focus on the crisis as an unfortunate detour into madness that quickly ushered in a peaceful period of integration that avoided the federal intervention and televised unpleasantness of Little Rock, Arkansas. This accepted version, helped by two CBS documentaries, one narrated by the legendary Edward R. Murrow, has nourished the entrenched self-image of Norfolk as a particularly progressive port, but it is only partially accurate. It is true that many whites complained about the inconvenience caused by the overreaction of school closures, but they did so believing that real integration would never come. It is true that white ministers in Tidewater rallied to oppose Massive Resistance, but only a few openly embraced the NAACP. It is also true that the school closures made Norfolk look particularly bad to businessmen, the navy, and *Business Week,* and thus the public schools could not be closed for long due to the concerns expressed by Norfolk's main industries. What gets lost in this official story of the school closures is the courage of those local African Americans who could not be persuaded, through patronage or otherwise, to settle for second-class citizenship. Indeed, this persistent courage and its accompanying sense of inevitability would be sorely needed for the long haul.[8]

What also gets lost is that not much changed in the immediate months and years after the hallowed date of February 2, 1959, the day that schools reopened on a desegregated basis in Norfolk. As we shall see, the reopening of the schools that February meant the continuation, invention, and recasting of every procedural obstacle erected by Norfolk's white officialdom to prevent true integration, usually with the seal of approval from Judge Hoffman himself. On a personal note for the Norfolk 17 and their successors, it meant both facing hostile classmates and indifferent teachers in formerly all-white schools and protesting deteriorating conditions in those schools that remained all-black. Hence, Duckworth and his supporters lost the main battle predictably and dramatically by early 1959, but he and his successors continued to fight the war on many different fronts, both public and personal, with success throughout the 1960s. Thus, this chapter seeks to de-emphasize the date of February 2, 1959, by placing it in context, connecting the important narratives that proceeded and followed it.

TO UNDERSTAND the courage of the Norfolk 17 and position them in their proper context requires that we revisit the causes, turning points, and consequences of the school closures in Norfolk based upon a wider variety of available sources than previous accounts have examined. And the best place to begin is Judge Walter Hoffman's courtroom on the eve of the school closures. The court transcripts keenly reveal the mechanisms by which the Norfolk 151 was whittled down to the Norfolk 87 and then to the Norfolk 17, and through this "sifting process" we get to see the first documented and relatively in-depth glimpses of the 17 and their fellow applicants.[9]

By August 1958, Judge Hoffman was losing patience with the dilatory tactics of the school board. On August 18, the attorneys for the school board — elderly veteran W. R. C. Cocke,[10] along with rising stars Leigh D. Williams and Leonard H. Davis — insisted that doing a makeup examination for 26 of the 151 plaintiffs would be logistically impossible.[11] At the same time, ironically, the school board's star witnesses maintained that testing students for placement was routine and that the school district had one of the best-resourced centers for testing in the country, with four full-time psychologists and "a psychometrist who assists the psychologists in scoring and in doing the statistical work in connection with test giving."[12]

In fact, the only real inconveniences caused by the testing and interviews were borne by the African American parents, who had to take off work on at least two days to escort their children to the testing and interview sessions; for the school board, it just meant canceling a planned summer retreat for school principals and revising the opening conference of the school year for administrators, many of whom were scheduled to be in court instead.[13] Thus, if all or nearly all of the applicants had been tested according to the ordinary operating procedures in the district, and if the retesting and interviews were simply a minor enhancement of previous efforts, then that begged the obvious question of why the tests and interviews mandated by the school board's resolution of July 17 were necessary at all. At least 62 of the 151 plaintiffs did not take the additional battery of tests, and, as previously noted, many parents and their attorneys had objected to this newly minted obstacle as a showing of contempt. While Hoffman was not sympathetic to those who had not taken the tests in July, he was certainly interested in prodding the board to notify the eighty-seven applicants who had dutifully taken those tests in order that they might learn their status for the fall.[14]

The courtroom minuet over testing and retesting was abruptly interrupted by the school board's decision on August 20 to deny all 151 applicants admission, whether they had taken the additional layer of tests and interviews or not. That decision, while expected, forced counselor Cocke on behalf of the school board to promise to present "a synopsis of the reasons for rejecting as to each child,"[15] which, in turn, gives us the best look at the applicants as individuals rather than as an enumerated cohort. Among other items, the synopses presented the applicant's name, address, school, grades, attendance records, health ratings, and scores on the California Achievement Test administered in the summer of 1958.[16] Paul Schweitzer, the chair of the school board and the president of the Layne-Atlantic Company, a locally based water-supply firm with branches in other cities, got to comment upon them, while Oliver Hill, one of the NAACP's best attorneys, selected the most problematic cases to address in court.

The first example to be brought before Judge Hoffman was that of Patricia Godbolt, who, in the words of Schweitzer, was an "excellent" pupil who attained a "very remarkable" score on the achievement test given in the previous month.[17] School superintendent J. J. Brewbaker later in the transcripts specified her performance on the California Achievement Test as 11.3, "which is the eleventh grade and third month, so she was somewhat above, and in some areas she was quite a bit above her grade level."[18] Her health was good, and she had displayed the skills to adjust socially and emotionally. She lived in the area around Norview High School, to which she applied. Nevertheless, she had to go to Booker T. Washington High School, which was farther away from her home than Norview, because she was black. Both Brewbaker and Schweitzer readily admitted that the only reason that Patricia Godbolt had been turned down as an applicant to enter Norview was because she was an African American trying to get into an all-white school.[19]

Both men would claim that their decision to turn down Patricia was in her best interests. They testified that they did not want the combustible distractions of racial tensions to divert her from doing as well as she was doing at Booker T. Washington. Problems of social adjustment were much harder on transferring junior and senior high school students than on their younger counterparts. Since Patricia was going into the eleventh grade, it would be very rough on her being at Norview, a school that was surrounded by some of the most racially polarized and explosive neighborhoods in the city.

Indeed, the school closures crisis had only added to Norview's reputation for overt displays of racial hatred. Roughly two months before Brewbaker's assessment of the neighborhood in court, a crudely made effigy of a black person was hung on a flagpole outside Norview High School. Even cruder words — "No nigs wanted at Norview"— were painted on a bedsheet attached to the effigy. Police Chief Harold Anderson dismissed it as "a juvenile prank," but the message was loud and clear.[20] The *Ledger-Dispatch* carried the story on the front page, and reporter Jim Elliott surveyed the attitudes of white parents and students there, finding a spectrum of opinions ranging from reluctant acceptance of desegregation to vehement outrage at local integrationists. As Elliott noted, "two of the most outspoken and bitter opponents of integration were two junior high school girls, Betsy Faulkner, fifteen, and Brenda Anderson, fourteen, both of whom will attend Norview High this September." Allegedly more interested in boys than books, Betsy was most worried about mixed school dances and interracial dating, while Brenda, whose father worked alongside blacks at the naval base, pledged to walk out if an African American student even came into her classroom. Two other white girls — Kathy Dail and Linda Lovelace, both aged thirteen — were more tolerant of integrated schools, as long as blacks and whites kept to their own kind. Both girls insisted on separate bathrooms and eating arrangements for whites and blacks so that the standards of racial decorum might remain in place. Another friend — Sandy Joyner, thirteen — "emphatically" said no to desegregation, noting that her mother planned to put her in a parochial school to escape a potentially desegregated Norview that fall. What Sandy and her mother apparently did not know was that local Catholic schools had desegregated several years earlier. Two white boys interviewed — Wallace Watson, sixteen, and Bill Carnes, twelve — were willing to put up with integration if it meant that the public schools would stay open. The two younger boys questioned — Bobby Rose, nine, and Ricky

This effigy appeared in a tree outside Maury High School in Ghent during the school closures crisis. (Courtesy of the *Virginian-Pilot*)

Curles, probably the same age — were much more aggressively hostile to the idea that African Americans might integrate their school. In fact, Ricky got into "a boxer's stance" and predicted that he would get into fights with any new black kids at his school, Norview Elementary. That lack of tolerance at such a young age seemed to undercut the position of Superintendent Brewbaker, who argued in court that if desegregation had to happen at all, then it ought to begin with the elementary school children.[21]

Yet despite any evidence to the contrary, Brewbaker said he was concerned for Patricia Godbolt and other excellent African American students hoping to transfer to the Norview area schools. The superintendent predicted in his courtroom testimony that nearly all white students at Norview would exclude Patricia from social and extracurricular activities, and thus he implied that any benefits to her from using more convenient and up-to-date facilities would be far outweighed by daily ostracism and harassment.[22]

Schweitzer supported his argument for protecting Patricia and, more directly, fellow applicant James A. Turner with a personal and revealing anecdote. Schweitzer was no Lewis Powell Jr., his counterpart in Richmond who would later go on to be a Nixon appointee on the U.S. Supreme Court. He was not born a Virginia aristocrat, and he was not limited by the accompanying pretensions of that ruling class. Nevertheless, despite being a self-made man in the manner of Duckworth, he supported segregation for different and more paternalistic reasons than the mercurial mayor did. He himself had been the "victim" of racial isolation in Arizona forty-five years earlier, having been only one of two white children attending a Hispanic elementary school. His academic progress, and that of his sister, was limited by the lack of social acceptance by the other students, and he eventually had to repeat the fourth grade. Indeed, his father "gave up the job as manager of this big ranch and moved back to Tucson because he could feel that his two children had to be in an environment that they could be accepted in." This "horrible" experience made Schweitzer resolve to avoid putting any other child of whatever background in that situation of facing a hostile or indifferent racial majority.[23]

Despite Schweitzer's paternalistic concern for Norfolk's African American students, the young applicants simply would not go away. The court transcript reveals a little of the stamina and excellence of the individual applicants who kept coming up. The Norfolk 17 proved to be an unusually well prepared sampling of students of whatever background. Even Delores Johnson, who was deemed in open court as the least academically proficient, was a solid student. She would have been transferred to Norview by school board officials if she were white, according to their own testimony and documents. Delores had no record of discipline problems and had an agreeable disposition.[24] What also probably came out in the interview done by the school board and what she recently expressed in an interview many years later was that she was also a busy caregiver who had had experience in a desegregated high school setting outside of the Old Dominion. The previous year, Delores had moved to West Orange, New Jersey, to help her older sister raise her nieces. Once there, she had started high school as one of only four blacks at West Orange High School. She fit in well, however, and was apparently accepted by her classmates. Yet she had to move back to Norfolk when her mother had been burned on her hands by an exploding gas stove that November. Taking care of her mother, she had transferred to Booker T. Washington, but, of course, Norview was closer to her home than the all-black school across town. That early sense of responsibility apparently made up for any minor deficiencies noted by the tests.[25]

Nearly all of the other applicants had strong academic credentials. James A. Turner was deemed to be a great student. He and his sister Patricia, another academically sound pupil, had benefited from the guidance of a strict mother and navy father, who had sometimes brought his children to the brave new world of the integrated naval base when he was stationed in Panama. That upbringing would serve them both well.[26] In the same vein, Johnnie Anita Rouse was dubbed "a good product" by a sincerely proud assistant superintendent, Edwin Lamberth. And the superintendent presented a laundry list of other good students who were qualified to transfer to Norview Junior or Senior High — Claudia Wellington, Carol Wellington, LaVera E. Forbes, Edward F. Jordan, Olivia Driver, Andrew Heidelberg, and Alveraze Frederick Gonsouland. These students were all denied, however, because the school board feared that their admittance would contribute to racial friction that would disrupt student learning.[27]

With the futures of so many good students at stake, the number of applicants to be heard and the individual details to be pondered were so overwhelming to Judge Hoffman that he allowed the defense counsel on August 25, 1958, to group their cases in the following ways: the "racial tension at Norview" group, the "isolation" group at Maury and Granby high schools and at Blair Junior High, the "too frequent transfer" group, which featured mainly elementary school students in the Rosemont-Oakwood area, and the "geographical boundaries" group that had only one person in it at that time. There was also the "lacking scholastic achievement" group for twenty-eight other applicants, and even that did not account for the Tatem children or the twenty-one others who had refused to participate in the interviews or examinations. Finally, there was the handful of applications in which the taking of either the interview or the test was in dispute.[28]

The "racial tension at Norview" group became the main nucleus of the Norfolk 17. LaVera Forbes, James Turner, Patricia Turner, Edward Jordan, and Claudia Wellington would attend Norview Junior High School, while Andrew Heidelberg, Alveraze Gonsouland, Delores Johnson, Johnnie Rouse,

Olivia Driver, Carol Wellington, and the oldest and brightest, Patricia God-bolt, would go to Norview Senior High. As expected by their parents and advocates, they all did well academically after the school closures crisis had ended and after they finally got to attend the school closest to their homes. As the *Journal and Guide* proudly revealed on the first anniversary of the desegregation of Norfolk's schools, by-then senior Patricia Godbolt was so ahead of her classmates that she had been exempted from taking three examinations, and she was already planning on getting scholarships to college. The Turners were getting good grades, too, with Patricia averaging B's and C's at Norview High and her little brother James becoming an honor student at Norview Junior High. Nevertheless, the same glowing article hinted at the difficulties and tensions that these overachievers had to deal with on a constant basis: "Extracurricular activities have been somewhat curtailed."[29] What an understatement that turned out to be!

The problems and obstacles that the admitted applicants had to face were much worse than either school officials or parents wanted to admit. Norview's reputation as a particularly Negrophobic place turned out to be all too true, but the 17 all suffered, whether they went to Norview High School or not. Rising stars Patricia Godbolt and Louis Cousins both had crosses burned on their lawns. Having had a knife thrown at her by a classmate, Patricia was so scared of her fellow students that she refused to use the school bathroom. Delores Brown was chased by a random mob on her way home from school. She and Olivia Driver were humiliated by teachers who put on gloves when handling anything they had touched. Andrew Heidelberg reported that he had to encounter every known racial epithet every hour of every day until he graduated. Only his prowess at football allowed him some degree of acceptance by his senior year. Olivia Driver ducked from the periodic volleys of rocks and spit. So did Betty Jean Reed at allegedly upscale Granby. Olivia also had to deal with teachers purposely calling her Oliver in a bizarre, gender-bending insult to an impressionable young girl. The youngest of the 17, Lolita Portis, ate alone at Blair — to this day she still dreads eating by herself in public. Teachers ignored and belittled their new charges; the nurturing ethos of Ruffner and Booker T. Washington was not obviously present at Norview or any other of the formerly white schools for the African American transfers. History teacher Hal Bonney at Norview would bait his new black students by showing movies with hurtful stereotypes of Africans and African Americans over and over again. When Carol

Wellington suffered a lab accident, her teacher did not care about her. Instead, the teacher was only concerned about Carol getting the teacher's hair wet. Patricia Godbolt and Johnnie Rouse both qualified for the National Honor Society, but their bids were blocked by the chapter's faculty advisers. Thanks to the majority of both white teachers and students, being the first African Americans to desegregate public schools was a searing gauntlet that no remaining member of the 17 can recall today without tremendous pain.[30]

The isolation and harassment predicted by defense witnesses in Hoffman's courtroom, therefore, came to pass in the reopened schools, only to be glossed over by the same officials after court-ordered desegregation. On the first anniversary of the reopening of the schools in February 1960, Brewbaker dismissed any sign of trouble, noting, "Some of the possible annoyances suffered by colored pupils could be attributed to adolescent behavior in no way related to race." Parents also publicly kept a brave face, with one father placing an especially positive spin on racially based ostracism: "We were interested in them receiving an education, not participating in social activities." The sweeping assessments of NAACP officials and attorneys on the first anniversary also contributed to this adult sense of smooth normalcy at the schools, even if the experiences of the African American transfers themselves were anything but smooth and normal. It was politically correct for those supporting integration and, ironically, for Brewbaker in the immediate aftermath of the schools being reopened to deny the existence of the predicted isolation and harassment. The children, unfortunately, were not in a position to deny those ubiquitous terrors.[31]

The defense witnesses had claimed that a sufficient cohort could mitigate isolation and harassment to a point, and, of course, the NAACP training of the 17 to be a family during the autumn of 1958 led to lasting group cohesion. Nevertheless, the identified "isolation" group at Granby and Maury high schools, and Blair and Northside junior high schools did not have the benefit of having a group of other African American students at their new schools. The original "isolation group" of August 22 featured only three members: Reginald Young and Lolita Portis, who had applied to Blair Junior High School in fashionable Ghent, and Betty Jean Reed, who had applied to Granby High School, which was located well north of the downtown area in relatively middle-class surroundings.[32] Only later would Louis Cousins, going to Maury High School in Ghent, and Geraldine Talley, going to the modern Northside Junior High School in newly annexed suburbs, be added to this classification. As with the Norview group, the "isolates" were judged to be scholastically adequate,[33] but the big problem to Brewbaker and the other defense witnesses remained the deleterious effects on good students of being the only African American in a sea of white faces. In Ghent or in the far north, Brewbaker and others implied that the atmosphere might be less overtly hostile than the shouting mobs possible at Norview, yet to the imagination of the school board officials, that overwhelming majority of whites would be intimidating just in its mere presence. At least four to eight suitable African American applicants to a single school in the west and north of the city were needed for comfort, judged the superintendent, and that was not possible at this time due to housing patterns, socioeconomic trends, and test scores. Brewbaker and the school board's attorneys suggested that it was better to wait until a critical mass of screened African American transfers, preferably in the lower grades, developed to implement desegregation in middle- and upper-class areas.[34]

To rebut the isolation theory, the plaintiffs called Thomas Howard Henderson of Virginia Union University, an African American and Baptist institution of higher learning in Richmond. In the pay-parity contests of the late 1930s, Henderson had been the secretary of the Virginia State Teachers Association and had assisted the NAACP with its lawsuits, pushing that organization's accommodationist president Winston Douglas of Booker T. Washington High School to take a definite, public stand. A specialist in educational psychology and a dean at the college by the 1950s, he noted that isolation could motivate good students to do better without social distractions. That was true, he deduced, in his own graduate education as one African American student out of a cohort of twenty-one taking a comprehensive exam. Indeed, to Henderson, since the transfers were conditioned by custom and experience to expect rude or indifferent behavior from white people, they would not be unduly shocked by the isolation that they might find at formerly all-white schools.[35]

While the "isolates" may have garnered the most attention from the court, the "too frequent transfer" group occupied a large and unreported chunk of Hoffman's time and would be significant long after the schools reopened. In late August 1958, this group included eight applicants: Glenda Gale Brothers, Charlene Butts, Melvin G. Green, Minnie Alice Green, Cloraten Harris, Rosa Mae Harris, Sharon Venita Smith, and Edward H. Smith III. Brewbaker explained that the members of this group were students at all-black Oakwood Elementary seeking transfer to Norview Elementary. Importantly, however, all members of this group were slated to go to the new Rosemont Elementary-Junior High to be opened in September 1959. Overcrowding had forced both Oakwood and Norview to go on a double-shift, part-time schedule, and the new Rosemont combined school for blacks was designed to relieve the situation at Oakwood while keeping segregation intact. Melvin G. Green and his sister Minnie, however, lived just a block and a half from Norview, and they had to go farther to attend Oakwood. Although Rosemont was closer to their house than Oakwood, it was still not as close as Norview. Brewbaker rejected the Norview option for Green and the others because it meant one too many transfers for these children, quick and abrupt changes that might disrupt the children's development.[36] He also went out of his way to reject geographical proximity as the most important factor in school transfers, citing the example of Charlene Butts, who lived closer to Norview, yet who would have to cross the dangerous Sewell's Point Road to attend it. The school board was just looking out for the child's safety when it had rejected Charlene's application, Brewbaker insisted.[37] Despite opposition from the NAACP attorneys on this point, Judge Hoffman eventually bought Brewbaker's line about the Oakwood-Norview-Rosemont question.[38]

The "geographical boundaries" group held only one member: Daniel Bryant, applying to Norview Elementary. This case was directly related to the Oakwood-Norview-Rosemont situation. Brewbaker testified, "Mr. Bryant said that his son lived four blocks closer to the Norview Elementary School, he thought, than he did to the Oakwood school." The superintendent himself thought that could not have been the case, and he had a Mr. Pollaneck, "our supervisor of custodians, who lived out there," actually measure the distances with his car's odometer. Pollaneck dutifully reported back to his boss that Daniel's family lived "seven and a half-tenths of a mile from Oakwood and nine-tenths of a mile from Norview Elementary." Well, the superintendent did not consider that difference of one-and-a-half-tenths mile significant, but he did claim that Daniel, like Charlene Butts, would have to cross Sewell's Point Road if he chose to go to Norview. Victor Ashe, for the plaintiffs, countered that both Daniel and Charlene could have gone through the Coronado neighborhood to get to Norview Elementary without crossing the dangerous highway. At any rate, Judge Hoffman eventually upheld the difference of one-and-a-half-tenths mile as sufficient to reject Daniel's application.[39]

The "lacking scholastic achievement" group was the largest and eventually consisted of twenty-eight members.[40] The questioning of Henderson revealed the criteria by which these students were assessed to be "slow." The board and its staff had placed all students who had scores on the summer's standardized test below the fiftieth percentile into this classification, with the implication that they were at least a semester to a year behind their purported grade level. Henderson responded that the board's standards in determining placement in the "lacking scholastic achievement" were overly stringent.[41] Furthermore, he pointed out that the board and its staff had presented no data to show that "these norms would be the norms for the children at those schools that they are seeking to enter."[42] Henderson noted that southern schools, whether for whites or African Americans, had separate, unequal, and "dumbed-down" averages that were provided by the publishers of the tests. So, holding the transfers to a national average, not a lower and regional average, unfairly condemned many of these students to the "lacking scholastic achievement" classification.[43] Finally, Henderson also thought that the conscious exclusion of African American teachers and staff from the testing and interview process skewed the assessments of the students' abilities. To him, using national norms and white interviewers who had no personal knowledge of individual student abilities for success inflated the number of applicants who were considered too academically deficient to transfer. Judge Hoffman, for his part, quickly dismissed the exclusion of African American teachers and staff "as an administrative matter that the Board has no control over," but, given the board's aversion to any transfers, the dean rather than the judge was spot-on correct.[44]

From the sheer size of the "lacking scholastic achievement" group, only hints of individual stories surfaced in the court testimony. For instance, Geraldine (or Jeraldine, as the transcripts and newspapers consistently misspelled her name) V. Talley was eventually admitted as one of the Norfolk 17. Geraldine, age twelve, and her family had been among the most outspoken advocates for transferring on principle as well as convenience. On June 11, 1958, in their home in Titustown, the whole Talley family was photographed and interviewed for a *Virginian-Pilot* story that explained the reasons black students wanted to transfer. From their facial expressions and body language in the resulting front-page picture, they did not seem pleased to be photographed. Despite any displeasure, however, Geraldine's mother, Mrs. W. E. Talley, was very candid in her responses, complaining that her daughters, Geraldine and her older sister, Dorothy, fifteen, had to endure long bus rides to get to their present schools. Dorothy was enrolled in a math class at Booker T. Washington that had no textbooks. "I'm just tired of it," said Mrs. Talley. Her husband agreed and added that "there's more to it than just convenience. There's a principle involved." The president of the Titustown Parent-Teacher Association (PTA), Mr. Talley thought that he deserved to send his children to the nearest and most appropriate school because of his extensive military and community service.[45] Despite the best efforts of the Talleys, Dorothy did not make the Norfolk 17, and Geraldine almost did not make it either. How the younger Talley sister became a member of the 17 is hard to discern for sure, but here are the available facts. Under cross-examination from Oliver Hill, Assistant Superintendent Lamberth admitted that Geraldine would have automatically transferred to Northside Junior High if she were white and newly transplanted into Norfolk. Yet he refused to say if there were specific individual or groups of white students already at Northside that had better or worse test scores than Geraldine. At any rate, Hill got Lamberth to admit that Geraldine had the same test scores as white children in the same grade at Northside. Later on, Hill pressed Geraldine's case by calling her mother to the stand. Mrs. Talley testified that she and her own father had accompanied Geraldine to her interview. Just before young Geraldine was to be interviewed, the switchboard operator brought chairs to the lobby for the group. The operator thought and then reported that Geraldine's mother had stuck her tongue out at the operator in a show of disrespect. For her part, Mrs. Talley denied doing so under oath. Judge Hoffman thought that this line of questioning was comedic relief from a long day, but Hill effectively showed how petty and biased the interviewing process could be. Geraldine then moved mysteriously from the "lacking scholastic achievement" group to the reluctantly accepted "isolates" cohort; she was the only one.[46]

After hearing case after case, Judge Hoffman went along with the geographical limitations, the scholastic achievement, and eventually the "too frequent transfer" excuses as valid legal reasons for denial, but he refused to go along with racial friction or isolation. Thus, the eventual selection of the Norfolk 17 on August 29, 1958, came out of the "racial tension at Norview" and "isolation" groups; the other 134 were denied. The school board then asked for one more semester to prepare everyone for this change, but Judge Hoffman refused. Facing this decision, the school board appealed its case to the Fourth Circuit Court and delayed the opening of all schools until later in the month. When news arrived that the appellate judges had deferred to Hoffman's ruling, the school board on Saturday, September 27, had no choice but to announce the opening of the schools on the following Monday with the seventeen African American applicants in attendance at six previously all-white schools. In response, Governor Almond, citing the Massive Resistance laws of the previous spring, quickly intervened to stop the process. On Sunday, September 29, 1958, he issued an executive order closing the six formerly all-white schools to which the seventeen African American transfers had been assigned. He said that he was only protecting the children, all of the children.[47]

IN FACT, the Norfolk 17 would need protecting, thanks in part to Governor Almond's brinkmanship. To steel the selected seventeen for the expected tension they would face when the schools reopened, Hortense R. Wells, an African American supervisor within the district, urged attorneys Madison and Ashe to conduct classes for them at Bute Street Baptist Church. Wells did not stop there, however. She followed through to buy supplies and books at her own expense and to put together a course of study for the students. During the first week, Wells and the attorneys had to rely upon a substitute schoolteacher, Katherine Quarles Allen, but then the NAACP asked Vivian Carter Mason, the nationally prominent and well-connected social worker, to take the reins of this impromptu school. Just back from a Middle Eastern tour, Mason was particularly well suited for this new assignment. She was married to one of the first African American millionaires in Virginia, so she could not be bought off or easily intimidated. She was educated at the University of Chicago, so she was eloquent and well organized, qualities that had served her well as president of the National Association of Negro Women. Once the director of social services in New York City, she was running her own public relations firm by the late 1950s. Knowing from experience, therefore, that she could not do it all by herself, Mason hired Gertrude Perry, a retired African American schoolteacher with decades of experience, to manage an integrated teaching staff of six faculty members — Hortense R. Wells, Charles S. Corprew Jr., Rudolfo Cejas, LuElla S. Howard, Elizabeth Jones, and Eleanor G. Jones — spread over five grades and twelve topics.[48] Predictably, as fitting in a church setting, these special tutoring classes at Bute Street Baptist Church worked on forming character through a thoroughly spiritual basis. Each morning the students would take turns in leading an opening religious exercise in which they had chosen the songs and verses to be performed. As Mason later noted, "Climbing Jacob's Ladder" was probably their favorite hymn, but the one that really got them going was "We're Marching, We're Marching, We're Marching Upward to Zion, Beautiful Zion, the City of God." Learning the words of this song gave them all a hard core of confidence, that despite the pebbles, spit, and shouting, God was on their side, and they knew that he would not let them fail.[49]

Not letting things fall to Providence solely, however, Mason and Perry continued to work with the Norfolk 17 at least a year after the schools reopened. Mason apparently assisted Patricia Godbolt on her way to college, while Perry coached each of the seventeen to do his or her very best. Yet their positive, public spins on the experiences of the transfers, along with those of the NAACP attorneys, ironically gave the most strength to the official story of a smooth transition that did not match the students' actual experiences. Even in Mason's commendation of the Norfolk 17's "open-mindedness" and apparent lack of hatred for their tormentors, however, one can see glimpses of bigotry and violence that these students and their parents had to face.[50] Privately, of course, Mason was far more blunt and angry about the harassment of the transfers than her watered-down statements in the *Journal and Guide* had let on, a private candor that came to the fore in the mid-1960s.

While Mason, Perry, and their colleagues nurtured the Norfolk 17 to face their destiny, the nearly 10,000 white students who were locked out of school had to resort to tutoring groups set up by teachers and parents. One of the most sought-after groups was set up by the chair of the Department of Education of the Norfolk Division of William and Mary (now Old Dominion University). T. Ross Fink established a "makeshift" school on campus that was exclusively for the children of the university's all-white clerical staff and faculty members. The school was touted to prospective new faculty members as an incentive to come to Norfolk, even if many of its schools for whites were now closed. Although the school was advertised, it was truly "makeshift," however, as it was run entirely by volunteers from the School of Education and other members of the faculty. The Norfolk Division also offered noncredit courses in English and mathematics to prepare college-bound seniors, waiving admissions requirements to get these suddenly anxious white students into the college. Fink did not please everyone, though. Well-to-do citizens in the surrounding silk-stocking neighborhoods of Edgewater and Larchmont criticized Fink's decision to limit the school to the children of

Tutoring groups for displaced white students appeared in Norfolk during the school closures crisis. (Courtesy of the *Virginian-Pilot*)

university personnel. Some of those critics, in turn, set up the Greenberg School in a vacant store on Powhatan and Forty-Eighth Streets; it was named Greenberg after the owner of the store.[51]

It was estimated that about half of the white students affected joined informal tutoring groups that met in private homes, vacant stores, and available churches. One such group from Larchmont Methodist was filmed having a staged break at Gray's Pharmacy for the CBS-TV program on the school closures, which eventually aired on January 21.[52] But the relaxed scene in the program belied the real inconveniences and compromises that these groups entailed. Students of the tutoring group at Talbot Park Baptist Church complained about the lack of classes required for graduation. Others missed the school activities and spirit that could not be maintained in disparate classes of less than twenty students each of differing grades and abilities. The overall number of students in this umbrella of groups at Talbot stood at 228, but their coordinator, Kenneth Hodge, a Northside Junior High School teacher, maintained that the only advantages that these groups had over the public schools were the groups' small class sizes. Everything else was inferior.[53]

Preferring real campus facilities over church and private basements, many students chose to commute to South Norfolk with its staunchly segregationist superintendent, William Story, or to any of the other nearby towns in Tidewater. One white parent allegedly approached Superintendent C. Alton Lindsay of Hampton City Public Schools with an open checkbook, offering any amount to have his child enrolled in one of Hampton's all-white schools.[54] Only recently connected to Norfolk by the Hampton Roads Bridge-Tunnel, Hampton City Public Schools eventually took in just twenty displaced students; in contrast, South Norfolk and surrounding Norfolk county became the most popular destinations, with even Mark Schweitzer, son of the chair of Norfolk's school board, transferring to Great Bridge High School in the Norfolk county district to finish out his senior year.[55]

When, in January, the Norfolk city council voted to cut off funding for all of the city's secondary schools, South Norfolk was viewed as the probable place for even more white and, now for the first time, black students — over 7,000 in all.[56] For those who did not want to commute, smaller numbers of white students went to live with relatives in other states or other cities in Virginia.[57] A handful of teens may have even enrolled at Norfolk Catholic High, which had been desegregated since the fall of 1955 and which had been enlarged to take in more students during the summer of 1958.[58] Private schools, besides the Tidewater Educational Foundation's (TEF's) Tidewater Academy, did not rush to take in the largely working-class refugees from the public schools in part because they wanted paying customers and not charity cases. They were also already operating at or near capacity, and the number and size of local private schools grew only after the school closures crisis had ended.[59]

With few palatable options, many more of the oldest white students left school for good rather than enrolling in parochial or private school. Those who "lost" their chance at a diploma joined the military, got married, or got a full-time job.[60] At Norview High School, at least 57 of the 225 white pupils who did not return after the crisis either went to work, entered the armed services, or got married.[61] Typical was Myrna Fine, a Norview High School student who was so frustrated with commuting to South Norfolk that she moved up her wedding plans from June 1959 to December 1958, effectively dropping out of school before she graduated.[62] Overall, only 6,400 of the roughly 10,000 displaced white students returned, with 2,000 of those having had no schooling at all since August.[63] About one-third to one-half of the displaced whites, then, truly became the "Lost Class of '59."

With so many white children adversely affected, one would think that whites in Norfolk would clamor across class and denominational lines en masse to demand the reopening of the schools. That public outrage did not happen, however, until the very end of the crisis, when local elites issued inflammatory statements about bad publicity and lost sales. Only about 1,000 people, mostly white students with time on their hands, showed up for a pro-opening rally at the Norfolk Arena on October 13. The organizers had hoped for 3,500 attendees. Just about 6,000 whites in the city signed the petition urging reopened schools that was presented to Governor Almond by the all-white NCPS a week later. That was a small number, given how many whites lived in the city. Instead of public engagement, an air of "complacency" was noted, as the tutoring groups got into full swing. The president of the NCPS, the Reverend James C. Brewer, characterized this lack of concern as "frustration" at the Hobson's choice available to parents. Looking back, however, Brewer's explanation seems to be a half-hearted attempt to rationalize the lack of support for the public school cause.[64] It is true that the frequent exhortations of white ministers to reopen the schools and the steadfast actions of affected white teachers to keep their jobs kept proschools advocacy going throughout the fall; the ministers and teachers in particular clearly frustrated the attempts of segregationists in the TEF to set up a rival, consciously separate, private school system. Nevertheless, the pleas of the clergy, in addition to those of key navy officials, increasingly went unheeded at city hall and beyond.[65]

Voters in Norfolk instead bestowed legitimacy upon the governor's decision. In mid-November, an advisory referendum held by the city council had a margin of 12,340 to 8,712 votes to continue the shutdown of the schools.[66] This special election garnered a small turnout in an East Coast port of 300,000 residents, even in the era of poll taxes and other intentional obstacles to voting.[67] As Alexander Leidholdt points out, if one deducts the 3,500 or so African American votes from the 8,712 pro-opening ones, then most whites in Norfolk who had bothered to vote were solidly behind Almond, Duckworth, and the referendum.[68]

This electoral victory predictably emboldened the die-hard segregationists, but that boost of confidence to Duckworth and the Byrd machine led them to overplay their hand. The city council's vote to close all schools above the sixth grade in January was the most egregious overreach, with one councilman, George R. Abbott, essentially agreeing to disrupt the education of his own grandson to prevent desegregation.[69] This council action angered Norfolk's PTAs and teachers, turning the sentiment in Bayview, for example, from solidly pro-Byrd in November to overwhelming proschools in January.[70] It also further fractured the already strained relations between the council and the school board, leading the council to withdraw the legal services of counselors Williams, Davis, and Cocke from the board until the crisis had seemingly passed.[71]

More significant, however, this reactionary and mean-spirited populism alienated powerful business and media leaders, who increasingly urged begrudging compliance with the court orders of Judge Hoffman out of their own self-interest. Supported by the editorials of Lenoir Chambers, former mayor J. Pretlow Darden and young publisher Frank Batten galvanized this revolt of notables over the very real fears of contracts and customers moving out of state. They were obviously not moved to secure justice for the Norfolk 17. Their petition, presented to the city council on January 26, 1959, and then published as a full-page advertisement in the *Pilot* the next day, was signed by 100 of the city's business elite. This bold maneuver finally broke the hold of local Massive Resisters and put the city on the road to reform. But it soon became clear that local businessmen had done it for themselves. As the opening clause of their petition read, the elite "would strongly perfer [*sic*] to have segregated schools."[72] This line was just not politically correct boilerplate; this opener was the sincere expression of nearly all of the signers and showed the real limits of moderation in the city.

The signers represented the best and brightest that white Norfolk had to offer — Dr. Mason Andrews, the internationally known obstetric and gynecological expert, future father of the Eastern Virginia Medical School, and future mayor in the 1990s; Frank Batten, the founder of the Landmark Communications empire; distinguished lawyers Barron F. Black (president of the Norfolk Historic Foundation in the 1960s), Charles Kaufman (Norfolk Redevelopment and Housing Association director under Duckworth), Michael Wagenheim, and both Thomas H. Willcoxes of Willcox and Savage; real estate wizards Harvey Lindsay Sr., Herman Furr, and Hunter A. Hogan Jr.; appliance chain-store owner Harry B. Price Jr.; department store heir Richard F. Welton III; newspaper executive and philanthropist Paul S. Huber Jr.; John R. Sears, chairman of the board of the Home Federal Savings and Loan Association; nursery owner Wendell Winn, the father of future councilman Barclay Winn; and, most important, industrialist Henry Clay Hofheimer

II, Norfolk's "First Citizen" of 1958. Shipbuilder John Lonsdale Roper II, as well as three Burroughs from their family's fertilizer company, also put their names on the petition. Even a relatively lesser light such as Harry A. Terjen, the manager of the downtown W. R. Grant's store, joined them. Nonetheless, one really "big" name who had tried with Beef Hoffman's pal Lewis F. Powell Jr. to end Massive Resistance via semisecret meetings with Governor Almond himself was not on the list: Stuart T. Saunders, president of Norfolk and Western Railways, the only Fortune 500 company headquartered in the port city then or now. Saunders and his Virginia Industrialization Group, as well as the 100 signers, were most concerned that closed public schools put Virginia at a deleterious disadvantage vis-à-vis North Carolina, let alone the traditional manufacturing states in the Northeast and Middle West.[73] These "wise" men of the port city all strongly preferred segregated schools long past February 2, 1959, but defying the courts was just too bad, both for regional business and for the civic oligarchy's self-image.

For their part, the silent white majority remained quiet up to the end, while the ministers and members of the NCPS and other good government organizations verbally clashed with Mayor Duckworth and local figures in the Byrd machine. It is true that the litigation to reopen the schools in Hoffman's federal district court was started and won by concerned white parents such as real estate agent Ellis M. James, who filed the important suit known as *James v. Almond.* Governor Almond also ironically sued to get the Virginia Supreme Court to confirm his decision to close the schools, but that court ruled against him in *Harrison v. Day.* These two lawsuits, rather than *Beckett v. School Board of Norfolk,* which had precipitated the crisis, were decided on January 19, 1959, and set the stage for the reopening of the schools.[74] Yet most whites waited passively for events to unfold. When the legal and political controversy had finally settled and the schools had come into session again with the Norfolk 17 admitted on February 2, pediatrician Dr. Forrest White of the NCPS declared victory. The national and international media in attendance may have been disappointed at the lack of any story, but February 2 turned out to be a routine, dull day, "and that was that."[75]

That seemingly boring anticlimax to the dramatic crescendo of the fall and winter is where the official story of smooth, gradual desegregation in Norfolk usually stops. While Vivian Carter Mason saw opening day as a part of a systemic "crisis" in public education, Edward Breeden's reply to her assumed that everything would be just fine.[76] Indeed, it was "a fine thing,"

according to none other than President Eisenhower himself, who was relieved over the Virginian calm compared to the Little Rock crisis of the
previous two years. The General Assembly also commended the "Virginian" stoicism displayed not only in Norfolk but in Arlington as well, which
opened its schools on a desegregated basis that same day. Prominent lawyer
Toy D. Savage of Willcox and Savage gushed, "I am gratified at the actions
of the students, the parents, and citizens of Norfolk. It stands as a credit
to themselves, the city, and the state."[77] From the Pacific port of Seattle,
Washington, James A. Anderson credited Paul Schweitzer for the apparent racial equipoise of opening day in particular, echoing local sentiment
among whites that continues to this day. He predicted to the school board
chair that their great-grandchildren would still be thanking Schweitzer in
the twenty-first century. Apologists for Schweitzer still see him as a friend
to desegregation, but that selective memory leaves out both his August 1958
testimony in favor of segregation and his subsequent service as part of Roy
Martin's bloc on the city council to block any real moves toward integration
in the 1960s.[78]

Thankfully, both the testimonies of the Norfolk 17 and our own document-
based research have begun to challenge these carefully nurtured myths
about the "end" of Massive Resistance, myths that survive because of their
political utility, both then and now, for the port city's racial majority. The
painful truth is that whites all along the spectrum — from the rank and file
of the NCPS on the left through J. Pretlow Darden on the center-right —
convinced themselves that "that was that" on February 2, 1959, and that they
needed to move on. Judge Hoffman himself, in an Admiralty Day Luncheon
speech in San Francisco on July 28, 1960, marveled at the relative calm after
the storm, noting that "as lawyers and judges we know that we must adhere
to the law whether we like it or not."[79] Only maybe the Reverend Brewer,
real estate agent Ellis James and his children, and Forrest White himself
continued to harbor doubts about the real and complete "end" of Massive
Resistance in 1959, but their NCPS disbanded shortly thereafter. When segregationist teacher Hal Bonney had the sardonic audacity to call attention
to the racial tensions and harassments that he himself was orchestrating at
Norview, the school's principal and his boss, Charles W. "Bolo" Perdue, re-
assured the public that those tensions and harassments were not happening.
A former New York Giants linebacker from the 1930s who would remain as
head of Norview until the height of the busing crisis in 1982, Perdue gave

the necessary "gentleman-jock" believability to his opinion, which quickly became a usable gospel for civic leaders keeping as much as the dual system intact as possible.[80] Understandably, most whites congratulated themselves on weathering "the storm," and, like most of the "Lost Class of '59," they did move on. Again, it was the NAACP, African American parents, and their children who kept pushing the legal and cultural envelope, when, at the same time, nearly all of their erstwhile white allies were content to express satisfaction and gratitude that Norfolk had avoided a Little Rock and that they had achieved their goal of realistic, if token, desegregation.

THE DIVERGENCE between white "moderates" and local blacks was best displayed in the array of reactions to a speech delivered by Roy Wilkins, the executive secretary of the NAACP, less than two weeks after the desegregation of Norfolk's public schools. Speaking across the Elizabeth River in Portsmouth, Virginia, Wilkins called for continued vigilance in the fight against school segregation. In particular, he challenged black students and parents to seek admission to segregated schools, "not by twos and threes, but by the hundreds." Parents should "apply for transfers for their children and, if denied, should seek a decision in the courts," Wilkins said. Eventually, he predicted, school officials in Virginia would accept the large number of black students applying for transfers to white schools, or they would face legal challenges that would demonstrate the racial factors used to prohibit the transfers. Either way, black students would win. School officials would voluntarily approve the transferring students, or African American parents, students, and the NAACP would fight the pupil placement system until it was declared unconstitutional.[81]

Wilkins's speech sparked an immediate storm of controversy across Virginia. In Portsmouth, Inez Baker, the local member of the Virginia House of Delegates and the wife of Mayor B. W. Baker, said that Wilkins's speech should "stir the very soul" of people at home and around the state.[82] The Wilkins speech had confirmed her worst suspicions, and she wanted other opponents of integration to hear her message. "I urge all parents to realize the seriousness of the threat made by this Negro leader," Baker said. The NAACP and other civil rights organizations "are not going be satisfied with a little integration." They want "hundreds" of black students to seek transfers to white schools. In response, Baker told her constituents, "We must throw off the cloak of complacency" and "resist [further integration] with all [the] strength that can be mustered."[83]

Even moderate political and legal leaders in Virginia criticized Wilkins's speech. For instance, Delegate Robert Whitehead, the independent, anti-Byrd Democrat from Nelson County, complained to lawyer Oliver Hill that Wilkins's speech was "harmful and detrimental and contrary to the best interest of all [Virginians]." Judge Hoffman agreed. From his courtroom in Norfolk, he rejected the NAACP's position on desegregation, saying, "I don't agree with Mr. Wilkins that the idea is to push [integration] all in one day." Hoffman argued that planning and "gradual development" were the keys to success.[84]

The press also condemned Wilkins's Portsmouth address. At the conservative *Richmond Times-Dispatch,* editor Virginius Dabney, an architect of "the Virginia way," declared that "the NAACP seems determined to bulldoze its way ahead, and to refuse to heed the advice of its integrationist friends who have been urging it to slow down, or even to withdraw from the school cases entirely." After months of controversy and compromises, Dabney argued, moderation had proved triumphant. Schools in Norfolk, Arlington, and Alexandria were desegregated, and "Virginia's stand in the controversy ha[d] won widespread praise throughout the North and West." Now, however, "Mr. Wilkins' counsel to 'hundreds' of Virginia children threatens to poison the air all over again."[85] The *Virginian-Pilot* was only slightly less critical. There, Lenoir Chambers argued that black children undoubtedly had the right to apply for transfers to white schools "by the hundreds," but that it did not "necessarily follow that the advice is good, or that the results will be better education for more children, black or white." Chambers argued that Wilkins's loose language was unfortunate. This kind of talk made "the legal rights of Negro children more difficult to obtain," and increased "the hostility of already opposed white people." Indeed, Chambers insisted, "Moderation is—or ought to be—the goal on both sides."[86]

Even the *Journal and Guide* panned Wilkins's speech, which editor P. B. Young Sr. considered far too radical for most white Virginians to accept. Although Young shared Wilkins's desire to see desegregated public schools in Virginia, the relatively conservative newspaperman did not believe that local black families should be incited to launch a full frontal assault on the legal structure of Jim Crow. This might take the movement down a counterproductive road of radicalism and violence, where African American leaders would find themselves isolated from the white establishment types who controlled Norfolk and greater Virginia. In addition, Young said, "unfortunate" comments, like those made by Wilkins in his Portsmouth address, "release into the hands of an unsympathetic press, campaign material for the people who are directly opposed to . . . first-class citizenship for the Negro people in the South." In short, Young concluded, Wilkins's words incited white extremists and alienated moderate whites, leaving little hope that any substantial good could result from "mass meetings featuring outside speakers who unintentionally leave behind much ammunition for our enemies."[87]

The real enemy of integration, however, remained the moderation that had opposed both Massive Resistance and the implementation of the *Brown* decision. Even Governor Almond finally realized that this seemingly measured way of declaring desegregation over and done with was the most effective strategy in blocking its actualization. Indeed, on January 30, 1959, speaking before a special session of the Virginia General Assembly, Almond announced to legislators that Massive Resistance had ended; there was no legal way to halt public school integration in Virginia. "I have repeatedly stated," the governor declared, "that I did not possess the power and knew of none that could be evolved that would enable Virginia to overthrow or negate the overriding power of the Federal government." Thus, Almond said, those who oppose widespread integration "must begin now to lay the groundwork for a transition to other methods as effective or better than those which have served until the hammer of federal intervention fell with devastating force." With these simple words, the governor abandoned Massive Resistance and his political patron Senator Byrd, announcing the creation of a new Commission on Education, which was to begin work on a new strategy for the state government one week later.[88]

Known as the Perrow Commission for its chairman, state senator Mosby Perrow, the governor's forty-member education board was comprised of four legislators from each of Virginia's ten congressional districts. The commission's leadership and the bulk of its members were well-known moderates who, many whites hoped, might save the public schools of the state while maintaining as much segregation as possible. The commissioners worked on their study from February 5 to March 31, 1959. At the end of their time together, thirty-one of the board's forty members approved the majority report, which revealed both the hopes and the limits of white political moderation at the time.

In their report, the Perrow Commission's majority stated explicitly that they sought to "avoid integration" in Virginia, while preserving the public school system of the state.[89] To do so, the members of the commission suggested a radical departure from current practice. They put forward a "freedom-of-choice" plan, which was designed to give local school boards — rather than the state Pupil Placement Board — control over the time, location, and rate of desegregation in local communities. In addition, the commission's report included a host of other controversial proposals. It called for publicly funded "scholarships" for students wanting to attend nonsectarian private schools, a tailored "compulsory attendance law with adequate safeguards" for whites who opposed desegregation, "additional legislation for [the] disposal of surplus school property," and a new program that would allow localities to "withhold [financial] support from public schools" to create private ones. "Under these recommendations," the report emphasized, "no child will be forced to attend a racially mixed school [in Virginia]."[90]

The Perrow Commission's work was truly a moderate compromise; it angered integrationists and segregationists alike. Attorney Oliver Hill, one of the key civil rights lawyers in Norfolk's *Beckett* case, spoke out in opposition to the use of public tax dollars for private segregated schools, saying, "No one in a democratic society has the right to have his private prejudices financed at public expense."[91] On the other side, segregationists like Inez Baker in Portsmouth declared that the Perrow Commission's report was "an act of submission," a "so-called freedom-of-choice plan" aimed at "appeasement and containment." Baker, like many other segregationists, opposed this strategy, saying, "I am opposed to subjecting innocent children to the evils which exist in Washington, Philadelphia and other heavily populated Negro areas where integration has taken place."[92]

Despite the opposition of Massive Resisters, the hesitation of proschool activists, and the frustration of African American leaders, Governor Almond pushed the Perrow Commission's report before a special session of the Virginia General Assembly on Monday, April 6, 1959. "With commendable candor and frankness," the governor said, "the report portrays the truth to the people of Virginia. It deals with facts, not fiction. . . . It does not run from the problem [of desegregation]. It points a way to deal with it without total destruction of public education."[93] A majority of the members of the House of Delegates agreed, passing the Perrow Commission's recommendations by a narrow margin. Then, in an unprecedented move, Almond's supporters bypassed the Education Committee in the senate, which was dominated by hard-line Massive Resisters, and considered the Perrow bills as a committee of the whole, chaired by Norfolk's Eddie Breeden.[94] Under his stewardship, the controversial local option bill moved to the senate floor, where it passed along with the other major Perrow bills on Thursday, April 23.[95]

Two days later, in a blistering editorial, the *Journal and Guide* declared its disappointment with Virginia's new education bills. In a statement governed by as much fury as frustration, the paper said that there was "very little difference" between the new, local option program, and the old, Byrd organization resistance. "The only difference we can see," the editor said, "is that the Organization members of Virginia working under orders from Washington would kill the schools at once, while those who are working under orders from Richmond would let them pass after a lingering illness supported by opiates, while a state-wide system of 'private' schools supported by the state for white children is being set up."[96]

The effects of the Perrow Commission were clear in Norfolk even before its recommendations passed the House of Delegates. If there was to be local management of the desegregation process, then Mayor Duckworth and the members of the city council meant to gain tighter control of Norfolk's school board. On Monday, April 6, the council sent a request to the General Assembly seeking several amendments to the city charter; these changes would enlarge the school board from six to seven members, place all school board appointments on a citywide basis, and shorten the terms of school board members from three years to two.[97] If approved, these provisions would give the city council and its mayor greater freedom in choosing school board members and increased leverage when dealing with the board on controversial issues like desegregation.

Although many of Norfolk's proschool activists spoke out in opposition to the proposal, these protests failed to have much effect. With a crucial primary election approaching, Edward Breeden and all six of Norfolk's members of the House of Delegates supported the legislation requested by the city council, and the school board alteration bill passed in late April.[98] Then, Mayor Duckworth and the Norfolk city council quickly implemented their new powers. In June, the council released two moderates from the school board—Mildred Dallas and W. P. Ballard—when their terms expired. The city council then named Kathleen Griffin, Levi Roberts, and a seventh member, Stanley C. Walker, to the board. These appointments were intended to strengthen the board's minority bloc that favored resistance to integration. In response to the city council's actions, representatives of the

NCPS spoke out again, voicing their opposition to the new appointees at a heated city council meeting in early July. They noted that Kathleen Griffin was the former head of the TEF, the segregationist organization that had recently opened an all-white private academy in Norfolk, while Roberts and Walker had no formal experience in education.[99] The selection of these individuals was remarkable. Proschool advocates, although not avowedly integrationist, feared that the new school board members would sour racial relations in Norfolk rather than improve them.

Mayor Duckworth, as usual, was little concerned with the criticisms of the NCPS. He saw the reorganization of the school board as the first step in his own personal strategy for halting desegregation. Next on his agenda was promoting the construction of single-race, neighborhood schools that would be difficult, if not impossible, to integrate. He would solve the Oak-wood-Norview-Rosemont question of the previous fall, once and for all. In the winter and spring of 1959, he had encouraged the rapid construction of Rosemont Elementary and Junior High School, a new structure that would serve black students who lived in the immediate vicinity of two predominantly white schools, Norview Elementary and Norview Junior High.[100] When it became clear that Rosemont could not accommodate all the necessary pupils to prevent the additional enrollment of black students at the Norview schools, Duckworth and the city council approved funding for Coronado Elementary School. This site was one of a half-dozen new structures that the mayor nicknamed the "little red school houses." These neighborhood schools were considerably smaller than the traditional campuses built by the city. They were meant to keep construction time and costs to a minimum, while they replaced larger regional schools that were considered soft targets for desegregation suits.[101]

Taken together, the Rosemont and Coronado schools were especially revealing. They sat less than a mile apart, and were clearly intended to prevent African American students from applying to white schools in the Norview area. The Coronado school, moreover, represented the worst of all possible scenarios for students. Approved late in the year, it was hastily constructed; it lacked a playground, lunchroom, library, and other common facilities. The school was so bad, in fact, that in fall 1959, the NAACP launched a legal challenge to pupil assignments there.[102]

As the mayor and city council pursued policies intended to thwart integration, new procedures and organizations emerged to assist them. The first and most obvious of these was the state-supported tuition grant system put in place by the General Assembly at the recommendation of the Perrow Commission. The new tuition grants — now euphemistically called scholarships — avoided any reference to race or desegregation. To receive a grant, parents needed only to apply to their local school board, which was empowered to approve funding for students at private, nonsectarian schools or public schools in another district. The state set a $275 maximum for high school grants, and a $250 maximum for elementary schools, of which the state would provide $150 and $125, respectively.[103] In Norfolk, more than 1,200 tuition grants were issued for the 1959–60 school year, amounting to roughly $276,000.[104] As a percentage of the district's student body and total budget, these numbers were relatively minor. At the time, Norfolk enrolled 53,615 students and received more than $11.8 million in local, state, and federal funding.[105] Nevertheless, funds for the tuition grant program were drawn directly from the pool of public tax dollars available to the local school district, and thus the program had what many considered a direct and negative impact on the public schools.[106]

One of the principal recipients of local tuition grants was, of course, the TEF, which had emerged as the leading private organization locally to oppose school integration. As noted previously, the TEF was initially designed to educate white students who were affected by the school closures crisis. When the schools reopened in February 1959, however, attorney James G. Martin IV and the other directors of the TEF decided to make their hastily established Tidewater Academy a permanent private school for white children. That spring, Martin left a prosperous law practice and resigned as secretary-treasurer of the Norfolk-Portsmouth Bar Association to become full-time executive director of the TEF. In July, the organization purchased the twenty-six-room Bruce Mansion at Mowbray Arch and Fairfax Avenue in Norfolk's historic Ghent neighborhood. This $75,000 palatial site would become home to the new Tidewater Academy, which heralded a more ambitious program than the temporary one that had been in place at Bayview Baptist Church the previous year.[107]

In September, the TEF opened its new academy, and the school's director advertised "conservative, private, character-building, Christian education" for white boys and girls.[108] Only 175 students enrolled that September, however, and the school remained troubled by financial and public relations problems. Few wealthy white parents in Ghent were willing to send their children to such a hastily established, avowedly segregationist school. On the other hand, middle- and lower-income whites across town, who had made up the bulk of the enrollment at the original Tidewater Academy, found it difficult to send their children to Ghent every day. By moving the school, the TEF had unintentionally separated the academy from its principal source of students. This would prove to be a disastrous mistake in the long run.

As Mayor Duckworth and the city council attempted to hold the line on segregation in Norfolk, a new group of black students entered the struggle to dismantle it. In the summer of 1959, seventeen students completed the procedural requirements and academic tests necessary to transfer to all-white or predominantly white schools in the city.[109] Based on their test results, however, the Norfolk School Board rejected fifteen of the seventeen African American applicants. In its recommendation to the state Pupil Placement Board, Norfolk suggested that only two students receive transfers and that two of the original Norfolk 17 — Patricia Turner and Reginald Young — be promoted to desegregated high schools. The Pupil Placement Board refused even this small concession, however, rejecting each of the new transfer applicants and postponing action on the two promotions indefinitely. As a result, all seventeen of the applicants filed suit against the Norfolk School Board, and they were joined by eight additional pupils who objected to their assignment at the new Rosemont and Coronado schools.[110]

In court, the students' attorneys, Victor Ashe, J. Hugo Madison, and Joseph A. Jordan Jr., focused on three points. First, they argued that the Norfolk School Board had violated their clients' rights by requiring them to take academic tests from which "similarly situated" white applicants were exempted. Second, the lawyers argued that the state Pupil Placement Board clearly considered race as a factor when it denied their clients' applications for transfer — a clear violation of the law. Third, the attorneys argued that black students assigned to the Rosemont and Coronado schools had been denied their Fourteenth Amendment equal protection rights, since those schools were "of makeshift structure, with no playground area, [and] no cafeteria." The schools were "inadequate and not in conformity with the general outlay of schools similarly occupied and used by pupils in the City of Norfolk."[111]

The students' attorneys were only partially successful in their arguments against the Norfolk School Board. In a memorandum opinion dated September 8, 1959, Judge Hoffman found that the Norfolk School Board had "incorrectly, but not deliberately" exempted white applicants from transfer examinations, which it had required of black applicants. Hoffman was always willing to give his friends on the school board the benefit of the doubt. Yet to remedy this "unintended" violation, Hoffman ordered the temporary transfer and academic monitoring of three black students—Gloria Scott, Robert J. Neville (formerly in the "lacking scholastic achievement" group of August 1958), and Mary Rose Foxworth—whose transfer applications had been denied by the Norfolk School Board.[112] The temporary nature of these transfers and the insulting stigma of "academic monitoring" made this an incomplete victory at best.

Judge Hoffman was also hesitant to criticize the school board's placement of African American students at Rosemont and Coronado. Although he recognized the inadequacies at the two schools, he apparently convinced himself that they were simply minor problems in Norfolk's grander strategy "to meet the grave problem of racial mixing in public schools."[113] The deficiencies at Rosemont and Coronado were temporary and unintentional, and they would be rectified in due time, Hoffman believed. So, he ruled against the request of the eight black pupils who had protested assignment at the schools.

The students' attorneys had more success with their arguments against the state Pupil Placement Board, which Judge Hoffman ordered to appear in court alongside the Norfolk School Board. In his decision, Hoffman found that the state's three-man board—which included Andrew A. Farley, Hugh V. White, and Beverly H. Randolph Jr.—had pursued a policy "of routinely denying all applications of Negro children for placement in schools attended solely or predominantly by white children . . . and no reason other than the applicant's race is assigned or can be found for . . . denying the application." In fact, Hoffman wrote, Beverly Randolph "testified that he could not conceive of any circumstances which would cause him to vote in favor of granting the application of a Negro child for placement in a school attended solely or predominantly by white children."[114] The board's outright refusal to approve any of the transfer requests of black students seeking admittance to white schools, Hoffman found, denied those students their due process and equal protection rights under the Fourteenth Amendment. On this basis, he ordered that two members of the original Norfolk 17—Patricia Turner and Reginald Young—be promoted to the desegregated high schools of their choice, and that two students approved for transfer by the Norfolk School Board — Daphne Perminter and Anita Mayer — be admitted to the schools of their choice.[115] In addition, he ruled, "So long as the Pupil Placement Board pursues its present policies and practices . . . neither the School Board nor the Division Superintendent [in Norfolk] . . . is legally required to engage in any procedure involving the Pupil Placement Board."[116]

When schools opened again on September 8, 1959, twenty-two black students entered seven previously all-white or predominantly white schools in Norfolk. This event gave rise to multiple interpretations. On the one hand, it was seen as a victory for local black students, their parents, and the NAACP, which had secured some minor procedural concessions from the city of Norfolk and the state Pupil Placement Board. This interpretation gained added legitimacy the following February, when the three members of the Pupil Placement Board announced their resignations. By that time, it was clear that Judge Hoffman's decision in the *Beckett* case had provided federal reinforcement of the state's new local option plan, making it significantly more difficult for the Pupil Placement Board to pursue obstructionist policies.[117] Although African Americans in Norfolk found this development encouraging, many viewed the events of September 1959 from a different perspective. They saw continued enrollment at the substandard Rosemont and Coronado schools, continued (re)testing of all black students seeking transfers, and continued delay by the white power structure in Norfolk. Five years after *Brown v. Board of Education,* and one academic year after the school closures, little had changed. "That was that," indeed, with a different meaning here than the one that Dr. Forrest White had intended with those same dismissive words on February 2, 1959.

CHAPTER FOUR

PROTEST
AND THE ALL-AMERICAN CITY AND THE AGE OF TOKENISM, 1960–1968
PROGRESS

WHEN NORFOLK'S SCHOOLS opened on September 5, 1963, students at Booker T. Washington High School were furious at what they found. Conditions at the all-black school were appalling. Classes were overcrowded, with forty students stuffed into many of the rooms. The cafeteria was underfunded, with only one steam table to serve more than 2,400 students. And the physical plant was in dreadful condition. The restrooms were dilapidated; the laboratories were poorly equipped; and paint was peeling off the ceiling and the walls. "When we saw how bad conditions were," William Bagby, the vice president of the student body, recalled, "we . . . thought about [taking action]."[1]

Inspired by the historic March on Washington, which had occurred only a few weeks earlier, students at Booker T. Washington coordinated a simple but dramatic demonstration.[2] At nine o'clock in the morning on Thursday, September 19, more than 2,200 young people assembled on the athletic field behind the school. Led by members of the student council and the local National Association for the Advancement of Colored People (NAACP) youth chapter, the students marched two miles to Norfolk's school administration building, where they picketed and protested against conditions at their school. A delegation of five students — Kenneth Wilson, Eleanor Southall, Marvin Gay, Kenneth Norman, and Thomas Scott — presented a list of grievances to Edwin Lamberth, the new superintendent of Norfolk's schools. The students' petition complained that Booker T. Washington was outmoded and overcrowded. The heating system was ineffective, the gym and shower rooms were inadequate, and the deficiencies in the scientific laboratories were "too numerous to enumerate."[3]

As the student delegation presented its petition to Superintendent Lamberth, hundreds of young people picketed on the sidewalk outside the administration building. Many carried signs decrying the conditions at their school. "Booker T. is cold, dark, and drafty," one placard read. "No Seats for Students at Booker T.," another declared. The protesters went beyond the simple circumstances at their school, however. Some students carried signs questioning Norfolk's continued resistance to desegregation. "Why Can't I Go to School of My Choice," one sign read, while another declared simply, "Stop Token Integration."[4]

The Booker T. Washington demonstration represented a crucial part of Norfolk's school desegregation story. It was not only the city's largest student-led protest to that time, but it also served as a seminal community event that focused attention on the plight of black schools in a way that few other demonstrations could have. Here were the students themselves — the innocent, impressionable young people whom the city had taken the responsibility to educate — and they were presenting an indictment against their leaders. From the students' point of view, Norfolk's establishment had failed them. The students argued that no justice, no equality, and no true opportunity could exist in a city where the vast majority of African Americans were forced to attend a single high school, and that institution was as poorly maintained as Booker T. Washington.

The students' demonstration proved as controversial as it was significant, however, dividing Norfolk's community along racial lines. On the one hand, the city's white leadership condemned the protest. Editors at the *Virginian-Pilot* complained that the demonstration was "a poor way to promote a good cause," while Wayne Woodlief, a reporter at the rival *Ledger-Star,* suggested that conditions at Booker T. Washington were "largely the students' fault."[5] The superintendent and school board members shared these feelings. In an official report for the district, Superintendent Lamberth downplayed or dismissed most of the students' charges. He wrote that Booker T. Washington was as well funded and well maintained as the predominantly white high schools in the city and suggested that the students had little to complain about.[6]

Norfolk's African American leaders saw things from an entirely different perspective. Activists including P. B. Young Jr., Lyman Beecher Brooks, and Vivian Carter Mason supported the students and petitioned the school board to resolve the problems at Booker T. Washington. At the same time, Young, Brooks, and Mason joined with dozens of other local residents to form the Committee for the Best Booker T. Washington High School. This grassroots organization campaigned for the construction of a new school that would meet the needs of the city's growing African American community.

Although the Booker T. Washington demonstration played a pivotal role in Norfolk's school desegregation debate, all record of the protest has been stricken from the official history of Norfolk Public Schools. In the two standard works on the district, authors Henry Rorer and Gary Ruegsegger fail to mention the event at all.[7] In fact, a thorough review of the existing literature suggests that the Booker T. Washington demonstration is only the tip of the iceberg. Most scholars writing on Virginia during the 1960s have ignored school desegregation altogether.[8] With the exception of the inflammatory case in Prince Edward County, the 1960s have been treated as a brief and insignificant transition period between two critical events: the initial desegregation of schools in 1959 and the Supreme Court's landmark decision in *Green v. New Kent County* (1968). This chapter challenges such a dismissive account of the 1960s. Using long-overlooked African American sources alongside official and familiar documents from the white establishment, it presents a fresh approach to Norfolk's school desegregation story. Traditionally, Norfolk has been seen as a moderate southern city where school desegregation occurred smoothly and swiftly. In reality, however, desegregation occurred slowly and painfully in the 1960s, requiring constant legal and social agitation.

THE STORY OF Norfolk and the 1960s traditionally begins at the dawn of the decade, when *Look* magazine and the National Municipal League presented the city's leaders with the prestigious "All-American City" prize. Norfolk was one of only a handful of southern cities to receive the award in the early 1960s, and in many ways, it helped to confirm what most of the city's white professionals already believed: that Norfolk was a bastion of moderation where race relations were peaceful and progress was as sure as the wind and the tides. Mayor W. F. Duckworth summed up the spirit of many white leaders in the area when he declared that Norfolk was "the best city in Virginia . . . [especially] in regard to its colored population."[9]

Norfolk entered the 1960s as a booming metropolis. With the annexation of thirteen square miles from Princess Anne County in 1959, Norfolk became the largest city in Virginia and the eighth largest city in the South.

Since World War II, its population had doubled in size, jumping from 144,000 in 1940 to 305,000 in 1960. As the home of the U.S. Atlantic Fleet and the North Atlantic Treaty Organization's (NATO's) Supreme Allied Command, Norfolk attracted thousands of sailors and diplomats every year. The city also served as the business and financial center of Hampton Roads. Shipbuilding and trade were vital parts of the local economy, and the city's seaport handled millions of tons of cargo every month. Norfolk boasted two regional universities, three major newspapers, and one of the most successful urban redevelopment programs in the country.[10]

Norfolk's boosters also pointed to the city's school district as an example of local progressivism and goodwill. With sixty-one schools and 53,000 students, Norfolk's school system was the largest in the state.[11] In 1959, six of the city's junior and senior high schools had been among the first in Virginia to desegregate, and during the following years the media reported that "integration continued quietly" in Norfolk.[12] In a 1962 special report titled "The Other Face of Dixie," CBS News cited Norfolk as one of the South's most successful sites in the implementation of school desegregation. A local teacher named Margaret White, who was featured prominently in the CBS program, said, "I have never really been more proud of anything . . . than the way the people of Norfolk took to [desegregation]. . . . We've had no incidents [in the schools]. . . . The children, their parents, and the teachers have cooperated, and I really am proud." When asked what made the desegregation process so successful, White responded that the races in Norfolk had arrived at "a mutual respect that comes with understanding."[13]

Norfolk's African American activists viewed this official story of progress and understanding as an elitist fiction, designed by those in power to maintain their political authority and white supremacy. One of the earliest examples of this point of view played out on March 3, 1960, when Norfolk's service clubs sponsored a gala luncheon at the downtown arena to celebrate the presentation of the All-American City award. More than 1,000 people attended the event, which included keynote presentations by Vernon Myers, the publisher of *Look* magazine, and Cecil Morgan, a leading executive at Standard Oil of New Jersey. As these speakers rose to the podium to congratulate Mayor Duckworth and the leaders of Norfolk's business community, a different scene was unfolding outside the award luncheon. Joseph A. Jordan Jr., the African American attorney, local activist, and well-known World War II veteran, was leading a protest with Edward Dawley, Leonard

Holt, and other members of the Norfolk chapter of the Congress of Racial Equality (CORE). From his wheelchair, Jordan carried a sign that read, "Discrimination and Segregation are not All-American." He and other protesters were enraged by the city's decision to keep the award luncheon a whites-only affair. No African American leaders—no ministers, no lawyers, not even P. B. Young Sr., the venerable publisher of the *Journal and Guide*—had been invited to the luncheon. The bitter irony of the event was almost too much: as Mayor Duckworth and Norfolk's white elite accepted the All-American City award, forty prominent African American citizens marched outside demanding equal treatment and fair play—the most fundamental American values.[14]

The luncheon epitomized the official embrace of "malign neglect" with reference to local black concerns. Although African Americans accounted for 25 percent of Norfolk's population, Mayor Duckworth and the city fathers purposefully excluded members of the black community from policy-making roles in city government. African Americans were barred from the school board and the port authority, and Norfolk's police force had no blacks above the rank of patrolman. Visitors to the city's administrative offices encountered white staff members and city officials, and the mayor liked it that way. As a firm believer in white supremacy, Duckworth opposed the creation of a biracial committee or other furtive "concessions" to the city's black community. Instead, he insisted, "Equality should be earned not legislated."[15]

IF DUCKWORTH believed that African Americans should pursue equality more vigorously, then Norfolk's "Bulldozer Mayor" was about to get his way. On February 1, 1960, a new phase of the civil rights movement began in Greensboro, North Carolina, less than 250 miles from Norfolk. That afternoon, four African American college students from North Carolina A&T sat down at a whites-only lunch counter in a demonstration against Jim Crow segregation. In less than a week, hundreds of other students had joined the burgeoning nonviolent resistance movement against segregation. Young people participated in dozens of "sit-ins" throughout North Carolina, and soon the protest had spread across the South, forever transforming the civil rights movement.[16]

Young people in Norfolk found the developments in Greensboro exhilarating. At the local branch of Virginia State College, students quickly coordinated their own sit-in demonstrations for the downtown business district. Milton Gay Jr., a college freshman and president of Virginia's NAACP Youth Council, emerged as the leader of the local movement. Within days, he had organized a crack team of student-activists, including Eric Jones, Winston Williams, Oscar Waller, and Jan Filhiol. These college students received additional reinforcements from Milton's younger brother, James Gay, and his friends at nearby Booker T. Washington High School. Together, these young people gravitated to the sit-ins because they offered a nonviolent means "to confront the system [of segregation] head-on in a collective manner."[17]

Sit-in demonstrations and picketing lines provided the backdrop for Norfolk's school desegregation debates in the early 1960s. Although the city's flirtation with Massive Resistance had run its course, many whites in Norfolk continued to speak out against desegregation. For example, Wayne Dick and his wife wrote to Governor J. Lindsay Almond, pleading with him "to stop this [school desegregation] mess!" "We do not dislike the colored people," they wrote, "but it is a proven fact that the majority of them are not sanitary." The Dicks were deeply racist people who worried "about the restrooms . . . clubs, social events, sports teams, and activities that would have to be open to the colored as well as the white" if desegregation continued. And they were not alone. A week rarely went by without an editorial appearing on the pages of the city's newspapers bemoaning school desegregation or the NAACP. In fact, many whites in Norfolk agreed with longtime resident Victor Buhr, who complained that "when integration takes place, education is retarded."[18]

At the same time, however, dozens of white liberals in Norfolk rejected the bigotry and belligerency of the racists. Activists like Ellis James Sr. and Forrest White spoke out in defense of African Americans who participated in the city's sit-in demonstrations and voter registration drives. Indeed, Ellis James Jr. would go on to found Tidewater Fair Housing in 1965, and he has never stopped advocating social justice, even when it went out of style during the Reagan and Clinton eras. Closer to the center, many white moderates pressured for the desegregation of Seashore State Park, while energetic gadflies such as Henry F. Howell Jr. helped to change the dynamics of Norfolk politics during the 1960s. At first glance, Howell seemed an unlikely tribune for the common people. Like so many in Norfolk's elite, he had graduated from Maury High School and then the University of Virginia. He came home to the port city to cofound the law firm of Jett, Sikes, and Howell in 1950, specializing in admiralty and tort law. Howell and his wife, Betty, would go on to live in Larchmont on the city's wealthy west side. Yet even before the school closures crisis, there were signs of him betraying his own class, as he campaigned for anti–Organization Democrats such as Colonel Francis Pickens Miller and Delegate Robert Whitehead, before running himself as an unsuccessful candidate for the assembly in 1953. In 1959, on an anti–Massive Resistance platform, Howell finally won election, only to lose a bruising fight to be renominated two years later. As the happy warrior-tribune, Howell was elected to the state house in 1963, and the state senate in 1965 and 1967, and finally to statewide office as lieutenant governor in 1971 at the height of the busing battle. Yet his memorable tagline, "Keep the Big Boys Honest," pertained much more to labor, consumer, and ethics issues rather to those of civil rights.[19]

Indeed, when it came to school desegregation, the moderates, including Howell, remained remarkably quiet. The Norfolk Committee for Public Schools (NCPS), which had been one of the most important agents for change during the school closures crisis of 1958, shut its operations in the early 1960s. Jim Brewer left Norfolk for missionary work in South Africa; his successor at the Unitarian Church, James H. Curtis, was committed to civil rights causes, yet he was not as successful as Brewer had been in drawing attention to the need for further action. The Unitarian Church itself eventually left deteriorating East Ghent for Ghent proper in 1971. In fact, Forrest White, the former head of the NCPS, actually sent his son to private school with one of the state's $250 tuition grants. This action, and others like it, sent a clear message to the city's African American community: now that the school closures crisis was over and white children were back at school, further desegregation was a job for black leaders.[20]

It might be said that the members of the Norfolk School Board shared the view of the city's white establishment. While the board did not reject all desegregation out of hand, it intended to do as Richmond journalist Virginius Dabney suggested and "hold the mixing of the races in the schools to an absolute minimum."[21] In the early 1960s, this meant that the board needed only to maintain the status quo, since the vast majority of Norfolk's schools remained segregated. That at least was the view of the school board's chairman, Francis Crenshaw (1961–64), who insisted that the administration had no affirmative duty to "initiate desegregation." A native of Washington, D.C., and a graduate of the University of Virginia Law School, Crenshaw was an attorney who had ingratiated himself with the local business elite.

He declared that, under his leadership, the board would "not initiate any action to force any child to go to any school he doesn't want to go to."[22] And there was little doubt that he meant it. Although Crenshaw had opposed the school closings of 1958, and was a well-known critic of Mayor Duckworth, the school board chairman was no radical on racial issues. He opposed court-ordered desegregation and for many years had sent his own children to private schools.[23]

With Crenshaw at the head of the school board, Norfolk maintained its traditional pupil assignment process for as long as possible. Under the established procedures, no desegregation occurred unless black students sought transfers to white schools. In such cases, black parents were responsible for filing the necessary transfer application on behalf of their children by May 31 of the year in which the transfer was requested. Once the application was submitted to the superintendent's office, all children seeking transfers were required to complete a standardized achievement test, while school officials examined their academic and behavioral records. If these factors demonstrated that a student could perform at his or her requested school — and the student lived closer to that school than to his or her assigned location — then the school board often approved the student's application. If, however, any problems were found in the student's test scores, school record, or residential location, then the school board denied the child's request.[24]

During the early 1960s, the school board's system of procedural deterrence proved remarkably successful in limiting the number of African American students admitted to white schools. Between February 1959 and May 1963, the Norfolk School Board approved the transfer requests of only 134 out of 455 African American students — 29 percent.[25] Of this number, fifteen students received insulting "probationary" placements, which required that they submit to additional surveillance and academic monitoring. In the most infamous case involving a probationary student, the Norfolk School Board ordered that a young African American pupil named Gloria Scott be removed from Blair Junior High and returned to a black school because of poor academic performance. Members of the African American community were outraged by the board's action. At the *Journal and Guide,* P. B. Young Sr. placed the story on the front page of the paper and declared it a travesty of justice.[26] Meanwhile, Vivian Carter Mason sent a scathing letter to the members of the school board. She lambasted them for their "illogic[al]" and "insulting" order, and demanded to know where they were "sending the white failures from Blair — to Princess Anne County . . . or Moscow?" Then, in one of the most remarkable statements ever written on school desegregation in Norfolk, Mason provided an eloquent and moving refutation of the school board's official story of progress and goodwill. She wrote, "The general atmosphere of school paradise you describe so blandly . . . does not in any way cover the situation."

> All the Negro children who are attending integrated schools have suffered from innate and senseless cruelties. There are students in all the schools who have done their best to drive the Negro students out — by deliberate and overt acts of meanness, ill breeding, insulting behavior and small terrors. They met their match however for the Negro students have been spiritually and psychologically immunized against such manifestations. Many fine [white] students, teachers and principals had no part in this underground movement. They are a bulwark of decency and courage but even they have been powerless against the convulsions of the lunatic fringe. However Negroes in this day and time are not intimidated by morons whatever their guise.[27]

The frustration, pain, and sheer emotional power of Mason's words still resonate with readers to this day. Her willingness to speak out and confront the white establishment on matters of significance made her one of the most important activists of her day. As she later said, "You must try to be a rebel. Anyone who sees the inequities of our times and the slowness of change must not think [rebellion] a terrible thing, but see it as his duty."[28]

Civil rights attorneys in Norfolk found developments at the school board as troubling as Vivian Carter Mason did. Many black lawyers worried that the city's insulting probationary procedures and high rates of rejection for transfer students might have a chilling effect, discouraging other African American students from pursuing their constitutional right to equal education. The NAACP did not intend to allow this process to occur, however. Roy Wilkins, the organization's executive secretary, emphatically rejected the "token integration plan" that Norfolk and other cities in Virginia had enacted. In a speech before the state NAACP convention, Wilkins declared that African Americans in Virginia would not be satisfied "with even the best tokenism."[29]

Norfolk's African American attorneys initiated the local effort against token integration in the fall of 1960, when the city's school board denied frican American transfers to white schools in Norfolk, 1959-1963

ear	Students applying for transfer	Students initially approved by school board	Additional students suggested by court for transfer	Students who received probationary transfer	Students finally approved for transfer	Percentage of applicants finally approved
ebruary 1959	151	0	17	0	17	11
eptember 1959	17	2	3	3	5	29
960–1961	31	1	5	0	6	19
961–1962	113	31	2	0	33	29
962–1963	143	73	0	12	73	51
otal by May 1963	455	107	27	15	134	29

the transfer requests of thirty out of thirty-one black applicants. In court, NAACP lawyers Victor Ashe and J. Hugo Madison challenged Norfolk's pupil placement procedures. Specifically, Ashe and Madison argued that the school board required African American students to take academic tests for admission to white public schools, while similarly situated white students were exempted from the tests. In a heated courtroom discussion, U.S. District Judge Walter E. Hoffman rebuked the school board for its failure to apply the tests equally to both races, but he refused to order any other changes to the district's policy. Rather, he requested that the school board admit five additional African American students whose rights had been violated. The board speedily met this request, and six of the thirty-one transfer applicants moved to new schools in September 1960.[30]

Hoffman's stopgap measure failed to satisfy Ashe and Madison, however. They viewed the judge's action as a temporary expedient that failed to confront Norfolk's entrenched program of discriminatory behavior. In the fall of 1961, when the school board denied the transfer requests of 81 out of 113 African American students, Ashe and Madison returned to Judge Hoffman's courtroom. This time the lawyers argued that Norfolk's entire pupil placement program was unconstitutional. The school board illegally characterized all African American transfer requests as "unusual circumstances," requiring that black children meet academic standards that were not required of white children. Ashe and Madison requested that the court overturn the school board's testing procedure and order that pupil assignment be initiated on a strict geographic basis. Hoffman refused to do so, however. He declared that the school board had constructed a "very fine and progressive" integration program, and that scholastic achievement tests would be discontinued as a prerequisite for transferring students "within a reasonable length of time."[31]

Although Hoffman failed to act on Ashe and Madison's request in 1961 — admitting only two of the transfer students that the school board had denied — the lawyers continued to pressure the city the following year. In the fall of 1962, the Norfolk School Board approved thirty-six of sixty-three African American transfer requests and granted eight additional probationary transfers. Although the high percentage of successful applicants seemed to signal a new trend in Norfolk's pupil placement procedures, a legal controversy developed when seventy-five additional African American students requested transfers to white schools in August — long after the May 31 deadline. Sixty-three of the new applicants were elementary school children living in the East Ghent area. According to the school board's traditional placement program, these children were enrolled at Young Park Elementary, an all-black school that was approximately a mile from the students' homes. In walking to school, however, many of these children — some as young as six — had to cross several hazardous roadways, including Llewellyn Avenue, Boush and Granby Streets, and Monticello Avenue. Attorney J. Hugo Madison requested that the school board grant these students a transfer to attend Robert E. Lee Elementary, a white school that was closer to their homes. The school board turned down fifty-one of these applicants, however, citing the fact that they were submitted after the posted deadline. In all, the board approved only twenty-four of the seventy-five late submissions, and five additional new arrivals in Norfolk, which brought the total number of transfer students to seventy-three for the 1962–63 school year.[32]

Despite the controversy over Norfolk's pupil placement procedures, the vast majority of the city's African American parents never applied for a school transfer on behalf of their children. Indeed, most African Americans took pride in their neighborhood schools, which they considered vital institutions of learning and community. Patricia Turner, a student, remembered, "Teachers [at black schools] were always very nurturing. . . . They were highly qualified ... [and] they wanted us to become someone." Delores Johnson Brown echoed this sentiment: "You knew you were loved [at the black school]. . . . You knew someone cared about you" and had "your best interest at heart."[33]

Although many African Americans cherished the black schools they had grown up with, there was an undercurrent of resentment and frustration within Norfolk's black community. Almost a decade after *Brown v. Board of Education,* many African Americans believed that the city's white leadership had done too little to improve conditions at black schools. In fact, ample evidence reveals that — in spite of increased funding — many black schools remained structurally deficient and poorly equipped. Douglas Park Elementary School serves as one example. Situated in the center of a poor black neighborhood, Douglas Park was the home to many African American students, including future city councilman Paul Riddick. Despite its obvious role in the African American community, however, the school sat across the street from a major industrial site, the Globe Iron Construction Company. In a formal petition to the school board, parents from Douglas Park complained that "pounding noises" emanating from the construction company continued "almost all day," and that the company's trucks "travel[ed] on school grounds when entering or leaving the plant." In addition, the parents cited numerous problems at the school that had resulted from overcrowding. Six classes were forced into four rooms. The nurse and speech teacher conducted all of their therapeutic activities in the hallway. Physical education classes were carried out in traditional classrooms because there was no gym. Furthermore, teachers, parents, and the principal had to use the same restroom facilities as the children.[34]

Superintendent Lamberth responded to the concerns of the Douglas Park parents with a polite, but dismissive, memorandum, which was distributed to the school board on March 8, 1962. "The deficiencies of this school have already been recognized by the administration," Lamberth wrote, "and we plan to abandon this building as soon as [Roberts Park] elementary school is constructed." In the meantime, however, the superintendent suggested that teachers at Douglas Park should "continue to work . . . with the children just as they have done in previous years."[35] Lamberth's suggestion meant that, regardless of the recognized "deficiencies" at the school, the Norfolk School Board took no action to improve conditions for the students. Indeed, the new facility that the superintendent promised — Roberts Park Elementary —

was not completed until September 1964, thirty-two months after the Douglas Park petition was submitted.[36]

Unfortunately, the circumstances at Douglas Park were disturbingly common. As enrollments in Norfolk's schools rose during the baby boom generation of the early 1960s, overcrowding became a universal problem. Classes were filled to capacity at many of the city's schools, and inventive scheduling practices were introduced at several sites to reduce the problems associated with large class sizes. Nevertheless, the record makes it clear that African Americans suffered the worst effects of overcrowding. Average class sizes at some black elementary schools reached into the thirties. More than 2,000 African American students attended part-time or split-shift classes. And resources at black schools were so limited that students often had to share textbooks and other essential supplies with their classmates.[37]

By 1962, many of Norfolk's African American parents had tired of waiting for new buildings and resources to become available. That spring, representatives from the twenty-four black schools in Norfolk formed the Parent Teacher Association Council (PTAC), a grassroots organization that sought to improve conditions at local schools. In May, the PTAC presented a petition to the school board, stating that the district faced "a lack of 'togetherness' in our focus on . . . child development." Overcrowding at black schools, part-time classes, inadequate libraries, and poor district leadership were among the problems cited by the petition. PTAC's spokespeople complained that, "generally, in discussing such problems with the Superintendent . . . he has approached them in a lackadaisical manner." Rather than facing the "more readily soluble problems" of the city's black schools, Lamberth was "avoiding [the] realities" of the district.[38]

IN SPITE OF the continuing racial tension in Norfolk's schools, the city entered a new political era in September 1962, when Roy B. Martin Jr. was selected to fill the seat of retiring mayor W. F. Duckworth. A graduate of Maury High School and the University of Virginia, Martin was a forty-one-year-old business executive who had served on the city council for nine years. In his day, the new mayor was known as a pro-business centrist and a racial moderate. For instance, in 1959, as a city councilman, Martin had cast the lone vote in opposition to the most controversial measure in the school closures crisis, the last-minute, vengeful bid to close Norfolk's black schools for the duration of Massive Resistance. As with Judge Hoffman's brief stay in social purgatory, Martin's vote would be worn by its progenitor as his badge of moral courage, inoculating him from any future charges of undue racial prejudice.[39]

In truth, however, race relations during Mayor Martin's tenure proved to be as complex and contradictory as ever. On the one hand, the city's citizens witnessed numerous positive developments that seemed to fore-shadow an era of growing interracial harmony. For instance, many members of the Norfolk 17 graduated from integrated high schools and enrolled in college.[40] Schools in surrounding communities, such as Portsmouth and Princess Anne County, began the long process toward integration. And, at the state level, public pressure and legal proceedings forced Virginia's government to eliminate several types of discriminatory behavior. The state's anti-NAACP laws were struck down; the "Blank Sheet" voter registration form was eliminated; and facilities at public venues, such as Seashore State Park, were moving swiftly toward integration.[41]

For every step forward, however, there seemed to be a corresponding step backward. For instance, in September 1961, representatives from the Virginia Committee on Offenses against the Administration of Justice attempted to raid the law offices of Joseph Jordan, Edward Dawley, and Leonard Holt in an attempt to intimidate three of Norfolk's most militant civil rights attorneys.[42] The law partners refused to open their offices to the committee's representatives, however, and soon the attorneys were forced to bring a lawsuit against the committee. Ultimately, it took more than two years to resolve the case, and, even then, the decision brought little satisfaction. Judge Hoffman, usually the decisive football referee, provided little more than Jesuitical cover for official skullduggery here. Thanks to both legislative intransigence and judicial inertia, Jordan, Dawley, and Holt were forced to suspend their partnership in Norfolk in September 1962, and Dawley and Holt eventually left the port city for California. Only Jordan remained, licking his wounds before a successful bid for city council six years later.[43]

As racial tensions in Norfolk continued to fester in 1963, Mayor Martin and the city's ruling oligarchy introduced a biracial advisory board, which had long been an aim of conservative members of the black bourgeoisie. Called the Citizens Advisory Committee (CAC), the twenty-five-member board had originally been established to meet federal housing and re-development guidelines. With racial conflict on the rise, however, Martin requested that the CAC study Norfolk's racial problems so that it could

"make recommendations to the City Council."[44] Although Robert Robertson, the local president of the NAACP, and other civil rights leaders saw
the CAC as nothing more than a bureaucratic stumbling block, Norfolk's
white establishment sought to portray the committee as a legitimate venue
for discussion. Indeed, the CAC did make serious gains in July 1963, when
thirty-two of the forty-five hotel operators in Norfolk agreed to accept all
clients without regard to race.[45]

Despite the CAC's progress on public accommodations, however, school
desegregation remained an important topic of controversy in Norfolk. In
April 1963, NAACP lawyers Victor Ashe and J. Hugo Madison filed a formal
complaint with the school board, requesting an immediate modification in
pupil placement procedures. The attorneys asked the members of the board
to adopt a new pupil assignment plan that would "afford all children . . . the
opportunity to receive an education on a nonracial, nonsegregated basis."[46]
Such a plan clearly did not exist in Norfolk in the spring of 1963. Ashe and
Madison alleged that Norfolk had "no uniform nonracial method of . . .
assigning pupils to schools." Rather, the district continued to use race as
the determining factor in assigning students, teachers, and other personnel to local schools, and the administration continued to require African
American transfer applicants to meet academic standards not required of
white students.[47]

The Norfolk School Board responded to the Ashe-Madison petition on
June 13, 1963. In a letter signed by Chairman Crenshaw, Norfolk's school
officials "den[ied] that the [district's] . . . assignment practices [we]re unconstitutional." On the contrary, the board insisted that Norfolk had one of the
most fair-minded desegregation programs in the state. Although students
were initially assigned to schools based on race and geographical region,
the city had liberalized the pupil placement process over the previous four
years. Specifically, the school board had relaxed its academic standards for
transferring students; it had eliminated the onerous personal interview process; and it had approved a "substantial percentage" of African American
students who had applied for admission to white schools. The members of
the school board considered these to be significant achievements, which
demonstrated that the "Administration [was] proceeding effectively to remove racial barriers in public education."[48]

Ashe and Madison disagreed with the school board's assessment. In July
1963, the attorneys filed a motion on behalf of six school-age children who

sought to intervene in the *Beckett* case. In court, the lawyers asked Judge Hoffman to "do away with the pupil assignment machinery" that had been in operation in Norfolk since 1959. In its place, Ashe and Madison requested that the court order the school board to assign all children to the schools nearest to their homes. In addition, the lawyers asked that Hoffman order the district to begin immediate desegregation of the faculty, so that principals, teachers, and other professional personnel could begin the long process toward integration.[49]

Facing a sweeping desegregation suit in federal court, Norfolk's city government took swift action to improve its legal standing before Judge Hoffman. The city's first major step came in July 1963, when the terms of appointment for four members of the school board expired. At that time, local African American activists renewed their efforts to desegregate the school board. In public presentations before the CAC, Evelyn Butts, the president of the Rosemont-Oakwood Civic League, urged the city to do as so many of its neighbors had done and name an African American member to the school board. In Richmond, she pointed out, Booker T. Bradshaw, a prominent figure in the local black community, had been elected to serve as vice chairman of the school board. Indeed, "most of the larger cities in Virginia," including Portsmouth, Newport News, and Hampton, had "appoint[ed] Negroes to their important commissions and boards," the *Journal and Guide* reported. Now, the African American community insisted, it was Norfolk's turn. The members of the CAC agreed, and they recommended that the city council select a black member for the school board.[50]

Two weeks later, on July 30, Mayor Martin led a unanimous city council in appointing Hilary H. Jones Jr., a forty-year-old attorney, as the first African American member of the school board. Born in Norfolk, Jones attended law school at Boston University before returning home to begin his practice. He was a member of the NAACP, the Virginia Bar Association, and the CAC's subcommittee on education. His son Jerrauld had been in the second wave of transfers to formerly all-white schools, having been trained at Jim Brewer's Unitarian Church the previous summer. Even though, as a parent, Jones had decided to buck the segregated system, Mayor Martin and the members of the city council considered him a solid, but safe, man for the job. After all, he had backed the CAC over the objections of the local NAACP. "His appointment is based on the belief that he will represent all the people of Norfolk," Martin said, "and that each of his decisions will be

In July 1963, as Norfolk faced a major desegregation suit in federal court, Mayor Roy B. Martin Jr. and the city council selected Hilary H. Jones Jr. to serve as the city's first African American school board member. Pictured here (back row, l–r): Joseph C. Nelson, Vincent Thomas, Hilary Jones; (front row, l–r): George S. Hughes, Joseph Leslie, Mrs. C. E. Griffin. (Courtesy of the *New Journal and Guide*)

predicated on his judgment of what is best for the Norfolk school system as a whole." Certainly, Norfolk's establishment tried to secure Jones's safety and social position by shepherding young Jerrauld (a future assemblyman and judge) to a series of appointments as a state senatorial page. Jerrauld Jones, in turn, won a Stouffer Foundation scholarship in 1969 to attend Virginia Episcopal School in Lynchburg. Despite these coveted entrees for his talented son into the world of the modern-day cavaliers, Hilary Jones turned out to be a thoughtful and challenging member of the board who often voted against his fellow members on matters pertaining to race and desegregation.[51]

Although the appointment of Hilary Jones was certainly a step in the right direction, it did little, if anything, to address the allegations of discrimination lodged by the NAACP. In fact, as Ashe and Madison applied legal pressure on the Norfolk School Board, local students and their families took to the streets. On September 19, 1963, more than 2,200 young people marched out of Booker T. Washington High School in protest of conditions at the school. At the same time, dozens of local parents and activists picketed the school administration building downtown. Evelyn Butts and Mary Humphrey were among the organizers of the protest. They carried signs denouncing "discrimination" and "token integration," in hopes that the school board might reverse its decision to reject almost 100 African American requests for school transfers.[52]

Facing intense public and legal pressure, the Norfolk city attorney, Leonard Davis, emerged as the point man in the city's attempt to answer the charges filed by the NAACP. Although Davis is largely forgotten today, he worked as city attorney in Norfolk for twenty years. A native of Portsmouth, Virginia, Davis served in World War II and received his law degree from Washington and Lee University, the same alma mater as Walter Hoffman and Lewis F. Powell Jr. As a young man on the make, Davis had close ties to the Organization Democrats. None other than Dr. C. J. Andrews—the father of Dr. Mason Andrews—recommended Davis to the Byrd machine's Billy Prieur for the position of police justice during the war; George Abbott, the city councilman who would go on to vote for shutting down all schools above the sixth grade in 1959, did so as well, saying that he was a close friend. In 1955, Davis was selected for the city attorney's position, and over the next two decades he represented Norfolk in each of its school desegregation cases. Lucy Rockwood, Davis's daughter, was a student in Norfolk's public schools throughout the 1960s. She remembers that her father was a "conscientious and fair-minded person" who found the school desegregation process "very difficult emotionally."[53]

In the summer of 1963, Davis put forward a new proposal intended to end the school desegregation debate in Norfolk. His plan promised a substantial change in the school board's existing enrollment procedures. It eliminated all academic testing and other procedures formerly used to determine placement. In their stead, the new plan called for a slate of geographical attendance zones in Norfolk, which would determine pupil assignments. Students residing in zones served by a single school would attend that school no matter what their race. Meanwhile, students residing in zones served by two or more schools would have the opportunity to choose the location they wanted to attend. This proposal, which went into effect in the winter of 1963, established

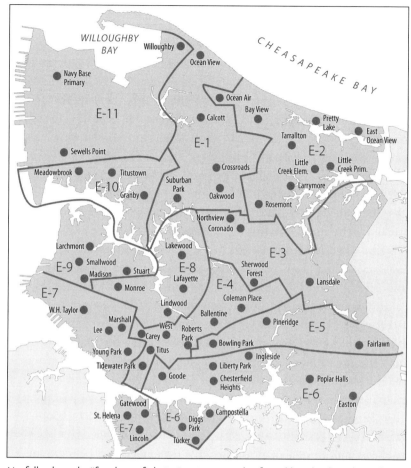

Norfolk adopted a "freedom-of-choice" assignment plan for public schools in the mid-1960s. This map depicts the zones at the elementary level, where official assignments placed the burden of desegregation on black students and their families. {Courtesy of the *Virginian-Pilot*}

"freedom of choice" for the first time in Norfolk. The new assignment plan made it possible for hundreds of African American students to transfer to white schools that previously had been off-limits. Indeed, in the 1963–64 academic year, the Norfolk School Board approved the transfer requests of 517 African American students. This meant that more young people attended desegregated schools in Norfolk than in Mississippi, South Carolina, Alabama, Georgia, and Arkansas — combined![54]

In October 1963, Samuel Edmonds posed for this photograph at a bus stop in front of Granby High School. Edmonds was forced to take city buses across town to attend the all-black Booker T. Washington High School. For Edmonds, this was particularly absurd, since he lived across the street from Granby High. (Courtesy of the *New Journal and Guide*)

Despite this startling statistic, Norfolk continued to operate a dual system of education in which race remained the determining factor in pupil assignments. In fact, from the African American perspective, the statistics looked quite different.[55] In the ten years since *Brown v. Board of Education,* only 651 of Norfolk's 19,800 African American students had been admitted to desegregated schools. And few blacks believed that freedom of choice promised anything better. "You insult the intelligence of Norfolk's parents and students," Joseph A. Jordan wrote to Superintendent Lamberth in March 1964, "when you suggest that your 'Choice of Schools' scheme will do anything more than create needless confusion, and maintain racial discrimination." Jordan and his NAACP associates viewed the new plan as another "sleight of hand" gimmick meant to delay desegregation through an illusionary procedure of choice. "It is time to grow up," he told the superintendent. "Put away your administrative knee pants, hula hoops and bob jacks. . . . Send Norfolk's students to the schools nearest their homes and let's get on with the real problems of Quality education."[56]

In spite of the nuances and complications presented by the freedom-of-choice assignment plan, Judge Hoffman found it more than satisfactory. In his memorandum decision issued on July 30, 1964, the judge voiced his support for the members of the Norfolk School Board. "They have moved cautiously but steadily forward," he said, "to the point where they now present . . . a plan of operation and procedure which goes far — and this Court believes the entire way — in removing all elements of racial discrimination in the school system." Hoffman believed that the freedom-of-choice assignment plan met *all* of the constitutional standards established by the U.S. Supreme Court in *Brown v. Board of Education*. In addition, he hoped that the plan might bring an end to litigation as the district made a smooth transition to desegregation. "Despite a natural reluctance to accept racial mixture in the public schools," the judge wrote, betraying his own deep-seated beliefs, "the people of Norfolk and its governing body have redoubled efforts to establish and maintain a more effective" school system in the city.[57]

As developments occurred, Norfolk turned out to be roughly six months ahead of national trends. In May 1964, the U.S. Supreme Court ruled that school desegregation in the South was proceeding far too slowly. In his decision in the famous *Prince Edward County* case, Justice Hugo Black wrote that the "time for mere 'deliberate speed' has run out." He declared that there had been "entirely too much deliberation . . . and not enough speed in enforcing the constitutional rights" of children seeking a fair and equitable education.[58]

In the summer of 1964, the other branches of the federal government joined with the Supreme Court in demanding swifter movement in favor of civil rights. That July, Congress passed and President Lyndon Johnson signed the groundbreaking Civil Rights Act of 1964, which outlawed segregation in U.S. schools and public places. Specifically, Title II of the act prohibited discrimination in public accommodations, including restaurants, hotels, theaters, and sporting venues. In addition, Title IV of the act authorized the attorney general to file suits "for the orderly achievement of desegregation in public education." The NAACP viewed these changes with a sense of welcomed relief. For more than a decade, the organization had been fighting segregation on its own. Now, the Justice Department and federal government could intervene. As J. Harvie Wilkinson III wrote, "The [Justice] Department's entry into school desegregation meant much more than legal manpower. Its presence meant integration was not only something blacks were seeking but something the United States government stood behind."[59]

The Justice Department was not the only federal agency drawn into school desegregation by the 1964 act. The Department of Health, Education, and Welfare (HEW) created desegregation guidelines in response to the act. The first guidelines, issued in April 1965, were relatively mild, accepting both geographic zoning and freedom of choice. By 1966, however, the guidelines were "considerably tougher." In fact, new standards empowered the federal government to withhold or discontinue funding to local school districts that failed to meet desegregation guidelines.[60]

With the new Civil Rights Act in place and a local freedom-of-choice plan governing pupil assignments, Norfolk's citizens moved boldly into the 1964–65 academic year. An unprecedented 1,251 African American students were approved for transfers to desegregated schools, and this dramatic upswing signaled a new era in the city's school desegregation story. In a June 9 article that appeared in the *Virginian-Pilot,* former governor J. Lindsay Almond Jr. declared that Massive Resistance and the school closings in Virginia had been a mistake. And later that October, the all-white Virginia Education Association for teachers and administrators voted to allow African American membership for the first time in the organization's history.[61]

In spite of the clear progress being made in Norfolk, the city's citizens remained divided on one aspect of the freedom-of-choice program: tuition grants. Originally established by the Almond administration in 1959, the grant program provided $250 in public funds for each student who desired to attend a private, nonsectarian school or a public school outside his or her assigned district. Although the program made no mention of race or desegregation, it was clearly intended to provide an outlet for those students who sought to avoid racial mixing in the public schools. Between May 1959 and May 1964, 8,840 students in Norfolk received tuition grants, totaling more than $2 million in state and local funds.[62]

Supporters of the tuition grant program argued that it was a legitimate, democratic extension of the freedom-of-choice plan, which was open to all members of society without regard to race or class. For instance, in February 1961 Idella Owens, a white working-class mother of two, wrote to Governor Almond to express her support for the program: "It has enabled my children to obtain first rate teaching and subject matter that they would not have been exposed to otherwise."[63] Three months later, Marjorie Claud struck a similar note with Governor Almond. Claud was an opponent of integration and had enrolled her daughter in a private academy "solely because of the integration of Maury High School." She was thrilled that the city and state had supported her daughter's previous request to attend the Country Day School for Girls in Virginia Beach and requested that Governor Almond take action to ensure that additional funds would continue to be available.[64]

With thousands of students taking public funds to enroll in private academies, however, the financial impact of the tuition grant program became a topic of heated debate. Although Mayor Duckworth had been an outspoken proponent of the program,[65] local parent-teacher organizations at Lakewood, Larrymore, and W. H. Taylor petitioned Governor Almond in hopes that he would review the grant process. The parents complained that the tuition program took desperately needed taxpayer money from the public schools and wasted it on well-funded private academies that enrolled the children of the wealthy. Editors at the *Virginian-Pilot* and *Ledger-Dispatch* agreed.[66] In a series of pointed editorials, the *Pilot* declared that the grants had become a "joke."[67] "The purpose [of the grants] was to assure that children could move out of desegregated public schools if they wanted to and go to other schools." Nevertheless, the *Pilot* pointed out, "Many scores of pupils are attending private schools in Norfolk and using state and city funds for that purpose when their parents are well able to pay the tuition and are not sending their children to private schools to avoid integrated schools. The state and the city offer the money. They take it. And taxpayers pay for it."[68]

Although moderate whites spoke out against the tuition grant program during the early 1960s, they were principally concerned with the "misuse" of the system. For instance, the Larrymore Elementary School Parent-Teacher Association (PTA) complained to Governor Almond that the "intent of the Tuition-Grant Act was to assist those facing serious problems of integration," but that the grants were "being used almost entirely by parents with no integration problems." The Larrymore parents opposed this "abuse" of the program — a sentiment that was echoed by the other parent-teacher organizations in Norfolk, including the Lakewood and Taylor PTAs.[69]

In contrast to moderate white opinion, the NAACP had consistently opposed all tuition grants in Virginia. In the summer of 1964, S. W. Tucker, the senior legal counsel of the Virginia NAACP, and Henry Marsh III, an African American attorney from Richmond, challenged the tuition grant program in a series of lawsuits. Initially, Tucker and Marsh targeted Prince

Edward and Surry Counties, where the white citizenry had replaced the public schools with segregated private academies funded by tuition grants. In a series of precedent-setting decisions, the U.S. District Court in Richmond and the Fourth Circuit Court of Appeals ruled that Virginia's tuition grant program as applied in Prince Edward and Surry Counties was unconstitutional. Specifically, the Fourth Circuit Court said that the two counties had created a system of schooling "tailor-made to continue [the] . . . policy of segregation." The counties' actions represented "a transparent evasion of the Fourteenth Amendment," and upon remand to the U.S. District Court, the local school boards were enjoined from paying tuition grants to support segregated private schools.[70]

On August 17, 1964, as the Prince Edward and Surry county cases wound their way through the courts, Tucker and Marsh filed another, more ambitious suit — *Griffin v. State Board of Education* (1965). In papers submitted to the U.S. District Court in Richmond, the NAACP attorneys asked that a three-judge panel be convened to consider the constitutionality of the tuition grant program as it was employed statewide. The lawyers alleged that the State Board of Education and the governing bodies of nine Virginia localities, including Norfolk, were engaged in state-sponsored acts of discrimination that violated the Fourteenth Amendment. To halt the abuse, Tucker and Marsh requested that an immediate injunction be issued to prevent the state and the local school boards from paying tuition grants for the 1964 school year.[71]

Although a three-judge panel was convened in October, Judges Albert Bryan, Walter Hoffman, and John Butzner Jr. refused to issue an injunction banning tuition grants in Virginia. Instead, the court scheduled oral arguments on the matter for December 14. Addressing the court at that time, Tucker argued that the purpose of the tuition grants law and related statutes was to ensure "that no child be required to attend an integrated school." This objective was clearly in violation of the Supreme Court's ruling in *Brown v. Board of Education,* Tucker declared, since many private schools that accepted tuition grants refused to admit African Americans. The state cannot "feign ignorance" of these admission policies, Tucker declared. "When the state ties its own hands and says it is not responsible, we must untie the state's mantles."[72]

On March 9, 1965, the three-judge panel ruled that tuition grants were "not unconstitutional on their face," and that they "may lawfully be used in a private, segregated, nonsectarian school if they do not constitute the preponderant financial support of the schools." However, if the grants were "paid by the governmental authorities knowing the funds will be used to provide the whole or the greater part of the cost of operation of a segregated school . . . then such disbursement of public moneys is impermissible."[73] This problematic ruling proved hard to enforce. Although it certainly made it more difficult for schools like Norfolk's Tidewater Academy to receive funding, many of them were able to circumvent the decision by making minor changes in operating procedures.

Four years later, however, this decision was overturned by the same three-judge panel. In *Griffin v. State Board of Education* (1969), the court held that recent decisions by the U.S. Supreme Court provided a more stringent tuition grant standard, which outlawed any state-sponsored assistance to racially segregated schools. Under the new standard, neither the motive nor the purpose of the grants saved them as a matter of law if they supported segregation. The court therefore declared the Virginia statutes invalid, but permitted the grants to continue for the remainder of the 1968–69 school year.[74]

AS THE TUITION DEBATE continued to simmer in the spring of 1965, civil rights activists in Norfolk returned their attention to desegregation. At the local branch of Virginia State College, members of the Student Committee Against Discrimination joined with representatives from the NAACP to force the integration of Norfolk's Young Men's Christian Association (YMCA).[75] At the same time, on the political front, Evelyn Butts and Joseph Jordan Jr. fought their way to the U.S. Supreme Court, where they proved victorious in a landmark case outlawing the use of poll taxes in Virginia's state and local elections.[76]

With pressure against discrimination mounting on all sides, local NAACP attorneys decided to push the envelope one step further. In the fall of 1965, they returned to court to challenge Norfolk's freedom-of-choice assignment plan. Originally established in 1963, the city's plan was approved by Judge Hoffman and the U.S. District Court in July 1964. The NAACP appealed Hoffman's ruling, however, arguing that it allowed faculty and student segregation to continue. The Fourth Circuit Court agreed with the NAACP, and in July 1965 the appellate court sent the case back to the district level, directing Hoffman to reconsider the city's school desegregation plan.[77] Then, four months later, the U.S. Supreme Court gave Hoffman a further rebuff when it vacated and remanded his decisions on faculty desegregation in *Bradley v. School Board of City of Richmond* and *Gilliam v. School Board of Hopewell.*[78] The quintessential referee had been too lax in his position on faculty desegregation, and now Hoffman would need all his judicial insights to find a solution that would please the High Court in Washington, D.C.

In light of the recent appellate decisions, Judge Hoffman moved swiftly to address the Norfolk case. On September 30, he ordered the local school board to submit its 1966–67 desegregation plan to the district court within two months. Then, in November, after the Supreme Court's *Bradley* decision, Hoffman ordered the Norfolk School Board and the NAACP to prepare evidence on the impact of faculty desegregation. He was determined to be right this time.

The Norfolk School Board filed its modified desegregation plan with the U.S. District Court on December 1, 1965. The new proposal made no provisions for faculty desegregation, however, and it provided for only minor alterations to the city's existing pupil assignment plan. Students residing in attendance zones served by a single school would still attend that school no matter what their race, while students residing in zones served by two or more schools could select the site they wanted to attend. Although the school board's proposal seemed to be little more than a continuation of the status quo, Norfolk's leaders highlighted one important innovation included in the plan. Beginning in the fall of 1966, they insisted, all African American children in Norfolk could attend a school with white students if they chose to do so.[79]

Despite the rosy picture presented by the school district, the NAACP filed exceptions to Norfolk's desegregation plan on January 3, 1966. Led by attorney Henry Marsh, the NAACP argued that Norfolk's plan was unconstitutional because it failed to provide any program for faculty desegregation. In addition, Marsh and his team cited specific problems with the city's pupil assignment plan. At the high school level, Maury, Granby, and Norview —the three predominantly white schools—had discrete geographic attendance zones, while Booker T. Washington, the all-black school, drew students from the entire city. This attendance scheme made it unlikely that white students would ever transfer to Booker T. Washington, which was attended by all but 680 of the city's 2,994 black high school students. At the intermediate level, six of the city's eleven junior high schools remained entirely segregated, while four additional junior high schools had 222 African

Americans enrolled in classes with 5,898 white students. And, finally, at the elementary level, at least thirty-one of the city's fifty-three primary schools remained entirely segregated. In sixteen of the remaining twenty-two schools, racial minorities represented less than 5 percent of the total enrollment.[80]

The statistical analysis presented by the NAACP described a school district that remained deeply segregated, despite the implementation of an enrollment program based on choice. "The problem with freedom of choice," J. Harvie Wilkinson wrote in 1979, "was the variance between theory and practice. In theory, each child's school choice was free; in practice, it was often anything but."[81] On the one hand, white children almost never chose to enroll in black schools. The reasons for this hesitation were deeply ingrained in the hearts and culture of southern whites. Racism, residential segregation, educational advantage, and simple convenience converged to keep most white children at their traditional schools. On the other hand, most African American students refused to enroll in white schools. Here again, culture proved as important as personality. At a July 1967 meeting of the Southside Virginia Institute on Desegregation, school administrators noted that blacks were hesitant to enroll in white schools because of a variety of reasons—from "a subtle type of harassment," to the despicable "language of prejudice."[82] These were the "deliberate and overt acts of meanness"—the "small terrors"—that Vivian Carter Mason had described five years earlier.

As the NAACP filed exceptions to Norfolk's new school desegregation program, the federal government, acting through the attorney general and the Civil Rights Division of the Department of Justice, requested to intervene in the case against the Norfolk School Board. Attorney General Nicholas Katzenbach said that the Norfolk situation was of "general public importance," and he sent St. John Barrett, a Justice Department attorney, to deal with the case. Barrett told local officials that Norfolk had been chosen as a site of particular legal significance for two reasons: "The issues were the same as those in many other [school] desegregation cases, and the litigation was far enough along to constitute a worthy landmark."[83]

On February 22, Judge Hoffman admitted the Justice Department to the case. At the initial hearing, however, things did not go well for Barrett and his assistants. In court, Hoffman reprimanded the Justice Department officials when they asked to call more than fifteen witnesses who were not listed on the pretrial conference order, which had been agreed to by all the parties. Although Barrett withdrew his request, Henry Marsh and the attorneys from the NAACP requested a continuance when it became apparent that more preparation time was needed. Hoffman granted the NAACP's request and instructed the parties to meet in conference so that they could work out their differences before court resumed on March 22.[84]

The following week, the parties began a series of marathon closed-door meetings at the U.S. District Court law library in Norfolk. On one side of the table sat Barrett, his two assistants, and NAACP attorneys Henry Marsh, Victor Ashe, and J. Hugo Madison. On the other side sat negotiators for the local administration: City Attorney Leonard Davis, Superintendent Edwin Lamberth, and school board chairman Vincent Thomas. At the beginning of the negotiations, the two sides moved hesitantly, hoping to come to some agreement on minor issues. Soon, however, it became apparent that both sides had a vested interest in resolving their differences outside of court. The Justice Department and NAACP knew that Judge Hoffman supported a go-slow approach to desegregation, and they hoped to negotiate a settlement that would provide for a more rapid, comprehensive plan than he might require. On the other hand, the city attorney's office and school board wanted to keep control over local operations and avoid an appeal to the Fourth Circuit Court, which had proved far more demanding than Judge Hoffman in recent decisions.[85]

Because of the difficulties and desires on both sides, the negotiators established a compromise plan that provided a middle road toward desegregation. First, Norfolk's leaders agreed to reform the high school attendance policy. Three geographic attendance zones were created: one for Granby, one for Norview, and one for Maury and Booker T. Washington. Under the plan, students living in the Granby and Norview districts received no school choice; they had to attend their assigned location. Meanwhile, young people in the Maury–Booker T. Washington zone could select either school, without regard to race. In addition, African American students living in the Maury–Booker T. Washington zone could select to enroll at any of the city's high schools, including Granby and Maury, to further desegregation.[86]

For the second element in the compromise plan, the negotiators turned to the intermediate and elementary schools. Here, they made dramatic changes to the existing desegregation plan. Drawing on suggestions first made by the NAACP, the negotiators redrew attendance lines, creating three junior high school and eleven elementary school zones, which each included two or more schools. In addition, each zone was specifically designed to include a rough balance between white and black students. The entire effort at the intermediate and elementary levels was intended to spur more rapid and thoroughgoing desegregation so that the city's young people could begin to grow up together.[87]

Finally, the negotiators turned to the difficult issue of faculty desegregation. Recently released school board records indicate that City Attorney Leonard Davis and W. R. C. Cocke, the school board's attorney, understood that recent federal court decisions made faculty desegregation inevitable.[88] In fact, in November 1965 Davis wrote to Cocke, stating that he believed "the Supreme Court may be taking the position that segregation of faculties and administrative staff is invalid *per se* and that no evidence or very little evidence is necessary to show the invalidity." In response, Cocke wrote that he was "satisfied that desegregation of both faculties and of administrative personnel w[ould] be required, at least to some extent," if Norfolk's desegregation plan was to be approved by the district court. Nevertheless, Cocke worried that Norfolk's white citizens would oppose faculty desegregation, and he suggested that Superintendent Lamberth testify about the difficulties of the process in order to "avoid the impression of total surrender, even though we may realize that a fight may be futile."[89]

In the conference room, we may assume that Davis never let on about these private conversations with Cocke. We do know, however, that he, Lamberth, and Chairman Thomas opposed the NAACP's proposal that a quota system for transferring teachers be established. Instead, Norfolk's school officials suggested that a bold but simple declaration be added to the district's desegregation plan. It read: "The School Board of the City of Norfolk recognizes its responsibility to employ, assign, promote and discharge teachers and other professional personnel of the Norfolk City Public School System without regard to race or color. It further recognizes its obligation to take all reasonable steps to eliminate existing racial segregation of faculty that has resulted from the past operation of a dual school system based on race and color."[90]

With an agreement in hand, attorneys from the Justice Department, the NAACP, and the city of Norfolk returned to Judge Hoffman to secure his blessing.[91] Although the judge had serious reservations about the agreement — calling it "a racial plan"— he approved the negotiated settlement on March 17, the same day it was signed by the school board.[92] Norfolk's leaders then quickly implemented the plan to provide for the smoothest transition possible — especially where faculty desegregation was concerned. On March 23, Superintendent Lamberth and school board chairman Vincent Thomas appeared on a school television program to explain the voluntary nature of faculty desegregation. At the same time, Walter Brewster, the director of personnel, requested that all teachers inform him of their willingness to serve on an integrated faculty. Approximately 1,000 teachers, principals, and other professional personnel responded to Brewster's request, and interviews were conducted with roughly 300 personnel in order to select those most qualified to transfer into a mixed-race faculty settings.[93]

As the district's leaders prepared for the first stage of faculty desegregation, they also distributed and processed more than 50,000 school choice forms for the fall of 1966.[94] Despite the modest changes that had been made in the district's assignment policies, however, numerous whites in Norfolk spoke out in opposition to the new plan. "Why do our children have the choice of two high schools," Mrs. C. V. Stephens complained, "and the Negro children have the choice of all four?" As a parent, she considered this terribly unequal. "I do not understand the compromise," she said. "The Negroes should have a right to choose their schools, but so must we. This is not what the Constitution is built on." Robert Jones, another white parent, agreed. Although he supported integration, Jones complained that the district's new assignment plan was impractical. "There have not been any riots in Norfolk," Jones told the school board, but there "are a lot of dissatisfied people" in town.[95]

Despite the criticism of some disenchanted souls, Norfolk's school district took another hesitant step forward in September 1966. The faculties in all the senior and junior high schools began the desegregation process, and incremental progress was being made at the elementary level as well. Norfolk's leaders portrayed this development as a bold, voluntary step away from discrimination — one that promised "a better education for all [the city's] children." Indeed, in an official enrollment report on the progress of the district, Norfolk's officials showed that a majority of the city's 55,851 students now attended integrated schools. In these new laboratories of democracy, the "cooperative attitude of dedicated teachers and the persuasive powers of . . . school administrators" made for a smooth transition to desegregation.[96]

At least that was one way to look at it. From another perspective, it seemed that change in Norfolk had been more difficult than dramatic. Although civil rights activists, NAACP attorneys, and even the Justice Department had pressured Norfolk to desegregate its schools, almost 26,000 students remained enrolled in single-race schools. But even this statistic failed to tell the whole story. In September 1966, forty of the city's seventy-one schools remained completely segregated; seven more schools were 99 percent white or black; and fifteen additional sites were 90 to 98 percent white or black. This meant that — more than twelve years after *Brown v. Board of Education* — sixty-two of the seventy-one schools in Norfolk remained at least 90 percent single-race, with more than 45,000 of the district's 55,851 students. From this vantage point, progress had indeed been slight.[97]

IN JUNE 1966, frustrated by the slow pace of desegregation, a group of 160 African American parents petitioned Attorney General Katzenbach, requesting that he take "immediate action" to rescind Norfolk's school desegregation plan. The parents insisted that the plan gerrymandered numerous school zones in the city and encouraged segregation rather than integration.[98] Although the attorney general took no apparent action on the matter, the parents did not have long to wait for further legal action to ensue. In March 1967, a new court fight began in Norfolk as the school board revised its desegregation plan for the 1967–68 academic year. What followed was a hard-fought two-year legal battle, pitting the school board and city attorney's office against local parents, the U.S. government, and the NAACP.

This latest phase in Norfolk's debate began on March 28, 1967, when the school board proposed modifications to its desegregation plan to account for the newly constructed Lake Taylor High School. This new site required that a fifth attendance zone be created for senior high schools and that the four existing zones be redrawn to accommodate the new location. Therein lie the rub. Although the majority of Norfolk's freedom-of-choice program remained in place, lawyers for the NAACP filed exceptions to the amended plan in U.S. District Court on April 13. Represented by a team of six attorneys — J. Hugo Madison and Victor Ashe from Norfolk, Henry Marsh III and S. W. Tucker from Richmond, and James Nabrit III and Jack Greenberg from New York — the NAACP took Norfolk to task. The civil rights lawyers alleged that the school board's new desegregation plan was devised to continue and expand segregation. Specifically, the attorneys objected to the zoning line separating Booker T. Washington and Lake Taylor high schools. They argued that the line was drawn in such a way that it "divide[d] the Negro and white community, thereby contributing to racial segregation" in the schools.[99]

More was at stake than a simple zoning issue, however. In a series of nine specific objections, NAACP lawyers alleged that Norfolk's desegregation plan ignored obvious issues of racial discrimination. In addition to detailed enrollment matters, the lawyers focused on three specific topics. First, they complained that the Norfolk School Board failed to provide for an integrated faculty at Lake Taylor High School. Second, the lawyers argued that Norfolk continued to avoid any specific goal or timetable for full faculty desegregation. And finally, the lawyers dropped a bombshell: they objected to the school board's recent decision to build a new Booker T. Washington High School on its current site, suggesting instead that a new site be selected "with a view of furthering racial desegregation of the school system."[100]

Many of Norfolk's black leaders were enraged by the NAACP's decision to challenge the city on the Booker T. Washington matter, which had been agreed to more than a year earlier after extensive negotiations between the school board and the Committee for the Best Booker T. Washington High School. At the *Journal and Guide,* Bernard Young complained that the NAACP had moved on the issue without consulting any of Norfolk's established black leaders. Young insisted that neither he nor any other member of the committee had any knowledge that the NAACP would challenge the city's plan for the new school. The *Virginian-Pilot* found this astonishing, since 70 percent of the committee was affiliated with the Norfolk branch of the NAACP. Indeed, Robert Robertson was an active member of the Committee for the Best Booker T. Washington High School and regularly participated in its work. Despite this "puzzling" lack of communication, however, Young insisted that the NAACP had taken the wrong position on the issue. Litigation, he said, would only delay the construction of a desperately needed new high school that would serve many of the city's black youth.[101]

Although Norfolk's white community showed little concern for the location of Booker T. Washington High School, many white citizens in the city spoke out against the school board's modified desegregation plan. As soon as the new proposal was announced, Oliver L. Rosso of Bayview challenged the revised high school attendance zones included in the plan. Echoing complaints made by Mrs. C. V. Stephens one year earlier, Rosso told the school board that the district's assignment policies were unfair. "[One] part of the population is going to have a choice of three [high] schools," he told the board, referring to black children living in the Booker T. Washington attendance area, while "my kids are going to have no choice [at all]." Rosso was enraged that the new assignment plan was going to force his children to transfer from Granby to Norview High School, and he meant to stop it.

When school board chairman Vincent Thomas responded that this type of redistricting was a necessary step to achieve further desegregation, Rosso promised to retain counsel and challenge the revised assignment plan in court.[102]

On Monday, April 17, as the U.S. District Court took up the latest stage of *Beckett v. School Board of Norfolk,* Rosso and a host of other white parents from the Winona and Riverview sections of the city appeared before Judge Hoffman with their attorney, Samuel Goldblatt.[103] Over the objections of the NAACP and the school board, Judge Hoffman granted the white parents leave to intervene in the case, and their complaints soon became the most significant part of the proceedings. After two days of hearings involving Superintendent Lambert, school board chairman Thomas, and other school administrators, Judge Hoffman issued a memorandum decision on May 12, 1967. He upheld the vast majority of the school board's revised desegregation plan, dismissing every one of the NAACP's nine objections. Nevertheless, Hoffman ruled against the board on the matter of high school attendance zones. He found that the assignment plans put forward by the board in 1966 and 1967 were "not true freedom-of-choice plans." Rather, Judge Hoffman said, the plans "present[ed] a Hobson's choice . . . afford[ing] a 'one-way ticket' for [predominantly white] students residing in Areas I, II, III and V, and a 'four-way ticket' for [African American] students residing in [the Booker T. Washington attendance area]."[104]

To remedy the situation, Judge Hoffman proposed that the school board choose one of three options for high school assignments — universal freedom of choice for all students, consolidation of the Booker T. Washington and Lake Taylor attendance zones, or strict geographic zoning without any student choice. On May 23, the school board adopted the final option, strict geographic zoning, largely for convenience's sake. It was late in the spring, and school was scheduled to begin anew in little more than three months. In discussing this option, members of the school board said that it was the "most desirable from an administrative standpoint." Not only would it keep the number of students at each school relatively equal, but this option also offered the quickest and simplest way to close the case on school assignments for the following year.[105]

Despite the simplicity of the school board's new assignment plan, it ruffled many feathers in Norfolk. Hilary Jones, the lone black member on the school board, voted against the plan, stating that it "would resegregate some schools," taking Norfolk "a step backwards."[106] Lawyers with the NAACP wholeheartedly agreed. From their perspective, the entire situation was a disaster. Not only had Judge Hoffman ruled against their objections to the revised desegregation plan, but he had now approved a geographic zoning program for the city's high schools that eliminated all choice for black students residing in inner-city Norfolk.

The NAACP had no intention of allowing Judge Hoffman's decision to go unchallenged. As soon as the judge issued the final order approving the school board's amended desegregation plan on May 29, 1967, lawyers for the NAACP filed an appeal with the Fourth Circuit Court.[107] Eight months later, the case appeared for argument before Chief Judge Clement F. Haynsworth Jr. and six other members of the court of appeals. In the courtroom, lawyers Marsh and Tucker reiterated the arguments they had made before Judge Hoffman only a few months earlier. In particular, the NAACP attorneys alleged that Norfolk's desegregation plan fell short on three counts: it did not establish a timeline for full faculty desegregation; it did not provide a means for desegregating the city's high schools; and it did not address the location of the new Booker T. Washington High School.[108]

Norfolk's city attorney, Leonard Davis, countered the NAACP at every point. He told the court that no hard timeline or statistical goal was needed to achieve faculty desegregation in Norfolk. Instead, he insisted, the city's vague objective — "to eliminate existing racial segregation of faculties" — was "just as good as a percentage goal."[109] In fact, Davis argued, Norfolk was moving swiftly to integrate its faculty. Desegregation was simply a complicated process that required time and patience. To emphasize this point, he turned to the Booker T. Washington issue. Davis noted that years of discussion between the school board and the Committee for the Best Booker T. Washington High School had produced a cordial agreement on the placement and layout of the school. Now, however, the national NAACP threatened to overturn this hard work, souring race relations in Norfolk and setting back the construction of the school by months if not years. In conclusion, Davis told the court, "I don't stand here, judge, and say to you that the job is complete, that we have fully and completely integrated." But, he insisted, "We are doing everything as quickly as we can."[110]

As the Fourth Circuit Court considered the Norfolk situation in the spring of 1968, the U.S. Supreme Court issued its landmark decision in *Green v. School Board of New Kent County*. Regarded by many scholars as the most important decision since *Brown* and *Brown II, Green* pushed far further than the High Court's previous opinions on school desegregation. The case originated in rural New Kent County, a sparsely populated enclave midway between Richmond and Norfolk. In 1965, school board officials in the county instituted a freedom-of-choice assignment plan to meet federal guidelines resulting from the Civil Rights Act of 1964. Since that time, however, the two schools in the county had seen little integration. Although 115 African American students had enrolled in the county's predominantly white school, faculty integration was virtually nil, and no white student attended the all-black George W. Watkins school. The question before the Supreme Court was simple, therefore: did New Kent County's freedom-of-choice assignment plan meet the constitutional requirements established in *Brown v. Board of Education?*[111]

Writing for the Supreme Court, Associate Justice William Brennan found that it did not. In a decision that would have wide-ranging implications for districts throughout the nation, Brennan wrote that New Kent County had an "affirmative duty to take whatever steps might be necessary" to eliminate racial discrimination "root and branch." The time for mere deliberate speed had long passed, Brennan said. Although the court refused to rule out all freedom-of-choice plans entirely, the justices agreed that all school districts must "come forward with a plan that promises realistically to work, and promises realistically to work now."[112]

The *Green* decision had an immediate impact in Norfolk. Four days after the Supreme Court had issued its opinion, the Fourth Circuit Court decided *Brewer v. School Board of Norfolk,* overturning Judge Hoffman's previous decisions on faculty desegregation and high school attendance zones. Once again, Hoffman had been overruled. Writing for the Fourth Circuit, Judge John D. Butzner insisted that the school board in Norfolk had an affirmative duty in light of the *Green* decision to establish a "realistic timetable" for faculty desegregation. In addition, Judge Butzner found that the school board's "strict geographical zoning" policy tended to perpetuate segregation at the high school level, rather than eliminate it.[113] He instructed the school board to propose "alternative plans for pupil assignment," which might then be considered and approved by the district court. Finally, the Fourth Circuit Court turned to the contentious issues surrounding Booker T. Washington High School. Rather than ruling on the matter itself, the court instructed Judge Hoffman to reconsider the location and plans for the school to determine whether it would "take its place in a non-discriminatory system or continue *de facto* the city's former *de jure* dual system of white and Negro schools."[114]

IN THE END, many scholars might argue that the 1960s resolved few issues in Norfolk. The city's freedom-of-choice assignment plan was remanded to the district court for further consideration in 1968, and no real resolution would present itself until busing began two years later. Although faculty and student integration had begun, progress was slow and tedious, with most court decisions calling for only minor adjustments to the city's school desegregation process. And many schools in the city remained racially identifiable, with little more than token integration taking place on most campuses in Norfolk.

What this perspective misses, however, is the dramatic transformation that African American activists brought to Norfolk in the years between 1960 and 1968. At the dawn of the era, segregation remained the standard practice throughout the city. Restaurants, libraries, hospitals, and parks routinely denied admittance to black citizens, and the city's school system reinforced this insidious form of racial discrimination. Despite years of legal pressure and dramatic courtroom decisions, only twenty-eight African American students had been admitted to predominantly white schools by 1960, and the faculty at each location remained entirely segregated. By 1968, however, African American activists had transformed Norfolk's social and political scene. Sit-in demonstrations, school walkouts, and constant legal and social agitation had made their mark. Many restaurants and libraries had begun the desegregation process, and parks and hospitals were not far behind. On the educational front, the situation was also much improved. More than 60 percent of the city's schools had at least taken the first step toward integration.

It would be wrong, though, to argue that all was well and good in Norfolk's schools. Despite the terrific advances that had been made, in 1968 the district remained divided by race. Of the seventy-three public schools in Norfolk, thirty remained 100 percent white or black; eight were 99 percent white or black; and twenty-three were more than 90 percent white or black. In total, then, sixty-one of seventy-three schools in Norfolk remained at least 90 percent single race. Such a situation could not stand.[115]

CHAPTER FIVE

BUSING
AND
THE AMBIVALENT HEYDAY OF
SCHOOL INTEGRATION, 1968–1975
BACKLASH

I N 1968, SEPTEMBER arrived hot and muggy in Norfolk. As the city's young people enjoyed the last days of summer vacation, school administrators and teachers prepared for a promising new academic year. In fact, there was much to be proud about in Norfolk. Since the city had introduced its Quality Education program in 1963, the school system had dramatically improved its offerings. For starters, the district's budget had grown by an astonishing 48.6 percent, and administrators were using this influx of new money to reduce class sizes and raise teachers' salaries. At the same time, Norfolk had implemented a number of trend-setting innovations to improve the quality of education in the district. Twenty-eight remedial reading centers had been constructed in the previous five years. An impressive enrichment program for disadvantaged children had been piloted to rave reviews. And a new Technical-Vocational Center was scheduled to open in the fall. All this led Superintendent Edwin Lamberth to the conclusion that the district was headed in the right direction. "The great majority of the parents I see are happy with the schools," he told a reporter from the *Virginian-Pilot.* But, he continued, "Maybe it's just the people I see. Maybe someone from the inner city would have something else to say."[1]

Indeed they did. In remarks before the school board in June 1968, Vivian Carter Mason spoke on behalf of dozens of African American parents who were members of the Norfolk Committee for the Improvement of Education. Mason told the board that her organization had serious questions about the quality and fairness of Norfolk's public schools. In particular, the group was concerned with three issues: the teaching of African American history; the preparation of teachers engaged in educating the economically disadvantaged; and the recognition of African American staff members. In each of these areas, Mason contended, the district had fallen short. To take only the most obvious example, Mason highlighted the "omissions [and] distortions" of African American history presented in the school curriculum. She complained that the schools presented a "one-sided, innocuous treatment of history," which failed to acknowledge "the wrongs, the terrors, [and] the misery" associated with racial slavery. As an illustration, she told the story of a fourth grade class in which the teacher asked the students, "How would you treat slaves, if you had them?" The students presented the expected answers, of course, suggesting that they would provide fair treatment, sound housing, and a well-rounded diet. Then, one African American student "had the superlative concept of humanity to answer, 'But I wouldn't have slaves, because it's wrong.'" This bold, refreshing statement brought a smile to Mason's face, but it did not last long. For, in the next breath she exclaimed, "What kind of teacher could propose such a question in the face of the outrageous crime of slavery?" Such action, Mason complained, showed a remarkable lack of historical understanding and an almost incomprehensible insensitivity to African American students and their heritage.[2]

To their credit, the superintendent and school board recognized many of the problems pointed out by Mason and took steps to correct them. During the summer of 1968, for instance, the school system conducted a two-week institute on teaching in an integrated setting. Approximately 250 teachers and principals attended the program, which was planned in association with the University of Virginia and the local branch of Virginia State College. When the institute came to a close in August, the district then encouraged teachers to participate in a televised college course on African American history. Designed and offered by Edgar Allan Toppin of Virginia State College, Petersburg, the course was entitled "Americans from Africa: A History." It appeared on WHRO-TV two times a week and could be viewed from home or school. In addition, the district organized several parent-teacher study groups to discuss the program and the broader issues of African American history. One result of these discussions was a pamphlet entitled *Epochs in the History of the Negro in America*, designed by Celestyne Diggs Porter, a longtime history teacher at Booker T. Washington High School and the sister of prominent lawyer T. Ione Diggs. Although brief and cursory, Porter's pamphlet offered teachers a chronological overview of African American history from the founding of Virginia to the mid-twentieth century.[3]

Despite these steps forward, Norfolk's schools continued to operate in a discriminatory fashion. The best illustration of this point may be found in an article that appeared in the *Virginian-Pilot* in September 1968, as students prepared to return to school. Written by Shirley Bolinaga, the piece presented a brief but poignant look at the story of Leola Pearl Beckett. Twelve years earlier, Beckett had been among the first African American students to pursue desegregation in the city's public schools. In 1956, at the age of fifteen, she had given her name to the landmark case, *Beckett v. School Board of Norfolk*. Even so, this brave young woman had never been admitted to an integrated school. In fact, Beckett was now married with three children of her own, and it seemed that they, too, would be relegated to segregated schools. Her oldest son, a second grader named Kelvin, was scheduled to begin the year at Smallwood elementary, an all-black school in Lamberts Point. To be sure, Beckett — now Mrs. Thomas Faulks — could have enrolled her son at either Larchmont or Stuart elementary school, which were both integrated. Under the city's freedom-of-choice plan, however, no free transportation was provided for students. This meant that young Kelvin would have been forced to walk more than a mile to Larchmont or Stuart, crossing Hampton Boulevard, one of the busiest streets in west Norfolk. For obvious reasons, therefore, the Faulks kept Kelvin at Smallwood, which was a safe, easy walk on the back streets of the area, less than half a mile from their home.[4]

As the Beckett-Faulks story makes clear, young Kelvin had many options that were never available to his mother. By filling out a simple freedom-of-choice form in the spring of each year, he and his parents could select any one of the schools in his attendance area. Yet in spite of the gains that had been made over the previous decade, the results were much the same. Like generations before him, Kelvin attended an all-black elementary school, which had never been integrated. Lingering patterns of residential segregation and the historical tendency to build schools in racially identifiable neighborhoods kept Kelvin and thousands of other young people from the benefits of integrated education. In fact, Norfolk's enrollment figures showed that twenty-eight of the city's fifty-seven elementary schools remained entirely segregated in 1968, while another twenty-two enrolled minority populations that accounted for less than 10 percent of the student body. This meant that fifty of the city's fifty-seven elementary schools remained at least 90 percent single race. And the story was much the same at the secondary level. Two of the city's eleven junior high schools remained entirely segregated; two more were 99 percent white or black; and four additional schools were over

In September 1968, Leola Pearl Beckett Faulks — for whom the *Beckett* case was named twelve years earlier — posed with her eldest son, a second grader named Kelvin, in front of Smallwood Elementary, an all-black school in the Lamberts Point neighborhood. (Courtesy of the *Virginian-Pilot*

90 percent single race. This same scenario held true at the majority of the city's five senior high schools. Booker T. Washington enrolled 2,396 African American students, but had only ten whites on the roster. Meanwhile, across town, Granby and Lake Taylor each enrolled student bodies that were more than 90 percent white.[5]

In light of these statistics, attorneys from the National Association for the Advancement of Colored People (NAACP) and the Civil Rights Division of the Department of Justice returned to federal court in Norfolk to challenge the city's school desegregation plan. Too little integration had been accomplished in the fourteen years since *Brown v. Board of Education,* the lawyers contended, and it was time for the federal courts to impose a new solution in Norfolk — it was time for crosstown busing. This chapter examines the legal, social, and political debates that developed in Norfolk as the city's citizens wrestled with busing and its attendant difficulties. What emerges most clearly from the narrative is the sense that many whites viewed busing as a traumatic, infuriating intrusion by the federal government, while many African Americans saw the process as a promising new opportunity to overcome white intransigence and racism. At the same time, however, it is clear that busing broke down long-held illusions of racial solidarity in both the white and black communities. As grassroots, working-class organizations highlighted the important socioeconomic factors at play in the city's busing scheme, infinite shades of gray appeared. While working-class whites and blacks complained that their children bore the brunt of the busing experiment, city leaders worried that middle-class flight would hinder their ability to manage and hence maintain white supremacy in Norfolk. Nevertheless, local black leaders, in concert with the national NAACP, insisted on moving full-speed ahead with busing because less compulsory schemes had failed to equalize or integrate the schools. The eyes of local black leaders were fixed on the prizes of educational equality and integration, and they averted their gaze from the quotidian and, in some ways, legitimate concerns about the federally mandated remedy for the sins of the past. To black leaders, crosstown busing had to be done, and it would eventually work, even if both oppressors and oppressed in Norfolk were suddenly taken out of their respective comfort zones.

ALTHOUGH FEW PEOPLE recognized it at the time, Norfolk's busing debate had its origins in 1968, as the nation struggled through a pivotal time of tension and tragedy. That February, President Lyndon Johnson's National Advisory Commission on Civil Disorders issued its landmark study, commonly known as the Kerner Report, warning that racism in America was causing the country to move "toward two societies, one black, one white — separate and unequal." This dramatic assessment of the nation's racial divide took on added poignancy during the following four months, as civil rights leader Martin Luther King Jr. and Democratic presidential candidate Robert F. Kennedy were gunned down in separate acts of brazen violence. Taken together, the King and Kennedy assassinations set the stage for a summer full of protests, including demonstrations in Chicago against the war in Vietnam, women's liberation marches in New York City, and student demonstrations in towns and cities around the nation.[6]

In Norfolk, the racial and cultural tensions of the era expressed themselves in a variety of ways. At the city's colleges and universities, students engaged in heated discussions about the Vietnam War, the draft, and the Black Power movement. In local politics, voters debated the election of Joseph Jordan Jr., the outspoken civil rights attorney who was selected as the city's first African American councilman since Reconstruction.[7] But it was on the public school front where tempers flared and temperatures reached their peak. As attorneys for the Justice Department and the NAACP returned to Norfolk for another year of school litigation, local citizens took sides in a raucous debate. The city's desegregation suit, *Beckett v. School Board of Norfolk,* was back before the court, and it featured some of the most pressing issues of the day.[8]

When U.S. District Judge Walter E. Hoffman took up the *Beckett* case in the fall of 1968, he expressed his frank exasperation with the matter. As a longtime resident of Norfolk and the husband of a career librarian in the school district, Hoffman resented the continual complaints filed by the Justice Department and the NAACP. In fact, he told Isle of Wight attorney Frederick Gray that "no school [desegregation] plan in the United States . . . ha[d] shown greater progress than Norfolk's."[9] The city's superintendent of schools and school board had made substantial efforts to overcome the district's history of discrimination, but repeated filings by the government and the NAACP threatened to create an environment of racial animosity and endless litigation in Norfolk. As Judge Hoffman was fond of saying at the time, it was all well and good for the government to pick on the South, but what was it doing to desegregate the schools of Harlem?

Many leaders in Norfolk's white community shared Judge Hoffman's frustration. At the *Ledger-Star,* for instance, editors ran an article lamenting Norfolk's continuing difficulties on the legal front. The city's problems were "especially regrettable," the paper said, since it was clear that Norfolk was rapidly "moving . . . toward a non-racial school system." Although the editors freely admitted that many schools in the city remained segregated, they insisted that "the racial make-up of the individual schools reflect[ed] the racial character of the surrounding residential areas." There was, in short, no attempt by the city's administration to perpetuate school segregation. On the contrary, school board chairman Vincent Thomas and Superintendent Edwin Lamberth had fought to desegregate the schools. Remaining segregation was simply the result of long-term consumer practices, which had created racially identifiable neighborhoods throughout Norfolk and the surrounding communities. In fact, the editors insisted, this housing trend could be seen throughout the South, and it was not the school board's job to reverse or overcome it. If whites and blacks chose to live in separate neighborhoods, then the city's school system should allow them to attend separate schools as well.[10]

Judges on the Fourth Circuit Court of Appeals rejected this rather benign interpretation of residential segregation. They knew, for instance, that the white citizens of Norfolk had employed various tactics, including local ordinances, racial covenants, and discriminatory redevelopment practices, to create a system of segregated housing in the city.[11] The court's May 1968 ruling in the Norfolk case noted that the city's planning districts continued to show a "wide variation in white and Negro racial distribution." Five of the city's planning districts had no black residents; fifty-one had less than 15 percent blacks; seven were mixed; and seventeen had more than 80 percent blacks. Upon remand to the district court, the appellate judges ordered Judge Hoffman to "determine whether the racial pattern of the districts result[ed] from racial discrimination with regard to housing." It was "immaterial," the circuit court told Hoffman, whether existing patterns of racial segregation resulted from private acts of residential discrimination or public acts requiring segregation. Both of these forms of prejudice were now illegal, and it was time for local leaders to realize it. The superintendent and school board in Norfolk could no longer cite lingering vestiges of residential segregation as justification for a school attendance plan that resulted in de facto segregation. In short, the court declared, it was time for Norfolk to take decisive action to integrate its faculty, student body, and administrative team.[12]

Although Judge Hoffman opposed the circuit court's decision in the Norfolk suit, he moved ahead with its enforcement. In November 1968, he scheduled a pretrial hearing in the *Beckett* case to take place on December 27. In preparation for the hearing, he ordered the Norfolk School Board to submit a status report on desegregation in the district. In addition, Hoffman informed attorneys with the Justice Department and the NAACP that they should be ready to consider all relevant issues that had emerged in the case following the U.S. Supreme Court's decision in *Green v. New Kent County*. Specifically, he said, school zoning, faculty desegregation, future construction, and the long-running Booker T. Washington matter would all be on the table for discussion.[13]

Administrators at Norfolk Public Schools moved swiftly to meet Judge Hoffman's order. On December 17, the school board passed a series of resolutions outlining the progress of desegregation in the district and providing plans for seven new construction projects. More important, however, the board adopted a formal timeline for faculty desegregation. This new proposal stated that each school in the district would employ at least two racial minorities—whether they be white or black—by September 1970. In addition, the board pledged to move "as rapidly as possible" to accomplish further faculty desegregation so that no school would be racially identified by its staff.[14]

In its initial response to the school board's proposals, the Justice Department was positive. At the pretrial hearing on December 27, lead attorney J. Harold Flannery suggested that the parties begin "good faith" negotiations to resolve their differences "without a hearing."[15] As a veteran of civil rights suits in some of the most recalcitrant areas in the South, including Grenada, Mississippi, and Danville, Virginia, Flannery believed that Norfolk's case presented an excellent opportunity for racial compromise and reconciliation.[16] There was good reason for this optimism. In March 1966, the Justice Department and the NAACP had reached an out-of-court agreement with the school board, settling that year's desegregation suit with a compromise plan. Now, however, the issues had become more complex and controversial. Although Judge Hoffmann approved the out-of-court negotiations between the parties, he expressed grave doubts about the possibilities that they presented, saying that Norfolk's school problems were "rapidly becoming insoluble."[17]

HOFFMAN'S ASSESSMENT of the situation proved to be prescient. In a statement reported in the *Virginian-Pilot* on March 18, 1969, City Attorney Leonard Davis noted that he and the lawyers from the Justice Department and the NAACP had met in five lengthy conferences, but had been unable to agree on a practical program for the city's public schools. In fact, more than a week earlier, lawyers for the Justice Department and the NAACP had requested that the district court resume proceedings in the case. Upon receiving this request, Judge Hoffman scheduled a pretrial conference for early April, and began preparations for a long, hard showdown.[18]

When Norfolk's lawyers met the Justice Department and the NAACP in district court on Wednesday, April 2, City Attorney Leonard Davis was suffering from an ulcer. He passed much of the responsibility for the school board's case to a new attorney, Toy D. Savage Jr. A well-known lawyer and former state legislator, Savage had grown up in Norfolk, served in World War II, and received a bachelor's and a law degree from the University of Virginia. He and his firm, Willcox and Savage, had been retained by the school board in early January to help with the city's case. Now, Savage told Judge Hoffman that Norfolk was developing a long-range desegregation plan to stabilize the district and reduce the likelihood that additional re-zoning would be required in the future. But, he insisted, the plan would take several weeks to complete, and the school board could not possibly implement it in September 1969. Savage requested, therefore, that the district be permitted to present an interim plan for the coming academic year.[19]

Henry Marsh and J. Harold Flannery both opposed Savage's proposal. They insisted that Norfolk's long-running desegregation suit demanded that the school board take swift action to end the city's dual system of education. Furthermore, the attorneys complained, Norfolk's representatives — including Savage — had been in conferences with the Justice Department and the NAACP for the past three months. During this time, the school district had drafted and presented the outlines of its new proposal, and any delays in its presentation to the court should be avoided. Despite these objections, Judge Hoffman agreed to the city's request. "If you don't like it," he told Henry Marsh, "you can go to the Fourth Circuit Court of Appeals."[20]

With Judge Hoffman continuing his longtime support for Norfolk's school board, administrators in the district were confident that they could secure approval of an interim desegregation plan. On April 3, Superintendent Lamberth, City Attorney Davis, and Assistant Superintendent John McLaulin presented a resolution to the school board that had been specifically drafted as an interim measure. The resolution ignored virtually every issue raised by the Justice Department and the NAACP. It left freedom-of-choice enrollments in place at the elementary and junior high schools levels, and it retained the faculty integration goal of two minority teachers per school. The only adjustment that the April resolution proposed was a slight alteration to high school attendance zones — a change that was required by the Fourth Circuit Court's previous decision in March 1968. Following a short presentation on the matter, led by attorney Leonard Davis, the school board approved the resolution by unanimous vote and sent it to the district court for consideration.[21]

Three weeks later, on April 22, the Norfolk case returned to Judge Hoffman's courtroom. In a lengthy, daylong hearing involving testimony from Superintendent Lamberth and Assistant Superintendent McLaulin, the Justice Department and the NAACP hammered at the city's interim plan. Henry Marsh complained that Norfolk's proposal did nothing to increase student or faculty integration in the district, and J. Harrold Flannery requested the right to call an expert witness who would present an alternative to the school district's proposal. Although the second and third days of the hearings became increasingly contentious, with school board chairman Vincent Thomas and other key administrators presenting testimony, the real fireworks in the case began on Thursday, April 24, when Flannery finally called his expert witness, Michael Stolee, to the stand.[22]

Stolee was a true outsider. A native of Minneapolis, Minnesota, he spent his early career in secondary education, serving as a teacher, principal, and superintendent of schools. In 1963, he received a Ph.D. in educational administration from the University of Minnesota and went to work as an assistant professor of education at the University of Miami. There, he codirected the Florida School Desegregation Consulting Center, the nation's first school desegregation institute funded under the Civil Rights Act of 1964. Over the next three years, Stolee and his colleagues performed vital consulting work for several of the largest urban areas in the region, including Jackson, Mississippi; Miami-Dade County, Florida; and Broward County, Florida.[23]

When Stolee appeared in Judge Hoffman's courtroom on April 24, few people were prepared for what he had to say. The Justice Department had provided him with ample enrollment and demographic figures on which to base his analysis of Norfolk's school system, and he had "driven extensively in the city" to develop a sense of the area and its issues. As a result of his study, Stolee proposed a broad new desegregation plan for Norfolk's schools, which called for a comprehensive overhauling of the city's current assignment plan. The Florida professor rejected freedom of choice entirely, saying that it had caused administrative chaos and confusion. "You don't know for sure who will go where," he told the court. "I have no sympathy for it. If it weren't for desegregation, no school board in the country would put up with freedom of choice."[24]

Stolee's plan called for a dramatic revision of elementary school assignments, with the pairing of many schools in racially identifiable neighborhoods. This meant that children attending a predominantly white school such as Ingleside Elementary would be matched with children attending a predominantly black school such as Liberty Park. In Stolee's proposal, the students in both schools would be placed in a single attendance zone, with the children in grades one through three going to Ingleside and those in grades four through six attending Liberty Park. With this system, Stolee promised to eradicate the "racial identity" of thirty of the city's fifty-five elementary schools. Furthermore, his proposal called for substantial integration at nine of the city's eleven junior high schools and all of the city's senior high schools. To achieve these results, Stolee suggested new zoning lines and crosstown busing for desegregation. Although these were certainly controversial suggestions, which promised to fundamentally alter the city's enrollment practices, Stolee's most divisive proposal called for the pairing of Booker T. Washington and Lake Taylor high schools, with tenth graders in both areas attending Booker T. Washington and eleventh and twelfth graders going to Lake Taylor.[25]

Attorney Toy Savage and administrators with the school district told Judge Hoffman that few whites in Norfolk would accept the Stolee plan. The school district's legal team then pressured Stolee to admit that his crosstown busing program would drive thousands of whites from the city. After repeatedly refusing to do so, Stolee became upset. "It's high time we in the schools stop monkeying around with desegregation and get back to educating the children," he said. "There are children presently being hurt by racial isolation in the Norfolk schools, and these children need help now." For his part, Judge Hoffman did not disagree with Stolee. "There's no question about it," he said. "In every district in the United States some children are suffering with racial isolation." But Hoffman wanted to know why the federal government was targeting Norfolk, where school desegregation was moving slowly but surely in a positive direction. The Justice Department kept filing cases in his court, Hoffman repeatedly complained in his deadpan voice, but "what are they doing about Harlem?"[26]

WHEN THE STOLEE PLAN hit Norfolk's newspapers on April 26, the public response was immediate. Opposition to the government's proposal began in the Ingleside area, a white middle-income neighborhood on the southeastern border of the city, where residents were deeply opposed to crosstown busing. There, the local parent-teacher association (PTA) met on Monday, April 28, and adopted a resolution protesting the government's proposal.

Parents from the PTA argued that the Stolee plan not only presented a great "hazard [to] the health and safety" of their children, but it also threatened the stability "of [their] community."[27]

A delegation from the Ingleside Civic League took the PTA's petition to the regularly scheduled city council meeting on Tuesday, April 29. Although they received little support from Mayor Roy Martin and the other council members, the delegation decided to take matters into their own hands.[28] On Friday, May 2, they packed more than 400 people into Squires Memorial Presbyterian Church to take part in a special meeting on crosstown busing. In a hot, crowded room, the spokesman for the group, Rev. John R. Hobson, led what amounted to a secular service against federal intervention in Norfolk. In place of sacraments and a sermon, the young pastor offered a homily on the dangers of busing. "School integration is not the issue," he told the crowd. What was at stake was something more serious, indeed more sacred, than simple schools. It was that "intangible something called a community." If Ingleside parents allowed the government to bus their children from the neighborhood, then the "common goals and commonly recognized symbols" of the area would fade away.[29] Of course, the young pastor was preaching to the converted, and it did not take long for them to sign on to the crusade he was proposing. By the end of the meeting, league members had passed a resolution questioning the constitutionality of the government's crosstown busing plan, and they had agreed to hire an attorney to represent them in the city's school desegregation suit.[30]

By Saturday, news of the Ingleside meeting had spread throughout Norfolk, and many parents in other parts of the city were calling for similar action. For instance, Mrs. J. S. Holmes of the Hollywood neighborhood called on Superintendent Lamberth to demand that he defend the "FAIR WAY" of desegregation—freedom of choice. Holmes was a typical white parent who had children at Lake Taylor High School. She claimed that the city's current zoning program was fair and equal, and she insisted that the plan to pair Lake Taylor and Booker T. Washington was "utterly ridiculous." If it came to that, Holmes told Lamberth, "we shall move or place [our children] in private schools rather than place them in such an unfair and detrimental position."[31] This last sentiment was echoed by hundreds of other white parents in Norfolk, and it soon evolved into something of a mantra. "White flight" was not only a fear of local politicians and policy wonks, it was a powerful weapon that middle-class whites wielded whenever their vision of the future was challenged. No better example of this may be found than the letter that Joan Warren of Ingleside wrote to U.S. senator William B. Spong Jr. on May 1, 1969. Warren told Spong in concise, clear language that the implementation of the Justice Department's busing plan would lead to a "mass exodus of residents" from Ingleside, which would ultimately result in "racial imbalance" and other alleged social pathologies for the city.[32]

With resistance to the Stolee plan running at an all-time high, Norfolk's anti-busing activists organized two large rallies for May 5.[33] The first meeting occurred at Virginia Heights Baptist Church, a white middle-class enclave in a bucolic setting, half a mile from Lake Taylor High School. E. G. Middleton Jr., a prominent engineer and local business leader, presided over the session, which drew a crowd of some 500 people. Many of the participants were neighborhood parents who simply wanted to express their frustration with the Justice Department's proposed desegregation plan. In addition, however, representatives from twenty-eight of Norfolk's civic leagues attended the meeting to voice their support for the Ingleside group and its stance against crosstown busing. By the end of the meeting, the neighborhood parents and civic league members had elected a six-person committee to confer with the Ingleside leaders so that the two organizations might forge a joint legal strategy to resist crosstown busing and school pairings.[34]

Although the Virginia Heights session remained calm and orderly, a second meeting at nearby Easton Elementary School turned rowdy. Organized in association with the Norfolk Federation of Parent Teacher Associations, this session featured a rousing introductory speech by Sue Allgood, the president of the Easton PTA and the mother of a Lake Taylor High School student. Allgood was infuriated by the Justice Department's plan to link Lake Taylor with Booker T. Washington, and she complained that the federal government was trying to take over local education. In particular, Allgood attacked the government's chief expert, Stolee, who had prepared his study of Norfolk after a mere two days in town. "He knows what's best for our city," Allgood declared sarcastically. "HE DON'T KNOW ANYTHING," someone shouted in response from the audience.[35]

WHEN THE NORFOLK CASE returned to court on Wednesday, May 7, Toy Savage and John McLaulin countered the Stolee plan by presenting one of their own. The school district had decided after much internal discussion to introduce the first broad outlines of Norfolk's long-range desegregation plan, which would be officially submitted to the court at the end of June. With maps and charts, McLaulin argued that the city's plan promised to accomplish virtually the same degree of desegregation as the Stolee plan, but the city proposed to do it in a more judicious and economical manner. "It seems to me," Hoffman responded, "that the principal difference between you all is that the Justice Department insists on busing and busing all over the city." The school board had rejected this approach, Hoffman asserted, and "I've told you that I'm not buying that deal either."[36]

Although there is no indication that public pressure affected Hoffman's decision on the interim plan for 1969–70, he did note that a "great feeling of unrest" had come over the city since the introduction of the Stolee plan.[37] In a heated rebuke of the government's plan, the judge said that he was sorry to see "responsible members of the U.S. government . . . press for such a proposal." It was frankly absurd, he declared. The pairing of white and black schools would infuriate parents and lead to white flight. The costs of crosstown busing would strap the city and the school system, reducing the quality of education. And virtually no one in Norfolk would be happy. "Dr. Stolee may be an esteemed educator," Hoffman said, but his plan is "so asinine I can't even give any consideration to it."[38]

On May 19, Hoffman issued his opinion approving the school board's interim desegregation plan for the 1969–70 school year. It called for a continuation of the freedom-of-choice assignment plan at the elementary and junior high school levels, and the adoption of a revised geographic zoning program for the senior high schools. "In the City of Norfolk," Hoffman wrote, "we are long past the days of integration. With few exceptions, children (and their parents) expect to encounter children of different races at some point during their public education." Although the Justice Department and the NAACP argued that integration was moving too slowly, Hoffman found that the school board was proceeding "in a realistic manner." There was no need for racial balancing or crosstown busing in the city's public schools. On the contrary, what was needed was time and old-fashioned horse sense.[39]

AS SOON AS NORFOLK received approval for its interim desegregation plan, the district's administrative team turned to the next stage in the legal process. In a lengthy memo drafted on May 27, John McLaulin presented the members of the school board with a detailed status report outlining the development of the city's long-range desegregation plan. Along with Superintendent Lamberth and Norfolk's legal team, McLaulin hoped to provide for further student and faculty integration, while preserving a clear white majority at each of the city's integrated schools. As the district's administrative team redesigned the pupil placement system, however, McLaulin emphasized that the school system faced considerable difficulties. New pupil assignment zones necessitated more busing than was currently required. Further faculty desegregation threatened to drive some teachers out of Norfolk. And the district's most important construction projects required major modifications. In working through these problems, administrators moved assignment zones and building projects to meet the demands of the district, but their long-term proposal ultimately proved to be just as controversial as their interim plan had been.[40]

On Friday, June 20, Norfolk's administrators presented their long-range desegregation plan to the district court. The architect of the plan, Assistant Superintendent McLaulin, insisted that his proposal incorporated "the most sound research evidence [available]."[41] In particular, he cited the historic 1966 study, *Equality of Educational Opportunity*, by James Coleman of Johns Hopkins University, and the subsequent 1967 report, "Racial Isolation in the Public Schools," by the Civil Rights Commission. Taken together, these reports presented the largest core of statistical data and the most well respected sociological analysis of school desegregation that had ever been assembled. The reports' major finding was that racial inequities in school achievement were primarily a result of children's home environment, not school resources or government spending. Although the researchers demonstrated that black children achieved at a higher rate in desegregated schools, the "Racial Isolation" report cautioned districts to be aware of the dangers caused by white flight, which was exacerbating the "social, economic, and racial separation between central cities and suburbs." Relying on a selective reading of the statistical data and ignoring some of the more subtle points made by Coleman and his colleagues, McLaulin used these reports as the basis for Norfolk's new desegregation plan.[42]

An amalgam of research and resistance, the McLaulin plan opened with a revealing series of philosophical principles meant to prop up a program of more of the same. To begin with, the city's administrators rejected thoroughgoing desegregation of the district as a whole. Rather, they emphasized the need for a stable, effective educational program, which would offer each child "at least a substantial number of years ... in an optimally desegregated school." In practice, this translated into a system of neighborhood elementary schools that would participate in a "feeder system" with regional junior and senior high schools. The overriding objective at each level was to "provide the best educational opportunity for students of both races" by creating "schools with a predominant middle class milieu."[43]

At first glance, this new socioeconomic standard seemed both startling and refreshing. Norfolk's previous desegregation plans had not addressed economic issues at all, and it appeared that the district's new proposal might open a fresh avenue for progress. Unfortunately, however, Norfolk's administrators refused to see any long-term causal relationship between an individual's race and his or her economic status. Rather, district leaders simply looked at the city's population as it currently existed. "At this time," the administrators argued, there is "a high statistical correlation" linking whites to middle-class opportunity and blacks to working-class poverty. When viewed in light of the district's goal, this socioeconomic analysis yielded a profound result. "In order to achieve and maintain the benefits of desegregation," the district's leaders argued, each "school in the ... system must have a clear majority of white children." This requirement was necessary, the educators suggested, because the assignment of "white children to a predominantly Negro school would not foster equal educational opportunity for either race." In fact, the district was offering only a slight alteration to its existing desegregation policy. Although the old freedom-of-choice program was to be officially ended, the district's new feeder system placed a strict limitation on black enrollment in predominantly white schools. The plan explicitly stated that black enrollment at integrated schools could not exceed 30 to 40 percent of the total enrollment. Administrators argued that this approach was the only way to provide the advantages of desegregation, without reducing white middle-class performance in the classroom.[44]

Two weeks after the announcement of Norfolk's long-range desegregation plan, the Justice Department and the NAACP filed objections to the proposal in federal district court. Jerris Leonard, an assistant attorney general with the Justice Department, attacked the Norfolk plan, calling it "a collection of gratuitous assertions about mixed questions of fact and law" that failed to provide for true desegregation. At the NAACP, Henry Marsh echoed Leonard's point. He complained that the principles put forward in Norfolk's assignment plan contained "an assortment of erroneous, misleading, self-serving, or irrelevant statements, which [we]re not proper" for inclusion in a school desegregation program. Attorneys with the Justice Department and the NAACP found little that they liked in Norfolk's proposal. Not only did it leave half of the city's elementary and junior high schools entirely segregated, but Norfolk's plan failed to present any commitment to balance the races at Booker T. Washington or the city's other high schools. In addition, this failure was further compounded by the fact that Norfolk had refused to make any substantive move toward faculty desegregation. Most schools in the system already had two racial minorities on staff, but the city had presented no plan to move beyond this low threshold of token integration.[45]

Following several months of protracted public debate, Norfolk's school desegregation case returned to district court on October 8, 1969. In a series of eleven extended hearings, including more than sixty hours of testimony, Judge Hoffman compared the school board's desegregation plan with a series of rival proposals made by the Justice Department's expert witness, Michael Stolee. "In the final analysis," Hoffman wrote, "there is one primary question to resolve. Does good faith implementation of governing constitutional principles require racial balancing in each individual school . . . where it is freely conceded that massive compulsory busing will be required to accomplish such racial balancing?" According to Hoffman, the NAACP and the Justice Department answered this question in the affirmative, while the school board, with whom he agreed, contended that the answer was no.[46]

Hoffman's framing of the case, however, was disingenuous, revealing his rather obvious support for the school board and its long-range assignment plan. Under the school board's proposal, the majority of the city's elementary schools would remain entirely segregated, and junior and senior high schools would see little additional desegregation. In opposing this plan, the NAACP and the Justice Department argued that such a settlement hardly constituted what Hoffman called "good faith implementation of governing constitutional principles." Rather, civil rights attorneys insisted that the school board's proposal was a brazen attempt to maintain neighborhood elementary schools in spite of the Supreme Court's order that segregation be abolished "root and branch."[47]

Hoffman's support for the school board was not limited to his framing of the case, however. After hearing testimony from more than fifty witnesses in October and November, he took the unprecedented step of traveling to Cambridge, Massachusetts, to conduct a special hearing with the school board's star witness, Thomas Pettigrew, a professor of social psychology at Harvard University. The author of numerous books and more than seventy articles, Pettigrew was one of the nation's leading authorities on race relations and school desegregation. Having worked as a consultant for the U.S. Office of Education and the U.S. Commission on Civil Rights, Pettigrew had testified on behalf of civil rights groups in numerous cases across the country. In the Norfolk suit, however, he chose to support the school board, arguing that its plan had "a good chance" of achieving lasting integration in Norfolk. Although Pettigrew noted that the city's plan for elementary schools was the weakest part of the board's proposal, he opposed calls by the Justice Department and the NAACP for racial balancing in the city's schools. For his part, Pettigrew suggested that racial balancing flew "in the face of the best educational data" and would almost certainly result in white flight from Norfolk to the new suburban areas in Virginia Beach and Chesapeake.[48]

In contrast, NAACP attorney Louis Lucas argued that concerns about white flight were irrelevant. Although Vincent Thomas, John McLaulin, and James Bash of the Virginia Desegregation Center had each presented white flight as a major issue in Norfolk, Lucas said that the U.S. Supreme Court had addressed the issue in 1967, when it found that "the vitality of . . . constitutional principles cannot be allowed to yield simply because of disagreement with them." Interpreting this phrase for the court, Lucas argued that this statement clearly required Judge Hoffman to ignore all concerns about white flight and other forms of resistance to desegregation. The constitutional rights of his clients and their class could not be limited or delayed because of fears of opposition.[49]

Gordon Foster, the new director of the Florida School Desegregation Consulting Center, went even further. He complained that Norfolk's administrators were willing to relegate thousands of African American children "to the academic scrapheap" in order to prevent white flight and maintain the status quo. In highly charged language, he argued that the district's desegregation plan was actually designed to "take care of the middle class, the white children primarily, and as many black students as they can comfortably handle, which, parenthetically, [wa]s not too many."[50]

Michael Stolee, Foster's friend and the new dean of the School of Education at the University of Miami, presented two alternative desegregation plans for the court's consideration. The first, a short-range plan, called for

Norfolk's elementary schools to be divided into groups of three, including one black school and two white schools. Within each group, students would be bused to achieve a rough racial balance at each of the three schools. Then, from the elementary level, students would participate in a crosstown busing program to attend desegregated junior and senior high schools. Under Stolee's long-range plan, this assignment scenario would continue until Norfolk completed a new academic park, which was to be constructed over the course of the coming decade. The educational park would consist of a central complex for all of Norfolk's students in grades three through twelve. Every student would ride the bus to the central location, and the system would be entirely integrated.[51]

In an eighty-four-page decision, Judge Hoffman dismissed the Justice Department's Stolee plans, saying that they offered little of value to the children of Norfolk. For starters, Hoffman did not believe that any of the Supreme Court's recent rulings required racial balancing in the schools. In fact, Hoffman feared the effects of crosstown busing and racial balancing in Norfolk, suggesting that the city's middle-class residents might flee such a situation and move to Virginia Beach or Chesapeake. Such a development would leave "nothing left . . . [to] provide a solid basis for a sound educational system," Hoffman declared. In addition, he noted that it would cost the city $4 million to purchase a fleet of buses and a further $800,000 annually to operate a transportation system. Most of this money would come from local sources, Hoffman argued, and it seemed obvious that such a large expenditure would have a negative impact on funding for classroom teaching.[52]

On the other hand, Hoffman found the local desegregation plan more than satisfactory. "The good faith of the School Board cannot be questioned," he said. For more than a decade the members of the board had worked with local administrators to integrate the schools, and much progress had been made in Norfolk. Citing the testimony of Pettigrew, Hoffman argued that the school board had presented an "intelligent approach . . . to the problem of desegregation" that took into account "social class" and not solely the "mixing of racial bodies." Based on such beliefs, Hoffman issued an opinion in favor of the school board on December 30.[53]

The Justice Department and the NAACP quickly appealed Judge Hoffman's ruling, and on June 22, 1970, the Fourth Circuit Court of Appeals issued a six-to-one decision overturning the district court's opinion. Citing statistics from the current school year, Judge John D. Butzner found that more than 80 percent of Norfolk's elementary students attended schools that were effectively segregated. By itself, this statistic proved that Norfolk continued to operate "a dual system of schools," and Butzner complained that the district's most recent desegregation plan offered few improvements. Under the school board's new proposal, at least thirty elementary schools, four junior high schools, and one high school would have enrollments that were 98 to 100 percent single race. In short, the court declared, Norfolk was not doing enough to create a unitary system as was required by federal law. "Instead it effectively excludes many black pupils from integrated schools on account of their race, a result which is the antithesis of a racial unitary system." The Fourth Circuit Court remanded the case to Judge Hoffman and gave specific instructions requiring that the school board submit a new desegregation plan by July 27. "The plan may be based on suggestions made by . . . Dr. Michael J. Stolee," the court said, "or on any other method" that may be expected to provide a unitary system by the time classes began in September. "With respect to elementary and junior high schools," the court told Hoffman, "the board should explore reasonable methods of desegregation, including rezoning, pairing, grouping, school consolidation, and transportation." At the senior high level, the court ordered that Norfolk must "immediately desegregate" Booker T. Washington and the other high schools in the city. In addition, the court ordered that the city provide free transportation for students seeking a majority-to-minority transfer option, while simultaneously integrating all faculties so that the racial ratio in each school "shall be approximately the same as the ratio throughout the system."[54]

When the Fourth Circuit Court released its opinion in the Norfolk case, local citizens quickly divided over the issue. Many African American leaders were elated with the decision. City councilman Joseph Jordan said that the "court was able to look through the hypocrisy of the Norfolk school plan" and see it for what it was — a brazen attempt to avoid integration.[55] On the other hand, Mayor Martin expressed the view of many whites in Norfolk when he said that the city was now in a "very desperate situation."[56] As George Hebert, the editor of the editorial page at the *Ledger-Star,* explained, the appellate judges had "given the School Board and the District Court . . . only a month in which to create and present a new [desegregation] plan." To Hebert and many other people, this simply seemed too short a time for the administration to create anything resembling the "meticulously researched [and] carefully devised" plan the school board had approved the previous winter.[57]

In fact, the members of the school board and local administration took every possible step to counteract the circuit court's ruling. On June 25, the board voted unanimously to appeal the court's decision to the U.S. Supreme Court. When the Supreme Court refused to hear the case four days later, the school board was forced to try another tactic. Working with the members of the district's administrative team, the board met during the month of July to produce a new desegregation plan that provided a slight alteration to its earlier proposal. The new plan retained neighborhood elementary schools in order to keep young children close to home. At the same time, the plan called for a feeder system to desegregate eight of the city's ten junior high schools, and a geographical zoning system to integrate all five of the city's senior high schools. In light of Norfolk's segregated housing patterns, however, the board conceded that sixteen of the city's elementary schools would remain all-black, and nine would remain all-white.[58]

When the school board filed its plan with Judge Hoffman on July 27, it also submitted two of Michael Stolee's proposals to illustrate its opposition to the crosstown busing program he suggested. Toy Savage, the board's lawyer, obviously hoped that Judge Hoffman would continue his long-running support for the school board in opposition to the federal government and its dreaded Stolee plan. At a pretrial hearing, however, Hoffman reluctantly informed the board that its neighborhood assignment plan for elementary schools flew "directly in the teeth" of what the Fourth Circuit Court seemed to want. "It would be unfair of me," Hoffman told the board's attorney, "to say . . . that the plan submitted for elementary schools could possibly pass muster" with the appellate court. Hoffman noted that Judges Simon Sobeloff and Harrison Winter had submitted a concurring opinion in the recent Fourth Circuit case, calling the concept of neighborhood schools a "shibboleth" that prevented true desegregation. Although Hoffman "was in direct conflict" with this interpretation of neighborhood schools, he believed that Norfolk's new elementary plan had no possibility of approval and ordered the district to prepare a realistic estimate on busing. "I might come up with a neighborhood school plan for grades 1 and 2," Hoffman told the board, "and shift grades 3, 4, 5 and 6" through a busing program.[59]

As Judge Hoffman struggled to enforce the wishes of the Fourth Circuit Court, he also allowed six parents with the Concerned Citizens of Norfolk to intervene in the city's school desegregation case. Formed in July, the Concerned Citizens was a white anti-busing group that opposed crosstown transportation as a means to achieve racial balance in the schools. Although its lawyer, Marshall T. Bohannon Jr., submitted no desegregation plan of his own, the group asked that Hoffman throw out the school board's proposal because it "requires children of all ages to attend schools distant from their homes solely because of their race." This proposal was discriminatory, the Concerned Citizens argued. "In an apparent effort to secure to one class of people its constitutional rights, it violates the rights guaranteed by the Ninth and Fourteenth Amendments of the Constitution to the other classes." In light of this violation, Bohannon asked that the "Norfolk School Board be directed to assign children to the school closest to their homes."[60]

When the *Beckett* case finally returned to court on August 11, Judge Hoffman considered the school board's plan and three other proposals in a twelve-hour hearing that lasted late into the evening. The first counterproposal came from the NAACP, which put forward Michael Stolee's comprehensive desegregation plan calling for racial balance through a citywide busing program.[61] Second, the Justice Department suggested a revised Stolee plan, which was designed by Robert T. Morris, an Atlanta program officer with the Department of Health, Education, and Welfare (HEW), whom Judge Hoffman ridiculed as "a numbers man, just like the rest of them." According to Morris's proposal, the government accepted Norfolk's secondary assignment plan, but called for more integration and crosstown busing at the elementary level. Finally, members of the Concerned Citizens of Norfolk entered their opposition to all the plans. Although they put forward no proposal of their own, the Concerned Citizens asked Judge Hoffman to order the school board to implement an assignment plan based on neighborhood schools and freedom of choice.[62]

In a second day of hearings on August 12, Judge Hoffman approved Norfolk's proposal for limited busing at the junior and senior high school levels. The school board's plan called for significant racial mixing and the construction of a new Booker T. Washington high school on or near its present site. Having dealt with the secondary level, however, Hoffman turned to the more complicated issue of the city's elementary schools.[63] "Because of the gun at my back," Hoffman told the audience in his courtroom, "we must go into some type of grouping [and busing]" at the elementary level. In his official order, released on August 14, he placed fifteen elementary schools into five groupings of three schools each. Each grouping included one black and two white schools, with all students in grades one through four assigned to the former white schools and all pupils in grades five and six assigned to the former black school. School board chairman Vincent Thomas said that these groups would "strain the capacity" of the city's public busing line "to the utmost," but he promised that school officials would do all they could to ensure that school went forward as planned in September.[64]

AS THE FALL grew near, there was a lot to do. Schools in Norfolk were scheduled to open exactly three weeks after Judge Hoffman's August ruling, and transportation plans still had to be finalized. Under the school board's new court-ordered desegregation plan, roughly 12,000 of Norfolk's 56,000 students would ride buses to school. Although this figure seemed to present only a slight increase from the previous year, when 8,000 students rode buses to school, in fact the number of morning bus trips had grown from 115 in 1969 to 275 in 1970.[65] This increase in bus riding was particularly difficult to plan, since Norfolk had no yellow bus system of its own. Students were forced to pay $5.00 a month to buy "school tickets" from the Virginia Transit Company (VTC), which operated the local bus line. At a quarter a day for round-trip fare, students were receiving half-price tickets. Still, the cost of the tickets was disturbing, especially for disadvantaged parents who had trouble paying for them. Rev. Frederick M. Ritter Jr., pastor at St. Mathias Lutheran Church, joined with other religious leaders in the city to encourage the school board to provide funding for indigent parents. As an example, he told the board about the case of Carlena Jackson and her husband, who was a $68–a-week city garbage truck driver. The couple had five children, ages six to eleven, who formerly attended Bowling Park Elementary School a few blocks from their home. Under the new busing program, however, Jackson had to keep her children at home because she could not afford the tickets that were required to bus her children to Pine Ridge Elementary School every week. And Jackson was not alone. As an indication of the widespread poverty across the district, school officials noted that 17,406 children were receiving free and reduced lunches in Norfolk. Still, these children were required to pay for their own busing or provide their own transportation if they attended a school beyond their neighborhood borders.[66]

Despite the financial hardship created by the busing system, planners could not escape the fact that some 12,000 students would be riding buses

When court-ordered busing for desegregation began in 1970, the city of Norfolk had no yellow bus system. Pictured here is a city bus featuring the "Back to School, Keep It Cool" logo from September 1970. (Courtesy of the *Virginian-Pilot*)

in the fall. This required that the school administration work with the VTC to stagger school openings so that enough buses would be available for public use. The school board ultimately decided upon a plan that opened high schools at 7:45 in the morning, junior highs at 8:30, and elementary schools at 9:15.[67] Because of the rushed planning job, however, Sam Ray Jr., an assistant superintendent for general administration, told the press that there was "bound to be some confusion . . . and overcrowdedness at some places." He urged parents and students to "remain patient so that we can settle these problems and establish a normal routine as soon as possible."[68] School administrators established a telephone hotline to answer parents' questions, and the district worked with the Citizens Advisory Committee (CAC) to develop a public relations campaign to encourage compliance and patience. "Back to School, Keep it Cool" was the slogan the CAC selected to place on billboards and advertising strips around the city.[69]

As local officials worked to implement Norfolk's new busing program, a group of disgruntled white parents lashed out against the plan. "Call it prejudice. Call it racism. Call it whatever you want to. My daughter's not going to Booker T. Washington High School," one of the parents said.[70] Led by the Ingleside Civic League and its president, Jack Q. Lewis, this group of angry protesters included parents from six other civic leagues: Coleman Place, River Oaks, Sewells Point Road, Lansdale, North Fox Hall, and Easton Place. Together, these organizations formed a new private school called Eastern Academy. The school originally met at Fox Hall Baptist Church and enrolled 500 students in grades eight to eleven.[71]

In fact, private schools in Norfolk and the greater Tidewater region were bursting at the seams. Helen Walker, director of the Carolton Oaks School, said she had received "hundreds and hundreds of telephone calls" from parents seeking to avoid crosstown busing. Her school was full though, as was Tidewater Christian School. There, Mrs. Harold Richards, the principal, noted that she did "not feel equipped to handle the problem" of integration. Her school was all-white, as was the American Christian School and many of Norfolk's other private institutions. The oldest and most prestigious private school in Norfolk was desegregated, however. Norfolk Academy had admitted a handful of African American students, but headmaster James Massey insisted that they were "well-qualified" to handle the rigorous curriculum at the school.[72]

There were certainly many whites in Norfolk who wanted to forget about racism and the discrimination of the past — at least when it suited their own purposes. For instance, William Carol Baskett Sr., a local tax attorney, wrote to the *Virginian-Pilot,* suggesting that federal judges issue a new standard order in public school cases. "The school board . . . shall forthwith destroy all records and traces thereof relating to the race, religion, and national origin of each and every child presently attending public schools in their district."[73] Baskett's fictitious order was wrapped up in the new color-blind ideology that many of the South's white residents adopted, as busing threatened to end the "splendid isolation" of white middle-class neighborhoods. While it is not clear what Baskett's own racial views were, he argued that race-conscious desegregation plans and crosstown busing were not appropriate ways to end the legacy of discrimination in the South. Rather, he sent his own children to Norfolk Academy, where they enjoyed the small luxuries of white middle-class privilege. For the rest of the city's residents, especially its African Americans, Baskett called for forgetfulness and erasure. There was to be no apology for the decades of educational and residential discrimination, no period of reconciliation or effort to offer a helping hand to those less fortunate. It would be impolite to raise the fact that white racism had left the city a fractured patchwork of public housing projects and edgewater enclaves of elitism. Now that busing had appeared as a means to suture the racial and economic divide, whites such as Baskett grasped on to the color-blind ideology with a newfound appreciation for all it offered.[74]

DESPITE THE CRITICISM of Baskett and others like him, Norfolk's schools opened on September 4, 1970, and enrollments increased following the Labor Day holiday. Although figures for the fifth day of class showed that roughly 2,200 fewer students were enrolled in September 1970 than had been on the books the same time a year earlier, Superintendent Lambert and school board chairman Vincent Thomas emphasized that 96 percent of the students had returned to school.[75] In fact, several white parents expressed their happiness with the way school was progressing. E. Randolph Fraser Jr., a resident in the Larchmont-Edgewater area, wrote to the *Virginian-Pilot* to report that his children "were in a better situation than ever before." Although the youngsters now attended a predominantly black school, they were pleased with their teachers and newfound friends. "Classes are smaller," Fraser reported, and there had been "almost daily meetings at the schools to fully acquaint parents with teachers and the system."[76]

Despite the few positive reports by residents like Frasier, most of Norfolk's white residents went on record against the city's new busing program. At the most mundane level, many whites complained about the changes taking place around them. Some students, like Bonnie Beckroge, noted that young people would face many new "hardships" in the schools they were being "forced" to attend. "I am being sent to an unfamiliar high school," she wrote, "where I will lose two club offices and the feeling of school spirit. Along with many others, I will be separated from acquaintances made in the past year. Athletic teams and cheerleading squads are being torn apart — all to satisfy the 'powers that be.'" Meanwhile, parents like Jeanne Callahan emphasized other concerns. The new school hours for elementary students were "inconvenient," she said, and would cause many difficulties. As a den mother for several young boys, she was concerned that the children would be "walking home around 5 p.m.," when it would be dark in the winter.[77]

These practical concerns were heightened by a series of incidences at local schools that became a cause célèbre in the city's newspapers. In a report to the CAC, Lt. David M. Blair, head of the city's Youth Bureau, explained that there was "a whole lot of tension" in the city schools. Blair cited the arrests of two adults for disorderly conduct, the charging of one student with the molestation of another, the expelling of two students, the treatment of several students for minor injuries at a local hospital, and a total of fifteen assaults in the first three weeks of class. Also highlighted in the report was a walkout by some 175 black Lake Taylor students who encountered two "anti-Negro" signs spray painted on front of the school. The first sign said "niggers go home," and the other was so obscene the papers refused to print it.[78]

Although most whites refused to use racial epithets in their public attacks on busing, critics of the new policy pushed forward with a variety of other tactics. The parents at Eastern Academy had their all-white school up and running by the fall of 1970, while the Concerned Citizens of Norfolk prepared an appeal in the city's desegregation case. In addition, the Larchmont-Edgewater Civic League went on record against the statements of resident E. Randolph Fraser Jr. and his friends. In a resolution adopted at a meeting of more than 100 parents on October 1, the league said that the "recent court-ordered assignment of children, including provisions for busing, goes beyond the requirements of the law, defies the concept of the neighborhood school and does not promote high quality education." Although there was a clear undercurrent of opposition at the meeting, civic league president Wilbur Marshall said that he thought there was a "general feeling that we have lost control of our schools." He and his supporters sent this message to the judges on the Fourth Circuit Court of Appeals and to their congressional representative, Republican G. William Whitehurst.[79]

There is no doubt that Whitehurst and the other members of Norfolk's political establishment got the message. Unlike their populist friend, state senator Henry Howell, Whitehurst and his colleagues took an outspoken position against busing. Not only did Whitehurst send a telegram to Chief Justice Warren E. Burger, asking for an immediate injunction "to forestall mass busing," but he often took to the stump during his 1970 reelection campaign to note that he was "categorically and emphatically opposed to forced busing."[80]

Despite his high-profile position on the matter, Whitehurst was not the only Norfolk political figure who opposed crosstown busing. The city's most senior state legislator, the debonair and popular Senator Edward L. Breeden Jr., said that he was "opposed to busing" no matter what the case.[81] In fact, it was hard to find a member of the city government who did not condemn busing and what it was doing to Norfolk. Most shared the opinion of Michael B. Wagenheim, a former chairman of the Norfolk School Board and veteran of the Aline Black controversy. Wagenheim wrote to the *Virginian-Pilot* in mid-September, suggesting that "carting a young child away from his neighborhood school a few blocks distant to another school miles away simply to achieve a numerical racial balance is not the answer. It is satisfactory neither to blacks nor whites."[82]

Many members of the black community were furious that whites such as Wagenheim would dare to speak on their behalf. For instance, Mrs. R. A. Linyear complained that such actions were an affront to black dignity and represented the long train of white paternalism that had dominated local politics for a century. It seemed strange, she said, that so many "white politicians find it necessary to speak for the black population against the busing of students. No white politicians spoke for the black population when black parents footed the bill for busing when its purpose was to maintain segregation." In hot prose that leaped from the page, Linyear emphasized that busing was "nothing new." "Only the reason has changed," she said. "This time we'll all be sacrificing for the good of us all."[83]

Although Linyear represented a large pro-busing majority in the black community, there were other points of view as well. For instance, in September 1970 a *Journal and Guide* reporter found that most of the residents whom he interviewed opposed crosstown busing. Audrey Shands, a sales clerk, said that she believed busing was a big problem. "I don't believe in busing for small children," she said. "It is too dangerous. . . . I prefer the neighborhood school concept for the very young." William Palmer, a dry cleaner, expressed another point. "Busing is for the birds," he said. "The money that will have to be spent c[ould] do more to give children quality education, which they really need." He wanted children to go to school in their own neighborhoods, where they could receive "quality education and integration without all the confusion."[84]

Despite this piece on popular opinion, Berkley's predominantly black Beacon Light Civic League issued a stern statement signed by its president, George H. Banks, which said that its members had unanimously adopted a special resolution in support of busing. "We cannot and we shall not allow the voice of fear and unreason to do damage to our children" the resolution read. "It is a source of disquiet and alarm to us that some civic associations in our city which represent areas of affluence and opportunity are urging citizens to adopt a 'stay at home' policy [for schoolchildren]." In contrast to many of the other leagues of the city, the Beacon Light group declared that it supported "the principle of busing to achieve a unitary school system."[85]

MOTIVATED BY CALLS for continued busing and greater integration, NAACP attorney Henry Marsh appealed the Norfolk case to the Fourth Circuit Court in October 1970. Marsh's brief complained that the existing assignment plan that had been approved by the district court failed to produce a unitary school system in Norfolk. "Notwithstanding 14 years of litigation seeking to end racially segregated education in the city's public schools," Marsh wrote, more than half of Norfolk's children attended segregated schools. Using the district's own enrollment figures from September 1970, the NAACP showed that twenty-one of fifty-five elementary schools in Norfolk remained 100 percent white or black; two of ten junior high schools remained 99 percent white or black; and three of five high schools had a minority population of 25 percent or less. "It is clear that the board's decision to limit desegregation of the high schools and of the other levels of education has been based in part on the consideration of the opposition of white and black parents and children." The NAACP reminded the appellate court that in its own previous rulings it had "laid to rest all notions that community opposition can defeat the equal protection rights of black children to receive an integrated education." To address the constitutional violation in Norfolk, the NAACP asked that the circuit court order the district court and the local school board to implement a version of the Stolee plan or another similar program that would immediately remedy the violation of their clients' rights and create a unitary district in Norfolk.[86]

As the NAACP appealed Judge Hoffman's decision, so, too, did the Norfolk School Board. In a succinct brief submitted to the Fourth Circuit Court, attorneys Leonard Davis and Toy Savage argued that the board had satisfied its obligations under the appellate court's previous order, issued on June 22, 1970, and the board's attorneys took direct aim at the argument presented by the NAACP. Complaining that the civil rights organization had apparently adopted a threshold of 25 percent minority enrollment as the determinant of an integrated school, the school board insisted that a 10 percent standard would be more appropriate. Obviously, this interpretation of the statistics favored the board, dramatically reducing the degree of racial mixing that was required for an integrated school. Even following this interpretation, however, the school board's desegregation effort proved to be insufficient. The best case that Davis and Savage could present was that 53 percent of the city's schools, with 64 percent of the city's schoolchildren, met the 10 percent threshold.[87]

Despite the district's rather modest showing, however, Davis and Savage pushed even further, arguing that Judge Hoffman's August order had "required [more] of the School Board" than the Fourth Circuit Court had directed. "The judgment of the District Court not only requires that all reasonable methods of desegregation be employed, as directed by this Court, but it goes further and . . . requires all of the integration that is possible." In doing so, the board argued, the order of the district court had gone too far. As proof, attorneys put forward more statistics to illustrate the effects that busing had already had on the city's school system. "Approximately 8% of the number of white elementary pupils in the Norfolk system in May, 1970, are no longer enrolled," the lawyers pointed out. This dramatic loss was the result of white flight from crosstown busing, they alleged. To halt white flight and return a sense of equilibrium to Norfolk, the board asked that the Fourth Circuit Court allow it to implement a plan that was "(1) educationally sound, (2) reasonable, [and] (3) in the best interest of the children irrespective of race."[88]

Although the Justice Department did not necessarily agree with the arguments presented by the school board, government attorneys submitted no appeal of their own. This did not stop the Concerned Citizens of Norfolk and other white parents, however. Reiterating the same argument in defense of neighborhood schools, the Concerned Citizens challenged Judge Hoffman's decision before the Fourth Circuit Court, demanding that crosstown busing be eliminated as an unconstitutional infringement on citizens' rights. Roy L. Burton, chairman of the organization, was also instrumental in the formation of a new national anti-busing group, which was called the United Concerned Citizens of America. "We will not take any stand which disobeys the law," Burton told the press, but he insisted that the new group meant to stop busing by any legal means necessary. To pay for their effort, parents in the organization sold green outdoor light bulbs throughout the fall to raise awareness and public support. Mayor Roy Martin bought one of the bulbs, as did the newly elected vice mayor, V. H. Nusbaum Jr., and city councilman Robert Summers.[89]

AS THE PARTIES in the Norfolk case filed their appeals, judges on the Fourth Circuit Court awaited the Supreme Court's decision in *Swann v. Charlotte-Mecklenburg,* one of the most important school desegregation cases of the period.[90] The facts giving rise to the *Swann* case were involved and somewhat complicated. Reduced to their most basic elements, however, they centered on a single, intractable problem: approximately 14,000 African American students in the Charlotte-Mecklenburg school district in North Carolina attended schools that were either totally black or more than 99 percent black. Although lower federal courts had already suggested several solutions to the continuing problem of racial segregation in the district, the question before the Supreme Court was whether (and to what degree) federal courts were authorized to produce remedies for state-imposed segregation. In a unanimous decision that resulted from extensive negotiations between the justices, Chief Justice Warren Burger affirmed a lower court's opinion requiring the use of racial quotas and crosstown busing as a remedy for past discrimination. In short, the *Swann* decision was important because it recognized the broad and flexible powers that district courts had to remedy the wrongs of the past. Specifically, the Supreme Court ruled that mathematical ratios or quotas were legitimate "starting points" for desegregation; that single-race schools required close scrutiny by the federal courts; that noncontiguous attendance zones were legitimate interim measures to desegregate districts; and that busing was a reasonable and justifiable tool to achieve greater racial integration.[91]

Following the announcement of the *Swann* decision on April 20, 1971, judges on the Fourth Circuit Court of Appeals asked that all attorneys in pending school desegregation cases, including Norfolk's, prepare briefs that addressed their local situation in light of the Supreme Court's recent ruling.[92] The appellate court then heard arguments in these cases on June 7, but there was little doubt about the way the court would rule. In a per curiam order issued three days later, the court vacated and remanded cases from Norfolk and Roanoke, Virginia; Orangeburg County, South Carolina; and Winston-Salem, North Carolina. "It is now clear," the court declared, "that in school systems that have previously been operated separately as to the races by reason of state action, 'the district judge or school authorities should make every effort to achieve the greatest possible degree of actual desegregation, taking into account the practicalities of the situation.'" Accordingly, the circuit court established a timeline for each district judge to implement in his or her own jurisdiction so that compliance with the *Swann* decision would begin in September 1971. In the Norfolk case, the local school board was ordered to submit a new desegregation plan on or before July 1. The circuit court suggested that Norfolk's plan could be based on a revision of the Stolee plan or some other plan that would meet the requirements of *Swann*. Following the submission of the plan, all other parties were to file responses by July 9, and the district court was to conduct a hearing on or before July 16.[93]

Events in the busing drama proceeded faster than any of the local actors could have predicted. Following the circuit court's decision in early June, Assistant Superintendent John McLaulin worked with the school board to develop a new desegregation plan, which was submitted to the district court on July 1. The new plan offered a variation on the Stolee proposal that had been presented two years earlier. In particular, it called for school groupings and crosstown busing to integrate every school in Norfolk, save one. Under the new proposal, elementary schools in racially homogeneous neighborhoods were grouped with different schools in other regions of the city. Within each group, students would be bused to achieve a racial balance at each of the schools. A similar idea, without the groupings, held true at the junior and senior high school levels, where integration would be achieved by busing students from different parts of the city.[94]

The school board's proposal was extremely controversial. In place of a program that required roughly 12,000 students to ride buses in 1970–71, the new plan called for the transportation of some 24,000 students, with approximately 18,000 riding city buses. All of these students would be required to pay for transportation — 25 to 35 cents a day — and that was not the least of it. The plan also provided for a series of noncontiguous elementary groupings that infuriated parents throughout the city. In particular, white parents who lived along the northern and eastern borders of Norfolk complained that their children were being grouped with African American students who lived in distant neighborhoods in the downtown district. For example, one attendance area grouped white students who attended Pretty Lake and East Ocean View with black students who attended the Lott Carey School in downtown Norfolk. First and second graders in this attendance zone were assigned to Pretty Lake and East Ocean View, while students in grades three through six were assigned to Carey. Ignoring the concerns of many African Americans, white parents complained that this plan would require their children — some as young as seven — to ride the bus more than twenty miles a day to attend school in the midst of a series of public housing projects.[95]

Many African American parents shared the concerns of their white counterparts, but the region's black leaders insisted that crosstown busing was the only way to desegregate the schools. Speaking for members of the Norfolk Committee for the Improvement of Education, Vivian Carter Mason gave her full support to busing. "There is the usual annoyance of having to get up earlier," she told a reporter from the *Virginian-Pilot*, "but many Negro parents are willing to accept these inconveniences and the financial burden . . . because they feel their children are getting a better education."[96] Indeed, Mason's support for busing became even more critical in June 1971, when she was selected to replace the lone African American representative on the school board, outgoing member Rev. Godfrey L. Tate Jr. Although Mason abstained from the initial vote on the district's desegregation plan, she became a vocal proponent of the effort to achieve meaningful integration in the city.[97]

Despite the support of Mason and other black leaders, Henry Marsh and attorneys with the NAACP filed exceptions to Norfolk's desegregation proposal on July 9. Citing the continued segregation of a single school, Tucker Elementary in Berkley, and the financial burden that would be associated with paying for crosstown busing, Marsh said that it was "unthinkable that the victims of discrimination [would] have to pay . . . now that the board has decided to desegregate."[98] Although these objections were significant, they paled in comparison to those submitted by the Concerned Citizens of Norfolk and some of their supporters. Lawyers for these groups insisted that the school board's plan was unconstitutional because it was based on race and would cause white flight from the district. In a hearing before the district court on July 15, Marshall T. Bohannon, attorney for the Concerned Citizens, emphasized this point, saying that the city's new desegregation plan would "guarantee that in a short time the Norfolk school system will contain only black students."[99]

Judge Hoffman was not in Norfolk to hear this penultimate round in the city's desegregation suit. During the last week of June, the chief judge of Virginia's Eastern District Court had traveled to San Francisco with his staff of three assistants to help federal judges there "clear up a backlog of draft cases."[100] In Hoffman's stead, U.S. District Judge John A. MacKenzie took control of the Norfolk case. A native of Portsmouth, Virginia, MacKenzie received his law degree from Washington and Lee University in 1939. After serving as an officer in the Coast Guard during World War II, he was named an associate judge on the police court in Portsmouth and later served as a member of the Virginia General Assembly. MacKenzie's tenure as a federal judge began in 1967, when he was named to the Eastern District Court by President Lyndon Johnson.[101]

MacKenzie's position on the Norfolk suit differed only slightly from that held by Judge Hoffman. Dismissing the majority of the objections submitted by the various parties to the suit, MacKenzie issued an eleven-page decision on July 28, approving an amended crosstown busing plan that provided for a unitary system without any single-race schools. He refused to order the city to assume the cost of busing, however. Free transportation was "a legislative prerogative," MacKenzie insisted, and was "not the proper subject of judicial fiat." With that said, it immediately became clear to parents throughout the city that crosstown busing and major changes in local school assignments would be implemented over the course of the next six weeks.[102]

AS THE FEDERAL district court approved the basic outlines of Norfolk's new desegregation plan, many local whites took an active role in the anti-busing movement. To begin with, on July 14 dozens of parents met at the school administration building, where they protested against the expense and inconvenience of busing. One of their picket signs read, "I want quality education, not manipulation," while another declared simply, "Busing is the first step to a dictatorship."[103] Local residents of the Bayview area expressed similar feelings one week later. On July 21, more than 1,000 neighborhood parents attended an anti-busing rally at Bayview Elementary School, where they heard from numerous speakers, including Morton Fleet, the president of Tape City stores.[104]

Then, on Monday, July 26, anti-busing protests resumed at the Veterans of Foreign War (VFW) post in Ocean View. There, Morton Fleet chaired a meeting of some 160 anti-busers who joined together in a new organization called Save Our Neighborhood Schools (SONS). The participants in the organization quickly elected a twenty-two-member board of directors and began planning for a regionwide recruitment effort. Fleet told reporters with the *Virginian-Pilot* and the *Ledger-Star* that SONS was opposed to busing and hoped to preserve the bedrock of the public education system, the neighborhood elementary school. In addition, he hoped that the new organization might unify the various anti-busing groups then taking root in Norfolk and the surrounding areas.[105]

As the members of SONS began their outreach program, the Norfolk

Hundreds of local residents joined Save Our Neighborhood Schools (SONS) in an effort to forestall court-ordered busing at the dawn of the 1970s. (Courtesy of the *Virginian-Pilot*)

Federation of Civic Leagues hosted a mass anti-busing rally on July 27 at Center Theater in downtown Norfolk. More than 1,800 people attended the event, which chairman Melvin W. Dize billed as the "Freedom Forum." As local residents arrived for the evening's activities, they found a surreal scene depicted in front of them. Eleven dolls stuck with voodoo pins were arrayed across the stage; nine black-gowned dolls represented the justices of the Supreme Court, while one black and one white doll represented the local population. Dize intended the audience to discuss the topic, "To Bus or Not to Bus: That Is the Question." But many of the invited speakers, including Mayor Roy Martin and school board chairman Vincent Thomas, objected to the question. Thomas insisted that the school system had already submitted its assignment plan for the coming fall and that the federal district court was in the process of approving it. "Whether you like it or not," Thomas told the audience, "we are going to have a plan similar to the one presented to the court." Despite his insistence, however, the crowd responded with a swift and resounding, "No! No! No!"[106]

Emboldened by the growing opposition to busing, members of the Concerned Citizens of Norfolk announced that they would appeal Judge MacKenzie's ruling to the Fourth Circuit Court of Appeals.[107] In their effort, they received a good deal of support from national and local politicians. In Washington, President Richard M. Nixon announced in early August that he wanted federal law enforcement agencies to scale back on busing. "I have consistently opposed the busing of our nation's school children to achieve a racial balance," Nixon said, "and I am opposed to the busing of children simply for the sake of busing." The president directed Attorney General John Mitchell and HEW Secretary Elliot L. Richardson to "work with individual school districts to hold busing to the minimum required by law."[108]

Meanwhile, at the local level, almost every white politician representing Norfolk took a stand with the region's new anti-busing forces. U.S. representative G. William Whitehurst and state senator Stanley C. Walker reiterated their oft-quoted statements against busing, while Walker's colleague, state senator Peter K. Babalas, took the issue even further. Issuing a hotly worded condemnation of crosstown busing, Babalas went on to attack the Norfolk School Board for "throw[ing] in the towel" in the city's federal busing suit. This complaint resonated with local leaders in Norfolk, including Mayor Martin and the members of the city council, who asked the school board to appeal the busing suit to the Fourth Circuit Court.[109]

Despite the tremendous pressure being exerted on the school board, its members refused to act until a new procedural opportunity presented itself on August 15. That evening, President Nixon announced a ninety-day freeze on wages and prices, meant to curtail inflation and restore confidence in the nation's sluggish economy. Four days after the president's announcement, Norfolk's city attorney, Leonard Davis, informed the school board that the price freeze would likely affect a recent agreement the city had made with the VTC. Specifically, Davis said that the private busing company would not receive a five-cent increase in one-way fares that the city council had approved for student transportation. This meant that the VTC would refuse to transport the 18,000 students it had agreed to carry earlier in the year, since the company needed a fare increase to sustain its operations. Although the members of the school board recognized the seriousness of the situation — Norfolk still had no yellow bus system — they also understood the opportunity this crisis afforded them. On August 19, they voted five to one to use the president's price freeze as the basis of a legal filing in which their attorneys would request that Judge MacKenzie vacate his order requiring the implementation of a new busing program.[110]

Henry Marsh and attorneys with the NAACP fervently opposed the school board's request. Nevertheless, Judge MacKenzie lifted his busing order on August 25, allowing Norfolk to return to its 1970–71 assignment plan. Or so it seemed. The NAACP quickly appealed MacKenzie's opinion to a special three-judge panel of the Fourth Circuit Court, which was meeting in Alexandria. Judges Albert V. Bryan, John D. Butzner, and Baxter Craven overturned MacKenzie's decision on September 2, insisting that Norfolk move forward with the assignment plan that had been approved by Judge MacKenzie on July 28.[111]

Following the decision by the Fourth Circuit Court of Appeals, Norfolk's leaders made one last ditch effort to delay implementation of the new busing program. For his part, Mayor Martin sent a desperate telegram to President Nixon, requesting that he assist the city in its "impossible situation." Not to be outdone, Vincent Thomas flew to Washington, D.C., by private plane with the school board's attorneys in tow. On September 3, Thomas presented a petition to Chief Justice Warren Burger, requesting a swift review of the Norfolk case. With the Supreme Court in recess until October, it took the chief justice only two days to deny Norfolk's filing for a stay in the city's busing suit. With this decision finally in place, Norfolk's leaders realized that they must find a way to make busing work, at least in the short run.[112]

WHEN NORFOLK'S schools finally opened on September 15, after a weeklong delay, the chaos and confusion of the initial days exceeded that of the previous year. The VTC was one of the weakest links in this social experiment. Under a revised agreement with the city, it was supposed to convey the majority of the 24,000 students who needed transportation, but many of these students never got onto buses. Hundreds of young people waited endlessly at bus stops, only to have relatively empty buses inexplicably pass them by. As late as October 1971, the school district was forced to admit these inexcusable problems, which angered already worried middle-class parents, who viewed the transit snafus as yet another reason to flee to the surrounding suburban "cities" or to get their children into a private or parochial school.[113]

While students, parents, and teachers grappled with the maelstrom of emotions and dramas that came with crosstown busing,[114] Vincent Thomas emerged from the mess with his reputation boosted and his influence increased. Judge John A. MacKenzie, like his more celebrated predecessor, Walter Hoffman, saluted the school board leader and his noble efforts. In a decision dismissing a white parent's lawsuit against busing for integration, Judge MacKenzie singled out Thomas for special commendation, suggesting that "a monument" be erected in his honor. After all, to MacKenzie and his coterie, Thomas had stoically deferred, in form if not in spirit, to the unworkable and coercive dictates of the outside agitators in charge: the federal appeals court and the NAACP.[115]

Reading from MacKenzie's script, Vincent Thomas certainly played the sympathy card, portraying himself and his colleagues on the board as the victims of the unintended fiscal, cultural, and demographic effects of crosstown busing. At the September 30 school board meeting, which finally ratified Booker T. Washington's new resting place on Park Avenue between Princess Anne Avenue and Virginia Beach Boulevard, Thomas complained about the unfunded nature of crosstown busing. He cited what he considered the willful hubris of the appeals court and the NAACP, which both ignored the simple logistical problems that Norfolk faced because it had no yellow bus system of its own. The court and NAACP were dead wrong, Thomas argued, and now the school board was left in an impossible situation. Parents were complaining about their children being stranded at bus stops for hours; thousands of white students were fleeing the district; and organizations likes SONS were criticizing the board for "giving in" to the federal courts. The school board was not to blame for these developments, Thomas insisted; crosstown busing had been forced on the board against its better wishes, and now the city would simply have to live with the results.[116]

Despite the self-serving position that Thomas adopted, it is clear in retrospect that he and his allies bore a great deal of responsibility for the busing crisis they so eagerly condemned. By refusing to pursue a comprehensive desegregation plan and avoiding the adoption of a realistic transportation program, Thomas and the school board had created a difficult situation for the students they were supposed to serve. Indeed, statistics showed that more than 7,000 white students left Norfolk Public Schools between September 1969 and September 1971. Of course, Thomas insisted that the majority of the parents who moved their children from the district were "conscientious and sincere" people who were "genuinely concerned for the welfare of their children." Nevertheless, one month after the city's busing program began, Thomas called for an end to the "ruinous process" and put forward his own revised version of desegregation. It was just this mixture of frustrated resistance and inventive recapitulation that so endeared Thomas to the white citizens of Norfolk. Indeed, his efforts in September and October 1971 helped lay the groundwork for his successful run for mayor in 1976 and his subsequent campaign to reduce busing in the Reagan era.[117]

During the heyday of integration in the 1970s, Norfolk's civic oligarchy embraced not only Thomas but also even figures from the Massive Resistance movement. For instance, the former headmaster of the segregationist Tidewater and then MacArthur Academy, Hal Bonney, switched careers in his midthirties from secondary education to the law, and was ironically hired by Walter Hoffman to serve as a bankruptcy court judge in 1971. In the late 1980s, Bonney presided over the bankruptcy hearings of the *Journal and Guide,* one of his long-ago opponents. Upon the occasion of his retirement from the bench in 1995, the *Pilot* discreetly avoided any mention of Bonney's earlier arch-segregationist stance or his abusive behavior toward members of the Norfolk 17. Only in the new century with the commemoration coming near did Judge Bonney finally confess to his deep shame about his youthful extremism. In contrast, his more refined partner, James G. Martin IV, never came to regret his 1950s positions and even chided Mayor Roy Martin for being too liberal in reference to a wide array of social issues, including race. Yet like Bonney, Martin became a local judge, serving on the Juvenile and Domestic Relations bench with the full support of the local Democratic machinery. His former leadership of the Defenders of State Sovereignty and Individual Liberties was not held against him in any way; after all, it was the same decade that the creator of interposition, James J. Kilpatrick, gained celebrity status as the conservative foil on CBS's *60 Minutes.*[118]

Ironically, given their embrace of Bonney and Martin, the city's establishment briefly adopted a new, positive spin on their role in the busing controversy. This new "success story" seemed all the more plausible because of recent accomplishments in Norfolk. Vincent Thomas, the longtime head of the school board, was appointed to the State Board of Education in 1972 and then elevated to its chairmanship three years later. At the same time, Norfolk's assistant director of human resources, Martin Mendelsohn, proclaimed that race relations in the port city were improving as students, parents, and teachers adjusted to the new racial mores of the 1970s. Finally, there was the opening of the new $8 million Booker T. Washington High School in 1974 and the dismissal of the interminable *Beckett* suit in February 1975, which ended the era on a optimistic note.[119]

As the *Virginian-Pilot* and *Ledger-Star* accentuated the positive, inevitably noting the arrival of every new school year with a panegyric on the "calm and quiet" of Norfolk schools, the city's opinion makers insisted that Norfolk could "count itself fortunate" that it was no Boston, Chicago, or Las Vegas. The city had sailed through the dire straits posed by busing and desegregation without much of the unpleasant violence in other cities. Its teachers even refused to strike as their northern materialistic colleagues had done. This calm before the storm did not last, however; it would be just a few years until the competing sides clashed again and the official story on busing soured. In fact, the roots of the new round were already well in place. As Vincent Thomas assumed the reins of state authority, and the *Beckett* suit passed into the history books, Virginia Beach outpaced Norfolk, becoming the largest school district in the state, revealing the trend of middle-class suburbanization that would soon confront Norfolk's civic oligarchy and shake them out of their congratulatory mood.[120]

CHAPTER SIX

COWARDICE
AND COMPLACENCY

THE ROAD TO *RIDDICK* AND RESEGREGATION, 1975–1987

THE TWENTY-EIGHTH anniversary of *Brown v. Board of Education* generated little fanfare in Norfolk on May 17, 1982. Businesspeople went to work as usual. Navy personnel reported for duty at their posts. And students attended classes throughout the city. Few people discussed the Supreme Court's historic decision or its implications for the new Reagan era. That evening, however, all this changed, as Norfolk Public Schools hosted the first in a series of hearings to discuss the end of elementary school busing for desegregation. From amid a crowd of several hundred citizens gathered at Diggs Park Elementary School, LeVera Forbes White approached the microphone. A middle-aged woman with high school children of her own, White opened her statement with a simple declaration. "I was one of the Norfolk 17," she began. "I fought hard . . . to achieve quality education" in Norfolk, and "I am totally against falling back on busing." Channeling the spirit of her friend and mentor, Vivian Carter Mason, who had died one week earlier, White insisted that crosstown busing was an essential element in the city's school desegregation program. "We do not intend to stand by," she told the city's representatives, "and watch our rights be infringed upon again."[1]

Despite the impassioned pleas of LeVera Forbes White and dozens of other African American activists, Norfolk's school board voted to end crosstown busing for elementary schools in February 1983. This controversial move was orchestrated by board chairman Thomas G. ("Tommy") Johnson Jr., a convivial patrician attorney with the prestigious downtown law firm Willcox and Savage. Johnson was a friend of Norfolk mayor Vincent Thomas, longtime head of Johns Brothers Incorporated, and businessman Josh Darden, scion of one of the region's most powerful and influential families. Together, Johnson, Thomas, and Darden hoped to restore the pro-business, pro-growth days of an earlier era in Norfolk. Emboldened by the success of President Ronald Reagan and his conspicuous retreat from the civil rights agenda, Norfolk's business leaders called for an end to many of the social experiments that had been tested over the previous two decades. In particular, Johnson, Thomas, and Darden focused on crosstown busing, which they portrayed as a vital threat to Norfolk's fiscal and social order. Busing was "universally disliked," Mayor Thomas said. It was eroding the city's tax base, driving middle-income parents from the school district, and making it harder to attract new residents and businesses. A cursory analysis of the city's demographics seemed to confirm what Thomas and other business leaders were saying. Since busing for desegregation had been introduced thirteen years earlier, the city's population had declined by more than 40,000, and Norfolk's school enrollment had plummeted from 56,000 to 35,000. "As you look at the future of Norfolk," Josh Darden told the *Virginian-Pilot,* "busing has to be taken into consideration." Without some alteration in the existing transportation program, Darden and his friends feared that middle-class professionals would continue to move to Virginia Beach and Chesapeake, taking their children and their tax dollars with them.[2]

The anti-busing position taken by Norfolk's leaders proved to be remarkably divisive. On the one hand, the school board and its business allies received support from working-class whites such as W. Randy Wright and his grassroots organization, the Norfolk Tea Party. Wright had deep roots in Norfolk. A graduate of Norview High School and veteran member of the "Lost Class of '59," he had formed the Tea Party in 1978 to protest the city's high tax rates. By 1981, however, members of the Tea Party were appearing at school board meetings to highlight the inequities they saw in the city's busing program. Headquartered in East Ocean View, Wright's group argued that the "burden of busing" fell disproportionately on working-class families in the city's eastern and southern neighborhoods. Well-to-do families on the city's west side rarely, if ever, bused their children to school. For this reason, Wright and his friends welcomed the school board's decision to eliminate elementary school busing; to them, the move represented a return to equity and reason in Norfolk's schools.[3]

On the other hand, most African Americans in Norfolk opposed the decision to end elementary school busing. Led by Norfolk State University's King E. Davis, head of the Norfolk Citizens Coalition for Quality Public

As the effort to end crosstown busing in Norfolk gathered steam during the early 1980s, the NAACP and other civil rights groups came to the defense of mandated initiatives for diversity. (Courtesy of the *New Journal and Guide*)

Education, and Bishop L. E. Willis, a prominent minister with the Church of God in Christ and principal stockholder in two local radio stations, local African Americans argued that crosstown busing was an essential element in Norfolk's school desegregation plan. Without it, they insisted, the city's elementary schools would be resegregated, with black enrollment topping 95 percent in many of the city's downtown schools. "Unless you want the political, legal, economic, and psychological liability for returning Norfolk to a racially segregated school system," Davis told the school board, "[you] must abandon the biased search for ways to eliminate busing." In a respectful, but determined tone, he insisted that the Norfolk Coalition would "accept no less than quality education, equal opportunity, and attention to the major problems within the school system."[4]

This chapter examines the causes and consequences of the school busing debate that erupted in Norfolk at the dawn of the 1980s. It focuses on local demographic, educational, and political issues, as well as trends in federal politics and policies. In the end, we argue that local and national developments converged in Norfolk to create one of the city's most dramatic periods of conflict. When the business community and its supporters on the local school board advocated an end to busing for grades K–6, civil rights activists immediately went to work to halt the move. The resulting struggle ultimately played out in a landmark legal suit, *Riddick v. School Board of the City of Norfolk* (1986), which was the first federal court decision to allow a school district to end busing for desegregation. It then fell to the leaders of Norfolk's civic and educational bureaucracies to prove that they could achieve the elusive goal of educational equality within a resegregated public school system.

IN FEBRUARY 1975, a new era in Norfolk Public Schools began when U.S. District Judge John MacKenzie dismissed the long-running school desegregation suit, *Beckett v. School Board of Norfolk* (1956–75). In his ruling, MacKenzie found that Norfolk's school system had met its legal obligations under the Fourteenth Amendment's equal protection clause. Specifically, he ruled that the district's administrators had dismantled the old segregated system that had defined the school district for more than seven decades. In its place, administrators had created a new unitary enrollment program that incorporated crosstown busing and other techniques designed to integrate and equalize the schools.

Key among the city's administrators was the new superintendent of schools, Albert L. Ayars. A native of Washington State, Ayars was born in the tiny town of Kettle Falls in 1917. He received his bachelor's, master's, and doctoral degrees in education from Washington State University, and had extensive experience as a teacher, principal, and administrator. He had even served as superintendent of schools in Spokane, Washington, between 1965 and 1972. But the quality that seemed to interest Norfolk's leaders most was Ayars's twelve years of experience as director of the educational department at Hill and Knowlton, a large public relations firm headquartered in New York City. When Norfolk's school board selected Ayars as the new superintendent in 1972, Chairman Vincent Thomas remarked that the local schools were in "need of public relations." Indeed, the night that Ayars and his wife arrived in Norfolk, they found that the house they were renting had been broken into, and the set of keys they expected to find had been stolen. Such was the welcome for this soft-spoken supporter of civil rights, who promised to bring an outsider's perspective to Norfolk and its schools.[5]

By September 1976, it seemed as though the affable Ayars had actually accomplished some reform. That month the local district implemented a $2 million contract with ARA Transportation Group, a Philadelphia-based company that provided yellow buses to large school systems around the country. Before this move, Norfolk had purchased its school bus services from Tidewater Metro Transit, which simply ran standard commercial buses for the city's schoolchildren. The move to ARA Transportation signaled the city council's tacit, if resigned, acceptance of the need for a new busing system.[6]

Despite appearances, however, many people in Norfolk still opposed busing and viewed it as one of the city's most important problems. On September 29, 1976, for example, representatives from the Norfolk-Chesapeake Board of Realtors met with Superintendent Ayars at the Lake Wright Conference Center to express their concerns about the school district and busing. According to Ralph K. Anderson, vice president of the realtors' association, and Joan Gifford, head of a local-issues committee, many naval personnel viewed Norfolk in a negative light. Gifford told Ayars that the realtors were "getting really concerned" about consumers' anti-Norfolk attitude. She emphasized that the public schools were at the center of the issue. Critics of the city hang their concerns "on busing," she said. "They'll say, 'I don't want my kids to be bused,' and it stops there." This concern was familiar to Superintendent Ayars, but he tried to reassure the realtors, urging them to shift the focus from busing to other educational issues. Recent improvements had been made to the facilities at local schools, he told the audience, and new programming had been introduced. For instance, the district was pioneering the use of nine-week elective courses, as it reduced class sizes and offered new practical courses on family life issues.[7]

In spite of the superintendent's sanguine portrayal of the school system and its offerings, Mayor Thomas was concerned about the persistent criticisms of the district. Elected in 1976, Thomas, the one-time school board chairman and president of the State Board of Education, had always been critical of crosstown busing for desegregation. He believed that it cost Norfolk too much money, drove middle-income families from the city, and paid few, if any, educational dividends. For these reasons, the mayor suggested that Norfolk begin a review of its busing program in October 1978. Meeting in an informal session with the city council and school board, Thomas emphasized that "many of the conditions which led to . . . [court-ordered] busing are no longer there." State-supported segregation had been wiped away, and Norfolk's school system had been declared unitary three years earlier. More important, Thomas declared, many of the parents in the city wanted to have their "5-year olds closer to home."[8]

When the mayor's proposal hit the press, it elicited a variety of responses. Locally, the president of the Norfolk Council of Parent Teachers Associations, Evelyn Johnson, liked the idea. "Right now, busing is the law," she said. "But, if we could comply with the law without busing, this would be fine." On the other hand, George Banks, president of the local National Association for the Advancement of Colored People (NAACP), said that he would oppose any "piecemeal reduction" of the city's busing program. He feared that such a move would result in resegregation of the schools and a heightening of racial tension in the city. Nationally, David S. Tatel, the director of the Office of Civil Rights, responded to Mayor Thomas's suggestion with a firm declaration of his own. Any attempt to reduce busing in Norfolk, Tatel said, would embroil the city in extensive litigation. "To say that Norfolk has lost a large percentage of its white, middle-income families to the suburbs is not unusual," Tatel told the *Ledger-Star*. "I think the city would be sadly mistaken if it thinks that by returning to neighborhood schools it could somehow be able to attract those whites back to the public school system."[9]

AS TATEL'S COMMENTS began to sink in, the busing controversy in Norfolk was pushed aside by a more demanding crisis. Put simply, discipline problems in the city's schools were running at an all-time high, and students were failing in unprecedented numbers.[10] The first inkling of trouble appeared in September 1976, when a seventh grader was stabbed to death at Jacox Junior High School during print shop. This was the first murder in the history of the district, and it opened a public debate about the safety of the schools.[11] The following year, there were several brawls in the parking lots at various high schools in the district, and administrators even considered a "last chance" school to remove unruly teens from everyday enrollment. School board chairman Joseph H. Strelitz disliked the idea, however, saying that the new school would soon be overcrowded due to the large number of miscreants in the system.[12]

By 1978, the discipline issues had reached a new threshold of concern. At an open house early in October, Marion DeSalvo, a Lake Taylor High

School parent and volunteer, told more than 200 parents that the school had become "a jungle." Two weeks before the meeting, fights between blacks and whites had broken out at the school, resulting in thirty-two suspensions and seven arrests. But, DeSalvo told the parents, the trouble ran much deeper than the occasional big-time fight. Children were smoking and drinking in the bathrooms. Food fights in the cafeteria were a daily occurrence. Fires had been set in several rooms. And there was little teachers and administrators could do about it without more help from parents.[13]

Discipline problems were not confined to Lake Taylor, however. In 1978–79, the Norfolk school system issued more than 13,000 suspension notices for a school population of 38,000 students. In addition, the district expelled 434 students, nearly twice as many as the previous year's total of 232. Alcohol and drug use were a real problem on campus, and teen pregnancies were on the rise. In 1977–78, 1,935 teenagers in Norfolk had babies of their own. Taken together, these various factors contributed to one of the district's most startling statistics: Norfolk consistently had the highest dropout rate in Virginia. More than 14 percent of the city's students left school during 1978–79 alone, and nearly one-fifth of Norfolk's high school students dropped out.[14]

Compounding the district's terrible showing on discipline and retention reports was a general sense that the "school system [was] not doing a satisfactory job" on academic matters.[15] On December 15, 1978, when the results of the new Virginia competency tests were released, Norfolk's scores ranked among the lowest in the state. On both the reading and the math tests, almost one-third of the city's tenth graders received failing grades. Making matters worse, a subsequent report issued by Superintendent Ayars showed that African American students failed at a rate almost four times higher than their white counterparts.[16]

In an effort to rectify the significant disparities between white and black achievement, the Norfolk School Board took dramatic action in December 1978. Board member Thomas Johnson said that the city was facing "a crisis" of unprecedented proportions, and must begin "operat[ing] on a crisis basis." In a heated session with Superintendent Ayars, the school board agreed to begin meeting twice a month, instead of once, and to devote the second meeting to educational issues only. The board then called on Ayars to take aggressive action of his own to ensure that Norfolk's scores improved. Specifically, the board encouraged Ayars to introduce new courses on test taking, to increase classroom time for basic skills (such as reading, writing, and arithmetic), and to initiate an immediate review of the controversial phase elective system, which allowed students to select their own nine-week courses.[17]

Although Ayars recognized that he was "under the gun," the superintendent was unwilling to paper over the particular problems that Norfolk faced or to play the fall guy. He told reporters that millions of dollars in federal funds had been spent to educate the city's disadvantaged students, but that the money had produced little in the way of results. "I think so far as academic achievement is concerned," Ayars said, "it would be very difficult to demonstrate a continuing positive impact." The superintendent attributed Norfolk's high failure rate and achievement gap to a number of social factors, which had little or nothing to do with the classroom. He pointed to student absenteeism, crosstown busing, half-hearted parental involvement, and urban poverty as the major issues driving down test scores. In short, Ayars said, "an effective way to educate many black children and other culturally deprived students still eludes the Norfolk school system."[18]

Many white teachers in Norfolk shared the superintendent's assessment. One in particular, Joyce Drew, went even further than Ayars was willing to go. A seventeen-year veteran at Norview High School, Drew sent an inflammatory letter to the *Virginian-Pilot,* portraying black teens as "swinger[s]," drug users, and fast-food workers who cared little or nothing for school. "Bless the School Board members who refrained from crying that the [Virginia competency] test was 'racially biased,'" she said. "It was not." If Norfolk's citizens wanted to turn the schools around, Drew told them that they needed to address the sexual irresponsibility of black teenage mothers and the apathy of their parents. What was needed, she declared, was a new emphasis "on families, on responsibilities, [and] on moral obligations." Teachers and principals could do little to assist students who came to school hungry, tired, and unprepared.[19]

When Drew's letter was published on January 7, 1979, it acted as accelerant on an already raging fire. At Norview, several students mounted a demonstration against the teacher, throwing food and calling for her job. Meanwhile, Bishop L. E. Willis called Drew a "racist" and demanded that she be fired. On the other hand, members of the Norview Parent-Teacher Association (PTA) presented the administration with a petition supporting Drew and her right to free speech. In the end, it was left to Superintendent

Ayars to resolve the issue. He characterized the situation as "highly explosive," and ironically decided to reassign Drew to a new position at the school district's central office.[20]

Although conservative African Americans in Norfolk thanked Drew for her "constructive criticism,"[21] the majority of the city's black community agreed with George Banks and the local NAACP, which characterized Drew as a major part of the black academic problem. Drew and teachers like her did not understand black students, Banks said, and they did not have the success of all children in mind. Faced with a school system that was failing black students in unprecedented numbers — and then blaming those students for their failure — the Norfolk NAACP hired Samuel Banks, a professional educator, to conduct a top-to-bottom analysis of the local school system. Banks, a coordinator of social studies at Baltimore City Schools, happened to be the brother of George Banks and a 1949 graduate of Norfolk's Booker T. Washington High School. In preparing his report, Banks conducted a fourteen-day analysis of the city's schools, met with Superintendent Ayars and his staff, and consulted with Herman Brown, a psychology professor at the University of the District of Columbia. On April 16, 1979, Banks presented a blistering twenty-three-page report to the school board, attributing the poor showing of black students on the recent standardized tests to "a fundamental lack of congruence and pertinence in Norfolk's curricula and instruction." More specifically, Banks said that the city's curriculum did not prepare students for the tests offered by the state. He was especially critical of the district's phase electives, which he characterized as "largely redundant, disjointed and, in a number of instances . . . [of] no pertinence to a school district with a broad spectrum of students with serious educational disabilities." Banks said that his conception of disjointed electives included courses such as, "'Let's Entertain,' 'Monsters,' 'Promises, Promises,' 'Madness,' 'From the Couch to the Cage,' 'The Human Rat,' and 'Who Are You.'" As an educator, Banks suggested that these electives be immediately curtailed and that a new, rigorous academic curriculum be introduced in their place. In addition, he called on Norfolk administrators to initiate a new "management system that ensures accountability . . . [and] effect[s] a working educational partnership with the local community."[22]

Superintendent Ayars found the NAACP report infuriating. It was "filled with factual errors," he said, and presented a "totally superficial study" of the Norfolk school system. Despite this criticism, Ayars insisted that the district had already implemented "virtually all of the recommendations" made by the NAACP. These rather contradictory and confusing statements were in many ways representative of the course that the school system pursued in confronting its problems. Between January and June 1979, the superintendent's office implemented a new set of rigorous academic standards, which established high expectations for reading and math proficiencies.[23] In addition, the district set strict rules defining each grade level and the number of credits necessary for promotion. These new policies resulted in two immediate outcomes. First, the district's ninth graders scored "dramatically higher" on state competency tests in the spring of 1979 than tenth graders had done only a few months earlier. Of more than 2,200 students tested, 84 percent passed reading, and 86 percent passed math. Despite this remarkable improvement, however, it soon became clear that good statistics came at a cost. The second outcome of the district's new academic standards was the creation of a massive new underclass of students who did not meet the requirements to take standardized tests or move to the next grade level. For instance, Norfolk's new classification requirements kept more than 730 ninth graders from taking the Virginia competency test due to academic ineligibility or absenteeism. This meant almost a quarter of the city's ninth graders did not even qualify to take the test for their grade level. The true impact of this policy became apparent in June 1979, when more than a third of Norfolk's 38,000 students failed to meet the requirements for promotion to the next grade level. Based on the new standards of classification, some students were actually demoted a grade. At the ninth-grade level, 69.9 percent of students failed. At Granby High School, 52 percent were retained; at Lake Taylor, 50 percent; at Maury, 60 percent; and at Booker T. Washington, 56 percent.[24]

Norfolk's unprecedented failure rates sent shock waves throughout the city. Many parents complained that local school officials were using their children as pawns in an accreditation game. And there were calls to fire the superintendent and sack the principals and teachers. Many people who had the means simply left the district. In September 1979, the school system registered its second largest enrollment decline in history, as 3,831 students — more than 10 percent of the city's enrollment — left Norfolk for private schools or another school system. A further enrollment decline the following year led many of Norfolk's residents to demand that action be taken to "save the schools."[25] One of the most interesting calls for action was a political advertisement put forth by Charles Poston, a Democratic candidate running for commonwealth's attorney. Poston was a Norfolk lawyer who had become disgusted with the local school situation. In September 1981, his campaign ran an advertisement entitled "Monday They Went to War." It pictured a small white child carrying a book bag, with a soldier's helmet on his head. The ad was simple but provocative. It read: "Monday they went to war. Well, maybe not to war . . . just school. You see, in Norfolk's schools today, our children seem to be learning less about how to read and write and more about violence, drugs, and sex." It was little wonder, Poston argued, that parents were "afraid to send their children to Norfolk's schools." His campaign conjured the image of a combat zone with racial tension seething below the surface in an effort to win the law-and-order vote. As the ad put it, "We can't have a positive influence on our school system or our children if we keep closing our eyes to the fact that there's a war going on in Norfolk's schools."[26]

City and school officials responded to the Poston advertisement swiftly and sternly. From the school board, Thomas Johnson said that the ad was "the height of irresponsibility." Mayor Vincent Thomas agreed. "The public should be very apprehensive about voting for someone who would make such irresponsible and exaggerated statements," he said. Indeed, George Raiss, the clerk of the school board, complained, "If the schools were a person, in my opinion this ad would be grounds for a suit of libel."[27]

Despite the harsh criticism presented in the Poston advertisement, many white parents in Norfolk viewed the school situation in much the same way that he did. At the grassroots level, Randy Wright and his allies at the Norfolk Tea Party argued that crosstown busing and lax standards of discipline had caused a precipitous decline in students' academic performance. Meanwhile, local attorney Alan S. Balaban complained to Superintendent Ayars that the city's busing program had created an "unconscionable situation" for parents in River Point, Talbot Park, and Wexford Terrace. Students in these white middle-class neighborhoods were bused to predominantly black, inner-city schools: Monroe Elementary and Campostella Junior High School. Balaban requested that these busing routes be revisited, since white parents in his area believed they had "no realistic alternative . . . but to send [their] children to private school."[28]

In fact, Vincent Thomas and Thomas Johnson were already working behind the scenes to redirect recent criticism of the schools and focus it on crosstown busing. Busing was not only a terribly unpopular social ex-

MONDAY THEY WENT TO WAR.

Well, maybe not to war . . . just school. You see, in Norfolk's schools today, our children seem to be learning less about how to read and write and more about violence, drugs and sex. And they're learning it on their own.

It's no wonder parents are afraid to send their children to Norfolk's schools, and are thinking about a private education in a better learning environment. It's no wonder teachers are increasingly reluctant to have any interest in Norfolk's schools beyond leaving them.

Of course, there are those who say our schools are safe, and that what goes on during the school day is just kids "being kids." The commonwealth's attorney seems to be one of them. Otherwise, why hasn't he been active in the prosecution of the misdemeanors our children and teachers talk about all the time.

Children don't know the difference between a misdemeanor . . . possession of drugs or assault . . . and a felony. Should they? Do we? Should the commonwealth's attorney make that distinction? Charles Poston doesn't think we can afford to.

Joe Campbell isn't going to do anything about the problem because he doesn't want to admit we have one. We can't have a positive influence on our school system or our children if we keep closing our eyes to the fact that there's a war going on in Norfolk's schools.

We can do something about the problem, and take the first step toward safer schools and a safer Norfolk on September 8. We can elect a commonwealth's attorney who cares. We can elect Charles Poston, so that next year, our playgrounds won't be war zones.

POSTON
COMMONWEALTH'S ATTORNEY.

Political Advertisement Paid for by Poston for Commonwealth's Attorney Campaign Committee, T. Matthews, Treasurer.

On September 3, 1981, Charles Poston, a candidate for commonwealth's attorney, ran this political advertisement in the local newspaper. (Courtesy of the *Virginian-Pilot*)

periment, they contended, it was driving middle-class whites from the city in unprecedented numbers. Citing figures from the public schools, they showed that Norfolk's enrollment had changed dramatically over the last dozen years. In 1970, the year that busing began, Norfolk's schools enrolled 56,830 students, of which 57 percent (32,586) were white, and 43 percent

(24,244) were black. By the early 1980s, however, the situation had changed dramatically. Total enrollment in Norfolk's schools had declined by more than 20,000 to 35,540. In addition, the racial composition of the school system had changed. Now, 58 percent of the students (20,681) were black, and 42 percent (13,327) were white. This meant that the city had witnessed a 59 percent decline in white enrollment in roughly a dozen years. Following a compelling if simplistic line of argument — which ignored the growth and appeal of suburban areas in Virginia Beach and Chesapeake — Thomas and Johnson blamed Norfolk's enrollment decline on their favorite bugaboo, crosstown busing.[29]

BY THE SPRING of 1981, a new political environment had developed in America, encouraging critics of crosstown busing to oppose it both openly and vigorously. Nationally, Ronald Reagan, a Republican conservative, had swept into the White House, bringing with him a new spirit of reform. A former Hollywood actor and governor of California, Reagan promised to cut taxes, reduce the size of the federal government, and rebuild America's military establishment. Although the president insisted that he supported civil rights for all Americans, he made no secret of his belief "that busing ha[d] been a failure."[30] In fact, at every key post in law enforcement and education, Reagan appointed individuals who shared his opposition to busing. The first and most important figure in this regard was his friend from California, Attorney General William French Smith, who claimed that court-ordered busing had "neither produced significant educational benefits nor won the support of most Americans."[31] Smith's assistant attorney general at the Civil Rights Division, William Bradford Reynolds, was even more emphatic about his opposition to busing. In testimony before a congressional committee in 1981, Reynolds told members of Congress that "compulsory busing of students in order to achieve racial balance in the public schools [wa]s not an acceptable remedy [to previous discrimination]."[32] Although this position was controversial, the new anti-busing mandate was quickly implemented, and the Justice Department settled two high-profile school desegregation suits without recourse to busing. In both cases, Attorney General Smith insisted that negotiated plans "maintain[ed] the neighborhood school system" for the good of the students and their families.[33]

The political transformation taking place on the national stage resulted in a heated, divisive climate in Norfolk. During the presidential election of

November 1980, for instance, half of the city's fifty-two precincts voted for the Democratic incumbent, Jimmy Carter, while the other half voted for Republican candidate Ronald Reagan. In Norfolk's twelve primarily black precincts, Carter received 93.5 percent of the vote, while in the city's predominantly white districts, most voters cast their ballots in favor of Reagan.[34]

Although few of Norfolk's citizens considered busing a major topic during the election of 1980, Reagan's sweeping victory emboldened the city's business leaders and put the busing issue back on the table. Five months after Reagan's inauguration, Mayor Thomas and his business allies initiated a new campaign to reevaluate crosstown busing. This was a large-scale strategic endeavor, which played out in a series of well-choreographed tactical maneuvers. The first move occurred in June 1981, when Thomas "railroaded through" the appointment of two anti-busing advocates to replace outgoing school board members, Joseph Strelitz and Catherine Brinkley. The new appointees, Jean Bruce and Robert Hicks, were both from the underrepresented east side of Norfolk, but they were appointed for very different reasons.[35]

Jean Canolies Bruce was a society-type who worked as an administrator with the United Way. A graduate of Maury High School and the College of William and Mary, she was a consummate insider who dressed well and looked professional. Bruce and her husband, John, a certified public accountant, lived in a beautiful home in Larrymore Lawns. A former member of the city's Planning Commission, Bruce had also served as president of the William and Mary Alumni Association and had helped design the school district's family life program, called "Directions for Living." In addition, she had family connections to some of the leading figures in Norfolk's political and business communities. Her brother, Leroy T. Canoles Jr., was a well-respected downtown lawyer who cofounded Kaufman and Canoles, one of Norfolk's leading corporate firms. Through her brother, Bruce was connected to Charles L. Kaufman, the former chairman of the Norfolk Redevelopment and Housing Authority; Henry Clay Hofheimer II, the "leader, godfather, and grandfather" of Norfolk's business elite; and Mason C. Andrews, Norfolk's vice mayor and chairman of the Eastern Virginia Medical School's world-renowned obstetrics and gynecological programs.[36]

At forty-three, Robert Hicks was ten years younger than Bruce, and he shared few of her contacts or experiences. He was an outsider — a big, bearded man who wanted to challenge the traditional power structure in

Norfolk. The owner of several fast-food restaurants, he worked as a certified public accountant and was a prominent member of his local PTA. Most important, Hicks was a member of the Norfolk Tea Party, which had secured a post on the school board by supporting the candidacy of Vincent Thomas in the election of 1980. As such, Hicks was a beneficiary of the quid pro quo that had been agreed to by Thomas and Randy Wright a year-and-a-half earlier. Now, this obscure eastside accountant, who had two young sons and a wife who worked in the public schools, could give voice to the frustration that fueled the Tea Party's opposition to busing.[37]

Despite the stylistic differences between Bruce and Hicks, they became two of the most important players in the city's controversial effort to eliminate elementary school busing. One month after their appointment to the school board, they joined their fellow members in electing Thomas Johnson chairman of the board. This maneuver was critically important. Not only was Johnson a well-connected and accomplished lawyer, but he had been studying the trends in school desegregation law for almost a decade. In recent decisions, Johnson found hope that Norfolk could scale back or eliminate large parts of its busing program without encountering significant legal problems.[38] In particular, the school board chief cited the recent settlement between the U.S. Justice Department and Louisiana's Caddo Parish School Board, which had minimized the transportation of school children.[39] "I'm not sure the rest of the board was as aware of the Louisiana situation as I was," Johnson remarked later. "I had been thinking there wasn't any direction you could move (to reduce busing). Then I thought maybe there [wa]s some room."[40]

Although few people in Norfolk recognized the significant changes taking place on the school board, Randy Wright, the head of the Norfolk Tea Party, believed that the board's new leadership might now be amenable to his criticism of busing. On August 10, 1981, Wright accompanied Al Horton, the Tea Party's education chairman, to a critical school board meeting about teacher pay and the problems facing the district. On the sidewalk outside the session, dozens of teachers carried signs protesting low salaries and poor benefits. Meanwhile, inside the meeting hall, Horton made a formal presentation to the board, highlighting the inequities that the Tea Party found in the city's busing program. "It is in the predominantly black areas of the city where the students are bused," Horton told the school board. "It is in the distant white, middle-income areas where the student exchange

Norfolk School Board chairman Thomas G. Johnson Jr. oversaw the end of crosstown busing for Norfolk's elementary schools in 1986. (Courtesy of the *Virginian-Pilot*)

takes place." Using colorful maps to illustrate the routes employed by the district, Horton claimed that the city's busing program protected children in the wealthy western neighborhoods around Ghent and Larchmont, while it placed the "the burden of integration on the black community and middle income white neighborhoods."[41]

The school board made no immediate response to the Tea Party's presentation, but a few weeks later Chairman Johnson called a special meeting of the board to address the district's agenda for the coming year. "I thought we ought to arrive at a consensus among ourselves," Johnson told the *Virginian-Pilot*, "as to what [we] should be doing." In a closed-door session on September 11, Johnson outlined his goals for the 1981–82 school year. He suggested that the district was facing a dire economic situation, which would require a reexamination of expenditures, especially where busing was concerned. "When I threw the idea out," Johnson said, "I was surprised by how likeminded we were." All the members of the board—with the exception of

Vice Chairman John Foster, who was absent — agreed that the principal objective for the coming year should be the reexamination of the city's busing program. As Cynthia Heide, a health care administrator and member of the board, suggested, the financial strain on the city required that some action be taken to cut expenses. "The primary concern is money," Heide told the *Virginian-Pilot*. With the city's teachers threatening to strike for better salaries, and many basic needs going unfunded, the expenditure of $3.9 million for the annual operation of the city's busing program was simply too expensive.[42]

There was more at stake than mere money, however. Taking an early position on the transportation issue, Jean Bruce claimed that "busing ha[d] been responsible for many middle-class families, both black and white, choosing to put their children in other school systems." Faced with a declining school population and a dwindling tax base, Bruce said that the school board could not afford "to lose any more families . . . because of busing. I'm not sure the number of children with black or white skin in a classroom is now the most important concern."[43]

When the school board convened in open session on September 17, Chairman Johnson announced that the top priority for the coming year was the development of a plan to "substantially reduce busing" for elementary school children. Johnson followed this announcement by establishing a special school board committee to direct the effort. Jean Bruce, who had been on the board a short two months, was selected to chair the new transportation committee, which included four other members of the board: Robert Hicks, the Tea Party opponent of busing; Hortense Wells, a retired African American teacher; John Foster, a local African American minister; and Johnson, an ex-officio member on all committees. Once established, the transportation study group wasted no time in getting to work. It quickly instructed the superintendent and administration to formulate a new attendance plan for elementary schools. In addition, the committee directed the administration to visit three cities where busing issues were then being decided: Shreveport, Louisiana; Nashville, Tennessee; and Richmond, Virginia. These site visits were to be conducted by November 1, so that any useful information could quickly be incorporated into Norfolk's new elementary school plan.[44]

In October, John McLaulin, the assistant superintendent for pupil support services, attended the sites selected by the transportation committee. Accompanying him were a number of other individuals, including school board member John Foster and administrator Dan Hagemeister.[45] In each of the selected sites—Shreveport, Nashville, and Richmond—McLaulin and his group met with different approaches to desegregation. Nevertheless, the Norfolk team found that all of the other districts had used magnet schools and middle schools in a way that might facilitate the reduction of busing in Norfolk. On November 19, McLaulin presented his findings to the transportation committee in the form of two preliminary plans to reduce busing in Norfolk. These plans called for the city's elementary schools to be redesigned so that they housed students in grades K–4 or K–5. Children in the sixth grade would be moved to a new set of middle schools with students in the seventh and eighth grades. This new design would reduce enrollment and overcrowding at the elementary level, thereby enabling the youngest students in the district to attend neighborhood schools within a mile-and-a-half of their homes. In addition, this move would free up several elementary school buildings, which could then be used as magnet schools. This new magnet program "would not serve gifted children exclusively," McLaulin suggested, "but could possibly include physical education, fundamentals, science, and other subjects." In short, these schools would be crucially important, since roughly eight of the new elementary schools would be all-black. The magnet schools would serve as a siphon for any student who was dissatisfied with his or her neighborhood school and wanted to attend a different location.[46]

As McLaulin and the school board's transportation committee devised a plan to reduce busing, African American community leaders joined forces to stop the move. In a heated school board meeting on December 17, King Davis, the impassioned professor of sociology at Norfolk State University, lit into the board. "Your efforts [to eliminate busing] are stimulating a climate that will make Norfolk a divided city," he said. As the first of many representatives from a new pro-busing group called the Norfolk Citizens Coalition for Quality Public Education (Norfolk Coalition), Davis declared his outright opposition to any program that would resegregate the elementary schools of the city. "Segregation was a psychologically painful and educationally deplorably policy for all children, parents, and for this community," he told the board. "The previous policy of school segregation was conceived, promulgated, promoted, and sustained by previous school boards, city councils, members of the state legislature, the former governor, and some citizens of this community." After fighting a long, hard battle to integrate the schools, Davis and his associates did not intend to go back to segregation.[47]

Despite the emphatic opposition presented by the Norfolk Coalition, a number of African Americans in Norfolk offered at least halting approval for the reexamination of busing. One of the most important figures in this regard was the Reverend John Foster, pastor at Shiloh Baptist Church, vice-chairman of the school board, and a member of the transportation committee. Although Foster was out of town when the board voted to make busing its top priority in September, later that month he acknowledged that the issue was worthy of study. "We need to look at it," he said, so that we can "hold down the funds we use for busing." At the same time, however, Foster insisted that he would favor the reduction of busing "only to the point that we can remain fully integrated."[48] He maintained this position throughout the fall, and once the initial proposals to reduce busing were presented in November, Foster pursued a difficult, middle-of-the-road position. On the one hand, he told the *New Journal and Guide* that "neither of the plans to reduce busing [wa]s acceptable." In fact, he said, both plans would "cause us to lose significant gains that we [have] made in the last 10 years."[49] On the other hand, at the school board meeting on December 17, Foster said that he believed the school board and the Norfolk Coalition had "more to unite us than divide us."[50]

The other African American member of the school board, Hortense Wells, did not find the busing issue to be nearly as complicated. As a thirty-year veteran teacher in Norfolk Public Schools, Wells had worked with Vivian Carter Mason and the Norfolk 17 during the school closures crisis of 1958–59. Despite this, she supported a moderate, some said accommodationist, position on race relations, becoming incredibly popular with white administrators in the superintendent's office.[51] From the beginning of the busing controversy in the 1980s, Wells was an outspoken supporter of Thomas Johnson and the effort to eliminate busing in Norfolk. She argued that the return to neighborhood schools would improve academic quality, parental support, and overall achievement. "One of the most important advantages of the neighborhood school is the parent involvement it fosters," she said. "In the best performing schools, there are always a lot of parents going in and out."[52]

Although Wells was ignored or belittled by members of the Norfolk Coalition, she received support from another group of African American or-

Earlean and Nelson White founded the Parental Involvement Network (PIN) to bring an end to crosstown busing. (Courtesy of the *Virginian-Pilot*)

ganizers who formed the Parental Involvement Network (PIN). Founded in January 1982 by Nelson and Earlean White, the parents of four children in Norfolk Public Schools, PIN argued that busing was "ineffective and unnecessary in the pursuit of quality education." In a letter to the editor that appeared in the *Virginian-Pilot,* Nelson White, a proud house painter and committed advocate for the common man, cited the "test scores of minority students" and the continuing achievement gap as evidence that "busing ha[d] been an academic failure." He then suggested that funds "used for transportation would be better spent upgrading the salaries of underpaid Norfolk teachers and on intensified special programs that could be applied within neighborhood schools without a racial stigma."[53]

White's letter was tinged with an undercurrent of anger and frustration. "It is now time for black people in leadership positions to stop calling everyone opposed to busing a racist, for the opposition includes many black educators and parents." White was particularly angry with the leaders of the Norfolk Coalition. He noted that some of them did not "even live in Norfolk" and argued that they were "out of step with the masses of people affected [by busing]." This was a recurrent theme that members of PIN returned to time and again.

Finally, White and his group argued that the end of busing did not mean that all black children would be doomed to a second-rate education. "Personally I have always resented the implication that my children would somehow be better students because they are in a classroom with children of other races. I regard this as a defeatist and beggar mentality," White said. "It has been proven in other cities that quality schools can be nearly 100 percent black. Isn't quality really what we are after?"[54]

DESPITE THE deep divisions in Norfolk, the school board's transportation committee voted on January 28, 1982, to move forward with its effort to eliminate elementary school busing. Jean Bruce, the committee's chairwoman, said that a "consensus" on the issue had been reached, and she asked school administrators to prepare a formal proposal along the lines suggested by John McLaulin. Specifically, the transportation committee asked for a plan that would accomplish three tasks: return all children in grades K–5 to neighborhood schools; assign students in grades 6–8 to middle schools; and establish a "fundamental magnet school" for students with basic needs. The committee asked that this plan be submitted by March 1, so that it could be presented to the public and implemented in September 1982.[55]

John Foster was the only member of the committee who dissented from the proposal. "We are moving very rapidly," he said, and "I don't think it's enough to take one idea and run with it without exploring others."[56] Foster's misgivings about the elimination of busing required that other members of the committee address his concerns. In fact, the transportation committee invited several outside experts to Norfolk during the winter of 1982–83 to discuss the busing dilemma and what should be done about it. The first of these experts, Ronald Edmonds of Michigan State University, suggested that high academic goals could be achieved in schools that were predominantly black. In addition, he encouraged the city to implement a program of fundamental education for low-level students. Sara Lawrence-Lightfoot of Harvard University agreed with Edmonds. In her presentation to the transportation committee, she emphasized the importance of parental involvement and close community support for schools. Although some people viewed Lightfoot's presentation as an endorsement of neighborhood elementary schools, she refused to take a position on the busing matter in Norfolk. Robert Green of Michigan State University was not so reticent, however. Invited at the specific request of John Foster and other black leaders, Green offered a scathing twenty-eight-page indictment that foresaw dire consequences if the school board retreated from busing and resegregated elementary schools. This jeremiad warned that the end of busing would "turn back the clock," increase racial divisions and inequity, and reduce black achievement levels by isolating poor students in single-race schools.[57]

With the experts seemingly divided, the Norfolk Coalition called a mass meeting for Saturday, February 13, to be held at the historic First Cavalry Baptist Church on Henry Street. More than 500 people attended the meeting, which included speeches by Rev. John Foster, attorney Henry Marsh, Rev. James Harris, and Delegate William P. Robinson Jr. Acting as moderator of the whole affair was King Davis, who gave perhaps the best explanation of the need for action. "The school board started out on the premise that they were going to study how to reduce busing," he said. "However, no such study has been made," nor has the "black community . . . been involved." Instead, Davis told the crowd, the school board had proposed a plan that would resegregate the city's elementary schools on the premise that reduced busing would foster increased parental involvement. In devising this plan, however, the school board had "not involved parents" in the least. The obvious irony of the board's argument led many of the participants at the meeting to join the Norfolk Coalition and pledge their support for busing in the coming days.[58]

In spite of the resistance offered by the Norfolk Coalition, John McLaulin and the school administration presented two plans to reduce busing in April 1982. The first proposal called for the elimination of elementary school busing and the creation of thirty-six neighborhood schools, thirteen of which would be more than 80 percent single-race. The second proposal, based on concerns presented by John Foster, retained busing but redrew attendance lines and reduced the number of children who would take crosstown trips. Each plan cited significant cost-savings and called for the resulting funds to be spent for activities that would foster parental involvement and multicultural education. In addition, the proposals cited the need for a new middle school program and the adoption of a minority-to-majority transfer option, which would allow students to move from single-race neighborhood schools to other locations.[59]

With the announcement of the administration's new plans, the busing debate in Norfolk became increasingly polarized. In a public relations effort aimed at white middle-class professionals, Mayor Vincent Thomas and his allies went on the offensive. Thomas told Stephen Engelberg, a reporter with the *Virginian-Pilot*, that crosstown busing had to be reduced if Norfolk was to avoid becoming "another Richmond." In his most recent and explicit attempt to link the city's economic health to its racial makeup and school population, Thomas argued that crosstown busing was an "artificial irritant" that was driving middle-income professional families from the city. "We don't want Norfolk to be like Richmond," he said, referring to Virginia's capital city, which had become predominantly African American. "It's not going to be to anyone's advantage . . . to have our traditional racial makeup altered." In fact, Thomas said, "we certainly don't want our school system [to become] overwhelming black and to have everything in the political arena considered in those terms."[60]

At the Norfolk Coalition, Rev. James Harris, of Mt. Pleasant Baptist Church, was "outraged" by Thomas's comments. In a public statement, Harris claimed that the mayor's argument against busing was "based on speculation, faulty premises, and . . . derogatory racial overtones." With his cochairman, King Davis, by his side, Harris then linked the mayor to school board chairman Thomas Johnson and the broader business community. Specifically, Harris said that Thomas and Johnson had a "hidden motive to resegregate the Norfolk public school system for economic and political reasons." Then, in a tone of defiance, the minister called for Johnson to resign, charging that he had "abdicated the role of an independent school board by adopting the objectives and agenda of political and business leaders."[61]

When Johnson was questioned about the coalition's position, he shrugged it off. "I have no comment on that kind of stuff," he told the *Virginian-Pilot*. In fact, it seems clear in retrospect that Johnson had the backing of the city's most powerful business and political figures. Joshua P. Darden Jr., the president of Colonial Chevrolet and current titular head of the prestigious Darden family, supported Johnson's efforts. The nephew of a former governor and son of a former mayor, Darden's pedigree gave him considerable influence when it came to political and social issues. Together with other business leaders, including real estate developer Harvey Lindsay Jr., newspaper magnate Frank Batten, attorney Charles L. Kaufman, and the indispensable industrialist Henry Clay Hofheimer II, Darden called for an end to elementary school busing to preserve "the middle-class, tax-paying, home-owning" population in Norfolk.[62]

Just as in 1957–59, however, Norfolk's business elite kept a low profile on a controversial racial subject that was bad for business any way you looked at it. The leaders preferred neighborhood schools to busing, but many of them sent their own children to private schools and were not willing to take a public position on the issue. Moreover, a "Petition of 100" such as the one that appeared in the *Pilot* in January 1959 was never necessary because this time the city had selected its own Thomas Johnson to handle the issue for them in a race-neutral, professional manner. Unlike previous school board chairmen and mayors, such as Fred Duckworth and Vincent Thomas, no one could convincingly accuse Johnson of being a Massive Resister or overt racist. On the contrary, he represented a new "Virginia way" that ensured the longevity of white leadership in Norfolk long after the civil rights revolution.

Johnson found more vocal support for his efforts among the political candidates in the 1982 councilmanic elections. Although Joseph N. Green Jr., the African American rector of Grace Episcopal Church, supported busing and received the largest number of votes, he was the exception that proved the rule. Green's three principal opponents were white incumbents who favored a return to neighborhood schools. Claude "Bubba" Staylor, the seventy-year-old former police chief; Dr. Mason C. Andrews, the chairman of obstetrics at Eastern Virginia Medical School; and Robert E. Summers, an insurance executive and self-declared independent, all advocated the end of busing. In addition, political outsider and grassroots organizer Randy Wright portrayed the election as a referendum on "forced busing." At the various polling places throughout the northeastern section of the city, he and his Tea Party associates collected thousands of signatures on a petition calling for an end to crosstown transportation for elementary school students.[63]

In May 1982, the school board's transportation committee hosted six public hearings to gather feedback on the administration's busing proposals. The meetings were held at local elementary schools, including Bayside, Bowling Park, Diggs Park, Larchmont, Little Creek, and Monroe Elementary. Jean Bruce, the chairwoman of the transportation committee, presided over the sessions. She began each meeting with the same prepared statement: "These deliberations take place only in the context of an unswerving commitment to a unitary, desegregated school system, where our sole goal is educational excellence and equal opportunity for every child."[64]

Despite the noble sentiment expressed in Bruce's statement, the hearings exposed the raw feelings and general distrust that many people in Norfolk felt toward the school board. At the first meeting, on May 17, hundreds of African American parents gathered at Diggs Park to express their outrage with the administration's proposals. "The fact of the matter is this," Vernon Fareed, a local religious leader, told the school board. "We can't trust you. Years ago, we saw you stack the deck. We saw you deal to us from the bottom of the deck. And, we saw the chairman of the school board [Vincent Thomas] transform into the biggest joker of all, the mayor." Fareed's commentary brought the crowd to its feet, and for the rest of the evening the board members faced a group of hostile critics. All but three of the twenty-seven speakers that night were African American, and all but two favored the continuation of busing. The most vocal opponents of the school board included attorney Henry Marsh, the new mayor of Richmond; Rev. L. P. Watson, president of the Norfolk branch of the NAACP; and Leonard Giles, a citizen of Norfolk, who told the board, "We're going to fight you . . . even if we have to run you out of town."[65]

The strident tone of the opposition was tempered to some degree by the appearance of Earlean White, the cofounder of PIN. Amid boos and hisses, White presented a petition signed by 664 African American parents who favored the end of busing. "Busing may have been created by the courts to solve the problem of desegregation," she said, "but it did not alleviate the problems of racism our children are confronted with today." White told the board that, regardless of what others may say about her and PIN, she supported the effort to restore neighborhood schools so that she could play a greater role in her children's educational experiences.[66]

Although White and the members of PIN found little support at the Diggs Park meeting, they would have fit in perfectly the following evening at Little Creek. There, Randy Wright and the Norfolk Tea Party put on an elaborate show of support for neighborhood schools. Their display began early in the afternoon with a mile-long march from Roosevelt Gardens Civic League to Little Creek Elementary. Dozens of children and their parents participated in the march, carrying signs that read, "Let's put education back in our schools, and the schools back in our neighborhoods."[67]

At the meeting that evening, Wright and his allies continued their effort to halt busing in Norfolk. "Let's stop wasting our children's time and tax-payer dollars on busing," Douglas Seibert said. "Children are more secure and better adjusted when they are in schools in their own neighborhoods." This sentiment was echoed by twenty-three other speakers, all white, including Marie Julian, who said that busing had served the purpose of integration but was "no longer necessary." In fact, Randy Wright presented the board with a petition containing 9,103 signatures calling for a restoration of neighborhood schools in Norfolk.[68]

There were voices of dissenting opinion at the Little Creek meeting as well. Attorney Gwendolyn Jackson, with the Norfolk chapter of the NAACP, urged the school board to give additional thought to the current system. "Share with us some other options under the current plan," she said, "before spending tax dollars on unconstitutional efforts to resegregate our schools." Carolyn Bell concurred. "There are two choices on the menu — Plan I and Plan II," she said, and each reduces elementary school integration. "Such a choice is really analogous to choosing poison or cyanide. I urge you to reject both . . . and present us with a different menu — quality education."[69]

The fervor and fury exhibited at the first two hearings continued unabated at the last three sessions. At Bowling Park Elementary, on May 19, a predominantly African American audience divided on the busing issue, with roughly half of the speakers calling for neighborhood schools and the other half voicing their support for continued busing.[70] Six days later, on May 25, a biracial group at Larchmont Elementary pushed for the continuation of busing. "You are committed, you said, to a unitary system," Harrietta Eley told the board. "Yet, I do not see how you can be so committed if the plan [you propose] would segregate a large number of children." This position found additional support in the final hearing of the month at Monroe Elementary. There, on May 26, Norfolk delegate William P. Robinson Jr. condemned the school board and Mayor Thomas for abandoning the integrated system that the community had worked so hard to create.[71]

Although the public hearings sponsored by the school board had been open affairs, critics of the administration's busing proposals viewed the members of the school board as elitist individuals who cared little about the practical concerns of average Norfolk citizens. According to this view, the recent hearings were nothing more than superficial rituals meant to justify a preordained decision in favor of neighborhood schools. Despite this view, in the short run top administrators decided to delay action on the busing front. Following the hearings, in June 1982, Superintendent Ayars sent a confidential note to the members of the board, requesting that any action on crosstown busing be delayed until September 1983. In addition, John Foster, Cynthia Heide, and Clifford Adams — all members of the school board — indicated their belief that the current system of elementary schools should remain intact until additional study could be completed.[72]

The opinion of these administrators won further support when City Attorney Philip Trapani became involved. Trapani, who has most recently been lionized by the biographer of Walter Percy Chrysler Jr. for his important part in the making of the Chrysler Museum, played an even more significant role during the 1980s: he served as one of the local power elite's point guards in the reduction of busing and the consequent resegregation of Norfolk's public schools. In the spring of 1982, Trapani surreptitiously approached the tried and true anti-busing consultant David J. Armor, of California, to review Norfolk's transportation situation. Armor was a well-published Berkeley Ph.D. who had gained a national reputation for refuting the judicial resort to crosstown busing for integration. In 1982, he was just ending a stint as a senior social scientist at the Rand Corporation in Santa Monica, California, to devote all his energies to his lucrative consulting business. Once he received Trapani's request, Armor quickly issued a report suggesting that Norfolk delay action on the busing front while it undertook "a comprehensive study . . . of a return to neighborhood schools."[73]

When viewed together, these developments left little operating room for Thomas Johnson. On June 4, the chairman of the school board sent a memorandum to his fellow board members suggesting that they postpone any action on the busing front for another year. "Delay is a small price to pay if we arrive at a solution which is more nearly correct and more acceptable to our community," Johnson told his colleagues. With the exception of Robert Hicks, the members of the transportation committee agreed with Johnson. A few days later, on June 9, the school board voted to delay action on the busing issue and to hire David Armor to review the matter for the city.[74]

With the postponement of the busing decision, another debate arose. On June 9, only hours after the school board voted to delay action on the busing front, Clifford Adams announced that he would step down from the board when his term ended on July 1. "It's time for me to get out now," the sixty-seven-year-old retired professor from Old Dominion University said. "My wife and I want to do some traveling . . . before we get too old." The Adams resignation opened one slot on the board, and two other members, Thomas Johnson and Cynthia Heide, were up for reappointment that summer.[75]

Even before the announcement of Adams's resignation, pro-busing and anti-busing groups were pressuring the city council for new appointments.

The Norfolk Coalition called for the council to "appoint two additional black persons to the School Board" so that it would be "truly representative of the student population it serves." Although 59 percent of the students in the schools were black, the coalition complained that only two of the seven school board members were African American. This left the black community underrepresented and posed a vital threat to black interests in the future debates over busing and resegregation. On the other hand, Randy Wright and the Norfolk Tea Party expressed outrage at the suggestion that another pro-busing black activist should be appointed to the board. Such a position was ludicrous, Wright said, because it preferred one community over another. Then, in an ironic and perhaps facetious twist, Wright suggested that he would call for the replacement of Johnson and Heide if they did not pursue some immediate action to eliminate busing.[76]

At any rate, Mayor Thomas and the city's business elite decided to reappoint Johnson and Heide to the school board. Then, in a series of phone calls and closed-door meetings, Thomas met with councilmen Mason Andrews and Joseph Leafe to discuss the appointment of a candidate who could replace Clifford Adams. Their choice was Lucy R. Wilson, associate dean of education at Old Dominion University. At fifty-one, Wilson held a doctorate in guidance and counseling from Indiana University, and she had served as one of the first black professionals at the Educational Testing Service in Princeton, New Jersey. After teaching at a number of historically black colleges, including Tennessee State University, Wilson moved to Norfolk with her husband, Harrison, in 1975. As president of Norfolk State College, Harrison Wilson had worked with the Dardens and Frank Batten to successfully prevent the merger of Old Dominion College and Norfolk State in the late 1970s. Thus, local powerbrokers hoped that Lucy Wilson would be just as an effective collaborator as her husband had been in their efforts to reverse the effects of busing at the elementary school level. These hopes were dashed, at least at the very outset, however. Lucy Wilson was not the earthy and glorified athletic coach that her husband was; she had a distinguished academic pedigree in her own right and was a vocal critic of programs with which she disagreed. While it is true that Lucy Wilson's social pretensions sometimes eclipsed her real abilities, she did her very best to represent the local black community.[77]

Although Lucy Wilson claimed that she had "not crystallized [her] position in regards to busing,"[78] Randy Wright was livid about her appointment.

"We're not going to tolerate this," he told the *Ledger-Star*. "I'm upset that no one was appointed from our part of the city and our point of view." Wright then suggested that he would call a meeting for Tea Party members to plan an act of legal or political "retribution."[79] Ironically, it turned out that many members of the black community were as mad as Wright. At the NAACP, Rev. L. P. Watson was furious that the city council had ignored Joseph Green's nomination of Edward Delk. The council's action was "paternalistic," Watson complained. "They give you what they think you should have, not what you ask for."[80]

Indeed, Lucy Wilson found the same sort of paternalism on the school board. When she took her seat in the summer of 1982, it became clear that Thomas Johnson and the leaders of school system did not desire any substantive input from her. For instance, when Wilson questioned the hiring of David Armor to conduct the city's transportation analysis, Johnson and his associate, John McLaulin, shrugged off her concerns. In a later interview, Wilson recalled the situation. "I brought [Johnson and McLaulin] together," she said. Then she asked them, "Do you know who this guy is? . . . There are some things about this guy that I am sure you don't know." In response, Wilson remembered, the two men "looked at each other as if to say, 'Doesn't she understand what is happening?' And the fact that I didn't, and the fact that I then knew that this was a ploy all along, made me very, very angry."[81]

When shopping around for an academic doppelgänger to tell them what they wanted to hear, Norfolk's leaders could not have handpicked a more sympathetic authority than Armor. For his anti-busing testimonies in Norfolk as well as in Wilmington, Delaware; Tampa, Florida; and Dallas, Texas, he would be rewarded by President Ronald Reagan with the position of acting assistant secretary of defense from 1986 to 1989. Thus, he was a very known quantity by the time he picked up Trapani's phone calls, and even Lucy Wilson, whom Johnson and his cronies had underestimated as a lightweight, knew from where he was coming.[82]

When David Armor issued his $60,000 review of Norfolk's busing plan in December 1982, it contained few surprises. The report argued that continued busing in Norfolk would further exacerbate the problems caused by white flight, and it suggested that the city take immediate action to reduce crosstown transportation, especially for younger children. Supporters of busing countered the Armor report, but to little avail. At Old Dominion University, Leslie Carr, a white member of the Norfolk Coalition, and his colleague Paul

Schollaert presented a twenty-five-page evaluation of Armor's study, which they called "slipshod and perfunctory." In their review of the Armor report, the two sociologists charged that Armor had "consistently violate[d] professional research standards" and that his report was "a generally flawed and biased review of the situation in the Norfolk public schools." When their offer to conduct a more thorough examination (for $1) was ignored by the board, Lucy Wilson undertook her own study of the matter that winter.[83]

AS THE CITY debated the Armor report in December 1982, Thomas Johnson took another step in his effort to eliminate the city's busing program. With Superintendent Ayars set to retire at the end of the year, Johnson called an emergency school board meeting on Sunday, December 19, to consider hiring Gene Carter as a replacement. At the time, the district was running a national search to replace Ayars, and more than fifty qualified applicants had submitted résumés. When Johnson became aware that Carter had been offered the superintendent's position in Baltimore, however, he moved swiftly to stop the search. From Johnson's perspective, Carter seemed the perfect candidate. An African American male who held a master's degree from Boston University and a doctorate in education from Columbia University's Teachers College, Carter was an inside candidate who had worked his way up the chain of command from classroom teacher to assistant superintendent. After meeting with Carter in a private, one-on-one discussion, Johnson suggested that the board offer him the job without delay.[84] The board never interviewed Carter, nor did anyone publicly address his position on crosstown busing. Carter's position on the matter, however, was not too difficult to ferret out. When a reporter from the *Journal and Guide* asked him about the importance of racial balance in the schools, Carter responded by saying that "the bottom line is providing quality education . . . the setting in which that takes place may or may not be influential." Later, when he was pressed on the busing matter and the administration's neighborhood school plan, Carter responded simply: "If I did not feel I could support the school board's plan . . . I should not have accepted the superintendency."[85]

The promotion of Gene Carter proved to be a masterstroke by a brilliant strategist. Thomas Johnson had not only secured the appointment of the first African American superintendent in Norfolk's history, he had also used the six-month delay in the busing debate to select a man who would defend the Armor report and the return to neighborhood schools. In fact, if there was one crucial element in the campaign to eliminate busing, the selection of Gene Carter as superintendent may have been it, for having an African American administrator at the head of the district inoculated the school board and city council from virtually all allegations of racism.

With the Armor report and Gene Carter's appointment behind him, Johnson moved quickly to consolidate his gains. On January 26, 1983, the chairman sent a nine-page, single-spaced letter to fellow members of the school board. Citing recent court cases and the city's public hearings, his letter highlighted the many problems that busing posed for the district. According to Johnson, these included:

> loss of parental involvement and support; absorption of scarce resources . . . ; elimination of opportunities for educational advancement outside of normal school hours . . . ; disruption of communication between home and school; inordinate lengthening of the school day — as much as an hour and a half in some cases; inordinate travel — as much as 4,320 miles annually for some school children; inability of parents to reach child[ren] when illness or other emergency arises at school; the loss of middle class students, white and black, to private schools and/or surrounding communities . . . ; and last but not least, the imposition of busing on some children but not others because of the demographic makeup of Norfolk neighborhoods.[86]

Drawing on his years of legal experience, Johnson used these so-called drawbacks to push for a new assignment plan that called for the elimination of elementary school busing for desegregation. The new Johnson plan differed only slightly from the one that Norfolk's administrators had presented the previous May. It called for a system of thirty-five neighborhood elementary schools, with an additional magnet school for students with special circumstances. Under the proposed assignment system, ten of the city's elementary schools would be more than 95 percent black, while six of the schools would be at least 70 percent white. Without the slightest hint of irony or concern, however, Johnson scheduled the vote for his plan on February 2 — the same day that Norfolk had initiated desegregation in 1959. In addition, he banned any public comment on the matter. "There won't be any speaking by the public" at the school board meeting, Johnson told the *Virginian-Pilot*. "This meeting is to consider a proposal before the board and to act on it."[87]

In spite of Johnson's prohibition on public discussion, the members of the school board engaged in a spirited debate on February 2. From the start, it was clear that Johnson had the support of Jean Bruce, Robert Hicks, and Hortense Wells. This "Gang of Four" was strong enough to pass the new assignment plan, and soon the group added a fifth member when Cynthia Heide signed on to the cause. Together, these five members argued that busing "was an artificial and contrived tool that had served its purpose." As Wells noted, busing had "outlived its usefulness" in the education game, and it was time to "make adjustments." "Just as laws are not above re-examination," she explained, "the strategies employed in the implementation of those laws are not above scrutiny."[88]

Lucy Wilson and John Foster vehemently disagreed with the majority's position. Backed by a large group of pro-busing activists at the meeting — including King Davis and his allies from the Norfolk Coalition — the two dissenting members of the board tried to open the floor to debate. Their motion was defeated, however, and it fell to them to present the case against the Johnson plan. "It is readily apparent," Wilson told the board, "that Norfolk would be returning, however gradually, to a segregated school system," should the new assignment plan be adopted. John Foster echoed this sentiment. "I believe this plan strangles, spiritually and culturally, the academic experience of the students," he told his colleagues. Neither Wilson nor Foster believed that there was anything magical about black students sitting next to white students in an integrated setting, but their own experiences led them to believe that busing and integration created a more diverse, equitable, and challenging academic environment that was good for students of both races.[89]

In the end, however, the Wilson-Foster criticism was not enough to sway Johnson or his allies from the new assignment plan. The measure passed by a five-to-two vote, and the chairman left the session with a broad grin. "Now we go to court," he told the *Virginian-Pilot*.[90] Indeed, Johnson had already been working behind the scenes to form a legal team for the next stage of the anti-busing effort. Headed by longtime Norfolk attorney Jack E. Greer, a 1951 graduate of Washington and Lee School of Law and a former law partner of W. R. C. Cocke, the school board's legal team also included Johnson, City Attorney Philip Trapani, and two lawyers on Trapani's staff. On February 24, the members of this team traveled to Washington, D.C., to meet with William Bradford Reynolds, assistant attorney general for civil rights at the

U.S. Justice Department. Attorneys Greer, Trapani, and Johnson specifically requested that the Justice Department back Norfolk's move to eliminate its elementary school busing program. In turn, the assistant attorney general told Norfolk's legal team that he generally supported the reduction of busing, but he was concerned about the tactics that Greer, Trapani, and Johnson were suggesting. In particular, Reynolds told the Norfolk lawyers that any effort to get the federal courts to issue a decision on the busing matter before Norfolk had implemented its new neighborhood assignment plan would draw opposition from his department.[91]

When the members of the Norfolk Coalition learned that the city's legal team was meeting with the U.S. Justice Department, King Davis and his allies moved quickly to secure their own conference with Reynolds. On March 8, Davis and a distinguished group of attorneys, including Henry Marsh, Gwendolyn Jackson, and Elaine Jones from the NAACP Legal Defense Fund, traveled to Washington, D.C., to meet with the assistant attorney general. "We urged Mr. Reynolds to intervene on the side of black children and their parents," Henry Marsh told the *Journal and Guide*. He and the other lawyers wanted to ensure that the past support civil rights activists had received from the nation's top law enforcement agency continued. As Marsh told Reynolds, the busing case was a continuation of "18 years of litigation—a bitter struggle which at one point saw that the schools were closed."[92]

In spite of the disagreements between Norfolk's various constituencies, few people could have anticipated the startling sequence of events that occurred in the spring of 1983. To begin with, on March 23, the school board filed two legal actions in district court, seeking a ruling on the city's new elementary school plan. The board's first pleading asked the court to reopen the *Beckett* case so that the city could test its position against elementary school busing. In a second related pleading, the school board took the unprecedented step of filing a class action lawsuit against four black parents who had publicly opposed the return to neighborhood schools. Listed as defendants in the case were King Davis, chairman of the Norfolk Coalition, and his two daughters; Carolyn L. Bell, secretary of the Norfolk Coalition, and her son; Paul R. Riddick, a funeral director, and his son; and the Reverend Luther M. Ferebee, a Pentecostal Holiness minister, and his daughter. In a public statement issued to the press, City Attorney Philip Trapani insisted that the suit named these specific defendants "simply to fulfill the procedural requirement[s]" of a class action lawsuit. Despite this rather prosaic intention, however, the school board's case quickly became a lightning rod for criticism of the district. Black leaders alleged that Thomas Johnson and the city attorney intended to intimidate local figures who were willing to speak out in defense of busing. "The Norfolk School Board has sent the message," one editorial writer complained, that it "will not tolerate any interference from the black community in its effort to resegregate the Norfolk schools." Furthermore, critics of the board insisted, by enjoining parents and children as defendants in the case, the school board had forced local citizens to accept an adversarial role in a legal suit, which would be both expensive and time consuming.[93]

Ironically, many members of the school board were outraged by the suit. Lucy Wilson, Cynthia Heide, Robert Hicks, and John Foster complained that they were kept in the dark about the board's legal proceedings. The class action lawsuit was never discussed at a school board meeting, and board members did not receive notice of the suit until the day before it was announced to the press. Clearly, many school board members were angry that Chairman Johnson and the city attorney had filed a suit on their behalf without asking for their support or input. Lucy Wilson told the *Virginian-Pilot*, "I think it is terribly unfair to sue persons who have expressed their opinions about busing even if it is just a ploy to get the case into court. . . . It just seems preposterous that we would do this." Robert Hicks agreed. "People ask me what the strategy is," he complained, "and I say 'I have not talked to the city attorney . . . [or] board chairman, and I don't know what the strategy is.' I feel stupid. I don't like feeling stupid."[94]

In response to the school board's controversial lawsuit, Bishop L. E. Willis and King Davis formed an ad hoc Committee of Concerned Citizens, which included Ed Brown, of the International Longshoreman's Association, and Charles Reynolds, president of the Atlantic National Bank. Using his radio show, *Crusade for Christ*, and his network of churches, Willis mobilized hundreds of local citizens and raised thousands of dollars to support the busing cause. Then, on April 10, he and the Committee of Concerned Citizens announced plans for a protest march to draw national attention to the situation in Norfolk. The Reverend Jesse Jackson, head of Operation PUSH and veteran of numerous demonstrations, was invited to lead the march, which was scheduled for May 13.[95]

As Norfolk's pro-busing movement grew stronger, it appeared that the tide of events was turning its way. On April 6, for reasons of its own, the Justice Department filed a brief with the district court, opposing Norfolk's two recent pleadings. Specifically, lawyers with the Justice Department presented a procedural objection, which stated that federal courts could not issue a ruling on a school assignment plan before the district had attempted to implement it. As one official said, "You have to pay for your legal advice, and the School Board knows that."[96]

In fact, the school board did know this, or at least its members learned it afresh, for on April 19 the board bowed to public pressure and dropped its case against the parents and their children. Chairman Johnson told the *Ledger-Star* that the case was being dropped because of community opposition. "I think our real concern was that our action in the case had been misperceived by the public. We wanted to go to the courts out of the best motives, but somehow it has gotten turned around. There was never any intention to intimidate anyone, to discriminate against anyone or to impose any economic hardship on anyone."[97] These criticisms had regularly been leveled against the board, however, and when the Justice Department submitted its brief against the district, it proved to be too much. The school board and city attorney's office decided to walk away from the case and weigh their other options.

Although the school board dropped the most controversial of its two lawsuits, Norfolk's black community recognized that the board still had every intention of moving forward with its neighborhood assignment plan. To counter the move, on May 5 Henry Marsh and lawyers for six black parents and sixteen children filed a new class action lawsuit against the school board. Several of the plaintiffs — including Paul Riddick, Luther Ferebee, and their children — had been defendants in the previous case that was dropped by the school board. In this new class action suit, they alleged that the board's plan to establish a system of neighborhood elementary schools "illegally discriminate[d] against black students." The school board knew that Norfolk's neighborhoods were racially segregated, the plaintiffs claimed, and that adoption of a neighborhood assignment plan "would substantially separate children in the elementary schools by race." Thus, implementation of the plan was unconstitutional because it would "deny black students equal educational opportunities" as required by the Fourteenth Amendment.[98]

As the new class action lawsuit, now known as *Riddick v. School Board of the City of Norfolk,* moved forward, Mayor Thomas became practically apo-

Between 1983 and 1986, Paul Riddick (pictured with his son, Paul Jr.) and other parents in Norfolk challenged the city's decision to end busing for elementary school children. (Courtesy of the *Virginian-Pilot*)

plectic about the demonstration that the Committee of Concerned Citizens had scheduled for that spring. When the mayor learned that Rev. Jesse Jackson had accepted the Concerned Citizens' invitation to come to Norfolk, he quickly drafted a letter requesting a meeting with the civil rights leader. "I understand from the local press," Thomas wrote to Jackson, "that you are planning to be in Norfolk on May 13. . . . Since your public career, as well as your ministry, must have taught you . . . that there are two sides to every difficult question, I would deeply appreciate the opportunity of meeting with you before the march." Thomas told Jackson that he wanted to discuss the complicated dynamics of the busing situation in Norfolk and explain what the school board had proposed to do about it. "If you are coming to our

On May 12, 1983, civil rights leader Jesse Jackson came to Norfolk for a large public demonstration in support of crosstown busing. The evening Jackson arrived, he met with Mayor Vincent Thomas at the Norfolk airport. (Courtesy of the *Virginian-Pilot*)

fine city to give us the benefit of your experience and outside perspective," Thomas told Jackson, "then we shall be happy and honored to have you with us. If, however, it is your intention to exploit for political gain a most difficult and emotional matter in our community, then you will do a disservice both to our city and to yourself [by coming]."[99]

After two weeks of negotiations, Rev. Jackson agreed to meet with Mayor Thomas as requested. One problem remained, however. The mayor told Bishop Willis, the principal negotiator and organizer of the march, that he could not meet with Jackson on May 13 because he would be in Washington, D.C., speaking to Congress. This forced Willis to make arrangements for an unlikely meeting time: 11 p.m. at the Norfolk International Airport on May 12, the night Jackson was scheduled to arrive. Although Jackson's plane landed in Norfolk half an hour behind schedule, the meeting went ahead as planned. Mayor Thomas and school board clerk George Raiss met Jackson in one of the airport's many conference rooms. The civil rights leader was accompanied by local African American activists, including Bishop Willis, King Davis, and several of Norfolk's most prominent black ministers.[100]

Around one o'clock in the morning, Thomas and Jackson emerged from their closed-door meeting and prepared for a press conference with local media. As they did so, the mayor handed Jackson a poem he had written to lighten the mood. "We are not elated that our city is castigated," Thomas's work began. "Our School Board is berated, but our school system is integrated. We don't want to be segregated, so Jesse don't be irritated." The poem brought a smile to Jackson's face and set a tone of cordiality for the late-night press conference. Both men agreed that Norfolk's leadership faced a "crisis of trust," and they issued a joint call for better communication between the white and black communities. Despite these small steps forward, however, Mayor Thomas reiterated his point that school desegregation and busing were issues for the school board, an independent administrative group over which he had no direct control.[101]

Six hours after the airport press conference, at 7:30 on the morning of May 13, Rev. Jackson appeared at a breakfast meeting for more than 225 local civil rights leaders. He then traveled with Bishop Willis to Lafayette Park at the intersection of Granby and Thirty-Fifth Streets. Greeted by hordes of adoring supporters, Jackson led a "singing, chanting crowd" of some 6,000 people on a three-and-a-half-mile march to the school administration building and city hall. Some marchers carried signs reading "What comes after Segregation? The plantation." Others sang songs, including "The Battle Hymn of the Republic" and "We Shall Overcome." Jackson himself declared that he was not simply marching for school desegregation or busing; he wanted much more than that. "We are tired of paying our share of taxes but not getting our rightful number of members on the City Council and the Board of Education," he said. "We have to integrate the power." To have true equality, Jackson told the crowd, African Americans had to engage the political process and put their own representatives in the statehouse. "They're using an old game with a new name to lock us out of power," Jackson insisted. "But we are on a journey from the slave ship to the championship, and we will not turn back."[102]

The historic May 13 march represented the high point in a wave of local activism that had long been battering against the forces of conservatism in Norfolk. What made the march so significant was the number of important social and political elements that it revealed. First, it demonstrated that thousands, if not tens of thousands, of Norfolk's citizens viewed the city's social and political leaders with a good deal of resentment and suspicion.

Vincent Thomas and Thomas Johnson were the focus of much of this ill feeling, but it ran broader and deeper than these two men. Many of Norfolk's African American citizens had come to see the city's white leaders as conniving, self-serving politicians who would stop at nothing to maintain their positions of authority. As Ed Brown, president of Local 128 of the International Longshoreman's Association, argued, "The issue [in Norfolk] is not busing. The issue is the perpetuation of political power by those who are in power at this date." The maintenance of this political power required the management and continuation of white supremacy in a city that was becoming increasingly black.[103]

If resentment and distrust were contributing factors leading to the march, the event also revealed that Norfolk's citizens had a wide range of views on busing. A poll conducted for the city's major newspapers in 1982 showed that 84 percent of Norfolk's residents agreed with the statement: "Young people must go to school too far from home."[104] In stark contrast, however, the march illustrated that thousands of people not only supported busing but were willing to spend a day demonstrating on its behalf. This feeling grew from a deeply held conviction among many people in Norfolk that true educational equity could not be achieved without integrated facilities, and that integration could not be achieved without busing.

Motivated by these convictions, pro-busing forces threatened a second march for June 1 at the grand opening of the city's new conference center, Waterside, if the school board did not delay implementation of its neighborhood assignment plan. On May 24, Bishop Willis met behind closed doors with Thomas Johnson, Jean Bruce, Vincent Thomas, and other local leaders to discuss the matter. Although few details from the meeting ever became public, on May 25 the school board voted six to one to postpone implementation of the new elementary school assignment plan until September 1984. While acknowledging that the threatened protest on Waterside had been a concern, Johnson and the other members of the board also called for additional public comment on the busing issue.[105]

As Johnson and his multifaceted campaign maneuvered to reduce crosstown busing in the port city, G. William Whitehurst spearheaded a drive to have the old federal building on Granby Street renamed in honor of one of the biggest local critics of busing: Walter Hoffman. Although the lobbying efforts and resultant tributes never mentioned Hoffman's consistent and persistent hostility toward full-scale integration via busing, they reinforced the often-told tidbits about the judicial martyr of the late 1950s with his recent role as judge in the Spiro Agnew tax evasion mess. To the civic oligarchy and its reporters, Hoffman was as solid and plainspoken as "his" building, which had stood since 1934. Accordingly, Whitehurst had no problems in shepherding the renaming bill through Congress in late December 1982, and the actual naming ceremony was held on July 8, 1983, just as the busing debate entered its final stages.[106]

As white Norfolk commended Judge Hoffman and his legacy, the city's small but vocal collection of black anti-busers threw their own celebratory session. On July 17, Nelson and Earlean White hosted the members of PIN at Booker T. Washington High School, where they sponsored a program billed as a "Tribute to Black Educators." Among those recognized at the event were Tony Brown, the national syndicated columnist and television host; Hortense Wells, the outspoken local critic of busing; and Gene Carter, the superintendent-elect who favored neighborhood schools. These figures each shared at least some elements of the educational philosophy espoused by the members of PIN. As Earlean White said, they all recognized that there is "no magic formula that will cause poor African-American children to catch up with affluent white children overnight." Instead, these advocates of neighborhood schools hoped to address the racial achievement gap by "focusing on the problems that [we]re endemic to low income children, instilling in them positive attitudes toward learning and removing busing as a stumbling block to parental involvement."[107]

DEBATES OVER the achievement gap and parental involvement featured prominently in the drama surrounding *Riddick v. School Board of the City of Norfolk*. The suit finally appeared in U.S. District Court on February 6, 1984. Presiding over the case was Judge John MacKenzie, who heard an astonishing sixteen days of testimony in one of the era's most significant school desegregation suits. At issue was an important legal point that was sure to set a precedent no matter how the case turned out. Specifically, Judge MacKenzie was to decide whether a school district, once declared unitary, could return to a neighborhood assignment plan that would result in de facto segregation.[108]

Presenting the case for the school board, attorneys Philip Trapani and Jack Greer argued that Norfolk had every right to restore a neighborhood assignment plan. Legally speaking, they based their argument on the district court's 1975 ruling in the historic *Beckett* case, which had bestowed "unitary status" on the Norfolk school system. Trapani and Greer contended that such status relieved the local district from any current responsibility for past discrimination. In other words, Norfolk was not a segregated, dual district seeking to maintain its course of discriminatory conduct. Rather, it was a unitary, integrated system seeking to make a procedural change in the assignment of pupils based on educational and economic necessities.[109]

This last point—the need for an immediate revision in the pupil assignment plan—was reiterated time and time again by the school board's twenty-one witnesses. On the stand, Vincent Thomas and Thomas Johnson both insisted that busing was driving Norfolk's middle-class professionals from the city. According to the mayor and school board chief, Norfolk's "school system was resegregating" because of white flight. "We don't have enough children from the middle-class milieu," Johnson said at one point, returning to the anti-busing rhetoric of the 1970s. Soon, they insisted, Norfolk's schools would be "overwhelmingly black" like those in Richmond, preventing any opportunity for integration.[110]

Thomas and Johnson continued to receive support from the city's expert consultant, David Armor, who appeared in court to defend his study of the local school system. In 1982, Armor estimated that Norfolk had lost 19,000 white students between 1969 and 1981. Of that number, Armor suggested that roughly "8,000 white students appear to have been lost because of mandatory busing policies." He also suggested that if busing continued, the district would lose further white enrollment at a rate of "4.4 to 8 percent annually." In 1984, Armor stuck to his earlier findings. He argued that a neighborhood school policy with a voluntary minority-to-majority transfer option would stem white flight and thereby enable more long-term desegregation in Norfolk. This position received additional support when the new superintendent, Gene Carter, called for a return to neighborhood schools. He and other witnesses testified that such a move would improve the quality of education by increasing parental involvement and ending unnecessary busing. "Blacks don't need separate schools," Carter said, "nor do they need integrated schools. They need quality education."[111]

On the other side of the courtroom, attorneys Henry Marsh, Gwendolyn Jackson, John Goss, and Napoleon Williams Jr. represented the Norfolk parents who had filed suit against the school board. As lead attorney, Marsh assumed the greatest responsibility in the case. He argued that the school board's plan to eliminate elementary school busing was racially motivated and that its implementation would violate the Fourteenth Amendment equal protection rights of African American children. In making his case, Marsh and his team pressured the school board's witnesses, trying to ferret out the slightest hints of discriminatory intent or racial motivation. In addition, the plaintiffs called twenty-six witnesses of their own, including King Davis, head of the Norfolk Coalition; Albert Ayars, the recently retired superintendent; Gordon Foster, former director of the Florida School Desegregation Consulting Center; Robert Green, president of the University of the District of Columbia; and Robert Crain, the supervisor of research at the Center for Organization of Schools at Johns Hopkins University.[112]

Despite the variety of people called by the plaintiffs, Marsh's witnesses agreed on two essential points. First, they argued that Armor's research was "very misleading." It presented a "mathematically biased" account of the local demographic environment, which one of their number characterized as a right-wing "joke." Armor had overestimated the impact of busing and failed to appreciate the growth and appeal of the suburban areas in Virginia Beach and Chesapeake. New houses and jobs in these areas were enticing local residents to move from older neighborhoods and traditional places of employment in Norfolk to newly constructed subdivisions and high-tech industries in the area's wealthiest regions. To lay the blame for white flight predominantly on busing was to miss this obvious factor and distort the true gains that busing had ushered in.[113]

Second, Marsh's witnesses argued that the school board's neighborhood busing plan would initiate a process of resegregation that would have a negative impact on students' academic performance, especially in poor African American neighborhoods. Despite claims by the school board that neighborhood schools would foster greater parental involvement and provide the opportunity for additional extracurricular activities, the plaintiffs' witnesses argued that racial segregation was by its very nature discriminatory. "It's training [students] to become lower-class [citizens]," Robert Crain opined. Black students in segregated environments performed at a lower level on achievement tests and developed a "fatalistic and pessimistic" outlook on life that they transferred to their children. In fact, the negative effects of segregation were so well established in the social scientific literature that Crain believed the school board's "resegregation" plan was an obvious violation of the Constitution.[114]

The U.S. District Court for Eastern Virginia disagreed. In his opinion, Judge John Mackenzie said that the evidence presented by the plaintiffs fell "short of demonstrating the requisite discriminatory intent" necessary to halt the school board's return to neighborhood schools. In other words, there was no proof that the school board's plan was "racially motivated." On the contrary, Judge Mackenzie wrote, there was ample evidence to show that the school board was trying to "meet the threat posed by white flight . . . [and] to increase the level of parental involvement" in Norfolk Public Schools. The district court, therefore, found for the city of Norfolk.[115]

Following this setback for civil rights forces, racial tensions in Norfolk escalated, and the black community divided. During the high tide of Reaganism, local politics offered limited choices for African American voters. During the elections for city council in 1986, for example, even the most moderate white candidates, such as veteran physician Dr. Mason Andrews and newcomer lawyer Paul Fraim, supported the reduction of crosstown busing. To nearly all blacks, these figures from the white establishment were more palatable than energetic white populists such as W. Randy Wright, whose followers threatened to roll back the gains of the civil rights era. Although African American voters helped Andrews and Fraim defeat Wright, vocal critics of the establishment pushed for a new ward system, which further divided the black community by pitting old-line recipients of elite white patronage against those who dared to defy the leadership of both the white and black establishments. This new divide within the black community reduced the coherency and unity of the civil rights forces, but it also opened the way for two new developments that proved critical in defining Norfolk's future political landscape. First, Paul Riddick and his supporters rallied for another assault on the school board's plan to restore neighborhood elementary schools, filing suit in the Fourth Circuit Court of Appeals in 1985. And second, activists James Gay and Herbert Collins filed a similar civil rights suit aimed at establishing a ward system in Norfolk that would provide a greater voice for the city's African American voters.

In appealing their case, Riddick and his fellow plaintiffs continued to support the approach of Henry Marsh and the NAACP. In 1986, however, the Fourth Circuit Court ruled against Riddick, with Circuit Judge Hiram E. Widener Jr. upholding the decision of the district court and emphasizing many of the points the lower court had made. For instance, Judge Widener rejected the plaintiffs' allegation that the school board's decision to end elementary school busing was "racially motivated." On the contrary, the court found that the school board was "racially mixed," as was the administrative and teaching staff. Quoting from Judge Mackenzie's decision, Widener wrote: "The Superintendent of Schools, Dr. Gene R. Carter, is black. Two of the three Regional Assistant Superintendents are also black. There are 88 principals in the system, 59% are white, 41% are black. The faculty is likewise fully integrated, 56% white, 44% black. . . . Given that the staff is completely integrated and given that very qualified blacks are at the top of the organization, the fear that white students will stand to reap some benefit over black students is totally lacking in credence."[116] Since the plaintiffs could not show that the school board's decision to end crosstown busing was intended to benefit white elementary students at the expense of black elementary students — and thus was "racially motivated"— the Fourth Circuit Court of Appeals ruled that the decision was permissible. While it might have a deleterious effect on African American students, the plaintiffs had not proved an intent to discriminate, and so there was no constitutional violation. "This purpose, or intent to discriminate," Widener said, "marks the difference between de facto and de jure segregation"— the former being legal, the latter illegal.[117]

With these words, Judge Widener closed *Riddick v. School Board of the City of Norfolk* (1986), the first federal court decision to permit a school district to end busing for desegregation. From his offices in Washington, D.C., William Bradford Reynolds hailed the decision as "a much needed breath of fresh air," suggesting that it complied with both the Constitution and the Supreme Court's landmark decisions on school desegregation. Widener's ruling supported "the sound legal proposition," Reynolds said, "that court supervision of our public schools under aged court decrees must come to an end on a demonstrated record of continuing good faith compliance." Julius Levon Chambers, director counsel of the NAACP Legal Defense Fund, obviously disagreed. He pointed out that Widener's decision "would permit the Norfolk school board to implement a neighborhood student assignment plan in the city's public schools which would have the effect of resegregating the schools, after 14 years of progress achieved in desegregation."[118]

In fact, six months after the *Riddick* decision, in September 1986, crosstown busing for elementary schools came to an end in Norfolk, and ten all-black elementary schools appeared on the city's books. The long Tidewater Thermidor had begun, and the civic oligarchy had won a lasting victory with

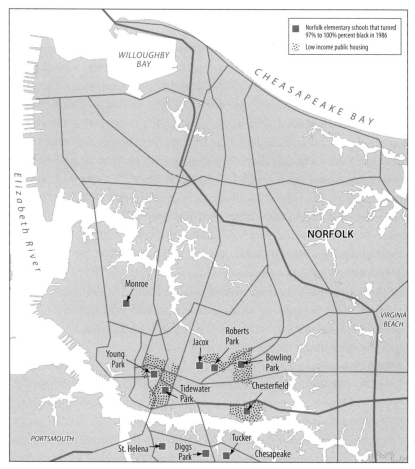

This map shows the alacrity and intensity of resegregation in Norfolk Public Schools following the Fourth Circuit Court's decision in *Riddick v. School Board of Norfolk* (1986). (Courtesy of the *Virginian-Pilot*)

key African American cover and support. Although Rev. G. Wesley Hardy's famous acceptance of neighborhood schools in exchange for small improvements in facilities and curricula — the so-called Hardy Compromise — was certainly implemented, it was so bogged down in the minutiae of test data and dollar figures that it missed the larger point. The city had taken its first step on the road to resegregation, and young people in the inner city were now trapped in an environment of concentrated poverty and deferred dreams. The cycle continued after the 2000 city council elections, when the election of Barclay C. Winn — the son of Wendell L. Winn, a signer of the 1959 petition — sealed the fate of middle school busing the following school year. This turning back of the clock at the turn of the century coincided with new bursts of urban renewal in Norfolk that displaced public housing and slum residents of whatever race with more affluent and educated citizens; in this new civic renaissance, talk of striving for educational equity and diversity seemed quaint and old-fashioned. In the New Jerusalem of condos and shopping centers, educational equity remained as elusive as ever, simply because most parents and leaders had either convinced themselves that the possible had already been achieved or had resigned themselves to cultivating their own gardens, their own neighborhood schools. New selective silences and memories regarding the heyday of integration joined those of the days of Massive Resistance: all upheld the entrenched image of Norfolk as an especially progressive port city with particularly harmonious race relations. We only wish that that image matched the historical reality, but, as the reader can tell on the road to *Riddick,* that simply was not the case.[119]

EPILOGUE

O VER THE PAST two decades, Norfolk, Virginia, has transformed its once-troubled school system into one of the nation's most acclaimed urban districts. School officials have raised standardized test scores, narrowed the achievement gap between white and black students in the district, and improved the high school graduation rate for all demographic groups. In recognition of these achievements, Norfolk received the 2005 Broad Prize, a $500,000 grant given to the best urban district in the nation. In 2008, *Newsweek* listed Norfolk's Maury High School (at 690) and Granby High School (at 1,020) in their ranking of the 1,300 best public schools in the nation. Indeed, a polished billboard, placed among those for other local treasures, greets travelers at the city's International Airport with these facts about Norfolk's "Nationally Recognized" and "Globally Competitive" public schools.[1]

The much-ballyhooed comeback of Norfolk's schools coincided with a generation of gentrification and urban renewal, improvements that displaced the poor of whatever race with the educated and affluent. While finally bringing families, shoppers, and students back to the downtown area with, among other things, the MacArthur Mall, posh condominiums, and a new community college, this renaissance secured "the middle-class milieu" in many areas of Norfolk. Ghent, Lafayette Shores, Robin Hood, Broad Creek Village, Brambleton, and East Ocean View were among the many neighborhoods — white, black, and mixed — that formed the backbone of middle-class moderation that Mayor Thomas had so desperately desired. By the end of the first decade of the twenty-first century, Norfolk was suddenly a livable city once again for professionals, managers, and entrepreneurs of any racial or ethnic background. No longer did middle- and upper-class families have to move to Virginia Beach or Chesapeake to avoid the perceived menaces of busing, blight, and crime, a troika of troubles bubbling up from the dangerous classes that seemed so intractable thirty years earlier.[2]

These often-trumpeted and well-advertised accolades, of course, belie a much more complicated and ambiguous story in the port city. The rising tide of civic self-confidence did not raise all ships, and the uneven nature of this renaissance was especially evident with reference to public education. Despite the undoubted success of some of Norfolk's schools, thousands of its students have yet to experience the gains made by the district as a whole. Most of these children attend neighborhood elementary and middle schools that suffer from de facto segregation. In the mid-1980s, as chapter 6 has shown, the district ended crosstown busing for its elementary schools, with its school board members insisting that they would maintain busing for diversity and equality at its middle and high schools. It would take another decade of urban renewal and removal before the city's white and black leadership backtracked on their Reagan-era promises and agreed to phase out the most hated remedy for integration. In 2001, the school board, with the protective covering offered by John Simpson — the district's second African American superintendent — finally ended crosstown busing for the middle schools. Seven years later, a new consultant's report under the auspices of the district's third African American superintendent — Stephen C. Jones — urged the end of the "vestiges" of busing to the high schools. This last recommendation has elicited surprisingly little public comment, but the consequences of the district's gradual retreat from busing have been very predictable. By 2004–5, four of the nine middle schools in the city were over 80 percent African American. Similarly, nine of Norfolk's thirty-four elementary schools were over 90 percent African American. In these resegregated, nearly all-black schools, students encountered the highest concentrations of poverty, the most frequent staff turnover, and recurrent lows on standardized tests. In fact, while beloved by the city's establishment, Superintendent Stephen Jones recently resigned under more than a little fire for failing to grapple with the effects of such racial and class segregation: grade inflation, social promotion, low test scores, and faculty cynicism. And, in late 2011, his white successor, Superintendent Richard Bentley, was fired for the same reasons after a mere sixteen months on the job.[3]

In many of these segregated, all–African American primary schools as well as their white-majority counterparts, the facilities are aged, crumbling, and/or cramped, according to a scathing 2008 report issued by the district's own Long-Range Citizen Advisory Committee. According to these findings — which were further highlighted in a concise op-ed and accompanying online video by committee member and Lake Taylor Civic League representative Charla Baucom — the former Roberts Park Elementary School, reincarnated as the Dreamkeepers Academy, was especially overcrowded, serving over 400 students in 2006–7 in a place designed for 315 students in 1964. Its art room served as a gymnasium; its ceilings had water damage and mold stains; it lacked a decent modicum of storage space. The school still had no sinks in its tiny bathrooms for children on its first floor. Things necessary for efficient learning that other children and teachers took for granted thus were still dreams at Dreamkeepers, which SchoolDigger.com subsequently ranked as 1,097 out of 1,115 public elementary schools surveyed in Virginia. Like its completely segregated forerunners, it had an overwhelming African American majority, even though its surrounding public housing project had been torn down in the early 2000s and was replaced with attractive mixed-income duplexes. A new principal has most recently brought new energy and much improved conditions for learning to Dreamkeepers, but sadly the school was slated for possible closure in 2011 because of budgetary constraints in the district. Another segregated, mostly black school, Lindenwood Elementary, had the same leakage and bathroom issues, according to the committee, with just one toilet for the seventy-three faculty and staff members who work there. The heating and cooling systems at Berkley-Campostella Early Childhood Center and Sewell's Point Elementary were found to be "poor," and neither building had an integrated sprinkler system for fire protection. Both facilities happen to be majority-minority in terms of their student clientele. White public schools in the most affluent neighborhoods were not exempt, however, from the committee's criticism. Larchmont Elementary, built in 1929, had some of the worst water damage and mold spots in the city. Most jaw dropping was the amount of money spent annually on school improvements in Norfolk compared with those moneys budgeted in suburban Chesapeake and Virginia Beach. As the report states, Norfolk budgeted a paltry $5.6 million in 2008–9 for renovations and construction, while Chesapeake allocated $77.5 million, and Virginia Beach set aside $64.5 million for those priorities. In her op-ed, Charla Baucom wondered why Norfolk was spending so little on its schools, when it was eagerly spending millions more on parking garages, cruise centers, light rail stops, and waterfront landscaping, all designed to continue to lure the affluent to the newly cosmopolitan downtown.[4]

The story is little different when these students move to Booker T. Washington High School, which is 87 percent African American. This school has the highest concentration of poverty, the lowest SAT averages, and the fewest number of Advanced Placement courses offered at any high school in the city.[5] Many of its graduates and more of its dropouts thus will experience the depressing "concentration effects" of both economic and social forces so clinically cataloged in the sociological work of Harvard's William Julius Wilson. Having been poorly prepared and/or alienated by segregated public schools with few academic aspirations, low-skill graduates become perpetually unemployable, as low-skill jobs disappear due to technological improvements, globalization, and immigration. For Tidewater, these are not merely Ivy League generalizations about long-term structural changes in the economy. Norfolk's Ford Motor Company plant just shut down after eighty years of operation, and the shipyards are not hiring as many people as they did in the past. Manufacturing and service jobs that required little reading and fewer math skills are gone forever, even for the longshoremen of the port city. While the Information Revolution has rewarded the well educated over the barely educated, the "oppositional culture" or defense mechanism of these youth — to characterize academic achievement as white and/or effeminate and to cast thuggish boorishness as being a real man — has doomed any piecemeal or episodic academic improvements to the ultimate dustbin of history. When viewed in light of these statistics and their sociological consequences, Norfolk's recent success seems much more tentative and circumscribed than its charm offensive would suggest. In fact, the statistics and stories from Norfolk raise new and fundamental questions about educational equality in the twenty-first century.[6]

Most recently in this ongoing discourse, private and charter schools, which may provide needed competition to keep urban public schools on the right path, have become the new panacea. After all, post-Katrina New Orleans used catastrophe to abandon many of its notoriously dysfunctional public schools for entirely new charters built from the ground up without any of the baggage of the past. The more uneven track record of Norfolk's schools has spared them a similar fate, but the competition has certainly arrived. At an impromptu event honoring the Norfolk 17 in February 2009, George "Billy" Cook, an African American member of the Norfolk school board, welcomed charter schools in particular "to bring it on." Yet, even there, the civic oligarchy has been less than helpful. In early 1994, the current mayor, Paul Fraim, and W. Randy Wright opposed the rezoning of ten acres along East Little Creek Road for Calvary Revival, a mostly black church, to build a 3,000–seat sanctuary. Fraim and Wright expressed the opposition of 14,000 residents in the nearby predominantly white neighborhoods around the property who had signed a petition against allowing the church to build. Then mayor Mason C. Andrews tried to deliver a compromise by steering Calvary to build in a more racially mixed area closer to traditionally African American enclaves. Calvary Revival, led by its formidable ministerial couple — Bishop B. Courtney and Pastor Janeen McBath — stood its ground, despite a drawn-out political and legal controversy. The church eventually built at the Little Creek site, choosing a school rather than a sanctuary. The new facility has been an aesthetic and cultural improvement hunched in between a bowling alley, a Shoney's Restaurant, and a onetime strip club. Nevertheless, many whites in the surrounding subdivisions, with their ranch homes built in the era between Massive Resistance and the end of busing, still think of Calvary as providing a fully accredited neighborhood school in the wrong neighborhood, even if the school can only help those lucky children of believers willing and able to pay for its Bible-based instruction.[7]

While the Calvary experience illustrates the limits of racial tolerance and private schooling in the port city, public education remains the path for most African American students in Norfolk. On April 11, 2009, the city of Norfolk and the *New Journal and Guide* cosponsored a symposium on the city's future. Few showed up for the afternoon event entitled "Trouble Don't Last Always," but those who did heard an array of possible solutions to present, pressing problems of achievement gaps, dropout rates, and outdated pedagogies. The keynote speaker, Reggie Weaver, the former president of the National Education Association, urged less confrontational, less authoritarian, and more respectful ways of discipline than the ways of forty years ago to engender more self-respect and fewer acts of defensive defiance on the part of inner-city students.[8]

Following Weaver, Charles H. Ford presented the principal arguments of this work, before passing the microphone to Congressman Robert Scott of Virginia's Third District. Always on target, Scott noted the unfortunate recent preference for locking up black and Hispanic youth rather than educating them. He then pointed to the obvious cost efficiencies of education over incarceration, hoping to reframe the horrible side effects of the law-and-order regime put in place by the wars on drugs and crime of the Second Gilded Age. Instead of building additional prisons to lock up youthful offenders, Scott suggested that more moneys should be directed into preschool and cocurricular programs that have worked to level the educational playing field.

While the congressman urged more fiscal and legislative help for struggling schools and pupils, Neal Holmes, the director of the "Call Me Mister" program at Longwood University in Farmville, Virginia, found that the best help for young black males from poor neighborhoods was to have role models as teachers who understood and cared about their problems. To Holmes, the most logical candidates for these role models would be young black men, who his program at Longwood molds into being educators in working- and middle-class communities.

Lillian Brinkley, the next panelist to speak and a thirty-seven-year veteran of working in Norfolk's public school district, lamented other unfortunate side effects of desegregation: particularly, the "color blindness" or artificially race-neutral stances that masked the indifference or hostility of white and even black teachers toward black students. If these seemingly objective teachers maintain that they do not see cultural differences in white and black students, and they teach all students the same Eurocentric content, then they are writing off students who do not see themselves in the material. Like Brinkley, George Banks, the last speaker and the author of *The Issue of Race: A Resolution for the 21st Century,* urged the appreciation of different ways of learning while raising faculty expectations for all students. In so doing, he recommended a practical and accessible approach to increase critical thinking at all grade levels, going far beyond the memorization needed to pass the ubiquitous testing in the age of Virginia's Standards of Learning and of the younger Bush's No Child Left Behind.

Yet despite the enthusiastic delivery of the learned panelists, the solutions they presented sounded depressingly familiar. Basically, they all wanted to spend more money on schools, to tell both white and black teachers to be respectful of the learning potentials of black students, and to "restore community involvement" in poor neighborhoods. These, of course, were all ideas espoused by Norfolk's white establishment in the 1980s. In fact, if busing was reduced or eliminated, the former board chair Tommy Johnson — most recently deemed one of Norfolk's Best Real Estate Lawyers for 2009 — had promised that the district would spend more money on inner-city schools and have teacher training to appreciate and respect cultural diversity.[9] As we know from chapter 6, however, the Hardy Compromise was hardly fol-

242 | ELUSIVE EQUALITY

lowed. Since integration had come and gone, there was no real need or legal pressure for the district to pursue any further affirmative steps to achieve equality. "That was that," as Forrest White had said on February 2, 1959, and similarly, "that's all, folks!," as the agenda to the last meeting of the Commemoration Commission on March 4, 2009, so cavalierly and unconsciously put it. As we have seen, an end to this century-old threat to racial harmony and hierarchy was what the civic oligarchy had wanted all along, and they finally got it during the benevolent calm of the Fraim years.

Johnson had also predicted that the end of busing would restore community involvement, which, of course, never happened and for which all of the "Trouble Don't Last Always" panelists were still pining twenty-five years after *Riddick*. Most ironically, in a 2008 interview with the coauthors in his well-appointed downtown office, Johnson says that, after retiring from the board in the late 1990s, he is now most passionate in lobbying for more money for preschool and even infant learning enhancement programs, which, of course, complements the efforts of Congressman Scott. Accordingly, if *Riddick* is to remain the legal lodestar of this landscape, then our first major recommendation is to urge the city's citizens, both black and white, to insist that the school board implement the promises and predictions of the previous generation's civic leadership. One purpose behind this work is to generate an outrage not at only exposing inconvenient truths about troubling continuities but also at getting leaders and parents to once again challenge a still unequal system in concert, just as the brave Norfolk 17 and their parents and their lawyers had done fifty years ago. The starting place for focusing that outrage is pressuring the city to live up to its progressive image and to do the various steps — outlined by the panelists — that it said that it would do in the Reagan era.

Furthermore, upon reflection, we offer a few recommendations of our own. First, as per Brinkley, the curriculum must become truly inclusive. Teachers of history and literature, for instance, must be prepared to teach the contributions of African Americans to broader American history. The continued token mention of Harriet Tubman, Sojourner Truth, Frederick Douglass, W. E. B. DuBois, Booker T. Washington, Martin Luther King Jr., and Malcolm X is tired and wanting. Little or nothing has been done to incorporate the story of Virginia's African American population into the story of civil rights, enabling the continued perpetuation of the official story of the "end" of Massive Resistance in the port city. Second, schools should enroll students year-round, especially in poor neighborhoods, where children are in dire need of academic and enrichment activities during the long summer months. Taking the period from May to August off is outdated and leaves students with few if any academic role models or organized, structured activities for long periods of time. Third, field trips, public history lessons, and academically connected cocurricular activities must become a part of the standard curriculum. Many of the poor, inner-city students in Norfolk and other communities have never traveled outside their immediate living area. Their horizons are terribly limited, and they have few opportunities to gain the perspective and experiences that other, wealthier children have. Finally, the problems with cramped and obsolete facilities, as detailed by the district's own advisory committee, need to be seriously addressed. As we have seen, overcrowding and antiquated facilities in part prompted the activism of the Norfolk 17 and their parents immediately after *Brown*, and such concerns remain a constant thorn in the side of quality education.

In recommending a grab bag of doable if limited improvements, we express no nostalgia for either the heyday of segregation or integration. A return to the "authoritative-supportive" or "Old School" pedagogy of black teachers under Jim Crow — so lovingly remembered by members of the Norfolk 17 — is not enough, given the same dilapidated classrooms and the intense, self-defeating anomie of the urban poor. Simple "body mixing" (in the words of Judge Hoffman) without addressing ingrained assumptions of black inferiority and white supremacy will not work either; the "dumbed-down," value-neutral curricula of the 1970s that coincided with the "body mixing" of busing made things much worse, not better. Simply put, as our research has shown, there has never been a golden age of equality and/or uniform excellence in public education in Norfolk. We remain hopeful, however. As Frederick Douglass said, "power concedes nothing without a demand," and we all need to start demanding more of ourselves, our students, our teachers, and our fellow citizens if the elusive goal of equality is to ever be attained.[10]

Abbreviations

ALP   Executive Papers, Governor J. Lindsay Almond, Jr., 1958–62, State
Government Records Collection, Library of Virginia, Richmond

ELBP   Edward Lebbaius Breeden Papers, 1932–72, Albert and Shirley Small
Special Collections Library, University of Virginia, Charlottesville

GWWCP G. William Whitehurst Papers, Leyburn Library, Special Collections,
Washington and Lee University, Lexington, Virginia

KHS   Kathryn H. Stone Papers, Albert and Shirley Small Special
Collections. Library, University of Virginia, Charlottesville

NCRB   Norfolk City Record Book, Sargeant Room, Norfolk Public Library,
Norfolk, Virginia

NJG   *Journal and Guide,* Norfolk, Virginia

NNJG   *New Journal and Guide,* Norfolk, Virginia

NPSDP   Norfolk Public Schools Desegregation Papers, Special Collections,
Old Dominion University, Norfolk, Virginia

NSBM   Norfolk School Board Minutes, Sargeant Room, Norfolk Public
Library, Norfolk, Virginia

SSN   *Southern School News*

Introduction

1. For the best parts of this series, see Denise Watson Batts, "When the Walls Came Tumbling Down," *Virginian-Pilot,* September 28, 2008, A10, 11; "Cracks in the Wall: A No-Nonsense Federal Judge Orders School Officials to Take Another Look at the Students They Have Barred from White Schools," *Virginian-Pilot,* October 1, 2008, A1.

2. Program, Commemoration of the End of Norfolk's Massive Resistance, 50 Years, MLK, Jr., Unity March, January 19, 2009, Scope Plaza, 10 a.m.; MLK, Jr., Unity Program, January 19, 2009, Chrysler Hall, 11 a.m.; Special Guest Parking Pass, Commemoration of the End of Norfolk's Massive Resistance, 50 Years, January 19, 2009. For an especially rosy version of the official story, see Gary Ruegsegger, "A Tale of Two School Districts, and the Giants in One of Them," *Virginian-Pilot,* August 12, 2003, B9.

3. Charles H. Ford observed the last meeting of the Commemoration Commission on March 4, 2009; a special thanks is extended to commission member and fellow Norfolk State professor Page Laws for inviting him to witness these proceed-

ings firsthand. See also Program, "The Triumph of the Rule of Law Over Massive Resistance: A Community Forum," January 28, 2009. For the civic sense of accomplishment, see the letter to the editor from leading members of the white "Lost Class of '59": "Healing, Closure, Unity," *Virginian-Pilot,* March 21, 2009, B6, as well as Leonard E. Colvin, "Unity Effort Begins for Norfolk 17 and 'Lost Class,'" *NNJG,* February 5–11, 2009, 1, 5. The commemoration events continued into the summer of 2009. For example, see "Massive Resistance Conference on C-Span 3," *NNJG,* August 6–12, 2009, 3.

4. For Mal Vincent's review, see his "Drama Exposes Norfolk's Dark History," *Virginian-Pilot,* February 28, 2009, E4. For the difficulties in the making of the play, see Teresa Annas, "A Massive Undertaking," *Virginian-Pilot,* February 25, 2009, E1, E4; Celia Wren, "Norfolk Play Revisits Life on Front 'Line' of Civil Rights," *Washington Post,* March 3, 2009, C1. For the earlier renditions of the play, on March 1, 2009, I had an interesting conversation with Sonia Yaco, archivist, Old Dominion University, who had witnessed the commission grill Chris Hanna over his earlier drafts and endings during the fall of 2008 and in January 2009. See also Program, *Line in the Sand,* February 24–March 15, 2009, Virginia State Company, Wells Theater, Norfolk, Virginia. Ironically, this program from a play about public schools featured three advertisements from private schools still catering to elite (if more multicultural than fifty years ago) audiences.

5. "Booker T.'s Class of 1959: A Look at Their Piece of Norfolk's History," *NNJG,* June 11–17, 2009, 1, 2; Lelia Hinton Crowder, "BTW Class of 1959," *NNJG,* June 25–July 1, 2009, 6.

6. For examples of the Norfolk 17's testimonies, see Andrew I. Heidelberg, *A Personal Narrative on Desegregation in Norfolk, Virginia in 1958–1962* (Pittsburgh: Rosedog Books, 2006); Leonard E. Colvin, "Louis Cousins Relives First Day at Maury — Without Jeers, Isolation," *NNJG,* February 12–18, 2009, 14. For the Library of Congress and Story Corps, see Leonard E. Colvin, "Norfolk 17 Member Is First to Record for Story Corps," *NNJG,* October 29–November 4, 2009, 1, 3. For the proposed monument, see Leonard E. Colvin, "HU Students Present Ideas for Norfolk 17 Monument," *NNJG,* December 17–23, 2009, 1, 3. For the controversy over the inclusion of Booker T. Washington alumni into the commemoration, see Lelia Hinton Crowders, "A Response from the BTW Class of 1959," *NNJG,* July 30–August 5, 2009, 6.

7. For the problematic proclamation, see "House Joint Resolution, No. 552, Offered March 3, 2008," at http://leg1.state.va.us/cgi-bin/legp504.exe?081+ful+HJ552, and then compare the text (written four years earlier) at http://www.littlejohnexplorers.com/jeff/brown/norfolk17.htm.

8. The transit of these records to Old Dominion is a story in itself, involving much stealth, guile, and skill on the part of the university staff. See Sonia Yaco, archivist, Old Dominion University, for more details.

9. For the "urban advantage," see http://www.improvehighschools.com/news/urbanadvantage/index.html

1. Discrimination and Dissent

1. "School Board Condemned by Negroes: Mass Meeting Asks Renewal of Contract for Aline Black; Petitioned Signed: Dozen White Persons at Gathering; Rev. G. E. Hopkins Speaker," *Virginian-Pilot*, June 26, 1939, back page; "School Board Gets Petition: 1,200 Ask Negro Teacher Be Reinstated," *Ledger-Dispatch*, June 26, 1939, 3; "1200 Score Board in Firing Teacher," *Richmond Afro-American*, July 1, 1939, 6; Earl Lewis, *In Their Own Interests: Race, Class, and Power in Twentieth-Century Virginia* (Berkeley: University of California Press, 1991), 159–60; Thomas C. Parramore, Peter C. Stewart, and Tommy Bogger, *Norfolk: The First Four Centuries* (Charlottesville: University Press of Virginia, 1994), 318–19. See the compelling photographs of the black schoolchildren and their placards in J. Douglas Smith, *Managing White Supremacy: Race, Politics, and Citizenship in Jim Crow Virginia* (Chapel Hill: University of North Carolina Press, 2002), ii, 257.

2. For a listing of the protest's organizers, see "Negroes Start Protest Move: Parade and Mass Meeting Sunday Afternoon," *Ledger-Dispatch*, June 24, 1939, 11.

3. Smith, *Managing White Supremacy*, 3–17.

4. "School Board Condemned by Negroes," back page.

5. Quoted in Mark V. Tushnet, *The NAACP's Legal Strategy against Segregated Education, 1925–1950* (Chapel Hill: University of North Carolina Press, 1987), 81.

6. "School Board Condemned by Negroes," back page; for Judge Cochran in 1939, see "Interracial Group Confers with Board: Committee Takes Up Teachers' Salary Matters," *NJG*, July 15, 1939, 2. Judge Cochran would go on to be a member of the Norfolk Committee for Public Schools (NCPS) during the schools closure crisis of 1958–59. For his career in context, see *Virginian-Pilot*, editorial, April 25, 1954, 6; *Ledger-Star*, November 20, 1969, A6; *Virginian-Pilot*, November 19, 1969, A18. For the listings of addresses for Hopkins and Keene, respectively, see the Summer-Fall 1939 Norfolk-Portsmouth and Vicinity Telephone Directory, 53, 59, Sargeant Memorial Room, Norfolk Public Library.

7. "School Board Condemned by Negroes," back page, 5.

8. "School Board and Teachers," *Ledger-Dispatch*, June 29, 1939, 10.

9. "Let the School Board Reconsider," *Virginian-Pilot*, June 27, 1939, 6. For Jaffe in this and related controversies, see Alexander S. Leidholdt, *Editor for Justice: The Life of Louis I. Jaffe* (Baton Rouge: Louisiana State University Press, 2002), 380–89.

10. "School Board Condemned by Negroes," 5.

11. Tushnet, *NAACP's Legal Strategy*, 77; Smith, *Managing White Supremacy*, 251–56.

12. Lewis, *In Their Own Interests*, 195–96.

13. Tushnet, *NAACP's Legal Strategy*, 81.

14. William Forsythe, "Praises Singer for Enjoyable Useful Talent: First Lady Gives Medal to Marian," *Pittsburgh Courier*, July 8, 1939. See also "Richmond Set to Entertain NAACP," *Richmond Afro-American*, June 24, 1939, 5. For Bright's letter, see "Mayor Bright Says City Has Interest in NAACP," *Richmond Afro-American*, July 1, 1939, 3.

15. For White, see "Sidelights of NAACP Conference," *Pittsburgh Courier,* July 8, 1939. For Houston, see Smith, *Managing White Supremacy,* 258–59.

16. For the best consideration of Young's life and work, see Henry Lewis Suggs, *P. B. Young, Newspaperman: Race, Politics, and Journalism in the New South, 1910–1962* (Charlottesville: University Press of Virginia, 1988).

17. For Young's exchange with Venable, see Lewis, *In Their Own Interests,* 155–56. For Young at the Richmond convention, see "Richmond Set to Entertain NAACP," *Richmond Afro-American,* June 24, 1939, 5. For the *NJG*'s circulation figures and motto, see "Growth of Guide at Peak Now: Its Circulation Over 65,000 Copies per Week," *NJG,* Peninsula Edition, March 3, 1945, 4. For an example of the *Journal and Guide*'s ongoing activism, see "Removal of Northampton County Jeanes Supervisor Is Asked," *NJG,* April 28, 1945, 2.

18. P. Bernard Young Jr. to Thurgood Marshall, October 13, 1939, 2, NAACP Papers, microfilm, Part 3, Series A, Reel 12, Legal Department Records, 1919–40, 00308–00309. For an example of early local efforts to raise the salaries of black schoolteachers, see "More Pay for School Teachers," *NJG,* April 13, 1929, 14.

19. B. T. Gillespie, "Some Norfolk Teachers Don't Want Increases: They Tell Board Present Pay Is Okey [*sic*], AFRO Learns," *Richmond Afro-American,* April 15, 1939, 2.

20. "Denies Offer to Miss Black: Dr. Gandy Disavows Tender of Virginia State Job in Exchange for Dropping NAACP Suit," *Richmond Afro-American,* May 6, 1939, 1. Winston Douglas, the principal of Booker T. Washington High School, had to quash a similar rumor about his trying to buy off or block Aline Black months earlier. "Principal Denies He Tried to Block Suit: Petitioner to Continue Action for Equal Pay," *NJG,* December 24, 1938, 20.

21. J. Robert Smith, "Echoes," *Richmond Afro-American,* March 4, 1939, 24.

22. Young to Marshall, October 13, 1939, 2.

23. Ibid.

24. For Alston's first bid for a soft landing if he became the plaintiff, see Melvin O. Alston to Thurgood Marshall, October 6, 1938, NAACP Papers, microfilm, Part 3, Series A, Reel 12, Legal Department Records, 1919–40, 00371. For the choice of Black, see Thurgood Marshall to Melvin O. Alston, October 31, 1938, NAACP Papers, microfilm, Part 3, Series A, Reel 12, Legal Department Records, 1919–40, 00372. For the inheritance angle, see Melvin O. Alston to Thurgood Marshall, September 21, 1939, NAACP Papers, microfilm, Part 3, Series A, Reel 12, Legal Department Records, 1919–40, 00538; Gilbert P. Swink to Melvin O. Alston, May 3, 1938, NAACP Papers, microfilm, Part 3, Series A, Reel 12, Legal Department Records, 1919–40, 00368.

25. Melvin O. Alston to Thurgood Marshall, July 28, 1939, NAACP Papers, microfilm, Part 3, Series A, Reel 12, Legal Department Records, 1919–40, 00517–00519; Melvin O. Alston to Thurgood Marshall, August 21, 1939, NAACP Papers, microfilm, Part 3, Series A, Reel 12, Legal Department Records, 1919–40, 00520–00521; Thurgood Marshall to Melvin O. Alston, August 29, 1939, NAACP Papers, micro-

film, Part 3, Series A, Reel 12, Legal Department Records, 1919–40, 00521; "Melvin Alston First to Win Doctorate," *NJG*, Home Edition, October 7, 1944; Lewis, *In Their Own Interests,* 161.

26. Lewis, *In Their Own Interests,* 162; for biographical details regarding Judge Way, see Charles Day, "Judge Way's Funeral Tuesday Afternoon; Many Pay Tribute to Federal Jurist," *Ledger-Dispatch,* October 25, 1943, 5; "Judge Luther B. Way," *Virginian-Pilot,* October 24, 1943, part 4, 4; "Judge Luther B. Way Dies; Funeral Services Tuesday — Eminent Jurist Succumbs After Few Weeks' Illness; Decisions Highly Regarded by Appellate Courts," *Virginian-Pilot,* October 24, 1943, part 2, 1.

27. Lewis, *In Their Own Interests,* 162–63; for the background information on Richard Dobie, see Gary Ruegsegger, *The History of Norfolk Public Schools, 1681–2000* (Norfolk, Va.: Letton Gooch, 2000), 27–29.

28. Tushnet, *NAACP's Legal Strategy,* 79–80.

29. Suggs, *P. B. Young,* 161–62; Lewis, *In Their Own Interests,* 163–65; Tushnet, *NAACP's Legal Strategy,* 80.

30. For Black, see Ruegsegger, *Norfolk Public Schools,* 49. See also Gil C. Hoffler, "Honor 'Courageous Teachers': 2 Receive 'Backbone Awards': Belated Salute to Mrs. Aline Black, Mrs. Mary Johnson," *NJG,* December 25, 1971, 9. For Alston, see "Melvin Alston First to Win Doctorate," 1–2.

31. Suggs, *P. B. Young,* 163; Lewis, *In Their Own Interests,* 173.

32. This low view of black teachers as selfish and petty did seem to dissipate a bit — see Luther P. Jackson, "Rights and Duties in a Democracy: Honor to the Teachers of Virginia," *NJG,* May 12, 1945, 6.

33. For the best look at the making of the first black schools, see Evelyn Sears Taylor, "The History of Public Secondary Education for Negroes in Norfolk, Virginia" (master's thesis, Hampton Institute, 1950), 5–6, 12–13. I would like to thank my colleague Cassandra Newby-Alexander for drawing my attention to this invaluable source. See also Ruegsegger, *Norfolk Public Schools,* 31–32.

34. Taylor, "Public Secondary Education," 60–63. In particular, for the West School, see Rorer, *Norfolk Public Schools,* 67; Klara James and Karen Winston, Oral History Transcript of Mrs. G. W. C. Brown, June 25, 1978, 15–21, Special Collections, Norfolk State University Archives. For pictures of the final demolition of the school in 2006, see "John West School: Huntersville Section, Norfolk, VA," Norfolk Public Schools, Photographs file #2, 57, 61, Sargeant Memorial Room, Norfolk Public Library.

35. See *City of Norfolk, Virginia* (Norfolk, Va.: City Council, 1924), 38–40, Sargeant Memorial Room, Norfolk Public Library. For a less flattering glimpse of the black high school just after it opened, see "Booker T. Washington High School, 1925," in Norfolk Public Schools, Photographs file #2, 77, Sargeant Memorial Room, Norfolk Public Library.

36. Winston Douglas, "Public School Education Here: Norfolk School System Is One of the South's Best," *NJG,* December 20, 1930, 21; for the hiring of Vivian Tucker, see Taylor, "Public Secondary Education," 28.

37. For the evolution of the building projects at Booker T. Washington, see the photographs and captions of "Construction Begins on New Gym," *NJG*, January 21, 1939, 4; "Progress Made on Gym, Cafeteria Project," *NJG*, March 18, 1939, 9. For the petitions in reference to overcrowding, see Taylor, "Public Secondary Education," 66, 69, 71.

38. "Booker T. Washington High School Lunchroom," November 8, 1939, in Norfolk Public Schools, Photographs file Boyes 151, 2, 49, Sargeant Memorial Room, Norfolk Public Library. For Douglas as a deft, if deferential, politician, see "Suspension of Bricklaying Course Here Explained: Classes Might Be Resumed Should Enough Students Indicate Interest," *NJG*, September 28, 1946, A13.

39. Lewis, *In Their Own Interests*, 29–38, 41, 67–70, 82, 149.

40. Jane Reif as quoted in Forrest R. White, *Pride and Prejudice: School Desegregation and Urban Renewal in Norfolk, 1950–1959* (Westport, Conn.: Praeger, 1992), 42.

41. "Cities of 25,000 or Over; United States Census of 1900 Shows 159 In This Class. Their Combined Population Is 19,694,624, a Gain of 4,839,136 Over 1890," *New York Times*, November 18, 1900, 17.

42. Parramore, Stewart, and Bogger, *Norfolk*, 336, 358.

43. See Nancy Martin-Perdue and Charles Perdue, eds., *Talk About Trouble: A New Deal Portrait of Virginians in the Great Depression* (Chapel Hill: University of North Carolina Press, 1996), 207–9.

44. For the Ghents, see Amy Waters Yarsinske, *Ghent: John Graham's Dream, Norfolk, Virginia's Treasure* (Charleston, S.C.: History Press, 2006). Otherwise, see Lewis, *In Their Own Interests*, 31; Parramore, Stewart, and Bogger, *Norfolk*, 266, 275.

45. Parramore, Stewart, and Bogger, *Norfolk*, 233, 249, 258, 414; Lewis, *In Their Own Interests*, 77–80; White, *Pride and Prejudice*, 43.

46. Lewis, *In Their Own Interests*, 31; Parramore, Stewart, and Bogger, *Norfolk*, 266, 311.

47. For the best overviews of black public schools in Norfolk, see Winston Douglas, "Forty Years with Norfolk's Public Schools for Negroes," *NJG*, November 23, 1940, 27; Willie Mae Watson, "Many Norfolk Schools Named for Prominent Leaders, Past and Present," *NJG*, February 18, 1961, 1–3. See also Willie Mae Watson, "Norfolk and the Negro: Supplement for Teachers," Fall Term 1959, 4–19, unpublished manuscript, Norfolk and the Negro/Willie Mae Watson File, Folder B, Special Collections, Norfolk State University Archives. For pictures that hint at the woefully inadequate facilities at Oakwood, see "Oakwood School 1947," Norfolk Public Schools, Photographs file #16; "Balloon Drill—Oakwood School, May 8, 1952, Second Grade," Norfolk Public Schools, Photographs file #26, Sargeant Memorial Room, Norfolk Public Library. For the official picture of the "new" Oakwood, see *Norfolk County Schools: Fifteen Years of Progress 1939–1954* (Norfolk, Va.: Norfolk County, 1954), 17, in Norfolk County Public Schools File, Wallace Memorial Room, Chesapeake Public Library, Chesapeake, Virginia.

48. "Clay School to Be Used by Negroes, Board Makes Decision to Effect Change in September," *Virginian-Pilot*, July 17, 1953, back page; "Era Ending," *Ledger-Star*, February 6, 1964, 15.

49. Watson, "Many Norfolk Schools Named for Prominent Leaders," 1–3. For a revealing picture of the Smythe School, see Henry S. Rorer, *History of Norfolk Public Schools, 1681–1968* (Norfolk, Va.: School Board of the City of Norfolk, 1968), 37. Rorer, a longtime teacher in the district, also compiled a useful listing of the naming and reassignment of Norfolk's public schools. Ibid., 55–58. For an approving editorial about the reassignment of Ruffner, see P. B. Young Sr., "Conversion of Ruffner Junior High," *NJG*, May 5, 1951, 1. For a picture of Ruffner around the time of its conversion, see "Ruffner Junior High, Norfolk, VA 1950s," Norfolk Public Schools, Photographs file #46, Sargeant Memorial Room, Norfolk Public Library.

50. For Dunbar, see *Norfolk Public Schools: Report of the Superintendent, 1924–1928* (Norfolk, Va.: School Board of the City of Norfolk, 1929), 67–69. See also "Dunbar School Meets Needs of Individual Pupil: Special Classes to Help Over-Age or Retarded Youth," *NJG*, November 11, 1944, 3; Watson, "Norfolk and the Negro," 9–10; "School Board Told Dunbar Unfit for Use — Powers Named Chairman; Allotted TV Channel to Be Retained," *Virginian-Pilot*, July 11, 1952, back page; "Aging Dunbar School Ends Long Service — Board Orders Closing; Scholarship Granted; Granby Bids Opened," *Virginian-Pilot*, May 27, 1955, back page.

51. Virginia Educational Commission, *Virginia Public Schools: A Survey of a Southern Public School System* (Yonkers-on-the-Hudson, N.Y.: World Book, 1921), 381–84.

52. For the making of Norview, see Ruegsegger, *Norfolk Public Schools*, 61–62; Rorer, *Norfolk Public Schools*, 50–51, 55–57, 58, 71. For the making of Granby, see Ruegsegger, *Norfolk Public Schools*, 49–50. See also "Maury, Blair Near Limit of Capacity, Too Heavy Pupil Load Indicated by 1956, P-TA Council Told," *Virginian-Pilot*, November 21, 1953, back page, 18; "Granby High Addition Bids Set for May, Gymnasium, Kitchen, Health Classrooms Included in Plans," *Virginian-Pilot*, April 15, 1955. For the overcrowding at Booker T. Washington for the intermediate grades, see this bluntly titled piece: Mary V. Ransom, "Norfolk's 'Intermediate School': Neither Elementary nor Jr. High — Where for Years Teachers and Principals Here Made Bricks without Straw. Occupies Wing of High School Building; Was without Lights for 18 Years," *NJG*, March 12, 1949, F13.

53. *Report of the Superintendent*, 38.

54. Cf. Ruegsegger, *Norfolk Public Schools*, 58–61.

55. For biographical details on each superintendent, see ibid., 39–41, 51–55, 56–58.

56. For the most complete and concise biography of Brewbaker, see his own "Affidavit" in *Leola Pearl Beckett, an infant, etc., et al., v. The School Board of the City of Norfolk, Virginia, Civil Action No. 2214, U.S. District Court for the Eastern District of Virginia, Norfolk Division*, February 12, 1957, Norfolk Public Schools Desegregation Files, Box 3, Folder 19, 1–2, Special Collections, Old Dominion University, Norfolk, Virginia. Otherwise, for Brewbaker, see Ruegsegger, *Norfolk Public Schools*, 56–58. For the Leonard Woods lynching, see Smith, *Managing White Supremacy*, 170–72. For Botetourt County, see "Botetourt's Loot from Schools Is $29,369," *Richmond Afro-American*, April 1, 1939, 12; Irwin B. Cohen, Robert N. Gilliam, William H. Hodill, Robert H. Kirkwood, and William Percy McDonald Jr., *An Economic and*

Social Survey of Botetourt County (Charlottesville: University Press of Virginia, 1942).

57. Brewbaker, "Affidavit," 2. For a great picture of Brewbaker upon his accession as superintendent, see "Named City Superintendent," *NJG*, April 9, 1949, D28B.

58. *The Public Schools of Norfolk, Virginia: A Brief Description* (Norfolk, Va.: School Board of the City of Norfolk, 1925), 14, 20, 25, 27, 32, 42, Sargeant Memorial Room, Norfolk Public Library.

59. *Report of the Superintendent*, 50, 58–59, 73–76, 91, 94.

60. *Growing Up in Norfolk Schools* (Norfolk, Va.: School Board of the City of Norfolk, 1937), 19, 50–52, Sargeant Memorial Room, Norfolk Public Library.

61. *Growing Up in Norfolk Schools, Volume II* (Norfolk, Va.: School Board of the City of Norfolk, 1951), 5, 11, 15, 18–19, 21, 35, Sargeant Memorial Room, Norfolk Public Library.

62. For the best collection of clippings and documents about these lawyers, see the Victor Ashe folder in "Prominent Blacks in Virginia A–C," 404; the Judge Joseph Jordan folder in "Prominent Blacks in Virginia J–K," 407; the J. Hugo Madison folder in "Prominent Blacks in Virginia M–N," 408, all in Norfolk State University Archives. For Madison as the vice president of his senior class, see "97 Graduate at Booker T. High School, Norfolk," *Richmond Afro-American*, June 17, 1939, 17. For Ashe and Madison initiating the Seashore State Park case, see "Suit Attacks Race Bars at Seashore State Park," *NJG*, June 30, 1951, 1, 2.

63. For the sheer seediness of Norfolk before and even after urban renewal, see Parramore, Stewart, and Bogger, *Norfolk*, 331–35; James T. Sears, *Rebels, Rubyfruit, and Rhinestones: Queering Space in the Stonewall South* (New Brunswick, N.J.: Rutgers University Press, 2001), 199.

64. Quoted in "Civil Liberties in Norfolk," *NJG*, March 25, 1939, 8.

65. William L. Tazewell, "The Making of the New Norfolk: A New Norfolk Has Arisen Out of the Blight," *Virginian-Pilot*, July 23, 1961, B1, B4; William L. Tazewell, "Renewal Men Spark City's Growth," *Virginian-Pilot*, July 26, 1961, 15, 23; White, *Pride and Prejudice*, 13–34. For a detailed listing of the highlights of urban renewal, see *Redevelopment in Norfolk: A Chronology* (Norfolk, Va.: NHRA, 1970).

66. William L. Tazewell, "Dominate Civic Posts with Cohesion and Direction: Businessmen Provide Push in Norfolk Development," *Virginian-Pilot*, July 25, 1961, 15.

67. Parramore, Stewart, and Bogger, *Norfolk*, 350; cf. Suggs, *P. B. Young*, 127–29; Lewis, *In Their Own Interests*, 188.

68. For Vivian Carter Mason's early life and work, see "Mrs. W. T. Mason to Represent Negro Women at World Meet," *Ledger-Dispatch*, November 23, 1945, 3; Shirley Bolinaga, "Civil Rights Veteran," *Virginian-Pilot*, February 16, 1969, C5; Carol Mather, "A Black Woman with Clout: Vivian Mason Still Has a Dream," *Virginian-Pilot and Ledger-Star*, May 25, 1980, G1, 2; Brad Bennett, "Vivian Mason: A Local Leader in Integration Battle," *Virginian-Pilot — The Compass*, February 12–13, 1992; Mervyn McLean, "Vivian Carter Mason: Civil Rights Activist and Educator," http://sola.nsu.edu/historywebsite/civiclife/mclean/earlylife.htm, 2005.

69. McLean, "Vivian Carter Mason."

70. For Mason in action, see "Democratic Club Hears Mrs. Vivian C. Mason Urge City Vote Increase," *NJG*, May 5, 1945, 5; "Laura E. Titus PTA Sponsors Conference," *NJG*, May 19, 1945, 4. Unfortunately, Virginia Carter Mason's leading role in the founding of the WCIC has been ignored recently—see Parramore, Stewart, and Bogger, *Norfolk*, 364; Leidholdt, *Editor for Justice*, 462.

71. For the WCIC's small victories at Booker T. Washington, see Taylor, "Public Secondary Education," 70. See also "Interracial Group to Hear Students," *Ledger-Dispatch*, December 13, 1951, 8.

72. "Negro Women to Be Headed by Mrs. Mason; National Organization Makes Selection at Washington Rally," *Virginian-Pilot*, November 21, 1953, 4.

73. White, *Pride and Prejudice*, 44–50.

74. For the background and ways of the Dardens, see Guy Friddell, *Colgate Darden: Conversations with Guy Friddell* (Charlottesville: University Press of Virginia, 1978). For Congressman Colgate Darden at St. John's AME, see "Calm Thinking Advised for World's Ills by Darden: Lauds American System of Government/ Guest Speaker for St. John's Brotherhood," *NJG*, April 8, 1939, 20.

75. Brewbaker, "Affidavit," 3. Cf. "An Exhibit in the Progress toward Equal Schools," *Ledger-Dispatch*, December 14, 1951, 6; "New School Districts Are Formed: Board Is Fixing Lines at Meeting This Afternoon," *Ledger-Dispatch*, December 13, 1951, 15. For the turnover of white teachers, see "Norfolk Has 79 Vacancies for Teachers," *Ledger-Dispatch*, July 10, 1956, 17. See also "In Norfolk School System: Annual Cost of Education Up Almost $10 per Pupil," *Virginian-Pilot*, July 31, 1958, 29.

76. Brewbaker, "Affidavit," 4.

77. Cf. "Exhibit in the Progress toward Equal Schools," 6; "New School Districts Are Formed," 15. For the turnover of white teachers, see "Norfolk Has 79 Vacancies for Teachers." See also "In Norfolk School System."

78. Brewbaker, "Affidavit," 5–6, 14–16.

79. Ibid., 8–9.

80. J. J. Brewbaker, "Progress in Racial Integration in the Norfolk Public Schools since July 1, 1949," April 1956 memorandum, Norfolk Public Schools Desegregation Files, Box 3, Folder 19, 1, Special Collections, Old Dominion University.

81. "Frontiers Commend Officials; Stand by Brewbaker and Chittum Wins Plaudits," *NJG*, June 18, 1955, 1. Curiously, Brewbaker and board chairman Paul Schweitzer did not mention their baby steps toward desegregation in their public, upbeat forecast about their district's future that same year. See "Schweitzer, Brewbaker View New Year: Norfolk School System Is Biggest in State, but Major Goal Is Making It 'Best Anywhere,'" *Virginian-Pilot*, September 4, 1955, 4E.

82. Brewbaker, "Progress in Racial Integration," 2–3.

83. Ibid., 3–4.

84. Ibid., 2; for a look at this "Training Center," see Rorer, *Norfolk Public Schools*, 71.

85. Brewbaker, "Progress in Racial Integration," 4.

86. Brewbaker, "Affidavit," 7.

2. Courage and Conviction

1. James E. Mays, "Among Students of Tax-Supported Colleges: No Integration Problems Seen as Negro Class Discusses Importance: Professor Marshall Leads Debate on Court Decision," *Virginian-Pilot*, May 19, 1954, back page.

2. For the best definition of "the Virginia way," see J. Douglas Smith, *Managing White Supremacy: Race, Politics, and Citizenship in Jim Crow Virginia* (Chapel Hill: University of North Carolina Press, 2002), 3–17.

3. "How Norfolk Opened Her Schools," February 2, 1959, 2, Women's Council for Interracial Cooperation Papers, Folder 20, MG-54, Special Collections, Old Dominion University.

4. For the Lakewood School workshop, see "Frontiers Commend Officials," 1.

5. "Schools Lauded for Racial Stand," *Ledger-Dispatch*, July 11, 1955, 17.

6. For the definitive look at Chambers, see Alexander S. Leidholdt, *Standing Before the Shouting Mob: Lenoir Chambers and Virginia's Massive Resistance to Public-School Integration* (Tuscaloosa: University of Alabama Press, 1997).

7. "Ministers Here Back Decision on Segregation," *Ledger-Dispatch*, May 24, 1954, 8A. For Brewbaker at First Christian, see John Joseph Brewbaker, *Autobiography, Including Brief Family Sketches of Close Relatives* (Norfolk, Va.: n.p., 1971), 28–29. For Schweitzer at First Christian, see Harry Nash, "Personality Sketch: Schweitzer: Realist," *Virginian-Pilot*, January 30, 1959, 5. Cf. Charles Ford, "Religious Support for Integrated Schools in Norfolk, 1954–1959," in *Voices from within the Veil: African Americans and the Experience of Democracy*, ed. William Alexander, Cassandra Newby-Alexander, and Charles Ford (Newcastle-upon-Tyne, U.K.: Cambridge Scholars Publishing, 2008), 316–17.

8. "What Ministers Said About Court Decision," *NJG*, May 22, 1954, 2.

9. For the quotes from Brewbaker, Powers, and Goodman, see "What Leaders Said on High Court Decision," *NJG*, May 22, 1954, 1. For Brewbaker and Brooks, see "Night School Graduates Hear Dr. Lyman Brooks," *NJG*, April 10, 1954, 3; see also Jean Bishop, "School Officials Unruffled: 1960 Seen Likely Date Before Segregation End Is Effective," *Ledger-Dispatch*, May 18, 1954, 15.

10. Stephen S. Mansfield, "Francis Joseph Blakely," in *Dictionary of Virginia Biography*, Vol. 1, *Aaroe–Blanchfield*, ed. John T. Kneebone, J. Jefferson Looney, Brent Tarter, and Sandra Gioia Treadway (Richmond: Library of Virginia, 1998), 553–54.

11. Luther J. Carter, "Disciplinary, Academic Standards Upheld: After a Year of Integration: A Report from Catholic High," *Virginian-Pilot*, June 17, 1956, 1C. In contrast to Norfolk Catholic, St. Paul's Catholic High School in nearby Portsmouth desegregated in 1959, four years after the bishop of Richmond's directive to do so. "Schools Open Today: Ding Dong, Summer's Gone," *Virginian-Pilot*, September 8, 1959, 15. See also Leonard E. Colvin, "Part One: 12 Norfolk Blacks Broke Private School Barriers in 1955," *NNJG*, April 9–15, 2009, 1, 4.

12. "Navy Will Obey Order to Integrate: Will Follow Wishes of President at Benmoreell School," *NJG*, April 3, 1954, 3. See also Floyd Pledger, "Navy-Norfolk's Ben-

moreell: 'City-Within-a-City' Opened a Decade Ago," *Virginian-Pilot*, March 11, 1951, part 5, 2; Jack Dorsey, "1 Million Called Benmoreell Home," *Virginian-Pilot*, April 8, 1992; Jack Dorsey, "Family Quarters in Norfolk May Be Torn Down," *Virginian-Pilot*, April 8, 1992, 4. See also White, *Pride and Prejudice*, 135–36, 143, 262.

13. For Stanley's move away from moderation, see Leidholdt, *Standing Before the Shouting Mob*, 66–67. For Darden's efforts, see "Darden Favors Commission Study of School Problem," *Ledger-Dispatch*, June 28, 1954, 3; John B. Henderson, "Action on Mr. Darden's Wise Counsel of Caution," *NJG*, April 24, 1954, 14. Darden would eventually leave the University of Virginia to come back to his native Norfolk on the eve of the schools closure crisis. "Darden to Leave University: President to End Public Life, Return to Norfolk," *Ledger-Dispatch*, June 14, 1958, 1. See also John B. Henderson, "Accepting the Decision in Good Sportsmanship," *NJG*, May 29, 1954, 14; "The Short Step from Lawmaker to Lawbreaker," *NJG*, June 5, 1954, 15.

14. For Seashore State Park, see "Seashore State Park Ruling to Be Appealed as Virginia Resists U.S. Infringement," *Virginian-Pilot*, May 4, 1956, 1; Leidholdt, *Standing Before the Shouting Mob*, 70.

15. Leidholdt, *Standing Before the Shouting Mob*, 68.

16. Virginia Council on Human Relations, *VCHR Newsletter* 3, no. 4 (April/May 1959): 3; Virginia Council on Human Relations, *VCHR Newsletter* 3, no. 5 (May/June 1959): 3.

17. "Mrs. Crawford Tells of Louisville Plan," *NJG*, November 30, 1957, 6. For the AAUW's involvement, for example, see Mrs. Robert Friend Boyd to Edward L. Breeden, March 5, 1958, Box 37, 1958 Political Correspondence, B, ELBP.

18. See also "Norfolk Women Told What 'Hate Groups' Are Really Made Of," *NJG*, March 22, 1958, 16. For the WCIC's membership numbers, see Mrs. Forrest P. "Edith" White to Kathryn Stone, March 22, 1958, KHS, Box 9.

19. Minutes, League of Women Voters, Norfolk chapter, January 15, 1957, in League of Women Voters, MG-72, Box 9, Folder 2, Special Collections, Old Dominion University.

20. For the panel, see "Integration Subject for St. Paul Church Panel," *NJG*, June 18, 1955, 3.

21. In particular, see "At Ministers' Wives Meet[ing]: Prepare for Integration, Dr. Martin Tells Group," *NJG*, November 23, 1957, 23. See also "Panel on School Crisis: Desegregation Called Phase of Social Change," *NJG*, September 20, 1958, 15. See also Ford, "Religious Support," 317–18.

22. "Frontiers in Appeal to Reason: Ask Leaders of Both Races to Solve School Crisis," *NJG*, April 20, 1957, 4.

23. "Frontiers Elect Officers," *NJG*, December 21, 1957, 20. Merritt also taught business courses at the Norfolk Division of Virginia State College. "Norfolk Division Offers Night Business Courses," *NJG*, September 27, 1958, 16.

24. Barbara S. Marx to Political Action Committee members, February 21, 1956, NAACP Papers, Part 27, Selected Branch File: 1956–65, Series A: The South, Reel 18.

25. Lucille Black to W. Lester Black, October 2, 1956, NAACP Papers, Part 27,

Selected Branch Files: 1956–65, Series A: The South, Reel 18. Only New York, California, and Michigan had more NAACP members.

26. NAACP Membership and Freedom Fund Contributions, January 1 to December 31, 1956, Virginia Branches, NAACP Papers, Part 27, Selected Branch Files: 1956–65, Series A: The South, Reel 18.

27. NAACP Membership and Freedom Fund Contributions, January 1 to September 15, 1958, Virginia Branches, 3, NAACP Papers, Part 27, Selected Branch Files: 1956–65, Series A: The South, Reel 18.

28. For the officer roster of the local chapter, see Local Branch Roster for 1958, NAACP Papers, Part 27, Selected Branch Files: 1956–65, Series A: The South, Reel 18.

29. Heidelberg, *Personal Narrative,* 2–4.

30. NAACP Membership and Freedom Fund Contributions, 1956, Virginia Branches, NAACP Papers, Part 27, Selected Branch Files: 1956–65, Series A: The South, Reel 18.

31. Herbert L. Wright to W. Lester Banks, October 14, 1957, NAACP Papers, Part 27, Selected Branch Files: 1956–65, Series A: The South, Reel 18.

32. Copy of G. W. C. Brown to the Honorable W. F. Duckworth, Mayor, August 19, 1955, NPSDP, Box 3, Folder 19.

33. Copy of G. W. C. Brown to J. J. Brewbaker, October 4, 1955, NPSDP, Box 3, Folder 19.

34. "Bi-Racial 'Bargaining' Repudiated," *Virginian-Pilot,* June 19, 1958, back page.

35. Leidholdt, *Standing Before the Shouting Mob,* 96.

36. For Tony and Marilyn Stein, see "Against the Times, They Spoke Out," *Virginian-Pilot,* January 19, 2009, B1, B3.

37. Leidholdt, *Standing Before the Shouting Mob,* 81.

38. Ibid., 68–70.

39. "The Resort to 'Interposition,'" *Virginian-Pilot,* February 4, 1956, 6, as quoted in Leidholdt, *Standing Before the Shouting Mob,* 76.

40. Leidholdt, *Standing Before the Shouting Mob,* 76.

41. "School Issue Stand Studied by Ministers: Committee to Consider Association Action on Referendum," *Virginian-Pilot,* December 6, 1955, 24.

42. "Summers Thinks Existing Schools, Teachers Enough: Present Forces Will Meet His Proposed Segregation Plan, Says Norfolk Councilman," *Ledger-Dispatch,* July 27, 1955, 19; George M. Kelley, "Parent Could Pick School Under 'Integration' Plan Summers Offers to Council: Surprise Resolution Sent to Redder for Further Study," *Virginian-Pilot,* July 27, 1955, back page.

43. "Segregation Supported by Summers: Cosmopolitans Hear Councilman Take Stands on Issues," *Virginian-Pilot,* May 11, 1956, back page, 41.

44. Leidholdt, *Standing Before the Shouting Mob,* 76.

45. Ibid., 77–79.

46. For this cartoon, see "Ridiculous? Ask the Oppressed Millions," *NJG,* August 5, 1956, 10. The former cartoon would be republished at least two more times: *NJG,* April 11, 1959, 13; and *NJG,* August 22, 1959, 12. See also "God and Science Explode a

Myth," *NJG,* August 11, 1956, 8, and the overt religious imagery in "God Speaks on Segregation," *NJG,* April 18, 1959, 8. See also Ford, "Religious Support," 318.

47. Leidholdt, *Standing Before the Shouting Mob,* 79.

48. Jim Henderson, "Negroes Ask for Injunction Ending School Segregation in Norfolk; Claim 'Injury,'" *Virginian-Pilot,* May 11, 1956, 1; Leidholdt, *Standing Before the Shouting Mob,* 80.

49. Leola Beckett Faulks still lives in Norfolk. For her family connections and context, see her aunt's obituary: "Willie B. Drummond," *Virginian-Pilot,* November 22, 1996, B8.

50. "Perhaps It's State Policy," *NJG,* August 3, 1957, 10.

51. "Text of Judge Hoffman's Opinion," *Virginian-Pilot,* February 13, 1957, 8.

52. Ibid.

53. Ralph Matthews, "2 Va. Cities Must Mix Schools 15 August," *Richmond Afro-American,* February 16, 1957.

54. Ibid.

55. "Contempt Charge Squashed After . . . Norfolk Lawyers Irk Probe Group," *NJG,* August 17, 1957, 1, 2.

56. "Birth of a Dictatorship," *NJG,* October 19, 1957, 1. See also "Virginia Veterans Group Decries 'Probe' Antics," *NJG,* October 5, 1957, 20; "By Norfolk Man: Report Given on Virginia's NAACP Inquisition," *NJG,* April 6, 1957, 1.

57. "Parents Map Pupil Placement Fight," *Richmond Afro-American,* April 6, 1957.

58. "To Sign or Not to Sign," *NJG,* May 25, 1957, 1.

59. "2 Students Are Expelled at Norfolk: Parents Refused to Sign New Pupil Placement Blanks," *NJG,* September 14, 1957, 1.

60. "Judge Hoffman Grants Injunction: Pupils Return to School in 3 Virginia Districts," *NJG,* October 5, 1957, 3.

61. "Upset Featured Primary; Close Call for Winners," *NJG,* July 13, 1957, 1.

62. "Attack on Court House Segregation Came as Surprise to Norfolk Lawyers," *NJG,* April 20, 1957, 14; "U.S. Circuit Court Rules: Segregation in Rest Rooms of Norfolk Court Sustained," *Virginian-Pilot,* October 16, 1958, back page. For Dawley's candidacy to be a delegate, see "Election Reflections," *NJG,* November 16, 1957, 5. For an example of Dawley's continuing street theater that was designed to criticize the effects of internalized racism, see "Norfolk Lawyer Tells Why He Launched His 'Renaissance Crusade,'" *NJG,* September 20, 1958, 11. Here he marched from the center of a black neighborhood at Goff and Church Streets to city hall and back wearing a toga and carrying a placard that stated, "When 5,000 have marched, the renaissance will come."

63. John B. Henderson, "Closing Schools No Way to Cope with Sputniks," *NJG,* November 23, 1957, 8. See also John B. Henderson, "Sense of Mission Lost in Schools of America," *NJG,* November 30, 1957, 9.

64. For Henderson's editorial on this gubernatorial speech, see his "For Whom Did Bell Toll during Almond's Address?" *NJG,* January 25, 1958, 8.

65. For a useful recap of these laws, see Virginia State Conference of the NAACP,

Candle 1, no. 6 (March 1958): 12–13, NAACP Papers, microfilm, Part 27, Selected Branch Files: 1956–65 Series A: The South, Reel 18.

66. James Elliott, "If Admitted to Norfolk White Schools: Negro Students See No Racial Troubles," *Ledger-Dispatch,* June 11, 1958, 23. For an update on the Welch sisters, see Lauren Lea, "Massive Resistance: Another View of the Efforts Toward Integration," *Spartan Echo,* February 16, 2009, 1, 3.

67. Charlton Harrell, "Negro School Bids Persist in Norfolk: 10 More Seek Transfer for Next September," *Ledger-Dispatch,* June 12, 1958, 27.

68. Charlton Harrell, "18 Norfolk Negroes Seek White Schools," *Ledger-Dispatch,* June 11, 1958, 1.

69. These guidelines were republished verbatim in John Brewbaker's self-congratulatory after-action brochure, "Desegregation in the Norfolk Public Schools" (July 1960), 5–6. See also "Text for Resolution for Norfolk Placement Plan," *NJG,* July 26, 1958, 9.

70. "Norfolk Police to Be on Hand," *NJG,* August 2, 1958, 2.

71. "Minutes of the Informal School Board Meeting," July 17, 1958, NSBM, Reel 1498, 1–4.

72. "Assignment Interviews Start for Admittance to Schools: 13 Negro Pupils Report for Tests Out of 22 Called," *Ledger-Dispatch,* August 1, 1958, 15; Tony Stein and Jean Bishop Porter, "School Assignment Hearing Set Aug. 18," *Ledger-Dispatch,* August 4, 1958, 13.

73. "Norfolk Parents Say They'll Ignore Tests," *NJG,* August 2, 1958, 11.

74. "School Test Data Query Is Refused: Negro Applicants' Attorneys Told Information Never Given," *Virginian-Pilot,* July 25, 1958, back page.

75. "Pupil Tests Are Called Routine," *NJG,* August 2, 1958, 2. See also "Usual Tests to Be Given to Negroes: Brewbaker Issues Statement About Tuesday Program," *Virginian-Pilot,* July 26, 1958, 13.

76. Luther J. Carter, "Despite New Court Action: Some Children Likely to Take Pupil Tests," *Virginian-Pilot,* July 29, 1958, back page, 22; Jean Bishop Porter, "16 Negro Pupils on Hand to Take High School Tests: 16 Others Called Fail to Appear at Proper Time," *Ledger-Dispatch,* July 29, 1958, 15.

77. Tony Stein, "19 Others Absent: 39 More Negro Students Report for Achievement Test," *Ledger-Dispatch,* July 30, 1958, 17. See also "Few Pupils Boycotting City Tests: 39 of 58 Slated for Examination Appear Wednesday: 29 More Scheduled Today; Board Due to Act in August," *Virginian-Pilot,* July 31, 1958, 29.

78. Jean Bishop Porter, "Negro Test Total Here Rises to 71: 16 More Students Report Today; 15 Others Absent," *Ledger-Dispatch,* July 31, 1958, 25.

79. "Applicants' Family Leaving," *Virginian-Pilot,* July 30, 1958, 22; "Army Calls Transfer 'Routine,'" *Ledger-Dispatch,* July 30, 1958, 30; "Negro Pupils Complete Test Boycott," *Ledger-Dispatch,* July 30, 1958, 2.

80. "Assignment Interviews Start for Admittance to Schools"; Stein and Porter, "School Assignment Hearing Set Aug. 18."

81. "Final Interviews of Negro Students Take Place Today," *Ledger-Dispatch,* August 6, 1958, 15.

82. Jean Bishop Porter, "In Federal Court Monday: 21 Subpoenaed to Appear at Assignment Hearing," *Ledger-Dispatch*, August 15, 1958, 17.

83. "Norfolk Plan Attacked, But: Judge Rejects Petition Against School Board," *NJG*, August 16, 1958, 1; "Norfolk's Assignment Plan Faces Second Court Action: White Parent to File in Circuit Court—Contends Only State Has Authority to Assign Students," *Ledger-Dispatch*, August 7, 1958, 21; Tony Stein, "4–Cornered Crossfire for Board: School Officials Face Problems from All Directions," *Ledger-Dispatch*, August 8, 1958, 17. For the Virginia context of this development, see Jean Bishop Porter, "Placement Injunction Sought: Suit Based on Assumption?" *Ledger-Dispatch*, August 12, 1958, 17. See also Jean Bishop Porter, "Placement Forms Going to State: Whether It's Mere Formality Being Discussed Here," *Ledger-Dispatch*, August 9, 1958, 13. For biographical information on Judge Jacobs, see his obituary, "Clyde Jacob Dies; Retired Circuit Judge," *Ledger-Star*, November 5, 1974, B1.

84. "Henderson Speaks: School Board Between Devil and Deep Blue Sea," *NJG*, August 30, 1958, 8; "Henderson Speaks: Virginia's Deadly Virus: Little Men in Big Places," *NJG*, September 30, 1958, 8. See also Ford, "Religious Support," 317.

85. Petition to City Council, Norfolk City Council Minutes, June 3, 1958, Sargeant Room, Norfolk Public Library.

86. Letter from W. T. Wood, Chairman of the Board, Defenders of State Sovereignty and Individual Liberties, presented to City Council, Norfolk City Council Minutes, June 12, 1958, Sargeant Room, Norfolk Public Library.

87. Norfolk City Council Minutes, June 3, 1958. Cf. White, *Pride and Prejudice*, 156–57. White claimed that this petition was presented on June 12 by Brooks, but it was actually done on June 3. Also, in his account, Duckworth cut Brooks off with a racist tirade, but that is not in the official minutes or in any newspaper account of that time.

88. "A Past Seven Backgrounder: Interracial Relations," *Virginian-Pilot*, June 15, 1958, 3D. Cf. White, *Pride and Prejudice*, 156–57. White incorrectly cited the date of this article as June 12.

89. Norfolk City Council Minutes, June 3, 1958.

90. "The Position of the 16," *Virginian-Pilot*, June 14, 1958, 4. For the letter to which Young was responding, see "16 with 'Flag of Truce,'" *Virginian-Pilot*, June 7, 1958, 4. For a tongue-in-cheek letter in support of Young in this exchange, see "How to Make NAACP Fold and Block Communists," *Virginian-Pilot*, June 29, 1958, 4. See also a later echo of this controversy in P. B. Young's letter to the editor, "Negro Leaders and Council," *Virginian-Pilot*, December 5, 1958, 4.

91. "Bi-Racial 'Bargaining' Repudiated: City Negro Baptist Ministers Adopt Resolution Against Compromise," *Virginian-Pilot*, June 19, 1958, back page.

92. "Norfolk Lawyer Tells Why He Launched His 'Renaissance Crusade,'" *NJG*, September 20, 1958, 11.

93. "Churchmen Will Not Allow Buildings to Be Used as Schools," *NJG*, August 9, 1958, 1–2; the article was repeated in *NJG* on August 16, 1958, 10.

94. "Two Pastors Accept Calls to Norfolk: Rev. J. C. Brewer and Rev. Odell J. Powell Will Serve Here," *Virginian-Pilot*, May 4, 1956, 48.

95. Virginia State Conference of the NAACP, *Candle* 1, no. 5 (December 1957): 3, NAACP Papers, microfilm, Part 27, Selected Branch Files: 1956–65, Series A: The South, Reel 18.

96. William B. Abbot to Kathryn Stone, Papers of Kathryn H. Stone, No. 10555-A, Box 9, Albert Small Special Collections Library, University of Virginia. For his activity during the school closures, see "'Open Our School' Pleas Sounded by Students Fall on the Deaf Ears of Governors," *NJG*, September 27, 1958, 19. For Abbot as plaintiff, see "Race Barriers in Public Places Contested in Suit," *NJG*, May 16, 1959, 1–2; "'Still Agree in Principle'— Rev. Abbot," *NJG*, May 16, 1959, 1–2. For Abbot as correspondent to Eddie Breeden, see William B. Abbot to Edward L. Breeden, late 1958, Box 36, 1958, Democratic District Committee Folder, ELBP, 1932–72, Accession #9825. See also William B. Abbot to Edward L. Breeden, January 29, 1958, and William B. Abbot to Edward L. Breeden, late 1958, both in Box 37, 1958 Political Correspondence, A, ELBP, 1932–72, Accession #9825. See also Ford, "Religious Support," 319.

97. Leidholdt, *Standing Before the Shouting Mob,* 86; "For School Locations: Foundation Asks Aid of Churches," *Ledger-Dispatch,* August 4, 1958, 13; Luther J. Carter, "A Past Seven Interpretive: Aid Lagging for Private Schools," *Virginian-Pilot,* August 10, 1958, 3D. For Martin's spin on the lack of interest in the TEF shown by local churches, see "700 School Rooms Ready in Churches," *Ledger-Dispatch,* August 15, 1958, 17.

98. See the 1959 yearbook for Tidewater Academy, *The Mariner,* 1–4, Sargeant Memorial Room, Norfolk Public Library. See also "For School Locations: Foundation Asks Aid of Churches," *Ledger-Dispatch,* August 4, 1958, 13; Ford, "Religious Support," 320.

99. "Methodists Bar Use of Churches to Keep Segregation," *NJG,* January 25, 1958, 13. See also Ford, "Religious Support," 320. For a remarkable apology from Bonney, see Denise Watson Batts, "Voice of Remorse: 'I Took It Too Far'— An Opponent of Integration in 1958 Gains Fresh Respect for the Rule of Law and for Equal Rights," *Virginian-Pilot,* October 1, 2008, A10.

100. Dick Mansfield to Time-Life Inc., telegram, May 22, 1958, sheets 3, 4, and 5, NAACP Papers, Part 22, Legal Department Administrative Files, 1956–65, Reel 1. The "nasty in-fighting" between PTA moderates and McKendree did come to pass, as predicted by Mansfield. See "In PTA, Foundation: M'Kendree Asked to Divide Roles," *Virginian-Pilot,* July 29, 1958, back page, 22.

101. "'Let Pupils Know Stand' Judge Says: Officials Chided for Not Following First Order of U.S. Court," *NJG,* August 23, 1958, 1.

102. Heidelberg, *Norfolk 17,* 6.

103. Program, "Testimonial Dinner Honoring Norfolk's Young Pioneers of Freedom: Our Fate Is in Your Hands," December 6, 1958, Dr. Floyd Crawford Papers, Archives, Norfolk State University, Norfolk, Virginia.

104. Heidelberg, *Norfolk 17,* 6.

105. For the best chronology of the countdown to the closures of the schools, see

Denise Watson Batts, "Schools Are Closed: Local Officials Run Out of Options, and State Steps In to Preserve Segregation," *Virginian-Pilot,* October 2, 2008, 1–8.

106. See Edward L. Breeden to W. Fred Duckworth, September 29, 1958, Box 36, 1958, Democratic District Committee Correspondence Folder, ELBP.

3. Conflict and Continuity

1. For the presession setup, Duckworth drama, and the phrase "predominately Negro side of the chamber," see Robert Smith, "Defensive Game," *Virginian-Pilot,* October 5, 1958, 3D. See also Gene Roberts, "Council Indicates: Negroes' Withdrawal Would Reopen the Schools," *Virginian-Pilot,* October 1, 1958, 1, 11; Johnnie A. Moore, "In Heated Session: City Council Turns Away Pleas to Reopen Schools," *NJG,* October 4, 1958, 1, 2.

2. Norfolk City Council Minutes, September 30, 1958, Sargeant Room, Norfolk Public Library. See also Paul Williams, "To Get Schools Reopened: Mayor Suggests Ministers Use Persuasion on Negroes," *Ledger Dispatch,* October 1, 1958, 19.

3. Norfolk City Council Minutes, September 30, 1958.

4. Malcolm Stern, "Living the Norfolk Story," 7, unpublished typed manuscript of speech given at Olef Sholom Synagogue in 1971 and 1976, Special Collections, Lyman Beecher Brooks Library, University Archives, Norfolk State University, Norfolk, Virginia. Stern, a local rabbi and member of the Interracial Ministers Fellowship, was an eyewitness to the meeting.

5. Norfolk City Council Minutes, September 30, 1958. See also Ford, "Religious Support," 322.

6. Norfolk City Council Minutes, September 30, 1958.

7. "In City Council: Rev. Martin Answers Norfolk Mayor's Slur," *NJG,* October 4, 1958, 1, 2.

8. The *Business Week* piece from October 4, 1958, on the school closings was typical of outside white-centered media coverage in its sympathetic portrayal of the moderate board under pressure from extreme segregationists and its complete ignoring of the black plaintiffs and their case against the board. It was reprinted in "Business Sharing the Bill: What Massive Resistance Costs City," *Virginian-Pilot,* October 16, 1958, 4.

9. Charles H. Ford found these transcripts at the National Archives in Philadelphia. These are the transcripts that I gave to journalist and friend Denise Watson Batts, providing the grist for her compelling narrative series commemorating the fiftieth anniversary of the schools closure crisis in the local paper. See, in particular, the fourth part of her six-part series: "Cracks in the Wall: A No-Nonsense Federal Judge Orders School Officials to Take Another Look at the Students They Have Barred from White Schools," *Virginian-Pilot,* October 1, 2008, A1, 10.

10. For biographical information on Cocke, see "Cocke President of Virginia Club: Attorney Succeeds Throckmorton; Washington Taylor Vice President," *Virginian-Pilot and Norfolk Landmark,* January 14, 1934, part 2, 3.

11. Transcript of Proceedings, *Leola Pearl Beckett, et al. v. The School Board of*

the City of Norfolk, Virginia, August 18–20, 1958, U.S. District Court for the Eastern District of Virginia, Norfolk Division, 165–66.

12. Ibid., 78.

13. Jean Bishop Porter, "Placement Injunction Sought: Suit Based Upon Assumption?" *Ledger-Dispatch,* August 12, 1958, 17.

14. Transcript of Proceedings, *Beckett v. Board,* 29, 45, 163.

15. Ibid., 169.

16. Transcript of Proceedings, *Leola Beckett, et al. v. The School Board of the City of Norfolk, Virginia,* Vol. 2, August 21, 1958, U.S. District Court for the Eastern District of Virginia, Norfolk Division, 185–86.

17. Ibid., 190–91. For more biographical information on Schweitzer, see his obituary, "Paul Schweitzer, Ex-councilman Dies at Home," *Ledger-Star,* November 1, 1976, B5.

18. Transcript of Proceedings, *Beckett v. Board,* Vol. 2, 201.

19. Ibid., 192, 203, 227.

20. "Effigy Hung on Flagpole at Norview," *Ledger-Dispatch,* June 12, 1958, 1.

21. Jim Elliott, "Negro Moves Stir Norview," *Ledger-Dispatch,* June 12, 1958, 1.

22. Transcript of Proceedings, *Beckett v. Board,* Vol. 2, 201–8.

23. Ibid., 253–54. For Powell, see Robert A. Pratt, *The Color of Their Skin: Education and Race in Richmond, Virginia 1954–1989* (Charlottesville: University Press of Virginia, 1993), 34–36. Cf. Watson Batts, "Cracks in the Wall."

24. Transcript of Proceedings, *Beckett v. Board,* Vol. 2, 269–78.

25. Delores Johnson Brown, interview with Jeffrey Littlejohn, Spring 2004; Delores Johnson Brown, interview with Charles Ford, June 28, 2009. See also George M. McKinley, "At Informative Meetings on Amendment: Integration Effect Minimized; Circumvention Effort Denied," *Virginian-Pilot,* January 5, 1956, 1, 9.

26. Patricia Turner, interview with Jeffrey Littlejohn, March 17, 2005. For the Turners' milieu, see Watson Batts, "When the Walls Came Tumbling Down." See also the revealing photograph of navy families — both black and white, including the Turners — in 1954 on Little Creek Beach, in *Virginian-Pilot,* September 29, 2008, A10.

27. Transcript of Proceedings, *Leola Beckett, et al. v. The School Board of the City of Norfolk, Virginia,* Vol. 3, August 22 and 25, 1958, U.S. District Court for the Eastern District of Virginia, Norfolk Division, 357–66.

28. Ibid., 357–79.

29. "Parents Satisfied with Their Children's Progress," *NJG,* February 6, 1960, 1.

30. For Godbolt urinating in a field to avoid the always dangerous school bathrooms, see Heidelberg, *Norfolk 17,* 35–36. For Patricia Godbolt White, see Jennifer Jiggetts, "Retired Teacher Remembers Hard Days," *Mix Magazine,* July 2008, 11–12. For Louis Cousins, see Wil LaVeist, "Picture of Pain . . . And Promise," *Mix Magazine,* July 2008, 12–13. For Reed's reception at Granby, see "'Lost Class of '59': Granby Reunion Recalls Bittersweet Memories of Closed Schools," *Ledger-Star,* July 28, 1979, B1, 7. For Portis, see Denise Watson Batts, "17 Students Break Through the Color Barrier: 17 Face Hostile Reception as Schools Reopen," *Virginian-Pilot,*

October 3, 2008, 14. See also Jaedda Armstrong, "Norfolk 17 Recall Their Struggles on Documentary," *Spartan Echo,* February 16, 2009, 1, 3.

31. "'On Road Toward Democracy:' Norfolk Desegregation Reaches First Birthday," *NJG,* February 6, 1960, 1. At the end of the second year of desegregation, Brewbaker was a little less sanguine and admitted the "ugly remarks" and ostracism were making some African American transfers unhappy, but he insisted that "there have been no serious incidents and no interruption in the normal processes of education." Brewbaker, "Desegregation in the Norfolk Public Schools," 14.

32. Transcript of Proceedings, *Beckett v. Board,* Vol. 3, 367–69.

33. Ibid., 405–7.

34. Ibid., 411–13, 464–93.

35. Ibid., 456–57. For the Cousins photograph, see *Mix Magazine,* July 2008, 12.

36. Transcript of Proceedings, *Beckett v. Board,* Vol. 3, 494–518, 553–55, 560.

37. Ibid., 518–20.

38. Ibid., 502–21.

39. Ibid., 562, 563–66.

40. Ibid., 372–79, 606–7.

41. Ibid., 433, 439–45.

42. Ibid., 432.

43. Ibid., 430–33.

44. Ibid., 462–63.

45. Luther J. Carter, "They Don't Expect Schools to Close; Why Did the Negroes Apply? 'A Matter of Principle,'" *Virginian-Pilot,* June 11, 1958, 1, 8. See also Luther J. Carter, "9 Negroes Apply for Norfolk White Schools: Each Case to Be Dealt 'On Merit,'" *Virginian-Pilot,* June 11, 1958, 1, 8.

46. Transcript of Proceedings, *Beckett v. Board,* Vol. 3, 576–80, 616–19. For the Talleys and Titustown, see Christy Holloman Frederick, *Titustown: The People, the Clothing, the Culture* (Norfolk, Va.: Titustown Historical Influence Project, 2004), 5–6.

47. The Virginia General Assembly in 1956 and again in 1958 empowered the governor to use his discretionary powers to close any school facing the imminent prospect of desegregation. For the specific legislation, see Chapter 68 of the acts of the 1956 Extra Session of the Virginia General Assembly, approved on September 29, 1956, and Chapter 631 of the acts of the 1958 Virginia General Assembly, approved on March 29, 1958.

48. Leidholdt, *Standing Before the Shouting Mob,* 95–96. For her Middle East trip, see "Will Seek Peace Formula: Mrs. Mason to Tour Middle East," *Virginian-Pilot,* June 22, 1958, 3A.

49. "How Norfolk Opened Her Schools, February 2, 1959," 14–15, Women's Council for Interracial Cooperation Papers, MG-54, Folder 20, Special Collections, Old Dominion University. For the spiritual mentoring and preparation of the Norfolk 17, see also Margaret L. Gordon and the History and Archives Committee, eds., *A Documented History of the First Baptist Church Bute Street, Norfolk, Virginia*

(Virginia Beach: n.p., 1988), 137–39. See also Leidholdt, *Standing Before the Shouting Mob,* 95–96. For the list of the faculty and staff of the Bute Street school, see the program, "208th Church Anniversary and Freedom Sunday," July 6, 2008, 4, in Charles Ford's possession. See also Ford, "Religious Support," 324.

50. "Tutoring Leaders Proud of 'Norfolk 17' Record," *NJG,* February 6, 1960, 1.

51. James Sweeney, Interview IV with Lewis W. Webb Jr., December 3, 1974, transcript, Special Collections, Perry Library, Old Dominion University. See also Minutes of Meeting, November 17, 1958, 2, Board of Visitors, Norfolk Division of William and Mary College, Miscellaneous File, Special Collections, Old Dominion University.

52. Ralph Mulford, "Many Rumors Popping: Forthcoming CBS-TV Norfolk School Program Exciting Much Curiosity," *Ledger-Dispatch,* January 10, 1959, 13.

53. Luther J. Carter, "Past Seven Backgrounder: Tutoring Group Feelings Mixed," *Virginian-Pilot* (late 1958), clippings file, MG-98, Box 1, Folder 10, Massive Resistance Printed Materials, 1958–60, Special Collections, Perry Library, Old Dominion University. See also "Fire Hazards Studied in Tutoring Schools," *Virginian-Pilot,* December 4, 1958, 9.

54. Louise Watson Todd, *C. Alton Lindsay, Educator and Community Leader* (Lawrenceville, Va.: Brunswick, 1994), 116.

55. Henry Nash, "Personality Sketch: Schweitzer: Realist," *Virginian-Pilot,* January 30, 1959, 5.

56. Chet Paschang, "S. Norfolk's Next Move Hinges on Developments," *Ledger-Dispatch,* January 14, 1959, 15. Even after it was apparent the schools in Norfolk would reopen, Story kept his night schools going. "South Norfolk Plans to Continue Night Schools, Story Announces," *Virginian-Pilot,* January 28, 1959, back page.

57. Wilma Dykeman and James Stokely, "Report on 'The Lost Class of '59,'" *New York Times Magazine,* January 4, 1959, 4.

58. "Coats, Ties a Must: Catholic High Adds 5 Classrooms, 2 New Policies for Incoming Pupils," *Ledger-Dispatch,* August 11, 1958, 13.

59. Jean Bishop Porter, "Private Schools Have Room: Enrollment Rates Not Considered Unusual So Far," *Ledger-Dispatch,* August 8, 1958, 17; Gene Roberts, "New Private Schools Going Up in Norfolk: Facilities Planned for 900 Pupils as 'Crisis' Continues," *Virginian-Pilot,* December 5, 1958, back page, 58.

60. Dorothy Mulligan, "Minister Leads Fight for Public Schools: Norfolk Unitarians Back Rev. James C. Brewer in Virginia's Integration Crisis," *Unitarian Register* (January 1959): 19.

61. Frank Adams, "560 Seniors Missing: Commencement Near at Last For the 'Lost Class' of 1959," *Virginian-Pilot,* June 7, 1959, 3B.

62. Margaret R. Wilkins, "Many May Not Be Back: The 'Lost Class of '59,'" *Virginian-Pilot,* October 19, 1958, 1D.

63. Leidholdt, *Standing Before the Shouting Mob,* 122.

64. Luther J. Carter, "A Past Seven Backgrounder: Is Norfolk 'Complacent' since the Schools Closed?" *Virginian-Pilot,* October 19, 1958, 3D.

65. Leidholdt, *Standing Before the Shouting Mob*, 95–101.

66. For the breakdown of the vote by precinct, see the table "Vote by Precincts," *Virginian-Pilot*, November 19, 1958, 8. See also Leidholdt, *Standing Before the Shouting Mob*, 109.

67. Leidholdt, *Standing Before the Shouting Mob*, 109. Cf. Bob Dodson, "Wensel Gets 3,500 Negro Votes in Defeat by Byrd: Surprisingly Large Off-Year Ballot Gives Senator 3–2 Victory," *Ledger-Dispatch*, November 5, 1958, 1. Dodson considered the number of votes cast in Norfolk in the senatorial race in early November "surprisingly large" at 22,683; so, the 21,052 votes cast on the referendum two weeks later would have been in that same range to him.

68. Leidholdt, *Standing Before the Shouting Mob*, 109.

69. "No School for Grandson?: 'Duty' Came First with City Father," *Ledger-Dispatch*, January 15, 1959, 1. Abbott would later serve on the board of directors for the segregationist TEF's Tidewater Academy.

70. "Virginia, North Carolina: The Past Seven," *Virginian-Pilot*, January 18, 1959, 3B.

71. Luther J. Carter, "Between Council and School Board: History of a Norfolk Tiff," *Virginian-Pilot*, January 25, 1959, 1C.

72. Paid advertisement, "A Public Petition to the Norfolk City Council," *Virginian-Pilot*, January 27, 1959, 11; cf. Leidholdt, *Standing Before the Shouting Mob*, 118. See also "Appeal by 100 Leaders: Reopen Schools, Council Urged," *Virginian-Pilot*, January 27, 1959, 1. Thirty-five junior white executives and professionals in the city immediately followed with their own proschools pronouncement. "New School Plea Aimed at Council: Young Men Urge Early Reopening," *Virginian-Pilot*, January 28, 1959, 13.

73. Cf. Leidholdt, *Standing Before the Shouting Mob*, 111–12, 118.

74. Watson Batts, "17 Students Break Through Color Barrier," 14.

75. Quoted in Leidholdt, *Standing Before the Shouting Mob*, 122. For the Norfolk 17's diverse reactions to their first day back, see Jim Henderson, "'Like Any Other Student, I Guess': 17 Who Broke Color Line Report Some Friendliness, a Few Gaffs," *Virginian-Pilot*, February 3, 1959, back page, 20.

76. Mrs. William Thomas Mason to Edward L. Breeden, February 2, 1959, Edward L. Breeden to Mrs. William Thomas Mason, February 9, 1959, both in Box 40–41, 1959 Perrow Commission File, ELBP.

77. For Savage's quote and the assembly's reaction, see George M. Kelley, "Conduct Praised: Tribute Paid by Assembly," *Virginian-Pilot*, February 3, 1959, back page. For the White House's approval, see "'A Fine Thing': Eisenhower Pleased with Norfolk," *Virginian-Pilot*, February 3, 1959, 1.

78. James A. Anderson, Campaign Associate of the United Good Neighbor Fund, to Paul T. Schweitzer, February 3, 1959, Paul T. Schweitzer Papers, Special Collections, Old Dominion University.

79. Transcript, "Are Shipowners Insurers for Unseaworthiness?" Address of the Honorable Walter E. Hoffman, U.S. District Judge, Norfolk, Virginia, Admiralty

Day Luncheon, Fourteenth Annual Convention, NACCA Bar Association, San Francisco, July 28, 1960, in Walter E. Hoffman Papers, Ms #015, Box 2004M: 001, 4, Hoffman Speeches, 1960–68, Lewis J. Powell, Jr., Archives, School of Law, Washington and Lee University, Lexington, Virginia.

80. "Name-Calling Admitted: Cover-Up of Race Incidents at Norview Denied by Perdue," *Virginian-Pilot,* May 26, 1959, back page.

81. Ibid.

82. "Inez Baker Raps Talk by Williams: Moderation Plans Reversal Urged," *Virginian-Pilot,* February 18, 1959, 8.

83. Ibid. For information on Delegate Baker, see "Mrs. Baker May Race Sen. Spong," *Virginian-Pilot,* April 14, 1959, 3; "To Offer Bill Today: Let Assembly Run Schools: Mrs. Baker," *Virginian-Pilot,* April 14, 1959, 1.

84. Walter E. Hoffman as quoted by Jim Henderson in "Hoffman Frowns on Mass Mixing: Judge May 'Invite' State Pupil Board," *Virginian-Pilot,* April 26, 1959, 1.

85. "Will the NAACP Take Heed?" *Richmond Times-Dispatch,* February 20, 1959.

86. "Moderation for the NAACP," *Virginian-Pilot,* February 18, 1959, 4.

87. "New Strategy Needed," *NJG,* May 2, 1959, 1. See also "Alerting the Opposition; Mr. Wilkins' Error," *NJG,* February 28, 1959, 8; G. W. C. Brown's letter to the editor, "An Endorsement on 'New Strategy Needed,'" *NJG,* May 16, 1959, 8.

88. J. Lindsay Almond Jr., January 30, 1959, Senate Document No. 1, Extra Session, 1959, House and Senate Documents, 1959, Commonwealth of Virginia, Richmond, 8.

89. Report on the Commission on Education to the Governor of Virginia, Senate Document No. 2, Extra Session 1959, House and Senate Documents, 1959, Commonwealth of Virginia, Richmond.

90. Ibid.

91. James H. Hershman Jr., "Massive Resistance Meets Its Match: The Emergence of a Pro–Public School Majority," in *The Moderate's Dilemma: Massive Resistance to School Desegregation in Virginia,* ed. Matthew D. Lassiter and Andrew B. Lewis (Charlottesville: University Press of Virginia, 1998), 129.

92. George M. Kelley, "Almond 'Force' Resisted: Inez Baker Rips Governor," *Virginian-Pilot,* April 4, 1959, back page.

93. J. Lindsay Almond Jr. quoted in George M. Kelley, "Perrow Bills Get Almond's Support: Hits Back at Critics of Report," *Virginian-Pilot,* April 7, 1959. On April 16, the local option bill passed the House of Delegates by a seven-vote margin (fifty-three to forty-six). All of Norfolk's members of the House of Delegates — James Roberts, Delamater Davis, Theodore Pilcher, John Rixey, Toy Savage, and John Harper — voted for the Perrow plan's local option bill to be included.

94. George M. Kelley, "Local Option to Get Whole Senate Study: Public Hearing Monday," *Virginian-Pilot,* April 18, 1959, 1, 5.

95. George M. Kelley, "Almond Forces Gain, Perrow Plan Enacted: Assignment Bill Radically Changed," *Virginian-Pilot,* April 24, 1959, 1, 8.

96. "What Is All the Shouting About?" *NJG,* April 25, 1959, 13.

97. "Council Asks Change in School Board Law," *Virginian-Pilot,* April 10, 1959, back page.

98. "Requested by Council: 5 Norfolk Delegates Introduce Bill to Change School Board," *Virginian-Pilot,* April 16, 1959, back page.

99. "Choice of Mrs. Griffin Defended by Duckworth," *NJG,* July 4, 1959, 15. In fact, Roberts, a supervisor in the navy's Regional Accounts Office, was so controversial that he resigned from the school board in 1960, after serving one year. He was then appointed to the Norfolk Port and Industrial Authority by Mayor Duckworth and the city council. See "The New Politics in Norfolk," *Virginian-Pilot,* July 2, 1960, 4. Stanley Walker, who would go on to be one of Norfolk's most respected voices in the General Assembly a generation in the future, was at the time a thirty-eight-year-old secretary of Standard Oil and Gas Company. On Griffin's position with the TEF, see "Martin Heads Organization to Set Up Private Schools," *Virginian-Pilot,* July 11, 1958, 12.

100. "Council Step Advances Rosemont School Plans," *Virginian-Pilot,* January 14, 1959, 45.

101. "Commission Invites Ideas on Schools," *Virginian-Pilot,* February 22, 1959, 1. Four of the schoolhouses—Easton, East Ocean View, Pretty Lake, and Fair-lawn—were built in a thirteen-square-mile area that Norfolk annexed from Princess Anne County in 1959.

102. See the photograph with the revealing title and caption: "Muddy Welcome: Children Waiting to Enter the New Coronado Elementary School Line Up on the Concrete Pavement to Avoid the Mud Surrounding the Buildings," *Ledger-Dispatch,* September 8, 1959, 17; "No 'New' Front on Schools," *NJG,* August 22, 1959, 1–2.

103. "Parents, Localities Affected: State Sets Deadlines on Student Grants," *Virginian-Pilot,* August 3, 1960, 2.

104. Forrest White, "Tuition Grants—Strange Fruit of Southern School Integration," Forrest White Papers, Special Collections, Perry Library, Old Dominion University.

105. The exact breakdown was as follows: 36,498 white students and 17,117 black students. Funding included $3.4 million from the state, $2.1 million from the federal government, and $6.3 million from local city/county funds. Superintendent's Report, Library of Virginia, Richmond.

106. On the tuition grant debate, see "Do Taxpayers Save by Tuition Money?" *Virginian-Pilot,* May 30, 1960, 4.

107. "School Charter Issued: TEF Plans New Financing," *Virginian-Pilot,* August 5, 1960, 29.

108. "Enrollment Extended by TEF: Registration Below Academy's Estimate," *Virginian-Pilot,* July 2, 1959, 45; "175 Enroll at Academy," *Ledger-Dispatch,* September 8, 1959, 17.

109. "Norfolk School 'Peace' Is Temporary: Councilmen Seen Biding Their Time," *NJG,* June 27, 1959, 3. For more information, see "School Transfer Tests for 19 Norfolk Students," *NJG,* June 20, 1959, 1.

110. "No 'New' Front on Schools."

111. Ibid., 2.

112. *Hill v. School Board of City of Norfolk*, 282 F.2d 473. For information on pupil assignment locations, see "'On Road to Democracy': Norfolk Desegregation Reaches First Birthday," *NJG*, February 13, 1960, 4; Lin Holloway, "Pupil Humiliated: Board Act Implies Schools Inferior: Heart-Sick 7th Grader Legal Pawn," *NJG*, June 4, 1960, 1–2. Gloria Scott was assigned to Blair Junior High, Bobby J. Neville to Norview Junior High, and Mary Rose Foxworth to Suburban Park Elementary. See *Beckett*, 185 F. Supp. 459.

113. See *Beckett*, 185 F. Supp. 459.

114. Ibid. See also "6 Win in Norfolk Court; N.C. Board Lowers Bars," *NJG*, September 5, 1959, 1–2; "Placement Member Admits Race Entered His Decision," *Virginian-Pilot*, August 28, 1959, 1.

115. *Beckett*, 185 F. Supp. 459. See also "6 Win in Norfolk Court." Patricia Turner went to Norview High, Reginald Young and Anita Mayer to Maury High, and Daphne Perminter to Suburban Park Elementary.

116. *Beckett*, 185 F. Supp. 459.

117. The members of the Pupil Placement Board did not believe that they were required to take affirmative steps toward desegregation. In fact, they resigned, effective June 1, 1960. See "Stymied by Courts: Pupil Placement Board Quits," *NJG*, February 27, 1960, B1.

4. Protest and Progress

1. William Bagby quoted in Malcolm Scully, "Negro Students March with List of Grievances," *Virginian-Pilot*, September 20, 1963, 33.

2. For students who participated in the March on Washington, see "Norfolk Youth Took Part in Big March, Too," *NJG*, August 31, 1963, B2.

3. For the students' petition, see NSBM, Reel 1510, 118; Malcolm Scully, "Negro Students March," *Virginian-Pilot*, September 20, 1963, 33.

4. Obie McCollum, "2,400 B-T Pupils March: Lack of Facilities and Crowded Conditions Hit," *NJG*, September 21, 1963, C1; Scully, "Negro Students March."

5. "The Overcrowded High Schools," *Virginian-Pilot*, September 20, 1963, 4; Wayne Woodlief, "School Condition Blame Shared by All, Says Ray," *Ledger-Star*, September 21, 1963, 11.

6. For Superintendent Lamberth's report, see NSBM, Reel 1510, 137.

7. Rorer, *History of Norfolk Public Schools*; Ruegsegger, *History of Norfolk Public Schools*. The Booker T. Washington demonstration was mentioned in *SSN* 10, no. 2 (October 1963): 3.

8. For instance, in an otherwise excellent article, Mary Doyle covered the period from 1959 to 1968 in a single paragraph. Mary Doyle, "From Desegregation to Resegregation: Public Schools in Norfolk, Virginia, 1954–2002," *Journal of African American History* 90, no. 1 (January 2005): 64–83.

9. Mayor Duckworth quoted in Parramore, Stewart, and Bogger, *Norfolk*, 374.

10. U.S. Census Bureau, "Number of Inhabitants: Population of Incorporated and Urban Places: 1940 and 1930," Vol. 1, Table 5, 1940, http://www2.census.gov/prod2/decennial/documents/33973538v1ch09.pdf; U.S. Census Bureau, "Number of Inhabitants: Population of Incorporated Places of 10,000 or More," Vol. 1, Part 48, Table 5, 1960, http://www2.census.gov/prod2/decennial/documents/09768066v1p48ch2.pdf.

11. "School Board of City of Norfolk Enrollment," June 1960, NSBM, Reel 1501A.

12. "Integration Goes On in 3 Virginia Areas," *New York Times,* September 7, 1962, 59.

13. *CBS Reports: The Other Face of Dixie,* first broadcast October 24, 1962. Copies are available from Films for the Humanities, 132 West 31st Street, New York, NY 10001.

14. Luther J. Carter, "All American City," *Virginian-Pilot,* March 4, 1960, 29.

15. In 1960, the population of Norfolk was 305,872. Of this number, 225,251 (74 percent) were white, and 78,806 (25 percent) were black. On race and city commissions, see "A Past Seven Backgrounder: Inter-Racial Relations," *Virginian-Pilot,* June 15, 1958, 3D. On the request for a biracial committee under Mayor Duckworth, see "Minutes, City Council Meeting, June 3, 1958," NCRB, Reel 83. On Duckworth's views on African Americans, see "Minutes, City Council Meeting, September 30, 1958," NCRB, Reel 83. See also "Duckworth Returns — Mayor: 'Equality Should Be Earned, Not Legislated,'" *NJG,* October 7, 1961, C1. Although Henry Louis Suggs suggests that Duckworth and P. B. Young Sr. were discussing interracial matters by private correspondence in 1960–61, there is no evidence that Duckworth wanted an interracial council. See, for comparison, Suggs, *P. B. Young,* 185–86.

16. William H. Chafe, *Civilities and Civil Rights: Greensboro, North Carolina, and the Black Struggle for Freedom* (New York: Oxford University Press, 1981).

17. Eric Jones quoted in Cindy Schreuder, "Color Barrier Fell 25 Years Ago," *Virginian-Pilot,* March 24, 1985, B1. For a complete review of the sit-in demonstrations in Norfolk, see Jeffrey Littlejohn, "'Sit Down Children, Sit Down': The Sit-In Movement in Norfolk, Virginia," in Alexander, Newby-Alexander, and Ford, *Voices from Within the Veil,* 330–44.

18. Mr. and Mrs. Wayne Dick to Governor J. Lindsay Almond Jr., February 4, 1959, ALP, Public Education, Sections 129 and 133, Box 37. See also Randolph McPherson, "BiRacial Commissions," *Virginian-Pilot,* August 18, 1960, 4; Victor Buhr, "Rickover on Education," *Virginian-Pilot,* August 25, 1960, 4.

19. See Henry Howell's papers in the Special Collections at Old Dominion University.

20. See, for example, Ellis James, "The Negro in Public Life," *Virginian-Pilot,* March 7, 1960, 4. On Seashore State Park, see "White Citizens Campaign to Open Park," *NJG,* July 28, 1962, B15; "Seashore Pk. Sets Camp Site Openings," *NJG,* August 18, 1962, C1. On Henry Howell and the People's Ticket, see "In Peoples Ticket Platform Racial Amity Group Proposed for Norfolk," *NJG,* March 17, 1962, C1; "Committee of 100 Women Backs Peoples Ticket," *NJG,* June 9, 1962, C1; "Election Re-

flections; Blank Sheet Killed," *NJG*, November 10, 1962, B15. On Forrest White, see "Tuition Grant's—Strange Fruit of Southern School Integration," Papers of Forrest White, Box 1, Folder 11, Special Collections, Old Dominion University. For the end of the Norfolk Committee for Public Schools, see Forrest White to All Members of the Board of Directors, Norfolk Committee for Public Schools, May 7, 1963, Papers of Forrest White, Box 1, Folder 5, Special Collections, Old Dominion University.

21. Virginius Dabney, "Next in the South's Schools: 'Limited Integration,'" *U.S. News and World Report*, January 19, 1960, 92–94.

22. Francis Crenshaw quoted in "A Legal Dilemma for Five More Years," *NJG*, August 26, 1961, D1.

23. "Five School Board Posts Filled; Colored Ignored," *NJG*, July 22, 1961, C27. On Crenshaw's children, see William Tazewell, "Next Move: 4 School Boardmen," *Virginian-Pilot*, July 13, 1963, 15–17.

24. For details of the testing procedure, see "Special Notice No. 540," May 26, 1961, NSBM, Reel 1504, 21; "Procedure for Granting or Denying Certain Applications," August 10, 1961, NSBM, Reel 1504, 20. Once the request was submitted, all children seeking transfers were required to complete the California Test of Mental Maturity (elementary) or the Henmon-Nelson Test of Mental Ability (secondary).

25. Twenty-two African American students were admitted to previously white schools in February and September 1959. In September 1960, thirty-one African American students applied for transfers, and one was approved by the school board. "Minutes," July 25, 1960, NSBM, Reel 1501. Judge Hoffman then requested that five more students be approved, and the school board met his request. "Resolution," September 8, 1960, NSBM, Reel 1502, 52. In September 1961, 113 African American students applied for transfers, and 31 were approved by the school board. "Minutes," July 27, 1961, NSBM, 1504, 11. Judge Hoffman then requested that two more students be approved, and the school board met his request. "Minutes," August 24, 1961, NSBM, Reel 1504, 41. In September 1962, sixty-three African American students applied for transfers to predominantly white schools; thirty-six students were granted transfers, and eight were granted probationary transfers. "Resolution," August 23, 1962, NSBM, Reel 1507, 34. Then, twenty-four of seventy-five late African American applicants were approved for transfers. "Resolution," September 6, 1962, NSBM, Reel 1507, 36. Finally, five African Americans who moved to Norfolk during the year were approved for transfers. "Resolution," October 11, 1962, NSBM, Reel 1507, 69; "Resolution," October 25, 1962, Reel 1507, 79; "Report on the 1962–63 School Year," March 12, 1963, NPSDP, Box 3, Folder 17.

26. Holloway, "Pupil Humiliated," 1–2.

27. Vivian Carter Mason to the Norfolk School Board, May 30, 1960, NPSDP, Box 2, Folder 13.

28. Vivian Carter Mason quoted in Mather, "Black Woman with Clout," G2.

29. Roy Wilkins quoted in Pratt, *Color of Their Skin*, 36.

30. "Minutes," July 25, 1960, NSBM, Reel 1501; "Resolution," September 8, 1960, NSBM, Reel 1502, 52; "Transfer of Negro Ratified," *Virginian-Pilot*, August 16, 1960,

15; Glenn Scott, "Negro Pupils Fight Denial of Transfers," *Virginian-Pilot*, August 17, 1960, 17; "August 31st Hearing Set; Test Methods Are Under Attack in School Suit," *NJG*, August 27, 1960, D2; "Negro Pupils Claim Inaccuracies: Pupil Tests Face Challenge," *Virginian-Pilot*, August 30, 1960, 15; "Tests in Desegregation Cases," *Virginian-Pilot*, September 2, 1960, 4.

31. "Minutes," July 27, 1961, NSBM, 1504, 11; "Minutes," August 24, 1961, NSBM, Reel 1504, 41; "25 Rejected Norfolk Pupils to Bring Suit," *NJG*, August 5, 1961, 1; "A Legal Dilemma for Five More Years," *NJG*, August 26, 1961, D1; "Norfolk Pupils Appeal Ruling Rejecting Them," *NJG*, September 9, 1961, A2.

32. "Resolution," August 23, 1962, NSBM, Reel 1507, 34; "Resolution," September 6, 1962, NSBM, Reel 1507, 36; "Resolution," October 11, 1962, NSBM, Reel 1507, 69; "Resolution," October 25, 1962, NSBM, Reel 1507, 79; "Report on the 1962–63 School Year"; "Is This Compliance with Court Order?" *NJG*, April 14, 1962, C1; "Delegates Elected; Norfolk NAACP Decries Slow School Desegregation," *NJG*, June 16, 1962, B20; "Eight Already Desegregated; Eleven Schools Involved in Norfolk Transfer Bids for Fall 1962," *NJG*, June 23, 1962, B1; "44 Negro Pupils Get Transfers," *NJG*, August 25, 1962, C1; "Early Board Action Due in Ghent School Appeals," *NJG*, September 1, 1962, C2; "To Lee, Marshall, Etc; 23 Additional Norfolk Pupils Given Assignment," *NJG*, September 8, 1962, C1.

33. Turner, interview; Brown, interview.

34. "Memo to Mr. Francis Crenshaw, Chairman of the Board and All Board Members," February 7, 1962, NSBM, Reel 1505, 170.

35. "Report to the School Board on Investigation of Matters Presented by the Douglas Park Parent Committee," March 8, 1962, NSBM, Reel 1505, 263; "In New Location: Board Sets Replacement of Douglas Park School, *NJG*, February 17, 1962, B15; "Douglas Park P-TA Protests Council Action," *NJG*, May 19, 1962, C1.

36. For information on Roberts Park Elementary, see "Opens in September; Roberts Park School Modern in Every Detail," *NJG*, August 1, 1964, B15. Roberts Park served the area previously served by Douglas Park (closed), Stonewall Jackson (closed), and a portion of the Bowling Park area.

37. "Petition on School Facilities," presented to the Norfolk School Board by the Oakwood Parent Association, April 12, 1962, NSBM, Reel 1505, 239. See also "Parent-Teacher Association Council Report," presented to the Norfolk School Board by the Parent Teacher Association Council Educational Committee, May 1962, NSBM, Reel 1506, 259. On inventive scheduling practices, see "Minutes," May 10, 1962, NSBM, Reel 1506, 75.

38. "Parent Teacher Association Council Report," NSBM, Reel 1506, 259.

39. Bill Sauder, "Norfolk Entering New Era, Says Newly Elected Mayor," *Ledger-Star*, September 3, 1962, 17. On the end of the Duckworth era, see "Duckworth Chooses Not to Run Again," *NJG*, March 17, 1962, B1; "Duckworth Era Fades, Mayor Bows Out with Blessing of Rev. Brown," *NJG*, September 1, 1962, B3; "Dawn of a New Era at City Hall," *NJG*, September 8, 1962, B11A.

40. Patricia Godbolt graduated from Norview in 1960 and went on to Wash-

ington College in Chestertown, Maryland, where she was the first black female graduate. Betty Jean Reed graduated from Granby in 1961; Carol Wellington graduated from Norview in 1961; Johnnie Anita Rouse graduated from Norview in 1961; Alveraze Frederick Gonsouland graduated from Booker T. Washington in 1961; Louis Cousins graduated from Maury in 1962; Andrew Heidelberg graduated from Norview in 1962; Reginald Young graduated from Maury in 1962; Geraldine Talley graduated from Granby in 1963; Patricia Turner graduated from Norview in 1963; Delores Johnson graduated from Booker T. Washington in 1963; James Turner graduated from Norview in 1964; Lolita Portis graduated from Maury in 1964; Claudia Wellington graduated from George Washington High in San Francisco; LeVera Forbes graduated from Norview High School; Olivia Driver and Edward Jordan, unknown. Linda Waller, "They Were the First to Integrate Norfolk Schools," *Virginian-Pilot*, December 21, 1974.

41. "Portsmouth and Princess Anne Show How Its Done," *NJG*, September 8, 1962, B11A; "Seashore Pk. Sets Camp Site Openings," C1; "Two VA Anti-NAACP Laws Declared Unconstitutional, One Restricted," *NJG*, September 22, 1962, 3; "Election Reflections; Blank Sheet Killed," *NJG*, November 10, 1962, B15; Mark Tushnet, *Making Constitutional Law: Thurgood Marshall and the Supreme Court, 1961–1991* (New York: Oxford University Press, 1997).

42. "Attorneys in Protest—State Committee 'Raids' Didn't Get Member Lists," *NJG*, September 16, 1961, 1.

43. "Jordan, Dawley, Holt: Law Firm Suspending Practice in VA," *NJG*, October 6, 1962, C2. For Judge Hoffman's nondecision decision, see his memorandum from August 27, 1962, *Joseph A. Jordan v. Joseph C. Hutcheson*, Civil Action 3688, U.S. District Court for the Eastern District of Virginia, Norfolk Division, in Walter E. Hoffman Papers, Ms #015, Box 2004M: 001, Opinions—(Civil 1962), Lewis F. Powell, Jr., Archives, School of Law, Washington and Lee University.

44. On a previous request for a biracial committee, see "NAACP Leader Proposes Bi-Racial School Study," *Virginian-Pilot*, January 28, 1959, 2. On Mayor Martin and the CAC, see "Advisors to Hear Racial Complaints: 25 Member Norfolk Group Asks 'What Do Negroes Want'?" *NJG*, July 6, 1963, B1; "Work Forces Integrated: Job Policy Changes Are Bared at CAC Meeting," *NJG*, November 9, 1963, B2.

45. "Most Hotels in Norfolk Open to All," *NJG*, July 27, 1963, 1. Jack Amory is quoted in "75% Mix Now—Race No Block to Inn Doors," *Virginian-Pilot*, July 23, 1963, 17.

46. Victor Ashe and J. Hugo Madison, "Petition to the School Board of the City of Norfolk," April 23, 1963, NSBM, Reel 1509, 218.

47. Ibid.

48. "Memo to Victor Ashe and J. Hugo Madison," June 13, 1963, NSBM, Reel 1509, 245.

49. William K. Stevens, "Token Mixing Ended," *Virginian-Pilot*, September 13, 1963, 35. This was the first time that faculty desegregation entered the litigation. At the beginning of the case, Judge Hoffman reminded the lawyers that "his wife [wa]s a public school librarian that might be affected by integration of the faculty.

He said he would not want to see any decision of his on that score appealed on grounds that he was an interested party. He said he was an interested party. He said he would withdraw if they wished. The attorneys agreed he should hear the entire suit." "Mixing Suit Delayed," *Virginian-Pilot,* July 24, 1963, 17. In his later memorandum opinion—filed July 30, 1964—Hoffman denied the request for an order to desegregate the faculties, holding that the issue was not clearly resolved by superior courts.

50. Bill Sauder, "Maneuvers Cause Delay," *Ledger-Star,* July 25, 1963, B1; J. R. Roseberry, "Advisers Vote for Negro on School Board," *Virginian-Pilot,* July 16, 1963, 15; *SSN* 10, no. 2 (August 1963): 15.

51. J. R. Roseberry, "Norfolk Attorney: Negro Put on School Board," *Virginian-Pilot,* July 31, 1963, 1, 15. When the CAC was designated as mediator of the city's racial problems, a number of African American leaders objected, charging that its members—including Jones and the other four black members—were not representative of the community. For criticism of Jones's appointment to the board, see Harvey E. White Sr., "Opposes Negro on School Board," *Virginian-Pilot,* July 28, 1963, B2. For Jerrauld Jones winning the Stouffer scholarship, see Wayne Woodlief, "5 Area Negro Students Attend South's Finest," *Ledger-Star,* January 9, 1969, 15.

52. Malcolm Scully, "Negro Students March," *Virginian-Pilot,* September 20, 1963, 33; "Norfolk Board Acts; 77 After-Deadline Pupils May Gain Transfers," *NJG,* September 14, 1963, B1.

53. Lucy Rockwood, telephone interview with Jeffrey Littlejohn, May 21, 2007; Obituary of Leonard Davis, *Virginian-Pilot,* May 31, 1997, B6. For the recommendations of Davis as police justice, see W. L. Prieur to Dr. C. J. Andrews, January 17, 1944, C. J. Andrews to J. D. Wood, January 14, 1944, George R. Abbott to Dr. C. J. Andrews, January 17, 1944, all in the Mason Andrews Papers, unprocessed folder, Special Collections, Old Dominion University.

54. William K. Stevens, "Integration of Schools Requested," *Virginian-Pilot,* July 12, 1963, 31; "Norfolk Mix Suit Delayed: Rights of 6 1st on Agenda," *Virginian-Pilot,* July 24, 1963, 17; "School Board Suggests: Allow Children to Pick Schools," *Virginian-Pilot,* August 9, 1963, 29; William K. Stevens, "Token Mixing Ended," *Virginian-Pilot,* September 13, 1963, 35; "Schools Answer NAACP," *Virginian-Pilot,* November 2, 1963, 19; "Minutes of the Public Meeting of the School Board, September 3, 1963," NSBM, Reel 1510, 67. See also the materials relating to Leonard Davis in NPSDP, Box 5, Folder 9. Other states reported these statistics in 1963: Mississippi had no African Americans enrolled in desegregated schools; South Carolina had 9; Alabama, 21; Georgia, 177; Arkansas, 366; Louisiana, 1,814; North Carolina, 1,865; and Florida, 3,650. Southern Education Reporting Services, Statistical Summary, November 1963, revised especially for the Commission on Civil Rights as of August 1, 1964, quoted in 1964 Staff Report, Submitted to the U.S. Commission on Civil Rights, October 1964, 231, 291.

55. A headline in the *NJG* summed up the story well: "205 Pupils since 1959; Integration Hits Record But Is a Drop in a Bucket," *NJG,* August 10, 1963, B16.

56. Joseph Jordan to Edwin Lamberth, March 25, 1964, NPSDP, Box 4, Folder 6.

57. *Beckett v. School Board,* Memorandum decision, July 30, 1964, NPSDP, Box 5, Folder 5; Hoffman quoted in *SSN* 11, no. 2 (August 1964): 5.

58. *Griffin v. County School Board of Prince Edward County,* 377 U.S. 218 (1964).

59. J. Harvie Wilkinson III, *From Brown to Bakke: The Supreme Court and School Integration, 1954–1978* (New York: Oxford University Press, 1979), 103.

60. Ibid., 104.

61. *SSN* 11, no. 1 (July 1964): 12; *SSN* 11, no. 4 (October 1964): 1; *SSN* 11, no. 5 (November 1964): 8.

62. "Controversy Centers on Tuition Grants," *SSN* 11, no. 5 (November 1964): 8. This article originally appeared in Robert P. Hilldrup, "Controversy Centers on Tuition Grants," *Richmond News Leader,* October 2, 1964.

63. Idella P. Owens to Governor J. Lindsay Almond, February 16, 1961, ALP, Public Education, Sections 129 and 133, Box 37.

64. Marjorie P. Claud to Governor J. Lindsay Almond, May 3, 1961, ALP, Public Education, Sections 129 and 133, Box 37.

65. W. F. Duckworth quoted in "Tuition Grants Save Money, Mayor Says," *Virginian-Pilot,* June 22, 1960, 17.

66. "The Locality's Stake in Tuition Grants," *Ledger-Dispatch,* May 25, 1960, 6.

67. *Virginian-Pilot* quoted in Staige Blackford, "Free Choice and Tuition Grants in Five Southern States," *New South* 19, no. 4 (April 1964): 5.

68. "Tuition Grants as Velvet," *Virginian-Pilot,* May 7, 1960, 4.

69. Larrymore Elementary School PTA to Governor J. Lindsay Almond Jr., February 1961; Lakewood Parent Teachers Association to J. Lindsay Almond Jr., February 14, 1961; W. H. Taylor Parent Teachers Association to J. Lindsay Almond Jr., May 1961, all in ALP, Public Education, Sections 129 and 133, Box 37.

70. 339 F.2d 486. See also *SSN* 11, no. 6 (December 1964): 1.

71. Tidewater Academy in Norfolk was one of twelve schools mentioned in the complaint. 1964 Staff Report, Submitted to the U.S. Commission on Civil Rights, October 1964, 277; *SSN* 11, no. 3 (September 1964): 8).

72. *SSN* 11, no. 4 (October 1964): 12; *SSN* 11, no. 6 (January 1965): 4.

73. *Griffin v. State Board of Education* 239 F. Supp. 560 (1965).

74. *Griffin v. State Board of Education* 296 F. Supp. 1178 (1969); *Race Relations Law Survey* 1, no. 2 (July 1969).

75. "Drive to Desegregate Norfolk YMCA Hits New Peak," *NJG,* February 27, 1965, A15; "Rights Act Employed against Central; Wide Impact Forecast in Norfolk YMCA Suit," *NJG,* February 27, 1965, C1; "Norfolk 'Y' Opens Doors to Negroes," *Washington Post,* March 27, 1965, B3. On March 26, the Central YMCA agreed to integrate, and the federal court in Norfolk dismissed an NAACP suit against the Norfolk YMCA.

76. Peter Wallenstein, *Blue Laws and Black Codes: Conflict, Courts, and Change in Twentieth-Century Virginia* (Charlottesville: University of Virginia Press, 2004), 188–91.

77. "Neighborhoods Cited: School 'Choice' Plan Hit," *Ledger-Star,* September 1, 1965, A10.

78. *Bradley v. School Board of City of Richmond,* 382 U.S. 103 (1965).

79. William K. Stevens, "All Negro Pupils Could Mix," *Virginian-Pilot,* December 2, 1965, 49, 54.

80. The January 3, 1966, objections of the NAACP may be found in the NPSDP, Box 6, Folder 9. For a secondary account, see William K. Stevens, "They Reasoned Together," *Virginian-Pilot,* May 29, 1966, B1, B5.

81. Wilkinson, *From Brown to Bakke,* 109.

82. Pratt, *Color of Their Skin,* 42.

83. Stevens, "They Reasoned Together."

84. *SSN* 13, no. 6 (January 1966): Va-4. For the motion admitting the Justice Department, see the Appendix for the Appellees, *Brewer v. School Board of Norfolk,* July 1966, for the Fourth Circuit Court of Appeals, in NPSDP, Box 8, Folder 2.

85. See St. John Barrett to Leonard Davis, April 28, 1966; Victor Ashe to Leonard Davis, July 21, 1966; Leonard Davis to Victor Ashe, July 25, 1966; Leonard Davis to St. John Barrett, August 11, 1966, all in NPSDP Box 8, Folder 1.

86. Stevens, "They Reasoned Together."

87. Ibid.

88. Davis and Cocke were principally concerned with the Supreme Court's decision in *Bradley v. School Board of City of Richmond,* 382 U.S. 103 (1965). Yet they were also aware of recent decisions at the district level as well. For instance, on January 5, 1966, U.S. District Judge Thomas Michie Jr. of Charlottesville established a formula for faculty desegregation in cases involving Staunton and Augusta county schools. *SSN* 12, no. 6 (January 1966): Va-2. Then, on January 28, 1966, U.S. District Judge John Butzner of Richmond issued orders for faculty desegregation in cases involving Greensville, Hanover, and Goochland schools. *SSN* 12, no. 6 (January 1966): Va-4.

89. Leonard Davis to W. R. C. Cocke, November 25, 1965; W. R. C. Cocke to Leonard Davis, NPSDP, December 1, 1965, both in NPSDP, Box 5, Folder 9.

90. "Plan of the School Board of the City of Norfolk for Desegregation of the Public Schools of the City," March 17, 1966, NSBM, Reel 1516, 320.

91. Henry Marsh said the plan was a "compromise . . . a consensus that was certainly not a victory." *SSN* 12, no. 8 (March 1966): VA-4.

92. *Beckett v. School Board of the City of Norfolk,* March 17, 1966, NPSDP, Box 6, Folder 15.

93. "Resolution of the School Board of the City of Norfolk," July 19, 1966, NSBM, Reel 1519, 69; William K. Stevens, "Help Asked of Teachers on Mixing," *Virginian-Pilot,* March 24, 1966, 63.

94. "Resolution Concerning the Plan of the School Board of the City of Norfolk for Desegregation of the Public Schools of the City," July 19, 1966, NSBM, Reel 1519, 3.

95. "Minutes," April 14, 1966, NSBM, Reel 1516, 356. For other complaints, see NPSDP, Box 7, Folder 4.

96. Vincent Thomas quoted in "Excerpt from Transcript of Trial Proceedings, April 17, 1967," 68, in "Appendix for Appellees," *Brewer v. School Board of Norfolk,* NPSDP, Box 7, Folder 10.

97. "The Public Schools of the City of Norfolk, Their Pupil Memberships and the Extent of Integration Therein," September 20, 1966, NSBM, Reel 1522, 400.

98. *SSN* 12, no. 12 (June 1966): Va-5.

99. "Booker T. Site Issue in U.S. Court—City's New School Plan Under Fire," *NJG*, April 15, 1967, 1; William K. Stevens, "Court Asked to Mix Schools NAACP Objects to Booker T. Site," *Virginian-Pilot*, April 14, 1967, 37, 45.

100. "Booker T. Site Issue in U.S. Court," 1.

101. Stevens, "Court Asked to Mix Schools."

102. "Minutes," April 13, 1967, NSBM, Reel 1522, 404. See also "Negroes Not for Plan," *Virginian-Pilot*, April 14, 1967, 37, 45.

103. "Brief of Appellees," *Brewer v. School Board of Norfolk*, No. 11,782, NPSDP, Box 7, Folder 10, 7.

104. *Beckett v. School Board of the City of Norfolk*, 269 F. Supp 118 (E.D. VA 1967).

105. "Minutes, Special Meeting of the School Board," May 19, 1967, NSBM, Reel 1522, 482–A; "Minutes Special Meeting of the School Board," May 23, 1967, NSBM, Reel 1522, 482–D.

106. "Minutes, Special Meeting of the School Board," May 19, 1967, 482–A.

107. "Brief of Appellees," *Brewer v. School Board of Norfolk*, 8–9. Judge Hoffman's supplemental memorandum approving Norfolk's desegregation plan (June 2, 1967) may be found in NSBM, Reel 1522, 537.

108. Shirley Bolinaga, "School Site Called Court Role—Booker T. Relocation at Issue," *Virginian-Pilot*, January 9, 1968, 1, 4.

109. The phrase "eliminate existing racial segregation of faculties" comes from the Norfolk desegregation plan. It is included in the "Brief of Appellees," *Brewer v. School Board of Norfolk*, 9. Davis's statement is quoted in Bolinaga, "School Site Called Court Role."

110. Davis quoted in Bolinaga, "School Site Called Court Role."

111. *Green v. School Board of New Kent County*, 391 U.S. 430 (1968).

112. Ibid.

113. Citing statistics presented by the NAACP, Judge John Butzner found that Norfolk's high school attendance plan required "all but 1,230 of the city's 3,632 Negro high school pupils" to attend Booker T. Washington, while it "excluded from Washington School all but 90 of the 7,235 white high school pupils." *Brewer v. School Board of the City of Norfolk*, 397 F.2d 37 (4th Cir. 1968).

114. Ibid.

115. "Special Report on Enrollment as of October 1, 1968," NPSDP, Box 7, Folder 98.

5. Busing and Backlash

1. Richard C. Bayer, "Norfolk Meets Some 1963 'Quality Education' Goals," *Ledger-Star*, March 2, 1968, 13; William K. Stevens, "Norfolk's Venture into Empathy," *Southern Education Report* 2, no. 6 (1967): 13–16.

2. "Presentation of Urgent Requests to Norfolk School Board," Vivian Carter Mason for the Norfolk Committee for the Improvement of Education, Incorporated, June 13, 1968, NSBM, Reel 1526, 460.

3. On Norfolk's summer teaching institute, see "Resolution of the School Board of the City of Norfolk," October 31, 1968, NSBM, Reel 1528, 256. On "Americans from Africa: A History," see NSBM, Reel 1528, 259. On Celestyne Porter's pamphlet, see NSBM, Reel 1528, 284.

4. Shirley Bolinaga, "Beckett: Name for History," *Virginian-Pilot*, September 1, 1968, B1. In 1968, Larchmont had an enrollment of 664 whites and 54 blacks; Stuart enrolled 337 whites and 437 blacks; Smallwood enrolled 450 blacks.

5. "Special Report on Enrollment as of October 1, 1968," NPSDP, Box 7, Folder 98.

6. Matthew D. Lassiter, *The Silent Majority: Suburban Politics in the Sunbelt* (Princeton, N.J.: Princeton University Press, 2006), 2, 232; Taylor Branch, *At Canaan's Edge: America in the King Years, 1965–1968* (New York: Simon & Schuster, 2006).

7. On events in 1968 in Norfolk, see Staige Blackford, "Norfolk March of 700 Peaceful," *Virginian-Pilot*, May 18, 1968, 1; Wayne Woodlief, "How to Get It? Area Voters Want Change; Viet War Causes Unrest," *Ledger-Star*, November 4, 1968, 21; "Jordan Files for Council," *Virginian-Pilot*, March 15, 1968, 33; Parramore, Stewart, and Bogger, *Norfolk*, 380, 388–89.

8. Shirley Bolinaga, "School Board Assigns Students: Court-Rejected Plan Used," *Virginian-Pilot*, June 11, 1968, 17; Shirley Bolinaga, "School Integration: Suits, Progress Roll," *Virginian-Pilot*, September 24, 1968, 15, 23; "CAC Help Sought: Booker T. Faculty Pushes New School," *Ledger-Star*, November 19, 1968, 21. Judge Hoffman always referred to the Norfolk case as *Beckett v. School Board of Norfolk*. For instance, he referred to *Beckett v. School Board of Norfolk*, 302 F. Supp. 18 (E.D. VA 1969). On the other hand, the Fourth Circuit Court referred to the case as *Brewer v. School Board of the City of Norfolk*. See, for instance, *Brewer v. School Board of the City of Norfolk*, 397 F.2d 37 (4th Cir. 1968), and *Brewer v. School Board of the City of Norfolk*, 434 F.2d 408 (4th Cir. 1970).

9. Walter Hoffman quoted in "U.S. Suggests New School Be Built at Barraud Park," *Ledger-Star*, December 27, 1968, 17.

10. "School Snarl in the Courts," *Ledger-Star*, January 6, 1969, 6.

11. On Norfolk's residential segregation ordinance, see Gilbert T. Stephenson, "The Segregation of the White and Negro Races in Cities," *South Atlantic Quarterly* 13, no. 1 (1914): 13–14; Earl Lewis, *In Their Own Interests: Race, Class, and Power in Twentieth-Century Norfolk, Virginia* (Berkeley: University of California Press, 1991), 69–70; R. L. Rice, "Residential Segregation by Law, 1910–1919," *Journal of Southern History* 34 (May 1968): 179–99; "Norfolk's Segregation Law Unconstitutional: Police Court Test Strikes Blow at Law," *NJG*, February 20, 1926, 1. On racial covenants, see Michael Klarman, *From Jim Crow to Civil Rights: The Supreme Court and the Struggle for Racial Equality* (New York: Oxford University Press, 2004), 144–46. On segregated public housing for military families during World War II, see James T. Sparrow, "A Nation in Motion: Norfolk, the Pentagon, and the Nationalization of the Metropolitan South, 1941–53," in *The Myth of Southern Exceptionalism*, ed. Matthew D. Lassiter and Joseph Crespino (New York: Oxford University Press, 2010), 171–73; "Norfolk Agency to Get Broad Creek; County Bid on Two Projects Blocked,"

Virginian-Pilot, August 5, 1954, back page, 32; "Council Speeds Broad Creek Purchase," *Virginian-Pilot,* January 25, 1956, back page, 19; "City Approves Agreement for BC Village Purchase," *Ledger-Dispatch,* January 25, 1956, 12. On redevelopment and interracial conflict, see White, *Pride and Prejudice;* Parramore, Stewart, and Bogger, *Norfolk,* 351–53, 366–67.

12. *Brewer v. School Board of the City of Norfolk,* 397 F.2d 37 (4th Cir. 1968).

13. "Order Denying Hearing En Banc," U.S. Court of Appeals for the Fourth Circuit, August 1968, NPSDP, Box 9, Folder 1; "Order in the United States District Court for the Eastern District of Virginia," November 29, 1968, NPSDP, Box 7, Folder 7.

14. "Resolution of the School Board of the City of Norfolk," December 17, 1968, NSBM, Reel 1528, 311; "Plans and Contemplated Plans Relating to the Construction of Future Schools," NSBM, Reel 1528, 311–A; Shirley Bolinaga, "Norfolk Board Vows Faculty Mix," *Virginian-Pilot,* December 18, 1968, 29.

15. Harold Flannery quoted in *Beckett v. School Board of the City of Norfolk,* 302 F. Supp. 18 (E.D. VA 1969).

16. Eric Pace, "J. Harold Flannery, 65, Rights Lawyer and Appellate Judge," *New York Times,* December 23, 1998, C19.

17. Judge Hoffman quoted in "Exceptions to Faculty Plan Filed," *Ledger-Star,* January 6, 1969, 13.

18. "Pretrial Conference Asked," *Virginian-Pilot,* March 19, 1969, 17.

19. "Pretrial Conference, April 2, 1969, Before Walter E. Hoffman," NPSDP, Box 10, Folder 2. For Davis's illness, see 4–5, 11; for Savage's presentation, see 11–36. On Toy D. Savage Jr., see http://www.willcoxandsavage.com/paa/attorney_profile.php?id=82.

20. "Pretrial Conference, April 2, 1969, Before Walter E. Hoffman." For a secondary report, see "Pupil Assignment Plan Alters 4 High School Areas," *Ledger-Star,* April 3, 1969, A5.

21. "Minutes, Special School Board Meeting," April 3, 1969, NSBM, Reel 1530, 469.

22. "Trial Proceedings, April 22, 1969, Before Walter E. Hoffman," NPSDP, Box 10, Folder 2.

23. Marilyn Stolee, interview with Jeffrey Littlejohn, July 31, 2008. See also the Michael J. Stolee papers, which were donated by Marilyn Stolee to Old Dominion University in 2009. Finally, on Stolee, see Abel A. Bartley, *Keeping the Faith: Race, Politics, and Social Development in Jacksonville, Florida, 1940–1970* (Westport, Conn.: Greenwood Press, 2000), 86.

24. Michael Stolee quoted in Richard C. Bayer, "Educator Says 'Freedom of Choice an Abomination,'" *Ledger-Star,* April 25, 1969, B1.

25. Ibid.

26. Richard C. Bayer, "Mixing Variables Pointed Up," *Ledger-Star,* April 26, 1969, A2.

27. "Resolution of the Ingleside PTA Board," April 28, 1969, attached to a letter from C. E. Kirchheimer, President, Ingleside PTA, to Norfolk City School Board, April 29, 1969, NPSDP, Box 9, Folder 12.

28. "Minutes, City Council Meeting, April 29, 1969," Norfolk City Record Book, Reel 99, 271, Sargeant Room, Norfolk Public Library. See also Don Allgood, "Parents Oppose Busing," *Ledger-Star,* April 30, 1969, A23.

29. Allgood, "Parents Oppose Busing"; Lawrence Maddry, "Ingleside to Fight U.S. Plan," *Virginian-Pilot,* May 5, 1969, B1, B3. For Hobson's quote, see his presentation before the city council: "Minutes, City Council Meeting, April 29, 1969," NCRB, Reel 99, 271.

30. Bob Willis, "Easton PTA Seeks Mix Suit Support," *Ledger-Star,* May 5, 1969, A2.

31. Mrs. J. S. Holmes to Edwin Lamberth, April 29, 1969, NPSDP, Box 9, Folder 12.

32. Joan Warren to Sen. William B. Spong Jr., May 1, 1969, NPSDP, Box 9, Folder 12.

33. Maddry, "Ingleside to Fight U.S. Plan."

34. Wayne Woodlief, "Anti-Busing Moves Grow," *Ledger-Star,* May 6, 1969, B1.

35. Ken Wheeler, "City Opposes, Parents Told," *Virginian-Pilot,* May 6, 1969, B1.

36. Shirley Bolinaga, "School Board Offers Plan," *Virginian-Pilot,* May 8, 1969, C1.

37. Walter Hoffman quoted in Richard C. Bayer, "U.S. Judge Says He'll Rule in Favor of School Board on Desegregation," *Ledger-Star,* May 9, 1969, A1.

38. Walter Hoffman quoted in Richard C. Bayer, "'I Can't Consider It: Lake Taylor, Booker T. Link Called 'Asinine' by Hoffman," *Ledger-Star,* May 8, 1969, A1.

39. *Beckett v. School Board of the City of Norfolk,* 302 F. Supp. 18 (E.D. VA 1969).

40. "Memorandum from John C. McLaulin to Members of the School Board," May 27, 1969, NPSDP, Box 14, Folder 4.

41. John C. McLaulin quoted in Ken Wheeler, "City Opposes, Parents Told," *Virginian-Pilot,* May 6, 1969, B1.

42. John Svicarovich, "Booker T. Switch Foreseen: 'Separatist' School Possible," *Virginian-Pilot,* October 16, 1969, F1, F4.

43. "Long Range Plan of the School Board of the City of Norfolk," NPSDP, Box 9, Folder 7.

44. Ibid.

45. "Objections of Plaintiff-Intervener, United States of America, to Defendants' Proposed Terminal Plan of Desegregation," NPSDP, Box 14, Folder 1; "Plaintiffs' Objections to Defendants' Long Range Plan of Desegregation," NPSDP, Box 9, Folder 9. See also Jack Kestner, "Objections Filed to School Plan," *Ledger-Star,* July 7, 1969, A1. The filing took place on Monday, July 7.

46. *Beckett v. School Board of the City of Norfolk,* 308 F. Supp. 1274 (E.D. VA 1969).

47. Shirley Bolinaga, "Booker T. Would Be Replaced: Tidewater Drive School in Board's Mixing Plan," *Virginian-Pilot,* June 21, 1969, 1; Kestner, "Objections Filed to School Plan"; *Brewer v. School Board of the City of Norfolk,* 434 F.2d 408 (4th Cir. 1970).

48. John C. McLaulin to Thomas Pettigrew, June 24, 1969, McLaulin to Pettigrew, August 6, 1969, both in NPSDP, Box 14, Folder 4; Testimony of Thomas Pettigrew at the Offices of Willcox, Savage, Lawrence, and Spindle, September 19, 1969, NPSDP, Box 11, Folder 1; John Svicarovich, "'Balancing' Could Cause Exodus: Court Hears Testimony at Harvard," *Virginian-Pilot,* November 12, 1969, B1.

49. John Svicarovich, "Key Issue: How Much Desegregation Is Enough," *Virginian-Pilot,* November 17, 1969, B1.

50. Ibid.

51. Ibid.

52. *Beckett v. School Board of the City of Norfolk*, 308 F. Supp. 1274 (E.D. VA 1969). See also "Hoffman Rejects Mass Busing," *Ledger-Star*, December 30, 1969, A1; John Svicarovich, "Hoffman Rejects Balance, Busing: Board's Proposal Upheld," *Virginian-Pilot*, December 31, 1969, A1; Richard C. Bayer, "How to Integrate Black Core? School Ruling Leads to Big Question," *Ledger-Star*, December 31, 1969, A2.

53. *Beckett v. School Board of the City of Norfolk*, 308 F. Supp. 1274 (E.D. VA 1969).

54. *Brewer v. School Board of the City of Norfolk*, 434 F.2d 408 (4th Cir. 1970); Tom Laughlin, "Court Orders Norfolk to Draw Up New School Desegregation Plan," *Ledger-Star*, June 23, 1970, A1.

55. Joseph Jordan quoted in "Integration Order: Court Verdict May Aid Effort to 'Save B.T.,'" *NJG*, June 27, 1970, B1.

56. Roy Martin quoted in Don Allgood and Gene Owens, "School Board Asks Backing of Citizens," *Ledger-Star*, June 30, 1970, B1.

57. [George J. Hebert], "Courts and Classrooms," *Ledger-Star*, June 24, 1970, A6.

58. "Petition for a Writ of Certiorari," June 26, 1970, NPSDP, Box 14, Folder 2; Richard C. Bayer, "Fast School Appeal Goes to High Court," *Ledger-Star*, June 26, 1970, A2; "Norfolk School Review Refused by High Court," *Ledger-Star*, June 29, 1970, A1; "School Board Plan Delayed Until Monday," *NJG*, July 25, 1970, 1; "The School Board of the City of Norfolk, Plan For Unitary Schools for the 1970–71 Year," NPSDP, Box 14, Folder 1; "Statement of Vincent J. Thomas, Chairman of Norfolk School Board," July 27, 1970, NPSDP, Box 9, Folder 7; Richard Bayer, "School Board Looks to Top Court," *Ledger-Star*, July 28, 1970, A1; "The Norfolk School Plan," *Ledger-Star*, July 28, 1970, A6.

59. "Hearings On Motions, Before Honorable Walter E. Hoffman," July 29, 1970, NPSDP, Box 15, Folder 19. For Hoffman's quoted comments, see 19 and 41. See also "Order," *Beckett v. School Board of Norfolk*, Judge Hoffman, July 29, 1970, NPSDP, Box 15, Folder 20; Simon Sobeloff and Harrison L. Winter special concurrence, *Brewer v. School Board of the City of Norfolk*, 434 F.2d 408 (4th Cir. 1970); Richard C. Bayer, "Neighborhood Concept Combined with Limited Busing Considered," *Ledger-Star*, July 30, 1970, A1.

60. "Objections of the Defendant-Intervenors, David E. Allgood, et. al., to the Plan for the Operation of Norfolk Public Schools Submitted by the Norfolk School Board," *Beckett v. School Board of Norfolk*, July 1970, NPSDP, Box 17, Folder 7; "Hearings on Motions, Before Honorable Walter E. Hoffman," July 29, 1970, NPSDP, Box 15, Folder 19; Don Hunt, "NAACP Presses For Buses," *Virginian-Pilot*, August 5, 1970, A1.

61. "Exceptions to Plan," filed by the NAACP in *Beckett v. School Board of Norfolk*, August 3, 1970, NPSDP, Box 17, Folder 1.

62. "Trial Proceedings," *Beckett v. School Board of Norfolk*, August 11, 1970, NPSDP, Box 16, Folder 1. For the HEW proposal, see Jerry Brader to David Norman, August 4, 1970, NPSDP, Box 17, Folder 1. See also Don Hunt, "U.S. Weakens Demand for Busing in Norfolk," *Virginian-Pilot*, August 12, 1970, B1.

63. Walter Hoffman quoted in "School Uproar in Va. Cities: Hoffman Hammers Out Plan for Desegregation," *NJG*, August 15, 1970, 1.

64. Memorandum decision, *Beckett v. School Board of Norfolk,* August 14, 1970, NPSDP, Box 9, Folder 14; Vincent Thomas quoted in Don Hunt, "15 Schools Mixed in 5 Groups of 3," *Virginian-Pilot,* August 14, 1970, A1.

65. The figure of 8,000 students for 1969–70 comes from "Brief for the Appellees (School Board)," in *Brewer v. School Board of Norfolk* for the Fourth Circuit Court of Appeals, May 22, 1970, NPSDP, Box 14, Folder 1, 21. The figure of 12,000 students for 1970–71 comes from a school estimate presented in October 1970. See Don Hunt, "3,500 Needy Pupils in Norfolk: U.S. Aid for Busing Poor Requested," *Virginian-Pilot,* October 22, 1970, C1. The required number of bus trips is discussed in the "Brief for the School Board," in *Brewer v. School Board of Norfolk* for the Fourth Circuit Court of Appeals, November 11, 1970, NPSDP, Box 15, Folder 5, 9.

66. Marvin Lake, "Bus Aid Sought for Poor: Plea Renewed by Minister," *Virginian-Pilot,* October 16, 1970, C5.

67. Don Hunt, "16,000 to Be Bused Under Court Plan," *Virginian-Pilot,* September 4, 1970, C1.

68. Ibid.

69. "Parents, Children Urged to Be 'Cool,'" *Virginian-Pilot,* August 14, 1970, C1.

70. Ken Wheeler, "Schools . . . And Norfolk's Future: White Flight and the Vision of a Poor City," *Virginian-Pilot,* September 6, 1970, B1.

71. "Ingleside League: School Boycott Voted," *Virginian-Pilot,* August 15, 1970, B1; "Founders Oppose Busing: Private School Being Formed," *Virginian-Pilot,* September 1, 1970, B1.

72. Tom Laughlin, "Private Schools in Norfolk Full," *Ledger-Star,* August 21, 1970, A1.

73. William Carol Baskett, "Orders," *Virginian-Pilot,* August 9, 1970, C4.

74. For a fascinating discussion of the color-blind philosophy, see Lassiter, *Silent Majority.*

75. Don Hunt, "Enrollment Figures Off 2,200," *Virginian-Pilot,* September 16, 1970, B3.

76. E. Randolph Fraser Jr., "Pulling Together," *Virginian-Pilot,* October 5, 1970, A18.

77. Bonnie Beckroge, "Problem," *Virginian-Pilot,* September 3, 1970, A14; Jeanne Callahan, "Rescheduled, Too," *Virginian-Pilot,* September 3, 1970, A14. See the analysis presented in chapter 9 of Pamela Grundy, *Learning to Win: Sports, Education, and Social Change in Twentieth-Century North Carolina* (Chapel Hill: University of North Carolina Press, 2001).

78. "Norfolkians Seek to Ease Bus Tensions," *NJG,* September 26, 1970, 1. See also Richard C. Bayer, "Signs Lead Students to Peaceful Protest," *Ledger-Star,* September 21, 1970, B1.

79. Don Hunt, "Neighborhood School Backed," *Virginian-Pilot,* October 2, 1970, C3.

80. Tom Reilly, "Whitehurst Rally: Anti-Busing Stand Emphasized," *Ledger-Star,*

August 20, 1970, B3; Jim Henderson, "'Circumvent Congress': Whitehurst Opposes U.S. Grant for Busing," *Virginian-Pilot*," October 24, 1970, B1; "Bus Money for the Poor," *Virginian-Pilot*, October 29, 1970, A14.

81. Edward L. Breeden Jr. quoted in Ken Wheeler, "Special Session on Schools: Local Legislators Oppose Recall," *Virginian-Pilot*, August 1, 1970, B1.

82. Michael B. Wagenheim, "May It Please the Court," *Virginian-Pilot*, September 16, 1970, A14.

83. Mrs. R. A. Linyear, "Old Practice," *Virginian-Pilot*, August 4, 1970, A12.

84. Audrey Shands and William Palmer quoted in Southall Bass III, "Inquiring Reporter: Question, School Desegregation; Do You Think 'Busing' Is Really a Big Problem or Is It Another Phony Issue to Delay Equality and Justice," *NJG*, September 5, 1970, 10.

85. "Berkley Civic League Deplores School Fears," *NJG*, August 22, 1970, 1.

86. "Brief for the Appellants (NAACP)," in *Brewer v. School Board of Norfolk*, filed October 12, 1970, NPSDP, Box 15, Folder 5; George M. Kelley, "NAACP for More Busing in Norfolk," *Virginian-Pilot*, October 16, 1970, C1.

87. See especially pages 2–5 of the "Brief for the School Board," in *Brewer v. School Board of Norfolk*, filed November 11, 1970, NPSDP, Box 15, Folder 5.

88. "Brief for the School Board," in *Brewer v. School Board of Norfolk*, NPSDP, Box 15, Folder 5.

89. "Antibus Sale Gets Mayor's $1," *Virginian-Pilot*, September 3, 1970, C7.

90. *Swann v. Charlotte-Mecklenburg Board of Education*, 399 U.S. 926 (1970); *School Board of Norfolk v. Brewer*, cert. denied 399 U.S. 929 (1970); Wilkinson, *From Brown to Bakke*, 78–160.

91. Wilkinson, *From Brown to Bakke*, 78–160.

92. "Supplemental Brief of Plaintiff-Appellants and Cross-Appellees (NAACP)," in *Brewer v. School Board of Norfolk*, June 1, 1971, NPSDP, Box 17, Folder 11; "Supplemental Brief on Behalf of the School Board," in *Brewer v. School Board of Norfolk*, June 4, 1971, NPSDP, Box 16, Folder 10.

93. *Brewer v. School Board of the City of Norfolk*, 444 F.2d 99 (4th Cir. 1970).

94. Ethel A. Steadman, "Busing of 18,000 in New Norfolk Mix: Arguments Set July 15 in U.S. District Court," *Virginian-Pilot*, July 1, 1971, 1.

95. Ibid.

96. Vivian Carter Mason quoted in Richard C. Bayer, "Integration: Understanding by All Needed," *Ledger-Star*, June 26, 1971, A1, A3.

97. "Given Oath of Office: Appointment of Mrs. Mason Is Big Surprise," *NJG*, July 3, 1971, 1.

98. "Exceptions to Norfolk's Plan," in *Beckett v. School Board of the City of Norfolk*, July 9, 1971, NPSDP, Box 18, Folder 10; Henry Marsh quoted in Richard C. Bayer, "NAACP Lawyer Asks Tax Aid: Busing Fares 'Unthinkable,'" *Ledger-Star*, July 16, 1971, B1.

99. Marshall T. Bohannon quoted in Don Hunt, "Norfolk School Case: More Pairings Advised," *Virginian-Pilot*, July 16, 1971, 1.

100. "Hoffman Runs Court with Iron Hand," *Ledger-Star*, July 22, 1971, A1; Richard C. Bayer, "Judge Foresees Case Finale in Okaying School Board Plan," *Ledger-Star*, July 29, 1971, B6.

101. "John A. MacKenzie," *Virginian-Pilot*, January 4, 2010, B6.

102. Bayer, "Judge Foresees Case Finale."

103. Richard C. Bayer, "Parents Protest Busing," *Ledger-Star*, July 14, 1971, A1.

104. Tom Laughlin, "Busing Meeting Jammed," *Ledger-Star*, July 22, 1971, B1.

105. Brown Carpenter, "Busing Foes Rallying Tonight as New Challenges Develop," *Ledger-Star*, July 27, 1971, B1.

106. Richard C. Bayer, "It's Noisy 'No, No, No,' to Busing," *Ledger-Star*, July 28, 1971, C1.

107. "Appeal Notice Filed in School Bus Case," *Ledger-Star*, July 31, 1971, A5; Richard C. Bayer, "Citizens to Appeal Bus Order; Board Weighs Similar Action," *Ledger-Star*, August 19, 1971, B1.

108. James M. Naughton, "Nixon Disavows H.E.W. Proposal on School Busing," *New York Times*, August 4, 1971, 1; Richard C. Bayer, "U.S. Inconsistent on Busing — Thomas," *Ledger-Star*, August 4, 1971, A1.

109. G. William Whitehurst quoted in Richard C. Bayer, "Busing Aid to All or None Urged," *Ledger-Star*, July 21, 1971, A1; Stanley C. Walker press release included with letter to Betty Raby, August 19, 1971, Stanley C. Walker Papers, Box 24, Folder 12, Special Collections, Old Dominion University; Peter K. Babalas quoted in Tom Reilly, "Bus Order Appeal Urged," *Ledger-Star*, August 11, 1971, D5; Tom Reilly, "McNamara Offers Petitions on Busing," *Ledger-Star*, September 7, 1971, D3; Arthur P. Henderson, "Busing Case Appeal Up for Study," *Ledger-Star*, August 18, 1971, A10.

110. Richard C. Bayer, "Price Freeze Eyed as Anti-Bus Weapon," *Ledger-Star*, August 20, 1971, B1; "Appeal from Busing Order," *Ledger-Star*, August 23, 1971, A6; Gene Owens, "VTC Manager Says Fare Hike Necessary," *Ledger-Star*, August 25, 1971, A1.

111. Gene Owens, "Judge Lifts Order of Massive Busing," *Ledger-Star*, August 25, 1971, A1; "Partial Busing Reprieve," *Ledger-Star*, August 26, 1971, A6; "Busing Appeal on Thursday," *Ledger-Star*, September 1, 1971, B1; "Norfolk Busing Stay Overturned," *Ledger-Star*, September 2, 1971, A1; "School Bewilderment," *Ledger-Star*, September 3, 1971, A6.

112. "SONS Plan Appeal at Capital," *Ledger-Star*, September 3, 1971, B1; Jack Kestner, "Burger Decision Awaited," *Ledger-Star*, September 4, 1971, A1; Brown Carpenter, "Transport Plan Sought for Schools," *Ledger-Star*, September 6, 1971, A1.

113. "Bus Schedule Snags Battled," *Ledger-Star*, September 17, 1971, B1.

114. Richard C. Bayer, "School Board Disappointed with Consultant's Findings," *Ledger-Star*, September 17, 1971, B1.

115. "Transcript of Proceedings," in *William Whitmore, III, v. School Board of Norfolk* in the U.S. District Court for the Eastern District of Virginia, September 28, 1971, NPSDP, Box 17, Folder 27; Don Hunt, "Suit Attacking Assignments by Race Dismissed," *Virginian-Pilot*, September 29, 1971, B3.

116. Don Hunt, "Thomas Discusses Busing: Problem to 'Unequipped' Board," *Virginian-Pilot,* October 1, 1971, D1, 8; Don Nunes, "Granby High: Disorderly Conduct Charged to Students," *Virginian-Pilot,* October 1, 1971, D1.

117. "Text of Thomas' Proposal on Norfolk School Situation," *Virginian-Pilot,* October 10, 1971, A10. Enrollment in Norfolk Public Schools on the fifth day of the academic year was as follows: 56,448 (1969); 54,132 (1970); 49,278 (1971). See Richard C. Bayer, "White Student Total Declines by 7,011," *Ledger-Star,* September 29, 1971. In contrast, statistics in the *Ledger-Star* showed that Virginia Beach public schools had grown from 34,706 students in 1965 to 46,792 in 1971. Chesapeake public schools showed a smaller, but significant increase, rising from 24,947 in 1965 to 26,352 in 1971. "School Enrollment Totals," *Ledger-Star,* December 27, 1971, A7.

118. Hal Bonney Jr., interview with Jeffrey Littlejohn and Charles Ford, March 12, 2007; Mylene Mangalindan, "Hal J. Bonney Jr., a Benchmark in Bankruptcy," *Virginian-Pilot,* January 15, 1995, D1; Denise Watson Batts, "Voice of Remorse: 'I Took It Too Far,'" *Virginian-Pilot,* October 1, 2008, A10. On James G. Martin and Roy Martin, see Amy Waters Yarsinske, *The Martin Years: Norfolk Will Always Remember Roy* (Gloucester Point, Va.: Hallmark, 2001), 79–84.

119. Don Hunt, "Norfolk Study: School-Enrollment Drop Called Natural," *Virginian-Pilot,* February 5, 1973, B1, B3; "Norfolk's Pupil Loss," *Ledger-Star,* February 9, 1973, A6; "Pupils Get Warm Welcome," *Ledger-Star,* September 3, 1974, A1; John Levin, "New Booker T. Opens; Students Impressed," *Ledger-Star,* September 3, 1974, B1; "Booker T. to Be Dedicated," *Ledger Star,* February 8, 1975, B1; "Norfolk Saw Massive Resistance, Busing: Long Suit Ended," *Ledger-Star,* February 15, 1975, A3; "A Seasoned School Leader," *Ledger-Star,* February 17, 1975, A6; Don Hunt, "Advisers Get a Close Look at the City," *Virginian-Pilot,* February 21, 1975, A3; "School Confrontations," *Ledger-Star,* September 4, 1975, A6; "School Enrollment Near Projection," *Ledger-Star,* September 10, 1975, B1.

120. "School Confrontations."

6. Cowardice and Complacency

1. Amy Goldstein, "Keep Busing, Blacks Urge Board," *Ledger-Star,* May 18, 1982, A1; "Vivian Mason Dies; Pioneer for Civil Rights," *Ledger-Star,* May 12, 1982, C10; "Progress of Blacks — Mrs. Mason's Legacy," *Ledger-Star,* May 17, 1982, A6.

2. All quotes from Stephen Engelberg, "Mayor Ties School Busing, Economic Ills," *Virginian-Pilot,* April 23, 1982, A1; see also Deborah Moira Jewell-Jackson's excellent dissertation, "Ending Mandatory Busing for Desegregation in Norfolk, Virginia: A Case Study Explaining the Decision Making Process in a Formerly *De Jure Southern School District*" (Ph.D. diss., *Harvard Graduate School of Education,* 1995), chapters 2–4.

3. W. Randy Wright, interview with Jeffrey Littlejohn and Charles Ford, July 17, 2008; Stephen Engelberg, "Plans Pondered for Busing in West Norfolk," *Virginian-Pilot,* April 9, 1982, D1; John McManus, "Tea Party Asks Curbs on Busing," *Ledger-Star,* August 18, 1981, C1.

4. King Davis, telephone interview with Jeffrey Littlejohn, March 23, 2009; King Davis quoted in Milton A. Reid, "Coalition Counters School Board on Busing Issue," *NJG*, December 21, 1981, 1. On Bishop Willis, see Leonard E. Colvin, "Bishop L. E. Willis, Dick Price, Prominent Area Leaders, Pass," *NNJG*, February 26–March 4, 2009, 1, 2.

5. Judy Parker, "For School Superintendent, Wife—First 'Guests' a Surprise," *Ledger-Star*, July 28, 1972, A10; Stacey Burling, "Sensitive Man Quitting Helm of City Schools," *Ledger-Star*, June 26, 1983, B1; Kristen Kromer, "Albert Ayars, Former Schools Chief, Dies," *Spokesman-Review* (Spokane, Wash.), June 12, 2004, 6B.

6. Herman A. Cox Jr., "Yellow School Buses Rolling," *NJG*, August 28, 1976, 1; Terry Carter, "Norfolk Busing Annually Covers 1.7 Million Miles," *Virginian-Pilot*, February 6, 1983, A4.

7. Marvin Leon Lake, "Unfounded Rumors Claimed: School System Good, Realtors Told," *Virginian-Pilot*, September 30, 1976, B3.

8. Peter A. Loomis, "Ayars Supports Review of Norfolk School Busing," *Ledger-Star*, October 11, 1978, B1. At the time, Norfolk spent $2.8 million to transport students to school. Of the 43,000 students enrolled, 22,000 rode buses to school. Since the initial busing order of 1971, thirteen of the city's forty-six elementary schools had been allowed to return to neighborhood schools because some neighborhoods had become more integrated.

9. Loomis, "Ayars Supports Review of Norfolk School Busing," B1; Peter A. Loomis, "U.S. Aide Warns Against Cuts in School Busing," *Ledger-Star*, October 17, 1978, B1.

10. William H. Wood, "Parents Request Improved Safety on School Buses," *Ledger-Star*, September 17, 1975, B1; Kay McGraw, "Maury Opens Quietly After Disturbances," *Ledger-Star*, September 25, 1975, B1; Kay McGraw, "School Officials, Parents to Discuss Trouble," *Ledger-Star*, September 29, 1975, B1.

11. Ethel A. Steadman and Mike Smith, "Boy Killed in School; Another Held," *Virginian-Pilot*, September 4, 1976.

12. Deby Weyermann, "'Last-Chance School Funds Being Sought," *Ledger-Star*, November 11, 1977, B1.

13. Anne Smith, "Lake Taylor School Called a Jungle," *Virginian-Pilot*, October 7, 1978, B1, B4.

14. Stacey Burling, "Norfolk Again Leads in Dropouts," *Virginian-Pilot*, September 20, 1979, A1.

15. Thomas Johnson Jr. quoted in Jeff Brown, "Low Black Scores Anger Norfolk School Board," *Virginian-Pilot*, December 30, 1978, A1.

16. Peter A. Loomis, "Results of Tests Put Pressure on Ayars," *Ledger-Star*, December 30, 1978, A1, A3. In all, 1,548 black students and 1,099 white students took the tests. The report by Ayars showed that 12 percent of white students and 40 percent of black students failed the state reading test, while 13 percent of white students and 46 percent of black students failed the mathematics test.

17. Peter A. Loomis, "Blacks' Poor Testing a 'Crisis' in Norfolk," *Ledger-Star*,

December 29, 1978, A1; Loomis, "Results of Tests Put Pressure on Ayars," A1, A3; Brown, "Low Black Scores Anger Norfolk School Board," A1.

18. Albert Ayars quoted in Peter A. Loomis, "Ayars 'Under Gun' to Boost Scores," *Ledger-Star*, January 4, 1979, A1.

19. Joyce Drew's full letter was reprinted in the *Ledger-Star*, January 10, 1979, B6. Drew had contended that her meaning had been distorted in the paper's revision process. Her edited letter to the editor had appeared in the *Virginian-Pilot* of January 7, 1979.

20. Wilford Kale, "Reaction to Competence Tests Stings System, Superintendent," *Richmond Times-Dispatch*, January 21, 1979, 1.

21. See, for instance, Ray T. Jones, "Students Taught to Suppress Truth," *NJG*, January 19, 1979, 8; William Bennett, "Supports Joyce Drew," *NJG*, January 26, 1979, 8; "Pinch Shoe Hurts," *NJG*, January 26, 1979, 8.

22. Stacey Burling, "Norfolk Chastised on Test Scores," *Virginian-Pilot*, April 17, 1979, C1, C3; Bettina Cromwell, "Investigation Finds Teachers, Not Students — Incompetent," *NJG*, April 20, 1979, 1.

23. Burling, "Norfolk Chastised on Test Scores"; "Ayars' Reply to NAACP School Critique," *Virginian-Pilot*, June 19, 1976.

24. Stacey Burling, "34% Not Promoted in Norfolk Schools," *Virginian-Pilot*, July 4, 1979, D1. See also Stacey Burling, "Failure Rate Rises in Norfolk Schools," *Virginian-Pilot*, June 29, 1979, D1.

25. Jane Eisner and Stacey Burling, "Pupil Enrollments Off Sharply," *Virginian-Pilot*, September 14, 1979, A1; John McManus and Janet Langston, "Norfolk Eyes More Aid as Pupil Drop Lessens," *Ledger-Star*, September 12, 1980, C3; Mark White, "The Competency Bomb," featured in the *Virginian-Pilot* supplement, *Norfolk Compass*, August 29–30, 1979, 1.

26. Poston for Commonwealth's Attorney Campaign Committee, "Monday They Went to War," political advertisement featured in the *Virginian-Pilot* supplement, *Norfolk Compass*, September 2–3, 1981, 5. Kent Jenkins Jr. discusses the advertisement in "Ad About City Schools Starts Volley of Charges," *Virginian-Pilot*, September 3, 1981, A1.

27. All quotes from Jenkins, "Ad About City Schools," A1.

28. Correspondence between Alan S. Balaban and Albert Ayars, June 1, 1981, to August 4, 1981, NPSDP, Box 20, Folder 9.

29. Figures from *Riddick v. School Board of the City of Norfolk*, 627 F. Supp, 814, 817 (U.S. Dist. 1984).

30. Ronald Reagan quoted in Steven R. Weisman, "Reagan Supports Measure to Curb Suits on Busing," *New York Times*, November 19, 1980, A1.

31. William French Smith quoted in Robert Pear, "Departure from Busing Pledged in Rights Cases," *New York Times*, May 23, 1981, 9.

32. William Bradford Reynolds quoted in Gary Orfield and Susan Eaton, eds., *Dismantling Desegregation: The Quiet Reversal of* Brown v. Board of Education (New York: New Press, 1996), 17.

33. William French Smith quoted in "Accord on Integration of Shreveport Schools Is Given to U.S. Judge," *New York Times*, May 7, 1981, A21.

34. Jerry Alley, "Tidewater Turnout Heavy: Many Areas Report Brisk Pace at Polls," *Ledger-Star*, November 4, 1980, 1. The 1980 election vote totals were as follows: twenty-six precincts went for Carter (35,281); twenty-six precincts went for Reagan (27,504). In the twelve predominantly black districts, 12,864 of 13,747 votes went for Carter. In the city's pressure points, especially where race, class, and busing were concerned, white voters favored Reagan in each case. "Voting Totals," 1976, *Ledger-Star*, November 3, 1976, A8.

35. See also Sharon Coleman, "Private Selection of Members Stirs Debate," *Norfolk Compass*, July 12, 1981, 4.

36. Anna Barron, "A Look at New Members: Mrs. Jean Bruce," *Norfolk Compass*, July 12, 1981, 3, 4. For more on Jean Bruce, see her interview with James Bertram Haugh in James Bertram Haugh Papers, Box 1, Folder 9, Old Dominion University.

37. Cliff Foster, "A Look at New Members: Robert Hicks," *Norfolk Compass*, July 12, 1981, 3, 4, 9.

38. Bill Nachman, "School Board Official Discusses Norfolk System," *NJG*, July 22, 1981, 2.

39. "Accord on Integration of Shreveport Schools Is Given to U.S. Judge," A21; *Jones v. Caddo Parish School Board*, 704 F.2d 206 (5th Circuit, May 6, 1983).

40. Thomas Johnson Jr. quoted in Kent Jenkins Jr. "Review Planned: Busing Issue Tops Board's Priorities," *Virginian-Pilot*, September 27, 1981, B1.

41. McManus, "Tea Party Asks Curbs on Busing."

42. Cynthia Heide quoted in Jenkins, "Review Planned."

43. Jean Bruce quoted in Jenkins, "Review Planned."

44. John McManus, "Norfolk School Board Takes First Step to Curtail Busing," *Ledger-Star*, September 17, 1981, A1; Jenkins, "Review Planned."

45. For notes on the trips, see Memorandum on Shreveport, Louisiana Trip, John C. McLaulin to Albert L. Ayars, October 20, 1981; Memorandum on Nashville, Tennessee Trip, John C. McLaulin to Albert L. Ayars, October 21, 1981; Memorandum on Richmond, Virginia Trip, John C. McLaulin to Albert L. Ayars, November 3, 1981, all in NPSDP, Box 20, Folder 9. See also Donna Schewel, "Norfolk Studies Nashville Plan to Cut Busing," *Ledger-Star*, October 22, 1981, D1.

46. Terry Carter, "Magnet-School Study Sought," *Ledger-Star*, November 19, 1981, D5.

47. Sam Barnes, "Blacks Warn of Bus Cuts," *Ledger-Star*, December 18, 1981, D1.

48. John Foster quoted in Jenkins, "Review Planned."

49. John Foster quoted in "Still Fussing over Busing," *NNJG*, November 25, 1981, 6.

50. John Foster quoted in Barnes, "Blacks Warn of Bus Cuts." For John Foster's career, see "Dr. John H. Foster: Noted Pastor, Civic Leader Succumbs," *NNJG*, August 20–26, 2009, 1.

51. See, for example, Hortense Wells's letter to the editor lambasting a local group

of parents for complaining about the conditions of their children's segregated school in 1962. Hortense Wells, "Principals Under Fire, Defended by Mrs. Wells," *NJG*, May 19, 1962, B13. Also significant was the portrait that Thomas Johnson, Jean Bruce, and Gary Ruegsegger painted of Wells. They portrayed her as friendly to white interests, which they associated with the good of the district. See Hortense R. Wells, "Stop Busing? Why Not?" *Virginian-Pilot*, June 6, 1982.

52. Hortense Wells quoted in Schewel, "Norfolk Studies Nashville Plan." As noted above, Wells had participated in many of the steps toward integration. "I was a protester when I was young," she said. "It's just a part of me, I'm definite about what should be mine just by my being a human being." Hortense Wells quoted in Jenkins, "Review Planned."

53. Nelson White and Earlean White, interview with Jeffrey Littlejohn, July 16, 2008; Nelson O. White Jr., "Blacks, Too, Oppose Busing," *Virginian-Pilot*, January 15, 1982, A14.

54. White, "Blacks, Too, Oppose Busing," A14.

55. Stephen Engelberg, "Panel Urges Dramatic Cuts in Busing," *Virginian-Pilot*, January 29, 1982, A1.

56. Ibid.

57. On Ronald Edmonds and Sara Lawrence-Lightfoot, see Engelberg, "Panel Urges Dramatic Cuts in Busing," A1; Stephen Engelberg, "Expert on Parents, Schools to Speak," *Virginian-Pilot*, February 5, 1982, A2. On Robert Green, see Stephen Engelberg, "Plan to Curb School Busing Criticized," *Virginian-Pilot*, April 2, 1982, A1.

58. King E. Davis quoted in Milton A. Reid, "Citizens Will Fight School Battle, Again," *NJG*, February 17, 1982, 1.

59. Amy Goldstein and Mildred Williams, "Bus Study Costs Criticized, Praised," *Ledger-Star*, May 25, 1982, C1.

60. Vincent Thomas quoted in Engelberg, "Mayor Ties School Busing, Economic Ills," A1.

61. "Coalition Criticizes Mayor, School Board Chairman," *NJG*, April 28, 1982, 1.

62. Engelberg, "Mayor Ties School Busing, Economic Ills," A1. As previously noted, Joshua Darden's family had long been influential in Norfolk. His uncle, Colgate Darden, had served as governor of Virginia (1942–46) and president of the state's flagship university (1947–59). In addition, his father, J. Pretlow Darden Sr., had been a member of the Norfolk city council (1946–50), mayor, and a leading figure in the local business community.

63. Alfreda James, "Green, Butts Pledge to Run as Team," *NJG*, February 10, 1982, 1; "For Norfolk Council," *Virginian-Pilot*, April 30, 1982, A16; Maravia Reid, "Citizens Respond to the Call," *NJG*, April 21, 1982, 1.

64. Amy Goldstein, "Bus Hearings Provide No Easy Answer," *Ledger-Star*, May 27, 1982, A1.

65. Amy Goldstein, "Keep Busing, Blacks Urge Board," *Ledger-Star*, May 18, 1982, A1.

66. Ibid.; Nelson White and Earlean White, interview.

67. Amy Goldstein, "Busing Foes Push for Closer Schools," *Ledger-Star,* May 19, 1982, A1.

68. Ibid.

69. Ibid.

70. Amy Goldstein, "Blacks Who Oppose Busing Jeered," *Ledger-Star,* May 20, 1982, A1.

71. Goldstein, "Bus Hearings Provide No Easy Answer." Tara Bragg, president of the Education Association of Norfolk, agreed with Eley. As the representative of more than 1,600 of the city's 2,300 teachers, Bragg encouraged the board to continue busing so that resegregation of the district could be avoided.

72. Amy Goldstein, "Johnson Wants Bus Decision Delayed," *Ledger-Star,* June 7, 1982, A1.

73. On David J. Armor, see Jeffrey A. Raffel, *Historical Dictionary of School Segregation and Desegregation: The American Experience* (Westport, Conn.: Greenwood Press, 1998), 14–15.

74. Thomas G. Johnson Jr., "Delay Is a Small Price for Correct Decision on School Busing Issue," *Virginian-Pilot,* June 9, 1982, A15; Pete Rowe, "Norfolk's Crosstown Busing Expected to Continue in Fall," *Virginian-Pilot,* June 8, 1982, A1.

75. Warren Fiske and Pete Rowe, "Resignation Clouds Debate Over Busing," *Virginian-Pilot,* June 10, 1982, A1.

76. Ibid.

77. Tim Wheeler, "ODU Dean Named to Board Post," *Ledger-Star,* July 2, 1982, C1; Pete Rowe, "Dr. Wilson Ready for School Board," *Virginian-Pilot,* July 7, 1982, C1.

78. Rowe, "Dr. Wilson Ready for School Board," C1.

79. Wheeler, "ODU Dean Named to Board Post," C1

80. Rowe, "Dr. Wilson Ready for School Board," C1.

81. Jewell-Jackson, "Ending Mandatory Busing," 67.

82. Raffel, *Historical Dictionary of School Segregation,* 14–15.

83. Carr and Schollaert report, quoted in Amy Goldstein, "2 Sociologists Call Busing Study Biased," *Virginian-Pilot,* February 1, 1983.

84. Thomas G. Johnson Jr., interview with Jeffrey Littlejohn and Charles Ford, July 23, 2008.

85. Alfreda James, "Dr. Gene Carter Will Head Norfolk City School System," *NJG,* December 22, 1982, 1; Alfreda James, "Carter Becomes First Black to Be Norfolk's School Superintendent," *NJG,* June 29, 1983, 1.

86. "Memorandum from Thomas Johnson to the Members of the School Board, Regarding the Proposal for a Voluntary, Stably-Desegregated School System," January 26, 1983, NPSDP, Box 20, Folder 9.

87. Thomas Johnson quoted in William Keesler and Amy Goldstein, "School Board Won't Allow Meeting Input," *Virginian-Pilot,* February 2, 1983.

88. William Keesler, "Plan to Curb Busing OK'd: School Board Ends Months of Debate," *Virginian-Pilot,* February 3, 1983, A1; Amy Goldstein, "Courts Will Weigh Return to Neighborhood Schools," *Virginian-Pilot,* February 3, 1983, A1.

89. Goldstein, "Courts Will Weigh Return to Neighborhood Schools"; Alfreda James, "Board Votes to Return to Neighborhood Schools and Federal Court," *NJG*, February 9, 1983, 1.

90. Goldstein, "Courts Will Weigh Return to Neighborhood Schools."

91. Johnson, interview; Jewell-Jackson, "Ending Mandatory Busing," 71–72, 174.

92. "Busing Forces Meet with Justice Department," *NNJG*, March 16, 1983, 1.

93. Alfreda James, "Norfolk Sues Pro-Busers: Names Four Parents in Class Action," *NNJG*, March 30, 1983, 1; Alfreda James, "Group Calls for Resignation of Tom Johnson: Plans March to Waterside," *NNJG*, April 13, 1983, 1; "The School Board's Suit," *Virginian-Pilot*, April 3, 1983, A6; "Statement by City Attorney Philip R. Trapani," *Virginian-Pilot*, April 3, 1983, A6; "Letter from Mr. Trapani to Dr. King E. Davis," *Virginian-Pilot*, April 3, 1983, A6; Walter R. Singleton, "Letter to the Editor," *NNJG*, April 6, 1983, 7.

94. William Keesler, "6 on School Board Were Kept in Dark," *Virginian-Pilot*, April 3, 1983.

95. See, for instance, Keesler, "Plan to Curb Busing OK'd"; Goldstein, "Courts Will Weigh Return to Neighborhood Schools"; "Coalition Criticizes Mayor"; Alfreda James, "Focus on Desegregation: Dr. King Davis Leads Coalition in Drive for Educational Equality," *NNJG*, March 2, 1983, 1; William Keesler and Marvin Leon Lake, "Busing Supporters: From Intellect to Power," *Ledger-Star*, May 12, 1983, A7a.

96. Bob Geske, "Norfolk Board May Be Forced to Take New Approach on Busing," *Virginian-Pilot*, April 8, 1983, D1. For more on the Justice Department's position, see Raymond Wolters, *Right Turn: William Bradford Reynolds, the Reagan Administration and Black Civil Rights* (New Brunswick, N.J.: Transaction Publishers, 1996), 441–44.

97. Johnson, interview; William Keesler, "Norfolk Drops One Busing Suit," *Ledger-Star*, April 19, 1983, 1.

98. William Keesler and Marvin Leon Lake, "Black Parents Sue Over Busing," *Ledger-Star*, May 6, 1983, A1.

99. Vincent Thomas, interview with Jeffrey Littlejohn and Charles Ford, July 21, 2008; Vincent Thomas to Jesse Jackson, April 22, 1983, quoted in Linda Wyche, "Norfolk Mayor Speaks Out on Pro-Busing March Plans," *NNJG*, April 27, 1983, 1.

100. Thomas, interview; Marvin Leon Lake and William Keesler, "Jesse Jackson Wants Others at Talk," *Ledger-Star*, May 6, 1983; William Keesler, "Mayor, Jackson to Meet Before March," *Virginian-Pilot*, May 11, 1983, A1.

101. William Keesler, "Jackson Meets with Mayor: Thomas Critical of Norfolk's Black Leadership," *Virginian-Pilot*, May 13, 1983, A1; Jerry Alley and Sharon Coleman, "Working Together Is Prime Issue, Jackson Declares," *Ledger-Star*, May 13, 1983, A1.

102. William Keesler and Steve Stone, "Thousands March for Busing: A Singing, Chanting Crowd Follows Jackson in Norfolk," *Ledger-Star*, May 13, 1983, A1; Jesse Jackson quoted in William Keesler, "Jackson Wants Talks on Busing, Vote System," *Virginian-Pilot*, May 14, 1983, A3.

103. Ed Brown quoted in Alley and Coleman, "Working Together Is Prime Issue."

104. Amy Goldstein, "City Split on Busing, Survey Indicates," *Virginian-Pilot,* June 13, 1982, A1.

105. William Kessler, "School Vote Tied to Waterside, Possible Pro-Busing Protest Is Called Factor in Decision," *Virginian-Pilot,* May 28, 1983, B1.

106. Frank Callahan, "Judge Hoffman's Courthouse Should Bear His Name," *Ledger-Star,* November 30, 1981, A6; Ford Reid and Donald Moore, "Congress Names Old Federal Building for Hoffman," *Virginian-Pilot,* December 24, 1982, C1; "Key to the Chambers," *Ledger-Star,* July 9, 1983, B4; Tony Stein, "Hoffman and Moments of Greatness," *Virginian-Pilot,* April 13, 1995, A14; Joseph P. Cosco and Lynn Waltz, "Walter Hoffman, Noted U.S. Judge in Norfolk, Dies," *Virginian-Pilot,* November 22, 1996, A1.

107. Alfred James, "Urban League, Parental Group Take Action on School Issues," *NNJG,* May 25, 1983, 1; Program, "The Parental Involvement Network Salutes Champion Role Models," July 17, 1983, in the Charles Ford's possession. See also Tony Brown, "Busing and Segregation," *NNJG,* July 6, 1983, 6.

108. A particularly good overview of the court proceedings may be found in "Report to the School Board of the City of Norfolk," March 15, 1984, NPSDP, Box 25, Folder 9.

109. William Kessler, "School Plan Foes Hire More Lawyers," *Virginian-Pilot,* February 3, 1984, D2.

110. William Kessler and Warren Fiske, "School Plan OK, Carter Testifies," *Ledger-Star,* February 9, 1984, D1. The plaintiffs called Vincent Thomas as a witness, but he supported the position of the school board.

111. David J. Armor, *Forced Justice: School Desegregation and the Law* (New York: Oxford University Press, 1995), 51. See also Orfield and Eaton, *Dismantling Desegregation,* 121, 375, note 26; Kessler and Fiske, "School Plan OK."

112. Keesler, "School Plan Foes Hire More Lawyers"; William Keesler, "Busing Witness Urges School Merger," *Ledger-Star,* February 14, 1984, C1.

113. Keesler, "Busing Witness Urges School Merger"; William Keesler, "Busing Report Biased, Professor Says," *Ledger-Star,* February 10, 1984, C1.

114. Robert Crain quoted in Keesler, "Busing Witness Urges School Merger."

115. *Riddick v. School Board of the City of Norfolk,* 627 F. Supp, 814, 816 (U.S. Dist. 1984).

116. *Riddick v. School Board of the City of Norfolk,* 784 F.2d 521, 543 (4th Cir. 1986).

117. Ibid.

118. William Bradford Reynolds and Julius Levon Chambers quoted in Lena Williams, "Norfolk Can Halt Busing of Pupils," *New York Times,* February 8, 1986, 32.

119. On the aftermath of the *Riddick* case in Norfolk, see Leonard E. Colvin, "40 Years After Brown, Part 2: Legal Challenge to Dismantle Decision on Desegregating Schools Began in Norfolk," *NNJG,* May 25, 1994, 1; Leonard E. Colvin, "Neighborhood Schools, Part 1: Has the Clock Turned Back?" *NNJG,* September 30, 1987, 1; Leonard E. Colvin, "Neighborhood Schools, Part 2," *NNJG,* October 7, 1987, 1; Susan E.

Eaton and Christina Meldrum, "Broken Promises: Resegregation in Norfolk, Virginia," in Orfield and Eaton, *Dismantling Desegregation*, 115–42.

Epilogue

1. Amy Jeter, "Norfolk Wins Top Award for Urban Education," *Virginian-Pilot*, September 21, 2005, A14; Theresa Whibley, "Celebrating the Success of Our Local Schools," *Virginian-Pilot*, November 9, 2005, B11; Amy Jeter, "Award Gives Norfolk Schools More Acclaim and Visibility," *Virginian-Pilot*, November 21, 2005, B1; "The Top of the Class 2008: The Complete List of the 1,300 Top U.S. High Schools," *Newsweek*, May 17, 2008, http://www.newsweek.com/id/39380. For the awards ceremony of January 2010, see its program, a copy of which Charles H. Ford has donated to the Wilson Archives, Norfolk State University, Norfolk, Virginia.

2. Alex Marshall, "Will Mall's Design Make or Break Downtown? Norfolk's MacArthur Center Will Look Mostly Like a Suburban Mall," *Virginian-Pilot*, December 24, 1995, A1; "The Year in Norfolk Stressed Still, But Moving," *Virginian-Pilot*, December 29, 1998, B8; Karen Weintraub, "Downtown Norfolk, March 1999: Bright Lights, Big City?" *Virginian-Pilot*, March 14, 1999, A1.

3. Leonard E. Colvin, "Norfolk Ends Middle School Busing," *NNJG*, April 25–May 1, 2001, 1; Amy Jeter, "Plan Calls for New Zones," *Virginian-Pilot*, September 1, 2008, B1; "End of Busing, End of an Era," *Virginian-Pilot*, September 8, 2008, B6. Norfolk's 2004–5 school performance reports may be found at the district website: http://www.nps.k12.va.us/index.php. For Stephen C. Jones, see Steven Vegh, "Norfolk Schools Chief to Retire," *Virginian-Pilot*, January 21, 2010, 1, 8; Steven Vegh, "Norfolk School Superintendent Leaving Prematurely," *Virginian-Pilot*, November 16, 2011, http://hamptonroads.com/2011/11/norfolk-schools-superintendent-leaving-prematurely.

4. "Report to the School Board: Long-Range Facilities Citizen Advisory Committee," September 17, 2008, http://www.boarddocs.com/vsba/nps/Board.nsf/05879 692c6bc4a848725731b0060cac7/b0f17a8efa108206872574f7006da2bb/$FILE/Facili ties%20Cmte%20rpt.pdf. For the op-ed, see Charla Baucom, "Norfolk's School Renovations Delayed," *Virginian-Pilot*, April 12, 2009, B7. The school board did try to address the problems at the worst facilities in 2009. See Cheryl Ross, "School Board OKS an Extra $650,000 for Madison Career Center," *Virginian-Pilot*, June 18, 2009, 3.

5. http://www.education.com/schoolfinder/us/virginia/norfolk/b-t-washington-high/; http://www.fixnorfolkschools.com/research-the-facts/statistics/graduation-rates.

6. William Julius Wilson, *More Than Just Race: Being Black and Poor in the Inner City* (New York: W. W. Norton, 2009), 62–94.

7. For a taste of the Calvary controversy, see Tony Wharton, "Judge OKs Request for Referendum on Church Rezoning," *Virginian-Pilot and Ledger-Star*, January 22, 1994, D3.

8. Charles M. Payne, *So Much Reform, So Little Change: The Persistence of Failure*

in Urban Schools (Cambridge, Mass.: Harvard Education Press, 2008), 17–47, 61–65; Leonard E. Colvin, "NJ&G Symposium Highlights Educational Challenges," *NNJG,* April 16–22, 2009, 1, 4.

9. For Tommy Johnson Jr.'s latest award, see the website of his firm, Willcox and Savage, http://www.willcoxsavage.com/.

10. Payne, *So Much Reform, So Little Change,* 96–108.

Duckworth, W. Fred (*cont.*)
oppose, 102; Hoffman and, 55; key
role in school closures crisis, 6; murder of, 4; on Norfolk as best city in
Virginia, 116; in racial incidents of
1950s, 41; "separate but equal" doctrine supported by, 42; takes greater
control of School Board, 108–9; on
tuition grants, 136; white support for
position of, 100

Edmunds, Valerie, 69
equalization: African American desire
for, 11, 40; Alston's demand for, 21,
22; Brewbaker's claims regarding,
42–47; NAACP efforts for, 14; pay
parity, 8, 9, 13, 15, 16–22, 34, 42; superintendents' reports on, 35

faculty desegregation, 129, 138–39, 142–
43, 145, 146, 148, 164, 166, 233
feeder system, 165, 170
Fink, T. Ross, 97–98
Forbes, LaVera E., *78*, 89, 272n40
Foster, John, 206, 207, 208, 210, 211,
215–16, 221, 223
Foxworth, Mary Rose, 112, 268n112
Fraim, Paul, 2, 3, 232, 239–40
Francis, G. Hamilton, 58
freedom of choice: Concerned Citizens
of Norfolk support, 171; in Davis
plan of 1963, 132–34, 135; *Green v.
School Board of New Kent County*
on, 148, 149; in interim desegregation plan for 1969–70, 158, 163;
Lamberth supports, 161; limitations
of, 152; in modified desegregation
plan for 1967–68, 144, 146; NAACP
challenges, 138–41; Norfolk School
Board ends, 165; Norfolk's plan remanded to district court, 148, 149;
Perrow Commission recommends,
107; Stolee opposes, 160; Summers's

voluntary choice method, 61; white
reaction to, 143
Frontiers, 57–58

Gay, Marvin, 114
Gifford, Joan, 194
Gilliam, Jerry O., 8, 16
Gilliam v. School Board of Hopewell
(1965), 139
Godbolt, Patricia, 69, *78*, 85–88, 90, 91,
97, 271n40
Gonsouland, Alveraze Frederick, *77*,
78, 89–90, 272n40
Grace Episcopal Church, 29, 40, 53, 82,
213
Granby High School, 32; black student denied admission to, *133;* black
students' failure rate at, 199; black
transfer students at, 69, 77, 89, 90,
91; geographical attendance zone for,
139, 141; map of Norfolk schools in
1954, *50;* in modified desegregation
plan for 1967–68, 145–46; as still seg-
regated in 1968, 153; transformation
of, 236
Gray Commission, 55, 56, 60, 62–63
Green, Joseph N., Jr., 3, 213, 218
Green, Melvin G., Jr., 69, 92, 93
Green, Minnie Alice, 92, 93
Greenberg School, 98
*Green v. School Board of New Kent
County* (1968), 116, 147–48, 156
Greer, Jack E., 221, 222, 229–30
Griffin, Crystal, 69
Griffin, Kathleen, 108, 109
Griffin v. State Board of Education, 137,
138

Hagemeister, Dan, 207
Hanckel, Allan Reeves, 9, 16, 17, 19, 20
Hanna, Chris, 3–4, 246n4
Hardy, G. Wesley, 234, 241–42
Harrell, Charlton, 69

Norfolk (Virginia): African Americans voting in, 13–14; as "All-American City," 11, 116, 117–18; annexations of, 26–29, 27, 116–17; as "conscripted city" in World War II, 28, 38; discrimination and dissent in, 1938–54, 8–47; growth of, 27–28, 117, 269n15; historical vignettes about, 1; low-skill jobs disappear, 239; NAACP activity in, 10; new ward system, 232; in 1960s, 116–18; population decline, 191; postwar transformation of, 10; progressive self-image of, 6, 235; race relations in early 1960s, 127–28; racial and cultural tensions of 1968 in, 154–55; racial equipoise as window dressing, 3; racial incidents of 1950s, 41; suburbanization, 167, 186, 189, 195, 202, 231, 236; as unlikely place for Massive Resistance, 49; urban geography of, 22–33; urban renewal in, 37–38, 235, 236. *See also* Norfolk schools
Norfolk Catholic High School, 54, 99
Norfolk Citizens Advisory Council, 45
Norfolk Citizens Coalition for Quality Public Education, 191–92, 207–8, 209, 211, 212, 217, 221, 222, 231
Norfolk Committee for Public Schools (NCPS), 3, 75, 81, 100, 102, 103, 109, 120
Norfolk Committee for the Improvement of Education, 150, 182
Norfolk School Board: African Americans on, 129–30, 217; all 151 transfer applicants rejected by, 85; *Alston v. School Board of the City of Norfolk,* 9, 11, 18–22; anti-busing advocates added to, 203–4; approves 517 transfer requests in 1963–64, 132; Ashe-Madison complaint of April 1963, 128–29; attempts to slow desegregation, 120–24; attempts to use price

freeze to vacate court order, 185–86; *Beckett v. The School Board of the City of Norfolk,* 63–67; Black suit against, 8–9, 11–14; crosstown busing opposed by, 163, 170; desegregation resolutions of December 1968, 157; Duckworth and city council take greater control of, 108–9; elementary school busing ended by, 190–95, 202–35, 237; enjoined from enrollment under Pupil Placement Board, 72; hedges its bets regarding *Brown,* 60; Hoffman's school desegregation ruling appealed by, 178–81; interim desegregation plan sought by, 158–59, 163; long-range desegregation plan of, 158, 162–72; middle school busing ended by, 237; modified desegregation plan for 1967–68, 144–49; modified desegregation plan of December 1965, 139–44; new desegregation plan of July 1971, 180–83; Norfolk 17 admitted by, 77; pupil assignment practices of, 63, 121, 124, 128–29, 143, 146, 164, 178, 230; transfer applicants of summer 1959 rejected by, 111–12. *See also members by name*
Norfolk schools: achievement gap in, 196–202, 236; for African Americans, 23–26, 30–33, 50, 125–27, 237–39; African American transfer applicants, 68–75, 111–13; in anti-Norfolk attitude, 194; continue to operate dual system ten years after *Brown,* 133; discipline problems in, 195–96; enrollment decline in, 191, 199–200, 202; equalization of black and white schools, 42–46; integration in, 233; map showing segregation in, 50; national rankings of, 37; official reports on, 35–36; overcrowding in, 126; postwar building boom, 49;

Quality Education program, 150; racial composition changes in, 201–2; recommendations for, 242–43; resegregation of, *234,* 234–35, 237; seen as example of progressivism and good will, 117; superintendents of, 33–36; transformation of, 236–37; unitary status of, 193, 230; white students leave, 187. *See also* Norfolk School Board; school closures crisis; school desegregation; *and schools by name*
Norfolk 16, 74
Norfolk 17: admitted to all-white schools, 77; African-American narrative of, 4–5; depiction in Hanna's *Line in the Sand,* 4; Duckworth on, 81–82; "geographical boundaries" group, 93, 95; hostility faced by, 83–84, 97; "isolation" group, 91–92, 95; at King Unity March and Program, 2; "lacking scholastic achievement" group, 93–94, 95; photograph of, *78;* "racial tensions at Norview" group, 85–90, 95; synopsis on each applicant, 85; "too frequent transfer" group, 92–93, 95; tutoring for, 76, 91; as in vanguard, 83; as well-prepared, 88–89; whittling 151 down to 17, 84–96
Norfolk 17, The: Their Story (television documentary), 4
Norfolk Teachers Association (NTA), 16, 18, 19, 21
Norfolk Tea Party, 191, 200, 204–5, 213, 214–15, 217
Norman, Kenneth, 114
Norview Elementary School, *50,* 69, 87, 92–93, 109
Norview High School, 32; black transfer students to, 68, 77, 85–92; Bonney as teacher at, 76, 103; map of Norfolk schools in 1954, *50;* in Norfolk's desegregation plans, 139, 141, 145–46;

racial conflict near, 41; after school closures crisis, 99
Norview Junior High School, *50,* 69, 72, 77, 89

overcrowding, 25–26, 126

Parental Involvement Network (PIN), 209–10, 214, 228
Parent Teacher Association Council (PTAC), 126
parent-teacher associations (PTAs), 64, 76, 77, 95, 101, 136, 160–61, 162, 195, 197
Parker, John J., 20
pay parity, 8, 9, 13, 15, 16–22, 34, 42
Perdue, Charles W. "Bolo," 103–4
Perminter, Daphne, 69, 113
Perrow Commission, 106–8, 110
Perry, Gertrude, 96, 97
Porter, Celestyne Diggs, 151
Portis, Lolita, *78,* 90, 91
Poston, Charles, 200, *201*
Potts, Edgar, 81
Powell, Lewis, Jr., 56, 88, 102, 131
Powers, J. Farley, 53
Price, Harry B., Jr., 101
Prieur, William L., Jr., 38, 80, 131
Prince Edward County case, 134
private schools, 60, 75–76, 100, 108, 110–11, 121, 135–38, 174, 199, 239–40
Pryor, Lawrence, 69
Pupil Placement Act, 62, 66–67, 72, 107, 111, 112–13, 268n117

Quality Education program, 150
quotas, 142, 180

"Racial Isolation in the Public Schools" (Civil Rights Commission), 164
Reed, Betty Jean, *78,* 90, 91, 272n40
Reese, Cloyde, 69
Reese, Thomas, 69

ing; faculty desegregation; freedom
of choice
school pairing, 159–60, 162, 163, 169
Schweitzer, Paul T., 52, 60, 85–86, 99,
103, 253n81
Scott, Gloria, 112, 121–22, 268n112
Scott, James L., Jr., 68, 69
Scott, Robert, 240–41, 242
Scott, Thomas, 114
Sears, John R., 101
segregation: as increasing since 1970,
6–7; in Norfolk, 1938–1954, 8–47; re-
segregation of Norfolk schools, 234,
234–35, 237. *See also* desegregation;
residential segregation
"separate but equal" doctrine, 20–21,
42, 64
Shiloh Baptist Church, 13, 29, 40, 208
Simmons, Joseph, 58
Simpson, John, 237
sit-ins, 118–19, 149
Smallwood, J. J., Elementary School,
30, *50*, 152
Smith, Edward H., III, 92
Smith, J. Robert, 17
Smith, Sharon Venita, 92
Southall, Eleanor, 114
"Southern Manifesto," 61–62
Southside Virginia Institute on Deseg-
regation, 140
standardized tests, 43, 121, 123, 124, 196,
198, 236, 241
Stanley, Thomas, 49, 55, 56, 62, 66–67
Stein, Tony, 59, 72
St. John's African Methodist Episcopal
Church rally, 8–9, *10*, 11–14, 16, 31
Stolee, Michael J., 159–63, 167–68, 169,
170, 171, 178, 181
Strelitz, Joseph H., 195, 203
Stuart, J. E. B., School, 46, *50*, 152
Summers, Ezra T., 61
Swann v. Charlotte-Mecklenburg (1970),
179–81

Talley, Dorothy E., 69, 94–95
Talley, Jeraldine (Geraldine) V., 69, *78*,
91, 94–95, 272n40
Teachers' Advisory Council, 44
Teachers' Salaries in Black and White
(NAACP), 11
Thomas, Vincent, *130;* becomes mayor,
188; in Carter appointment, 219; and
crosstown busing, 172, 184, 186–88,
190–91, 194–95, 200–201, 203, 211–12,
214, 215, 217, 227, 228; on faculty desegregation plan, 143; and Jackson,
224–27; *Ledger-Star* article supports,
155; and Norfolk desegregation
plans, 141, 142, 146, 159; Norfolk Tea
Party supports, 204; on opening of
schools in September 1970, 175; in
School Board appointments of 1982,
217; on State Board of Education, 188,
189, 194; on white flight, 167, 230
Thomson, James M., 65–66
Tidewater Christian School, 174
Tidewater Educational Foundation,
Inc. (TEF), 75–76, 99, 100, 109, 110–11
Titus, Laura E., Elementary School,
30–31, *50*
token integration, 122, 131
Toppin, Edgar Allan, 151
transfer applicants: in early 1960s, 121–
24, 270n25; established procedures
for, 121; majority of African Americans never apply for transfer, 124–25,
140; School Board approves 517 requests in 1963–64, 132; School Board
approves 1,251 requests in 1964–65,
135; in summer of 1958, 68–75; in
summer of 1959, 111–13; whittling 151
down to 17, 84–96. *See also* Norfolk
17; *and individuals by name*
Trapani, Philip, 216, 218, 221–23, 229–30
Tucker, Richard Allen, School, 22, 30,
50, 182
Tucker, S. W., 136–37, 144, 146

tuition grant system, 110, 135–38
Turner, James, Jr., *78*, 88, 89, 90, 272n40
Turner, Patricia A., 2, *78*, 89, 90, 111,
112–13, 124–25, 272n40
Twohy, John, II, 38

Venable, W. H., 15–16
Virginia competency tests, 196, 197, 199,
285n16
Virginia Human Relations Council,
56, 59
"Virginia way," 9; beginning of failure
of, 46; changes in, 10; Dabney and,
105; Jim Crow defenders pushed
beyond, 49; Johnson and, 213; Norfolk Housing and Redevelopment
Agency and, 38; Norfolk officialdom
committed to, 42; Norfolk school
superintendents support, 33; and
official reports on Norfolk schools,
35; Parker's support for, 20; school
closures crisis commemoration
commission and, 2; Women's Council for Interracial Cooperation and,
40; Young Sr. rebuts, 16; Young Sr.
supports, 21
vocation and industrial training, 24,
35, 43
voluntary choice method, 61

Walker, Stanley C., 108, 109, 185,
267n99
Walton, E. C., 57, 66
Washington, Booker T., High School:
Alston on faculty at, 18; Aline Black
on faculty of, 8, 22; black students'
failure rate at, 199; court orders immediate desegregation of, 169; current conditions in, 238–39; history
of, 23, 24–26; map of Norfolk schools
in 1954, *50;* Mason lobbies for improvements for, 40; new library and
cafeteria for, 34; Night School, 53; in

Norfolk's desegregation plans, 139,
141, 144, 146, 166; opposition to bus-
ing white students to, 173; protest of
September, 1963, 114–16, 131; rebuild-
ing of, 145, 146, 148–49, 156, 171, 187,
188; as still segregated in 1968, 153; in
Stolee plan, 160, 161, 162; "Tribute to
Black Educators" program at, 229;
white schools contrasted with, 32,
35, 36
Watson, Willie Mae, 57
Way, Luther Bynum, 20
Welch, Evelyn, 68, 69
Welch, Juanita, 68, 69
Wellington, Carol, 69, *78*, 89, 90–91,
272n40
Wellington, Claudia, 69, *78*, 89, 272n40
Wells, Hortense R., 96, 206, 208–9, 221,
229, 287n51, 288n52
Welton, Richard F., III, 101
White, Earlean, 209–10, 214, 229
White, Edith, 57
White, Forrest, 57, 102, 103, 113, 119, 120,
242
White, Forrest, Jr., 11, 120
White, Nelson, 209–10, 229
White, Walter E., 11, 13, 14
Whitehead, Robert, 61, 105, 120
white middle-class flight: busing seen
as leading to, 6, 154, 167, 179, 191,
218, 230, 231; ending of busing as
response to, 232; racial separation
caused by, 164, 230; school pairing
seen as leading to, 163; suburbanization of Norfolk, 189; threat used as
weapon, 161–62
white supremacy: African American
resistance to, 36; education for challenging, 39; interracial committees
of nobles for maintaining, 10–11;
middle-class flight threatens, 154;
white liberals reject, 119–20
Widener, Hiram E., Jr., 232–33